CAMBRIDGE STUDIES
IN ENGLISH LEGAL HISTORY

Edited by
S. J. BAILEY
Fellow of St John's College, Cambridge
and Rouse Ball Professor of English Law Emeritus;
Barrister-at-Law, Inner Temple

HISTORY OF THE LAW OF CHARITY 1532-1827

BY

GARETH JONES

Fellow of Trinity College and Lecturer in Law in the University of Cambridge;
Barrister-at-Law, Lincoln's Inn

CAMBRIDGE
AT THE UNIVERSITY PRESS
1969

Published by the Syndics of the Cambridge University Press
Bentley House, 200 Euston Road, London N.W.1
American Branch: 32 East 57th Street, New York, N.Y. 10022

Standard Book Number: 521 07347 2

Printed in Great Britain
at the University Press, Aberdeen

CONTENTS

Preface ix
List of Abbreviations x
Table of Statutes xiv
Table of Cases xvi

THE DEVELOPMENT OF THE LAW OF CHARITY
1532–1700

I Introduction: Charity Before the Reformation 3
II The Reformation and the Law of Charity 10
III The Statutes of Charitable Uses: 39 Elizabeth I c. 6 and 43 Elizabeth I c. 4 16
The common law background 16
The statutes of charitable uses 22
i The jurisdiction of the commissioners 26
ii The commission and the hearing 39
iii The powers of the commissioners and the Chancellor 47
iv The achievement of the commissioners 52
IV The Development of the Law of Charity 1545–1700: A Definition of Charity 57
V The Development of the Law of Charity 1545–1700: The Privileges of Charity 59
The perfection of imperfect instruments 60
i Defect of form 60
ii Incapacity at law 65
iii The limits of the Chancellor's indulgence 70
The application of charitable funds *cy-près* 72
i Illegal charitable objects 76
ii Indefinite charitable objects 88
The application of surplus funds 91

Limitation 93

The Chancellor would hear charity suits even though the value of the property was under forty shillings 94

Suits to enforce legacies to charities were not remitted to the ecclesiastical courts 95

Priority over creditors of a bankrupt feoffee to charitable uses 95

The commissioners for charitable uses were allowed to decree land to a corporation *in esse* without danger of infringing the mortmain statutes 96

Marshalling of assets in favour of charity 96

The restriction of the defence of *bona fide* purchase 97

THE DEVELOPMENT OF THE LAW OF CHARITY 1700–1827

VI Introduction 105

VII The Mortmain Act, 1736 109

The background to the Act 109

The interpretation of the Act 113

VIII The Preamble to the Charitable Uses Act, 1601, and the Definition of Charity 120

IX The Influence of the Mortmain Act, 1736, on the Definition of Charity 128

X The Development of the Law of Charity 1700–1827: The Privileges of Charity 134

The perfection of imperfect instruments 135

The application of charitable funds *cy-près* 1700–1827 138

i Initial failure of a charitable object 140

ii The element of general charitable intention 144

The application of surplus funds 153

Marshalling of assets in favour of charity 156

XI The Enforcement of Charitable Trusts 1700–1827 160

Appendixes

A Bills and Answers in Chancery relating to Charities: 1350–1601 171

B Selected Transcriptions 202

C The Charitable Uses Act, 1597: 39 Elizabeth I c. 6 221

D The Charitable Uses Act, 1601: 43 Elizabeth I c. 4 224

E A Bibliographical note on the Cambridge MS. of Francis Moore's *Reading* on the Statute of Charitable Uses: 43 Elizabeth I c. 4 229

F Francis Moore's Notes and his *Speech at the Beginninge* 240

G A Case from Francis Moore's *Reading* 247

H Inquisitions before the Charity Commissioners: 1597–1787 251

I Decrees made by the Charity Commissioners: 1597–1787 255

J The Mortmain Act, 1736: 9 George II c. 36 257

K The Poor Relation Cases 260

Index 263

PREFACE

In this book I have attempted to trace the history of the law of charity from the fall of Sir Thomas More (1532) to the last year of Lord Eldon's Chancellorship (1827), by which time the outlines of the modern law have firmly emerged. Few areas of English law more vividly illustrate the influence of contemporary forces, and one of my primary objects has been to trace the impact of social, economic and religious pressures on the development of the substantive law, on such questions as the definition of charity and the scope of the privileges awarded by the Chancellor to the charitable gift.

In transcribing the primary sources I have not sought to turn contemporary orthography into modern form, nor have I corrected, or burnished in translation, Francis Moore's often corrupt law French. Editorial alterations and emendations have been distinguished by square brackets; and abbreviations have generally been expanded.

Over the years I have received a great deal of help from many friends. I would particularly like to thank Professors J. P. Dawson, S. E. Thorne and A. W. Scott of the Harvard Law School, and, in this Cambridge, Professor S. J. Bailey of St John's College and Mr D. E. C. Yale of Christ's College, all of whom allowed me to draw freely on their patience and scholarship. My greatest debt of gratitude is to my wife who has constantly assisted and encouraged me when assistance and encouragement have been most needed.

Trinity College, Cambridge GARETH JONES
5 *November 1968*

LIST OF ABBREVIATIONS

1. REFERENCES TO RECORDS IN THE PUBLIC RECORD OFFICE, LONDON

Transcripts and translations of Crown copyright records in the following classes in the Public Record Office, London, appear by permission of the Controller of H.M. Stationery Office.

C. 1	Early Chancery Proceedings: 1350–1558
C. 2/Eliz. & C. 3	Chancery Proceedings: 1558–1601
C. 4–C. 10	Chancery Proceedings: 1600–1714
C. 205	Special Commissions in Chancery
C. 33	Chancery *Entry Books of Decrees and Orders*
S.P. Dom.	Calendar of State Papers, Domestic
E. 134	Exchequer Depositions
E. 178	Exchequer Special Commissions
E. 126	Exchequer *Entry Books of Decrees and Orders*
C. 91	Proceedings of the Commissioners for Charitable Uses: depositions
C. 92	exceptions
C. 93	inquisitions and decrees.

2. REFERENCES TO RECORDS IN THE LIBRARY OF THE HONOURABLE SOCIETY OF LINCOLN'S INN

Hale MS.	Manuscripts of Sir Mathew Hale (1609–76), Chief Justice of the King's Bench.
Hill MS.	Manuscripts of George Hill (1716–1808), Sergeant-at-Law.

Cases in the House of Lords: Arguments of cases before the House of Lords.

3. REFERENCE TO RECORDS IN THE CAMBRIDGE UNIVERSITY LIBRARY

Moore	*Reading* on the Statute of Charitable Uses (43 Eliz. I c. 4), MS. Hh. III 2(c).

4. REFERENCES TO PRINTED SECONDARY SOURCES

Calder	I. M. Calder, *Activities of the Puritan Faction of the Church of England* (London, 1957).
Co. Inst.	Sir Edward Coke, *Institutes of the Laws of England*, 4 parts (London, 1797).

Duke	George Duke, *Law of Charitable Uses* (London, 1676).
Duke (Moore)	Abridgement of Francis Moore's *Reading* on the Statute of Charitable Uses, which is to be found in George Duke, *Law of Charitable Uses* (London, 1676).
Monro	Cecil Monro, *Acta Cancellariae* (London, 1847).
Viner, Abr.	Charles Viner, *A General Abridgement of Law and Equity*, 2nd ed. (London, 1791).

5. REFERENCES TO REPORTS OF CASES IN PRINT

Ambl.	Ambler's Reports, Chancery, 1737–84.
Ambl. (ed. Blunt)	Ambler's Reports, 2nd edition by J. E. Blunt, 1828.
Anst.	Anstruther's Reports, 3 vols. Exchequer, 1792–7.
Atk.	Atkyns' Reports, 3 vols. Chancery, 1736–55.
Beav.	Beavan's Reports, 36 vols. Rolls Court, 1838–66.
Bli. N.S.	Bligh's Reports, New Series, 11 vols. House of Lords, 1827–37.
Bro. C. C.	Brown's Reports, 4 vols. Chancery, 1778–94.
Bro. C. C. (ed. Belt)	Brown's Reports, 5th edition by Robert Belt, 1820.
Carthew	Carthew's Reports, King's Bench, 1686–1701.
Cary	Cary's Reports, Chancery, 1557–1604.
Cas. in Chan.	Cases in Chancery, 3 vols. 1660–98.
Cases *temp.* Bacon	Reports of Cases decided by Francis Bacon, prepared by John Ritchie, 1932.
Chan. Rep.	Reports in Chancery, 1615–1712.
Cl. and F.	Clark and Finnelly's Reports, 12 vols. House of Lords, 1831–46.
Co.	Coke's Reports, 13 vols. Common Law, 1572–1616.
Coop. Ch.	Cooper's Reports, Chancery, 1815.
Cox	Cox's Reports, 2 vols. Chancery, 1783–96.
Cro. Car.	Croke's Reports, *temp.* Charles I.
Dick.	Dickens' Reports, 2 vols. Chancery, 1559–1798.
Dyer	Dyer's Reports, 3 vols. Common Law, 1513–82.
Eden	Eden's Reports, 2 vols. Chancery, 1757–66.
Eq. Cas. Abr.	Equity Cases Abridged, 2 vols. Chancery, 1667–1744
Finch	Finch's Reports, Chancery, 1673–81.
Freeman, Ch.	Freeman's Reports, Chancery, 1660–1706.
Gilb. Rep.	Gilbert's Reports, Chancery, 1705–27.
Godb.	Godbolt's Reports, King's Bench, 1575–1638.
Hare	Hare's Reports, 11 vols. Vice Chancellor's Court, 1841–53.

H.L.C.	House of Lords Cases, 11 vols. 1847–66.
Hobart	Hobart's Reports, Common Law, 1603–25.
Jac.	Jacob's Reports, Chancery, 1821–2.
Jac. and W.	Jacob and Walker's Reports, 2 vols. Chancery, 1819–21.
Wm. Jones	William Jones' Reports, King's Bench, 1620–41.
K. and J.	Kay and Johnson's Reports, 4 vols. Vice Chancellor's Court, 1854–8.
Keen	Keen's Reports, 2 vols. Rolls Court, 1836–8.
Lane	Lane's Reports, Exchequer, 1605–11.
Leonard	Leonard's Reports, 4 vols. King's Bench, 1540–1615.
Lev.	Levinz's Reports, 3 vols. King's Bench, 1660–97.
M. and S.	Maule and Selwyn's Reports, 6 vols. King's Bench, 1813–17.
Madd.	Maddock's Reports, 6 vols. Vice Chancellor's Court, 1815–22.
Mer.	Merivale's Reports, 3 vols. Chancery, 1815–17.
Mod.	Modern Reports, 12 vols. King's Bench, 1669–1732.
Moo. K. B.	Moore's King's Bench Reports, 1512–1621.
Mos.	Mosely's Reports, Chancery, 1726–31.
Myl. and Cr.	Mylne and Craig's Reports, 5 vols. Chancery, 1835–41.
Myl. and K.	Mylne and Keen's Reports, 3 vols. Chancery, 1832–5.
Nelson	Nelson's Reports, Chancery, 1625–93.
Owen	Owen's Reports, King's Bench, 1556–1615.
Popham	Popham's Reports, King's Bench, 1592–1627.
Prec. Ch.	Precedents in Chancery, 1689–1722.
Russ.	Russell's Reports, 5 vols. Chancery, 1823–9.
Russ. and Myl.	Russell and Mylne's Reports, 2 vols. Chancery, 1829–31.
Salkeld	Salkeld's King's Bench Cases, 3 vols. 1689–1712.
Shower, P. C.	Shower's Parliamentary Cases, 1694–9.
Sim. and Stu.	Simon and Stuart's Reports, 2 vols. Vice Chancellor's Court, 1822–6.
Swanst.	Swanston's Reports, 3 vols. Chancery, 1818–19.
Sch. and Lef.	Schoales and Lefroy Jr.'s Reports, 2 vols. Irish Chancery, 1802–6.
Tothill	Tothill's Reports, Chancery, 1559–64.
Turn. and Russ.	Turner and Russell's Reports, Chancery, 1822–4.
Vern.	Vernon's Reports, 2 vols. Chancery, 1681–1720.
Ves. Sen.	Vesey Senior's Reports, 2 vols. Chancery, 1746–56.

Ves. Sen. Supp.	Vesey Senior's Reports, supplement by Robert Belt, 1825.
Ves.	Vesey Junior's Reports, 19 vols. Chancery, 1789–1817.
Ves. Jun. Supp.	Vesey Junior's Reports, supplement by J. E. Hovenden, 2 vols., 1827.
West. *temp.* Hardwicke	West's Reports, Chancery, 1736–9.
P. Wms.	Peere Williams' Reports, 3 vols. Chancery, 1695–1736.
Wilm.	Wilmot's Notes of Cases, King's Bench, 1757–70.

TABLE OF STATUTES

1215 17 John (Magna Carta), 112
1279 7 Edw. I stat. 2 c. 3 (Mortmain), 112
1357 31 Edw. III stat. 1 c. 11 (Administrators), 5
1391 15 Rich. II c. 5 (Mortmain), 112
1489 4 Hen. VII c. 24 (Limitations), 93, 94
1532 23 Hen. VIII c. 10 (Mortmain), 11, 86, 112, 147
1536 27 Hen. VIII c. 10 (Uses), 63, 64, 239
1536 27 Hen. VIII c. 16 (Enrolments), 60
1540 32 Hen. VIII c. 1 (Wills), 50, 65, 71
1540 32 Hen. VIII c. 2 (Limitations), 93
1541 33 Hen. VIII c. 9 (Maintaining Artyllarie), 27, 29
1543 34 & 35 Hen. VIII c. 4 (Bankrupts), 95, 244
1545 37 Hen. VIII c. 4 (Chantries), 10,11
1547 1 Edw. VI c. 14 (Chantries), 12–13, 14, 31, 32, 77, 79, 83, 86, 147
1549 2 & 3 Edw. VI c. 1 (Uniformity), 14
1550 3 & 4 Edw. VI c. 10 (Abolition of Missals), 14
1554 1 & 2 Ph. and M. c. 8 (Chantry Lands), 13
1559 1 Eliz. I c. 2 (Common Prayer), 14
1559 1 Eliz. I c. 24 (Religious Houses), 13
1571 13 Eliz. I c. 4 (Accountants), 244
1571 13 Eliz. I c. 7 (Bankrupts), 95, 244
1572 14 Eliz. I c. 14 (Hospitals misnamed), 21, 66
1581 23 Eliz. I c. 1 (Roman Catholics), 15, 83
1585 27 Eliz. I c. 3 (Accountants), 244
1597 39 Eliz. I. c. 5 (Incorporation), 21, 66
1597 39 Eliz. I c. 6 (Charitable Uses), 19, 22–3, 31, 43, 57, 221–3, 234
1601 43 Eliz. I c. 4 (Charitable Uses), 18, 19, 23–56, 57, 59, 60, 61, 62, 65, 68, 71, 89–90, 97–101, 114, 121, 123, 124, 125, 126, 132–3, 135, 136, 160, 224–8, 229, 232, 234–9, 244, 247–50.
1604 1 Jac. I c. 15 (Bankrupts), 95, 244
1624 21 Jac. I c. 1 (Incorporation), 66
1624 21 Jac. I c. 16 (Limitations), 93
1624 21 Jac. I c. 19 (Bankrupts), 95
1628 3 Car. I c. 2 (Recusants), 83
1635 10 Car. I sess 3, c. I (Irish Charities), 25
1660 12 Car. II c. 24 (Tenures), 72
1670 22 & 23 Car. II c. 10 (Distributions), 260–2
1673 25 Car. II c. 2 (Recusants), 85
1677 29 Car. II c. 3 (Statute of Frauds), 115–16, 134, 136
1677 29 Car. II c. 8 (Augmentations of Vicarages), 121

1689 1 Will. & M. c. 18 (Toleration), 81, 140, 141, 142
1698 9 & 10 Will. III c. 32 (Toleration), 140
1736 9 Geo. II c. 36 (Mortmain), 107–119, 120–133, 134, 145, 147, 157–9, 257–9, 261
1786 26 Geo. III c. 58 (Charitable Donations), 165
1791 31 Geo. III c. 32 (Toleration), 143
1803 43 Geo. III c. 107 (Queen Anne's Bounty), 118
1812 52 Geo. III c. 101 (Charities), 165–7
1812 52 Geo. III c. 102 (Charitable Donations), 165
1813 53 Geo. III c. 160 (Unitarians), 142
1815 55 Geo. III c. 192 (Copyholds), 137
1818 58 Geo. III c. 91 (Charitable Trusts), 167
1819 59 Geo. III c. 81 (Charitable Trusts), 167–8
1819 59 Geo. III c. 91 (Charitable Trusts), 168
1846 9 & 10 Vict. c. 59 (Jewish Relief), 143
1888 51 & 52 Vict. c. 42 (Mortmain and Charitable Uses), 133
1960 8 & 9 Eliz. II c. 58 (Charities), 133, 144, 168

TABLE OF CASES[1]

Adams and Lambert's case, 13, 14, 63
Addlington v. Cann, 86, 116
Anon (1553), 66
Anon (1571), 66
Anon (1576), 63
Anon (1602), 48
Anon (1678), 90
Anon (1702), 148
Arnold v. Att.-Gen., 93, 154
Arnold v. Chapman, 157, 158, 159
Ascough v. Phillips, 72
Ashburnham v. Bradshaw, 115, 117
Att.-Gen. v. Andrew, 146, 148, 149
v. Andrews, 107, 115, 137
v. Arnold, 93, 154
v. Barnes (or Baines), 106, 136, 137
v. Baxter, 81, 139, 141, 143, 147
v. Berryman, 152
v. Bolton, 161, 162
v. Boultbee, 138, 144, 146, 148
v. Bowles, 114, 115, 116
v. Bowyer, 21
v. Bradley, 134, 135
v. Brereton, 58, 120
v. Brewers' Co., 162
v. Bristol, Mayor of, 107, 134, 154
v. Burdet, 135
v. Caldwell, 119, 158
v. Carte, 162
v. Catherine Hall, 154
v. Chester, Bishop of, 117, 140
v. Churchill, 82
v. Clarke, 151
v. Cock, 141
v. Combes, 81
v. Coopers' Co., 140, 154, 156

[1] This is a table of cases which proceeded to judgment. For interlocutory bills and answers, see appendix A.

Att.-Gen. v. Davies, 115, 117, 118, 119
v. Day, 112, 113, 114, 118
v. Dove, 161
v. Downing, Lady, 61, 74, 121, 137, 139, 147, 150
v. Eades, 141
v. Fishmongers' Co., 161
v. Fletcher, 153
v. Fowler, 126
v. Gleg, 162
v. Goddard, 117
v. Goldsmiths' Co., 162
v. Goulding, 119, 144, 146, 148, 149
v. Gower, Lord, 53, 106
v. Graves, 117–18, 157
v. Green, 138, 166
v. Guise, 75, 81
v. Haberdashers' Co., 154
v. Hartley, 14, 117, 162
v. Heartwell, 117, 118
v. Herrick, 107, 139, 151, 152, 154
v. Hewer, 55, 120
v. Hewitt, 160
v. Hickman, 135, 141, 150
v. Hicks, 138
v. Hinxman, 119
v. Hudson, 5, 156
v. Hughes, 81, 141 (*see also* Att.-Gen. v. Peacock)
v. Hurst, 119, 144, 146
v. Hyde, 115
v. Johnson, 154
v. Knight, 162
v. Lady Margaret Professors, 73, 75
v. London, Mayor etc. of, 144
v. Londonderry, Marchioness of, 153
v. Mansfield, Earl of, 140, 162
v. Mathews, 88
v. Meyrick, 107, 118, 119, 158
v. Middleton, 162
v. Minshull, 139, 146, 154
v. Montague, 144
v. Mountmorris, Lord, 159
v. Nash, 115
v. Newcombe, 162
v. Oakover, 131

Att.-Gen. v. Oglander, 140
v. Oxford, Bishop of, 144, 145, 146, 148
v. Painter-Stainers' Co., 148, 155, 156
v. Peacock, 55, 69, 70, 88–90, 139, 151 (*see also* Att.-Gen. v. Hughes)
v. Pearson, 142
v. Platt, 55, 69, 73 (*see also* Platt v. St John's College)
v. Portington, Lady, 86–7
v. Rochester, City of, 93
v. Ruper, 121
v. Rye and Warwick, 60, 62
v. Sawtell, 137
v. Skinners' Co., 65, 135, 154, 155
v. Smart, 162
v. Sparks, 154
v. Stepney, 142
v. Sutton, 106, 137
v. Syderfin, 90, 149, 151
v. Tancred, 113, 134, 135
v. Tomkins, 118, 157
v. Townsend, 37, 93
v. Tyndall, 115, 117, 157, 158
v. Wansay, 141, 154
v. Weymouth, Lord, 114, 117, 159
v. Whitchurch, 117, 118, 148
v. Whiteley, 140
v. Whorwood, 121, 123, 130–1
v. Williams, 117
v. Winchelsea, Earl of, 144, 146, 154, 155, 158
v. Worcester, Bishop of, 166
v. Yate, 82
Aylet v. Dodd, 46

Baylis and Church v. Att.-Gen., 151
Bedford Charity, *Re*, 143, 161
Bennett v. Hayter, 153
Blandford v. Fackerell, 129
Boson v. Statham, 116
Bourne v. Keane, 143
Bramble v. Havering, Poor of, 71
Brantham v. East Burgold, 144
Bristol, Mayor of, v. Whitton, 65
British Museum v. White, 129
Browne v. Ricards, 18

Browne v. Yeall, 123, 125, 131–2.
Burford Corp. v. Lenthall, 46–7

Campbell v. Radnor, Earl of, 118
Cary v. Abbott, 143, 147
Champion v. Smith, 68
Chapman v. Brown, 115, 119
Christ's Hospital v. Hawes, 72
Clergy Society, *Re*, 153
Coleman and Coleman's case, 46, 55, 69
Collison's (or Rolt's) case, 65
Commissioners of Income Tax v. Pemsel, 124
Cook v. Duckenfield, 152
Corbyn v. French, 117, 144, 145
Croft v. Jane Evetts, 14, 82, 86
Crooke v. Ibberton, Churchwardens of, 67–8
Cudrington v. Stokes, 36
Currie v. Pye, 158, 162
Curtis v. Hutton, 158

Da Costa v. De Paz, 143, 146, 148
Dacres' case, Lady, 64
Damus' case, 65, 97
De Garcin v. Lawson, 147
De Themmines v. De Bonneval, 143
Doe d. Thompson v. Pitcher, 126, 130
Dorset, Earl of, v. Bridewell, Governor of, 94
Doyley v. Att.-Gen., 135, 150
Durour v. Motteux, 130

East Greensted's case, 43, 48, 99, 100
East v. Ryall, 46
Eastham, Poor of, v. Kemp, 46
Egerton's case, Lady, 14, 82
Ellis v. Selby, 127
Eltham, Inhabitants of, v. Warreyn, 46, 47
Emmanuel College v. English, 74
Endacott, *Re*, 132
Eyre v. Shaftesbury, Countess of, 21

Feoffees to Impropriations' case, 77–81, 84, 139, 140, 151
Fielding v. Bound, 5
Finch v. Squire, 119
Fisher v. Hill, 27, 34

Frenche v. Tetter, 61, 92
Flood's case, 65, 72
Foster v. Blagden, 158

Glubb v. Att.-Gen., 115
Goffe v. Webb, 91
Grant v. Huish, 74
Gravenor v. Hallum, 130
Grieves v. Case, 118, 122, 129
Grimmett v. Grimmett, 116
Gwyn v. Parker, 70, 71
Gwynn v. Cardon, 123, 125, 132

Habergham v. Vincent, 137
Harding and Edge, 36
Harris v. Barnes, 117
Hayter v. Trego, 138, 153
Hellam's case, 65
Hereford, Bishop of, v. Adams, 154
Hide's case, 48, 100
Higgins v. Southampton, Town of, 72
Hillyard v. Taylor, 158
Hobson v. Blackburn, 159
Hopkins, *Re*, 133
Horde v. Suffolk, Earl of, 127
Howse v. Chapman, 128, 158, 159
Hussey's case, 64
Hynshaw v. Morpeth Corp., 38

I.R.C. v. Baddeley, 30
Isaac v. Gompertz, 143

James v. Allen, 126, 131
Jemmit v. Verril, 127
Jenner v. Harper, 136
Jesus College case, 71
Jones', Gaynor, case, 82, 83–6, 139
Jones v. Williams, 126, 128
Jortin, *Ex parte*, 154

Kennington Hastings Almshouse's case, 93
Kenson's case, 49

King v. Baldwin, 35
Knapp v. Williams, 119

Lawford Charity *Re*, 166
Lee v. Libb, 136
Legge v. Asgill, 106
Lilburn v. Turner, 69, 91
Lloyd v. Spillett, 135, 161
London's, Mayor of, case, 68
London, Mayor of, v. Alford, 71
Ludlow, Corp. of, v. Greenhouse, 160, 161

Makeham v. Hooper, 158
Man v. Ballett, 73
Marsh v. Att.-Gen., 133
Martidale v. Martin, 14
Masters v. Masters, 130, 156
Mellick v. President etc. of the Asylum, 126, 130
Michel, *Re*, 143
Middleton v. Clitherow, 118
Middleton v. Royal Navy, Master etc. of, 48
Middleton v. Spicer, 158
Mills v. Farmer, 139, 146, 148, 150
Mogg v. Hodges, 157, 158, 159
Moggridge v. Thackwell, 81, 90, 107, 117, 125, 143, 146, 147, 148, 150, 151, 152
Morice v. Durham, Bishop of, 120, 122–6, 128, 129, 131, 132, 133
Morris v. Glyn, 119
Mountague's case, 72
Muckleston v. Brown, 116

Negus v. Coulter, 158
Nelson v. Norton, 17

Oliphant v. Hendrie, 118
Ommanney v. Butcher, 126, 127
Osborne v. Denne, 162

Paice v. Canterbury, Archbishop of, 150, 158
Parrott v. Pawlinge, 94
Peacock v. Thewer, 100
Pember v. Kington, Inhabitants of, 33, 34–6
Pennyman v. Jenny, 61
Penstred v. Pavier, 35

Pewterers' Co. v. Christ's Hospital, 71
Phillips v. Bury, 38
Pickering v. Stamford, Lord, 106
Piggot v. Prentice, 135
Platt v. St John's College, 62, 69–70
Plymouth, Earl of, v. Hickman, 106
Porter's case, 14
Pritchard v. Arbouin, 115, 118

Queens' College v. Fabian, 55, 69

Ranshawe and Robottom's case, 49, 72
Reade v. Silles, 92
Reading, Mayor of, v. Lane, 68
R. v. Newman, 55, 69, 96
R. v. Nottingham, Earl of, 76
Ridges v. Morrison, 158
Rockley v. Keyley, 46
Rolt's (or Collison's) case, 65
Rolt v. Smith, 97
Rycardes v. Payne, 33

St Bartholomew's Hospital's case, 68
St Dunstan, Poor of, v. Beauchamp, 45
St Mary Magdalen, Oxford v. Att. Gen., 134
Salisbury, Mayor of, v. Oldefylde, 97
Sanford v. Gibbons, 152
Saul v. Wilson, 46
Sewell v. Crewe-Read, 133
Seymour v. Twyford, Poor of, 48
Shore v. Wilson, 142
Shrewsbury v. Hornby, 142
Slevin, *Re*, 153
Sorresby v. Hollins, 114
Steward v. Germyn, 48
Stickland v. Aldridge, 116
Stinkley v. Chamberlain, 6
Stoddard's case, 64
Straus v. Goldsmid, 143
Sutton Coalfield case, 93
Symons' case, 60–1

Tate v. Austin, 156
Tay v. Slaughter, 62

Thetford School case, 92–3, 154
Townley v. Bedwell, 122, 128
Tuffnell v. Page, 137
Turner v. Ogden, 121, 122, 128

Vaughan v. Farrer, 115, 116
Venables' case, 76–7, 79, 80, 82, 139
Vezey v. Jamson, 127, 131
Vintners' Co. v. Simmonds, 72

Wagstaff v. Wagstaff, 107, 137
Waldo v. Caley, 127
Walter v. Childs, 141, 158
Walthamstow's, Poor of, case, 48
Ware v. Att.-Gen., 152
Welkden v. Elkington, 66
West v. Knight, 69
West v. Shuttleworth, 143
Wharton v. Charles, 46
Wheeler v. Sheer, 149
White, *Re*, 84
White v. Evans, 119
White v. White, 149, 155
Widmore v. Woodroffe, 118
Willet v. Sandford, 115, 117
Williams v. Kershaw, 159
Windsor v. Hilton, 46
Wingfield's case, 88
Wivelescom case, 73
Woodford, Inhabitants of, v. Parkhurst, 48, 100, 101
Wray v. Sapcote, 96

THE DEVELOPMENT OF THE LAW OF CHARITY

1532-1700

CHAPTER I

INTRODUCTION: CHARITY BEFORE THE REFORMATION

A PAPAL DECRETAL of Gregory IX urged the faithful to seek their salvation by bequeathing part of their wealth to the support of pious causes: 'the day of harvest' should be anticipated 'with works of great mercy, and, for the sake of things eternal, to sow on earth what we should gather in Heaven, the Lord returning it with increased fruit.'[1] The impious testator, who refused to observe this exhortation, might be denied the Eucharist and interred in unconsecrated ground.[2] A similar fate might befall the person who died intestate, for he too had failed to make provision for works of great mercy before death, but to ensure his salvation the Church obtained the right to administer his estate[3] and to distribute a portion of it *ad pias causas*.[4]

Pious causes were causes which honoured God and his Church. Such were gifts for the saying of masses, for obits, for the foundation of chantries, for vestments, for candles and incense, for the

[1] *Letter of Authorisation for Collectors for Charitable Institutions*, approved by the 4th Lateran Council (1215) and included in the decretals of Gregory IX; quoted by Brian Tierney, *Medieval Poor Law* (Berkeley and Los Angeles, 1959), 46.

[2] F. Pollock and F. W. Maitland *The History of English Law*, 2nd ed. (Cambridge, 1898), II, 356; H. C. Coote, *The Practice of the Ecclesiastical Courts* (London, 1847), 35–7; Felix Makower, *The Constitutional History and Constitution of the Church of England* (London 1895), 426–7.

[3] Pollock and Maitland, *History of English Law*, II, 356–63. Indeed the Church actively discouraged donations *inter vivos* which might defraud the Church and result in the disherison of the donor's family; see Archbishop Stafford's canon, cited by W. Lyndwood, *Provinciale* (Oxford, 1679), bk. III, tit. 13, quoted below, n. 4; W. A. Pantin, *The English Church in the Fourteenth Century* (Cambridge, 1955), 155–6.

[4] Distribution on intestacy was governed by Archbishop Stafford's canon (cited by Lyndwood, *Provinciale*, bk. III, tit. 13), which read: '*Bona quae supererunt in pias causas et personis decedentium consanguineis servitoribus et propinquis, seu aliis, pro Defunctorum animarum salute* (*Ordinarii*) *distribuant et convertant.*' For a comment on this passage, see E. F. Jacob in his edition of *Registrum Henricii Chichele, Vol. II*, Canterbury and York Society Publications, XLII (1937), xxxiii. Cf. Pollock and Maitland, *History of English Law*, II, 361–2; Coote, *Practice of Ecclesiastical Courts*, 47, 52–3; but see William Blackstone, *Commentaries on the Laws of England*, 9th ed. (London, 1783), I, 300.

repair of churches and for the upkeep of religious houses. But the canonical conception of piety also embraced gifts for the relief of distress and suffering on earth; so, in the medieval will[1] are to be found bequests for the poor,[2] the maimed and suffering, and the upkeep and repair of hospitals,[3] bridges, roads and dykes.[4]

Bequests to pious causes were particularly favoured by the ecclesiastical courts,[5] which, by the reign of Henry III, had secured an exclusive jurisdiction over the testament of personalty.[6]

The Bishop or Ordinary of every Diocese, unto whom the execution of testaments and last wills, especially *ad pias causas* (no executor being appointed by the testator), hath appertained.... Hence it is, that every Bishop is called *Ordinary*, as if other judges were in this behalf incompetent or extraordinary.[7]

[1] The nature of the medieval will, and the character of the pious cause traditionally supported by testators, can be seen from a study of the wills contained in such printed collections as *Registrum Henricii Chichele*, ed. E. F. Jacob; *Calendar of Wills proved and enrolled in the Court of Husting*, ed. R. R. Sharpe (London, 1889); Bedfordshire Historical Record Society, II (1914); Surtees Society, CXVI (1908).

[2] William Ashley, *An Introduction to English Economic History and Theory*, 4th ed. (London, 1925), § 53.

[3] R. M. Clay, *The Medieval Hospitals of England* (London, 1909), xviii–xix.

[4] J. J. Jusserand, *English Wayfaring Life in the Middle Ages* (London, 1889), 18; C. T. Flower, *Public Works in Medieval Law*, Selden Society, XXXII (1915), xx–xxii.

[5] See generally, Andreas Tiraquellus, *De Privilegiis Piae Causae Tractatus* (Venice, 1561); H. Swinburne, *A Treatise of Testaments and Last Wills*, 6th ed. (London, 1743).

[6] In Glanvill's time there is evidence that the *Curia Regis* enjoyed a similar jurisdiction; see *De Legibus*, bk. VII, chap. 7 and bk. XII, chap. 17; F. W. Maitland, 'The History of the Register of Original Writs', *Harvard Law Review*, III (1889), 167, 168. But by the reign of Henry III the ecclesiastical courts were in exclusive control; see John Selden, *Collected Works* (London, 1726), III, 1665–73; Pollock and Maitland, *History of English Law*, II, 334; R. J. R. Goffin, *The Testamentary Executor in England and Elsewhere* (London, 1901), 64–5.

[7] Swinburne, *Testaments and Last Wills*, 379–80. It may well have been that the Bishop's particular responsibility as the guardian of charity led to the acquisition by the spiritual courts of their jurisdiction over the testament of personalty. Lyndwood found the origin of the ecclesiastical jurisdiction in C. 1.3.28.49, which nominated the Bishop as the protector of all legacies bequeathed for pious causes. See Lyndwood, *Provinciale*, bk. III, tit. 13; cf. W. F. Finlason's comment in his edition of John Reeves, *History of the English Law*, 2nd ed. (London, 1869), I, 330. On the other hand, Selden, *Collected Works*, III, 1666, thought that 'the original of this jurisdiction for legacies, was out of the canon law', possibly from the canon '*Si haeredes jussa testatoris non impleverint, ab episcopo loci illius omnis res quae eis relicta est canonice interdicatur, cum fructibus et caeteris emolumentis, ut vota defuncti impleantur.*' Selden then adds, 'of what Council of Mentz this is taken, I have not yet learned'.

Many privileges were granted to the charitable legacy which were denied to the private legacy. For example, no charitable legacy was allowed to fail because it was too indefinite, and generous rules of construction were developed to cure the uncertainty. So, a testator who had bequeathed property 'to the church' was deemed to have bequeathed it to his parish church;[1] while a legacy 'to the poor', who were appointed in the will the testator's executors, was distributed among the poor of his parish for 'it is likely that he did bear a great affection to the poor where he dwelled; especially also if the testator were buried in the same place'.[2] Other privileges given to the legacy *ad pias causas* also helped to mark out its specially favoured position in canon law: for example, a legacy *ad pias causas* might be applied to similar charitable objects if it was impossible to execute the testator's wishes in a lawful manner;[3] and if there was an insufficiency of assets, debts were first satisfied from private rather than from charitable legacies.[4]

By the beginning of the fifteenth century, however, the testamentary jurisdiction of the ecclesiastical courts had become unpopular with the laity.[5] Court fees were resented and officials were thought to be corrupt.[6] Complaints are heard about the cost and delay of litigation and the ineffectiveness of ecclesiastical remedies[7]; and many executors and administrators were prepared to bear ecclesiastical censure with equanimity if their dishonesty

[1] Swinburne, *Testaments and Last Wills*, 489; and see below, p. 88 ff.

[2] *Ibid.*

[3] *Ibid.* 518–19. The privileges normally given to military wills were also given to legacies *ad pias causas*. Consequently, if wills contained charitable bequests 'which being blotted or put forth by the testator, it is not presumed to have been done willingly'. See *ibid.* 67, 539.

The ecclesiastical courts would not, however, cure any lack of capacity, for 'here is defect of content, without which content no testament is good'. See *ibid.* 518; and cf. below, p. 71.

[4] Below, p. 96. See *Fielding* v. *Bound* (1683), 1 Vern. 230; *Att.-Gen.* v. *Hudson* (1720) 1 P. Wms. 674, 675, *per* Parker L.C. But cf. Swinburne, *Testaments and Last Wills*, 228.

[5] The ecclesiastical records remain relatively untapped, so that the role and influence of the courts spiritual must be, to some extent, conjectural; see F. W. Maitland, *Roman Canon Law in the Church of England* (London, 1898), 130. For an important, more recent, work, see B. L. Woodcock, *Medieval Ecclesiastical Courts in the Diocese of Canterbury* (London, 1952), *passim.*

[6] These suspicions are reflected in the enactment of such statutes as 31 Edw. III, stat. 1, c. 11, which compelled the Ordinary to appoint the administrator from 'the next and most lawful friends of the . . . intestate'.

[7] W. S. Holdsworth, *A History of English Law*, III (London, 1923), 582–3.

was likely to be rewarded in this life.[1] It is true that a royal writ *de excommunicato capiendo* could result in the outlawing of an excommunicate; but it was issued only after a cumbersome and tardy process and, consequently, was rarely invoked.[2] Not surprisingly complainants turned to the Chancellor for help, and from the beginning of the fifteenth century onwards there is a steady trickle of petitions asking him to compel an executor to carry out a private or charitable legacy.[3] Fifty years later such petitions are common; and from this date at the latest the Chancellor's testamentary jurisdiction appears to be established.

The Chancellor's jurisdiction over the charitable legacy, which always remained concurrent with that of the Bishop, plays an important part in the history of this topic. But it is his exclusive jurisdiction[4] over the '*use*' (or '*trust*')[5] which is to be of paramount importance; for it is behind the use that the bulk of charitable endowment was to shelter.[6] At common law it was not generally possible to devise land by will.[7] Land could, however, be conveyed by the testator in his lifetime to feoffees for such uses as he

[1] Cf. Woodcock, *Medieval Ecclesiastical Courts*, 101, citing a fifteenth-century figure, one John Gray, who boldly observed that he 'settith not a straw by the suspension of the commissary or officiall'.

[2] *Ibid.* 85–6, 93–102; Holdsworth, *History of English Law*, I, 631–2.

[3] See, generally, the Public Record Office, *Indexes to Early Chancery Proceedings, Richard II to Philip and Mary*, 10 vols. (London, 1901–36); *Calendar of the Proceedings in Chancery in the Reign of Queen Elizabeth, with earlier examples*, 3 vols. (London, 1827–32); *Guide to the Contents of the Public Record Office* (London, 1963), I, 33–4.

[4] The Ordinary could not compel the feoffee to apply property to charitable uses, although he could make the feoffee account to him; see *Stinkley* v. *Chamberlain* (1598), cited in Owen, 33, *per* Cordell M.R.

[5] At this period, and throughout the sixteenth century, 'use' and 'trust' were used synonymously. Francis Moore in his *Reading* (see below, p. 27, n. 1) did so, as did the draftsman of the Statute of Uses, 27 Hen. VII c. 10. See A. W. B. Simpson, *An Introduction to the History of the Land Law* (Oxford, 1961), 188–94. From the late sixteenth century onwards, however, lawyers did distinguish the *passive use*, which was caught by that statute's provisions, from the *active use* or *trust*, which was not: see D. E. C. Yale, 'The Revival of Equitable Estates in the Seventeenth Century: an explanation by Lord Nottingham', *Cambridge Law Journal* (1957), 72; G. W. Sanders, *An Essay on Uses and Trusts*, 5th ed. (London, 1844), I, 290–4; J. L. Barton, 'The Statute of Uses and the Trust of Freeholds', *Law Quarterly Review*, LXXXII (1966), 215. This distinction is not important in the law of charity. I have, following Moore, generally used 'use' and 'trust' interchangeably.

[6] W. K. Jordan, *Philanthropy in England, 1480–1600* (London, 1950), 119.

[7] Except in certain privileged cities, such as the City of London. See, generally, H. Swinburne, *Testaments and Last Wills*, 119 ff.

should declare in his last will (*ultima voluntas*), the feoffees holding to the testator's use until he died. The advantages of such a feoffment were considerable.[1] Not only could the beneficial ownership of land be thereby transferred on the feoffor's death-bed, but the mortmain statutes, the rigid common law remainder rules and the feudal claims of the mesne lord could be adroitly avoided. Moreover, property could be conveyed to feoffees to hold to the use of persons who were incapable of holding property at common law, a particularly valuable advantage when it is remembered that many objects of charity were not legal persons.[2]

Among the pre-Reformation Chancery records[3] are to be found a number of bills to enforce charitable uses and legacies. These bills (or petitions) set out the facts of the case and the nature of the complaint, and concluded with a prayer for relief. Their object was generally to compel a feoffee, an executor or legatee to carry out the terms of a charitable gift.[4] For example, the wardens of the brotherhood of Saint Katherine in East Grinstead church seek to subpoena a feoffee who has failed to find a priest to say masses at the altar of that church[5]; William Carlele, a chaplain, prays for a writ of subpoena to be issued against the executors of Symon Camps, who had bequeathed a pecuniary legacy and certain

[1] See generally, T. F. T. Plucknett, *A Concise History of the Common Law*, 5th ed. (London, 1956), 582–3; A. W. B. Simpson, *History of the Land Law*, 164.

[2] See below, pp. 65–70.

[3] Before 1535 these records are entirely interlocutory, and consequently must be used with some caution. Nevertheless, they are of considerable value. As W. T. Barbour pointed out in his *History of Contract in Early English Equity*, Oxford Studies in Social and Legal History, IV (Oxford, 1914), 70: 'where there are numerous petitions based upon the same or a similar state of facts . . . it may be reasonably inferred that relief sought was granted.'

The earliest petitions are written in law French but soon after the beginning of the fifteenth century they are in English. On early Chancery procedure, generally, see Barbour, *History of Contract*, 66–70; Holdsworth, *History of English Law*, II (London, 1923), 342–7; W. J. Jones, 'Due Process and Slow Process in the Elizabethan Chancery', *American Journal of Legal History*, VI (1962), 123, and *The Elizabethan Court of Chancery* (Oxford, 1967), 11–15. D. E. C. Yale's introduction to *Lord Nottingham's Manual of Chancery Practice and Prolegomena of Chancery and Equity* (Cambridge, 1965), *passim*.

[4] See appendix A below, p. 171.

[5] C. 1/139/3 (1486–93). In many cases a Chancery petition can only be dated from the name or title of the Chancellor to whom it is addressed. Dating becomes particularly difficult if the Chancellor is merely described by his ecclesiastical title, such as the 'Archbishop of York' or the 'Bishop of Durham'. Occasionally the date of the petition is noted in the margin.

fittings to the petitioner's chapel;[1] John Dekon stubbornly refuses to pay over a bequest of forty shillings to a church[2]; and Richard Rode and Richard Meryham, the churchwardens of Goudhurst,

with divers other of the parisshioners of the sayde parishe of Goudhurst as yn the right of the sayde church of Goudhurst have many tymes and often demanded and requyryd the same Thomas [Patenden, who had 'admynistrated many thinges concerninge the will of the said Henry Burges'] to pay unto theym the sayd £X to thuse and interest of the sayd last wyll of the sayd Henry Burges.[3]

All these bills are brought by private individuals who have some interest in the success of their petition; and there appears to have been no attempt to enforce a charitable use via an information in Chancery, brought by the Attorney-General on behalf of the Crown.[4] Among the petitioners are to be found the parson, chaplain and churchwardens of a parish church to which the testator had bequeathed a legacy;[5] an heir-at-law proceeds against feoffees requiring them to perform his ancestor's feoffment to the use of a church;[6] the inhabitants of Shenley seek to enforce a devise which will relieve them of subsidies;[7] the Mayor and communalty of Lynn wish to compel the executrix to complete a cistern;[8] and the Merchant Taylors' Company ask for the perfection of a gift, which the donor intended to make to the Company before he died.[9] These petitioners pray for relief not merely on their own behalf but that 'the honor of God's churche' might be augmented and

[1] C. 1/16/225 (uncertain; addressed to the Archbishop of Canterbury).

[2] C. 1/70/89 (uncertain: early fifteenth century?).

[3] C. 1/807/49–51 (uncertain, mutilated). For other examples, see appendix A below, pp. 171–84.

[4] See below, pp. 34–7, 54–6. Cf. the modern law, on which see A. W. Scott, *The Law of Trusts*, 3rd. ed. (Boston, 1967), §391.

[5] E.g. C. 1/10/249 (uncertain—1433–43?); C. 1/12/83 (1433).

[6] E.g. C. 1/23/2 (1452–4?). Conversely, an heir-at law might seek to prevent feoffees applying property to charitable uses. Such a person was Nicholas Rowley, who subpoenaed the defendant who intended to use property for the 'welthe of his [father's] sowle . . . to be prayed for': see C. 1/561/100 (1518–29).

[7] C. 1/463/19 (1518–29).

[8] C. 1/331/88 (1504–15).

[9] C. 1/331/23 (1504–15), where the Master and Wardens of the Merchant Taylors' Company of London declared that the deceased had promised money to enable them to found a chantry in St Mary Abchurch and to distribute coals in the parish; the money was never received because of his sudden death. There is no indication whether the bill was successful; but see below, pp. 62–4. Cf. Swinburne, *Testaments and Last Wills*, 518–19.

'that hereafter lay people then may be the gladder and better willed to helping.'[1]

Few answers to these bills are extant,[2] and replies to answers are even fewer. Only exceptionally is there any indorsement that a petition was or was not successful, and before 1534–5 there are no *Decree Rolls*[3] so that the fate of a particular bill usually remains conjectural. Moreover the number of bills, answers and replies touching charitable causes is relatively meagre. In the one hundred and thirty-two years from the beginning of the fifteenth century to the end of Thomas More's Chancellorship the bills which concern the application of charitable funds appear to be less than one hundred.[4] This is a surprisingly small figure, when it is remembered that the number of interlocutory documents extant for the same period amounts to some one hundred thousand, that only a small percentage of bills could have ever reached judgment and decree, and that at this time Englishmen were supporting with considerable generosity works of piety.[5] But there is no evidence that the Chancellor had surrendered jurisdiction over charitable suits to the Bishop and the ecclesiastical courts or that he would not grant to the charitable gift the privileges anciently awarded to legacies *ad pias causas* by canon law.

[1] C. 1/98/17 (1486–93). The bill is transcribed in appendix B below, pp. 202–3.

[2] It is puzzling that the number of answers is not larger. It is likely that the facts were challenged orally in court; and it is significant that answers become more frequent with the Chancellor's increasing reliance on the written document: cf. Holdsworth, *History of English Law*, II, 342–3; Jones, *Elizabethan Court of Chancery*, 12.

[3] The Chancery *Entry Books of Decrees and Orders* begin in 1544–5. 'Decisions came to be recorded in the decree rolls but subsequently it was also done, and in expanding form, in the entry books, which in many respects came to supersede the rolls. Orders, motions, and every minute facet of procedure were also entered in the books, and before the end of the sixteenth century they had become a near-complete record of the court's activities.' See Jones, *Elizabethan Court of Chancery*, 14; and see below, p. 18.

[4] Ninety-two bills are set out in appendix A below, pp. 171–84. These figures must be very approximate for the volume of interlocutory documents means that any calculation must inevitably be based on the Public Record Office, Lists and Indexes: see above, p. 6, n. 3. The indexes give a terse indication (often only in a word or two) of the content of the bill. I have read all the bills and answers which I have been able to identify from the Lists and Indexes as 'charitable'; and have catalogued them in appendix A.

[5] See below, pp. 18–22 for a discussion of this question.

CHAPTER II

THE REFORMATION AND THE LAW OF CHARITY

THE Reformation statutes were the legal culmination of a complex social and religious revolution which affected all aspects of English life. The overthrow of papal supremacy and the decline of the authority of organised religion was paralleled by, what Professor Dickens has called, 'a change of viewpoint concerning the nature and functions of religion, both in the individual and in society.'[1] One manifestation of such a change was in the character of man's philanthropy.[2] The objects of charity were to become more secular as the majority of Englishmen reflected less on the fate of their souls and became more concerned with the worldly needs of their fellow men.[3]

Englishmen had always devoted considerable property to the endowment of chantries,[4] but these endowments had not always been applied for the purposes intended by their founders. Complaints that chantries had been allowed to lapse and that their endowments had been appropriated by the priest, the founder or the founder's heirs were not infrequent, and their maladministration[5] was the principal reason given in the Henrician statute of 1545 for their eventual suppression.[6]

The destruction of the chantries had profound educational and religious consequences[7] which have tended to overshadow the

[1] A. G. Dickens, *The English Reformation* (London, 1964), 325.

[2] See, generally, the trilogy of W. K. Jordan, *Philanthropy in England, 1480–1660* (London, 1958); *The Charities of London, 1480–1660* (London, 1960); *The Charities of Rural England, 1480–1660* (London, 1961).

[3] Jordan, *Philanthropy in England, 1480–1660* (London, 1959), *passim.*

[4] K. L. Wood-Legh, *Studies in Church Life in England under Edward III* (Cambridge, 1934), chap. IV, and *Perpetual Chantries in Britain* (Cambridge, 1965), 305–8.

[5] To secure the proper application of chantry endowments, testators would often provide for a gift to a charity on condition that it maintained a chantry, with a gift over to another charity if it failed to do so: see, for example, the wills cited in *Wills in the Court of Husting*, ed. R. R. Sharpe (London, 1889), II, 182–3, 431, 473; and cf. C. 1/152/52 (1486–93), or (1504–15), below, p. 178.

[6] 37 Hen. VIII c. 4; below, p. 11.

[7] See, generally, Dickens, *English Reformation*, 205–17, 334; *The New Cambridge Modern History*, II, *The Reformation 1520–59*, ed. G. R. Elton (Cambridge, 1958), 244; A. F. Pollard, *The History of England, from the Accession of*

effect of the chantry statutes on the English law of charity. For lawyers the chantry statutes are significant in that with their enactment emerges the conception of the *superstitious* use, so-called because it was a use which supported false (superstitious), religious purposes. Such uses were to be held unlawful and void, and the lawful charitable use was to be sharply distinguished from the unlawful superstitious use.[1] An attempt had been made in 1532 to dissuade donors from transferring land to chantries. By a statute of that year,[2] all feoffments (other than assurances for less than twenty years) made, *inter alia*, 'to the uses and intentes to have obittes perpetuall, or a continuall service of a Priste for ever' were declared to be void, being much prejudicial to the King our Sovereign Lord, and to other Lords and Subjects; and land so conveyed was to escheat to the mesne lord. The objects of this statute were very limited. It was in the tradition of the earlier mortmain legislation which had sought to dissuade donors from conveying land into the dead-hand of perpetual corporations, and no attempt was made to appropriate to the Crown the endowments of existing chantry foundations. Not until 1545 did the Crown seek to do this.

The preamble of the 1545 statute[3] attempts to justify this royal act of appropriation in a number of ways. Founders and patrons had misapplied endowments; lands had been sold without royal licence, and leases had been made by chantry wardens at low rentals for their own profit; chantries had been 'clerely dissolved extincted or determyned, contrarye to the willes myndes intentes and purposes of the foundors donors or patrons of the same, and to the greate contempte of your Majestie and of your auctoritie royall,' who 'hathe had and susteyned and dayley doeth susteyne, [great expense] as well for the mayntenance of theis present warres againste the relmes of Fraunce and Scotlande, and for the preservacion and defence of us your said subjects againste the invasions and malice of your enemyes, the Frenchmen and Scotts.' But there is no hint in the preamble or the body of the statute that chantries were objectionable on theological grounds, as nurturing false religion. Moreover there is no

Edward VI to the Death of Elizabeth (London, 1910), 17–19; Joan Simon, *Education and Society in Tudor England* (Cambridge, 1966); and the authorities cited in these works.

[1] See below, pp. 82–7.

[2] 23 Hen. VIII c. 10.

[3] 37 Hen. VIII c. 4.

pretence that the chantry revenues would find their way into any treasury but the royal treasury; although Henry, in his speech on the dissolution of the 1545 Parliament, tried to alleviate the anxieties of subjects, vociferously unwilling to renounce property in favour of the Crown, by a promise that he would take care, 'both for the supplying the ministers, for encouraging learning, and relieving the poor; and they should quickly perceive that in these things their expectations should be answered, beyond what they either wished or desired'.[1]

On the death of Henry the Crown's power to appropriate chantry revenues lapsed, only to be immediately revived by the statute 1 Edward VI c.14.[2] The preamble to that statute, which was to be frequently cited by later generations of lawyers as expressing its sense and reason,[3] differed significantly in tone and language from that of its Henrician predecessor, and reflected how rapidly the theological revolution had gathered momentum since 1545.[4] The justification for the Edwardian statute was not the maladministration of chantries but the need to suppress superstitious errors in the Christian religion. Its preamble read as follows:

The King's most lovinge subjects, the Lordes spirituall and temporall and the Commons in this present Parlament assembled, consydering that a greate part of superstition and errors in Christian Religion hath byn brought into the myndes and estimacion of men, by reasone of the Ignoraunce of their verie trewe and perfecte salvacion throughe the deathe of Jesus Christ, and by devising and phantasinge vayne opynions of Purgatorye and Masses satisfactorie to be done for them which be departed, the which doctryne and vayn opynion by nothing more is mayntayned and upholden then by the abuse of Trentalls, Chauntries, and other provisions made for the contynuance of the saide blyndness and ignoraunce; And further considering and understanding that the alteracion chaunge and amendement of the same, and converting to good and godlie uses, as in erecting of Gramer Scoles to the educacion of Youthe in virtewe and godlinesse, the further augmenting of the Universities and better provision for the poore and nedye, cannot in this present Parlament be provyded and convenyentlie doon, nor cannot ne ought to anny other manner parsone be committed then to

[1] Gilbert Burnet, *The History of the Reformation of the Church of England*, 2nd ed. (London, 1679), I, 338. And see Simon, *Education and Society in Tudor England*, 193.

[2] See, generally, Simon, *Education and Society in Tudor England*, especially chap. IX.

[3] See below, pp. 82–7, 143.

[4] *New Cambridge Modern History*, II, 244.

the King's Highnes whose Majestie with and by the advice of his Highnes moste prudent Counsaile can and will moste wiseleye and beneficiallye bothe for the honnor of God and the weale of this his Majesties Realme, order alter converte and dispose the same.

The substantive provisions of the statute appeared to forfeit to the Crown the lands of 'all manner of Colleges, Free Chapells and Chauntries, having being or *in esse* within five yeres next before the firste day of this present parlament'[1] and of brotherhoods, guilds and fraternities.[2] Thus, many were led to believe that the property of brotherhoods, guilds and fraternities was forfeited to the Crown whether or not it was devoted to the support of superstitious purposes. There was consequently outspoken opposition to the statute, and it was only the Crown's assurance that property held to non-superstitious purposes was outside the equity of the Act and concessions to the City of Coventry and the town of Lynn, that secured its speedy enactment.[3]

The apparent object of the statute was to confiscate the land endowments of *existing* chantries, the Crown piously promising, as before, to sustain from them 'good and godlie uses, as in erecting of Gramer Scoles, to the educacion of Youthe in virtewe and godlinesse, the further augmenting of the Universities and better provision for the poore and nedye.' So its substantive provisions only forfeited to the Crown realty which had been conveyed to chantries before the enactment of the statute; they disdained, with one limited exception,[4] the gift of personalty and did not appropriate any prospective endowment of realty to superstitious purposes. For these reasons, perhaps, it had never been repealed by Mary,[5] and Elizabeth I was careful, on her accession, to annex to the Crown all lands belonging to religious houses, monasteries and chantries, restored or erected in her sister's reign.[6] Nevertheless Coke, in his report of *Adams* and *Lambert*'s case[7] in 1602, observed that *any* property transferred *at any time* to superstitious purposes was forfeit to the Crown, for the object of the Edwardian chantry statute was 'to extirpate out of men's minds these superstitious errors, and to take them utterly away.' Coke's extravagance

[1] § I.

[2] § VII.

[3] Simon, *Education and Society in Tudor England*, 223–4.

[4] 1 Edw. VI c. 14, § 17.

[5] Indeed the statute 1 & 2 Ph. and M. c. 8 expressly protected, in § xv, the title of purchasers of chantry lands.

[6] 1 Eliz. I c. 24.

[7] (1602), 4 Co. 104b, 106b.

of language was well known to his contemporaries, and it must be confessed with Egerton, no friend of the Chief Justice, that Coke did darken his report of *Adams* and *Lambert*'s case with 'many intricate differences whereof the Court that argued the same did never dream.'[1] But principles of statutory interpretation in the sixteenth century were fluid and flexible; yesterday's interpretation of the 'sense' and 'reason' of a statute might not be that of to-morrow.[2] In the England of Elizabeth no man could have known how far the judges would extend the equity of the chantry statute, and in *Porter's* case[3] in 1592 counsel had had the temerity to argue, albeit unsuccessfully, that its sense and reason effectively destroyed all charitable and godly uses.[4] Religion was as variable as the pleasure of succeeding princes,[5] and no Englishman still faithful to the Old Church would have been anxious to provide posterity with a clear answer to the question whether transfers of real or personal property made after 1547, to superstitious purposes were forfeit to the Crown. The question, moreover, would have been mildly academic; for a gift to a superstitious use was after Elizabeth's accession void at common law even if it was outside the equity of the Edwardian chantry statute,[6] so that the property

[1] *Observations on Lord Coke's Reports* (London, 1710), 21. The author of this work was probably Egerton; but the matter is not free from doubt.

[2] For a discussion, see S. E. Thorne's introduction to *A Discourse upon the Exposicion and Understandinge of Statutes, with Sir Thomas Egerton's Additions* (California, 1942), 57–8.

[3] (1592), 1 Co. 22b.

[4] *Ibid.* 24a; see also *Martidale* v. *Martin* (1592), Cro. Eliz. 288.

If the charitable use was inextricably intermingled with the superstitious use, then the property could be forfeited to the Crown: see the contemporary cases collected in George Duke's *Law of Charitable Uses* (London, 1676), 86–94; henceforth cited as Duke. Lord Eldon considered Duke a work of 'great authority': see *Att.-Gen.* v. *Hartley* (1820), 2 J. and W. 353, 370–1. Much of its authority is derived from the fact that it contains an abridgment of Francis Moore's *Reading* on the Statute of Charitable Uses (cited hereafter as Duke (Moore)): see below, p. 27, n. 1. Duke's own contribution was small, for his book is merely a 'new edition' of John Herne's treatise on *Charitable Uses*, first published in 1660. For a full bibliographical note on Duke's book, see appendix E below, pp. 232–4.

[5] Duke (Moore), 131–2; see below pp. 31–7.

[6] *Croft* v. *Jane Evetts* (1605), Duke, 127; *Lady Egerton*'s case (1606), Moo. K. B., 551; see below, pp. 82–7 for a full discussion. By 2 and 3 Edw. VI c. 1 all ministers were required to celebrate Divine Service according to the Book of Common Prayer; and by 3 & 4 Edw. VI c. 10, all missals, antyphons, etc., were 'utterlye abollished, extinguished and forbidden for ever'. These statutes were repealed by 1 Mary, stat. 2, c. 2. But the authority of the Book of Common Prayer was restored by 1 Eliz. I c. 2, which repealed all laws as to Divine Service

if not forfeitable to the Crown would have reverted to the grantor's heir or next-of-kin. The theology, if not the equity, of the Edwardian chantry statute had drawn a clear line between the charitable use, which the courts would continue to favour, and the superstitious use which the courts would strike down. Piety and charity could no longer be to all Englishmen synonymous conceptions.

established in Mary's reign. Penalties were not imposed on those who said or heard mass until 23 Eliz. I c. 1 § 3. It was by this statute, § 1, that persons who attempted to persuade any of the Queen's subjects to 'withdrawe . . . from the Relygeon nowe by her Highenes aucthoritie established within her Highenes Domynions, to the Romyshe Religeon' were declared guilty of High Treason.

I know of no case before the early seventeenth century where the courts were required to consider the fate of a transfer of property, made after 1547, to popish purposes. Express gifts to superstitious uses were, for reasons set out in the text, rare: cf. Jordan, *Charities of London*, 279. And see below, pp. 82–7 for a further discussion whether property devoted to superstitious uses was forfeited to the Crown.

CHAPTER III

THE STATUTES OF CHARITABLE USES: 39 ELIZABETH I c. 6 AND 43 ELIZABETH I c. 4

The common law background

THOUGH after the Reformation the objects of men's bounty are more secular, frequently the poor of a village or the scholars of the local grammar school,[1] the nature of the petitioners' complaints does not change. The parson and church-wardens of St Mary Maudlin in Milke Street, London, complain[2] to Lord Keeper Sir Nicholas Bacon that Thomas Altham and William Gray have omitted to

> distribute, yeld and deliver unto the poore sicke and nedye paryshyoners of the said poore paryshes and in and amongste the poore prysoners in Newgate . . . eight shillings, . . . to be bestowed in good newe and sweete breade.

The churchwardens of Whitchurch assert[3] that their vicar had failed to maintain their parish church from the revenues of certain lands which had been conveyed to him for such a purpose; he had cut off the seal of the conveyance and the 'same did embeasell', and had expelled them from the land, 'not suffering them to enjoy the profits thereof'. Consequently 'your said Orators cannot have anie remedye by the order of the common lawes of this realme and so are like to be remedyless for recovery of the said land to their grete hinderaunce and to the utter subvercion of such charitable dedes and workes wich were usually done with the profittes thereof.'[4]

[1] The changing character of man's philanthropy has been fully discussed by Professor Jordan in his trilogy on the history of English philanthropy: see above, p. 10, n. 2. The subject matter of the Chancery bills is further support for his general thesis.

[2] C. 3/118/60, 61 (1564). The bill is transcribed in appendix B, below, pp. 203–5.

[3] C. 3/119/23 (*temp.* Nicholas Bacon L.K., 1558–79).

[4] Other bills seek the appointment of new feoffees to hold to charitable uses; for example, that a 'deed of feoffment might be made and younger men might be put into the same for the better [performance] of the uses thereof for ever': see C. 2/Eliz./W.9/42 (1596). See also C. 2/Eliz./D.2/57 (1601).

Pleas in answer to such petitions are now frequent, and it is noticeable that Chancery pleading becomes more prolix and sophisticated as the sixteenth century progresses.[1] The answer generally commences with much that is common form:[2] a defendant pleads that the petitioner should have proceeded in the common law courts or in the ecclesiastical courts or in the court of the ancient demesne; the petition is 'incertayne and insufficient in law to be answered into'; or it is 'maliciously' brought to put the defendant 'to wrongfull costes and expenses in the lawe'. It then sets out the real defence to the petition: an executor pleads insufficiency of assets;[3] a feoffee denies that he claims any personal interest in a charitable endowment;[4] Benjamin Harris answers that he had not yet paid the testator's legacy to the poor of Burnham but has paid them £10 yearly;[5] Francis Dynne, executor of Robert Lambe, is detaining a legacy of £20 until the inhabitants of Halingbury Morley enter into a bond that the money should be spent for the 'best purposes' and distributed where there is 'most neede' among the poor;[6] and Robert Suckerman denied that the scrivener negligently failed to give effect to the testator's true intention, which was to benefit a charitable use.[7]

The majority of petitioners pray for the enforcement of charitable trusts. But the number of petitions to compel executors and legatees to carry out bequests for charitable purposes is rateably no less than before the Reformation.[8] This is significant, for there is evidence that after Nicholas Bacon had ceased to be Lord Keeper in 1579 suits to enforce legacies were in practice directed to be heard in the ecclesiastical courts.[9] 'None . . . ought to have recourse *ad extraordinarium remedium ubi competit et ordinarium*,'[10]

[1] Cf. W. J. Jones. *The Elizabethan Court of Chancery* (Oxford, 1967), chap. VII.

[2] For examples, see the answers transcribed in appendix B below, pp. 208–11, 213–15.

[3] C. 2/Eliz./B. 29/44 (1602).

[4] C. 2/Eliz./H. 7/57 (*temp.* Thomas Bromley L.K., 1579–87).

[5] C. 2/Eliz./B. 1/16 (1595).

[6] C. 2/Eliz./H. 20/35 (*temp.* Thomas Egerton L.K., 1596–1603).

[7] C. 3/214/75 (1586). See also C. 2/Eliz./M. 10/65 (1597).

[8] Appendix A, below, pp. 184–201.

[9] Though this tendency is particularly marked during Egerton's tenure as Lord Keeper, it is clear from a study of the Chancery records that there is a sharp decline after 1579 in the number of legatory matters which were heard by the Chancellor. See, too, Jones's comments in his *Elizabethan Court of Chancery*, 409 ff.

[10] *Nelson* v. *Norton* (1591), Cecil Monro's *Acta Cancellariae* (London, 1847), 10.

for it is 'more meet' that such matters should be heard 'in the Ecclesiastical Court than in this Court'.[1] Though the Chancellor required, therefore, the private legatee to take his suit for 'ordinary trial in those courts, where the same doth properly lie,'[2] he would take jurisdiction over a petition to enforce a charitable legacy. The petitioner on behalf of a charity would not have to incur the additional expense and further frustration of a suit in the ecclesiastical courts.[3]

This is but one example of the many privileges which the Chancellor was prepared to grant to the charitable gift. The evidence of the registrars' *Entry Books of Decrees and Orders*,[4] which are extant from 1544–5, reveals that the ancient privileges given by canon law to charity were confirmed by the Chancellor: for example, no charitable gift was allowed to fail for uncertainty; imperfect conveyances of land to charity were perfected; and debts were first marshalled against private legacies. Though the Reformation was to restrict the class of charitable objects,[5] it did not curtail in any way the privileges[6] which the law conferred on the gift *ad pias causas*.

The number of bills to enforce charitable uses and legacies between 1532 and 1601 (the date of the enactment of the second charity statute)[7] was, as far as can be judged from the Public Record Office Lists and Indexes, 131; so that for the period from

[1] *Browne* v. *Ricards* (1600), Monro, 761.

[2] *Nelson* v. *Norton* (1591), Monro, 10.

[3] Legacies payable to infants and married women were similarly favoured: see G. Spence, *The Equitable Jurisdiction of the Court of Chancery* (London, 1846), I, 581–2; W. S. Holdsworth, *A History of English Law*, V (London, 1924), 320.

[4] These exist only in MS. There are two books for each year, known respectively as the *A* and *B* books. Until 1629 each book contains suits commenced by any petitioner, and there are often duplicate entries. After that date, however, a suit commenced by a petitioner whose surname begins with the letters A–K will be found in the *A* book, and the remaining suits in the *B* book. The majority of entries deal with interlocutory matters; but demurrers and decrees are also recorded. See *Guide to the Contents of the Public Record Office*, I (London, 1963), 30; and above, p. 9 n. 3.

Decrees were also enrolled. But enrolment was never popular and by the end of Elizabeth's reign less than thirty decrees were being enrolled annually. For one explanation, see M. Birks, 'The Perfecting of Orders in Chancery', [1955] *Cambridge Law Journal*, 101; but cf. Jones, 'Due Process and Slow Process in the Elizabethan Chancery', *American Journal of Legal History*, VI (1962), 123, 147, n. 71, and *Elizabethan Court of Chancery*, 296.

[5] See above, p. 11 and below, pp. 57–8.

[6] See below, pp. 59–101 for a full discussion of these privileges.

[7] 43 Eliz. I c. 4; see below pp. 224–8.

1400 to 1601 the number of bills amounted to 223.[1] This calculation is, of course, approximate. Many bills may not have been traced or have been lost; but the *Entry Books of Decrees and Orders* confirm that the number of charitable suits heard by the Chancellor was very few, not more than one or two a year. Such figures could persuade a superficial inquirer to conclude that feoffees to charitable uses were distinguished by their integrity and honesty.[2] There is good reason to believe, however, that the traditional Chancery procedure of petition, answer, and decree, was an inadequate method of controlling their conduct and their application of charitable funds. For with the new procedure of supervision established by the charity statutes of 1597[3] and 1601,[4] there is a startling increase in the number of 'charity' decrees. So in the reign of James I alone as a result of the investigations of the charity commissioners the Chancellor made over one thousand decrees securing the proper application of charitable endowments and correcting the maladministration of charitable funds by individual feoffees.[5]

The procedure of the Court of Chancery was initially both simple and speedy.[6] There were no technical rules of pleading and the proceedings were characterised by informality. In the sixteenth century, however, there are indications that these advantages were beginning to disappear. Pleadings became progressively more verbose and delaying motions, both before and after judgment, more frequent. Thomas More's feat in clearing the back-log of cases that had accumulated during Wolsey's Chancellorship was a matter for comment among lawyers two generations later,[7] and by the end of the century there were audible murmurings

[1] See appendix A, below, pp. 171–201.

[2] Particularly if Professor Jordan's estimate of the volume of philanthropy between 1558 and 1601 is accepted: see *Philanthropy in England, 1480–1660* (London, 1959), chap. VII. It has been argued, however, that Jordan has not taken into account the startling price-rise which occurred during this period; in which case his figures require considerable readjustment: see *History*, XLIV (1959), 257 (L. Stone); *English Historical Review*, LXXVII (1962), 327 (L. Stone); *Historical Journal*, III (1960), 89 (G. R. Elton).

[3] 39 Eliz. I c. 6; see below, pp. 23–4.

[4] 43 Eliz. I c. 4; see below, pp. 24 ff.

[5] See below, pp. 52–3, for a full discussion. These figures are based on the statistical analysis contained in appendix I below, pp. 255–6.

[6] W. T. Barbour, *History of Contract in Early English Equity*, Oxford Studies in Social and Legal History, IV (Oxford, 1914), 72; Holdsworth, *History of English Law*, V, 285–6.

[7] 'Ro. Ba.', *Life of Sir Thomas More, Ecclesiastical Biography*, II (1559), 80, quoted by R. W. Chambers, *Thomas More* (London, 1935), 262.

directed against the expense and tardiness of Chancery procedure.[1] The enforcement of charitable gifts must have been peculiarly difficult. Often there was no single 'legal' person whose interests would be affected by the failure of feoffees to perform their trust. Representative actions (for example on behalf of the poor of Dale) were cumbersome; defendants could delay the hearing by objecting that the representatives were not 'apt parties',[2] and the representatives themselves would be well aware that they would have to bear the costs of the petition if it failed.[3] Moreover, a great many charitable gifts were relatively paltry, a few pounds annually or half an acre of land, and the expense of ensuring that such meagre endowments were applied according to the intent of the donors must have chilled the hearts of potential petitioners. A commission to examine witnesses, together with the fees of counsel and court officials, would soon eat up a small trust fund. It is not surprising that the proper application of charitable funds often depended on the intervention of feoffees who were corporate bodies or an affluent heir-at-law who could withstand the expense and delays of litigation.[4]

It has always been a 'peculiarity of Charitable Trusts', as the Victorian charity commissioners were to note in 1857, 'that the persons beneficially interested under them are seldom in a position to originate measures affecting their government, and the disposition of disinterested persons to undertake such measures with a single view to the benefit of their objects cannot always be relied on.'[5] In the ecclesiastical courts the Ordinary's responsibility as the guardian of charity was necessary because there was frequently no single person who was prepared to, or was in a position to,

[1] William Roper, *Life and Death of Sir Thomas More* (London, 1729), 44–5; G. Norburie, *The Abuses and Remedies of the High Court of Chancery*; Hargrave's *Collection of Tracts relative to the Law of England* (London, 1787), 425, which was written 'soon after the fall of Lord Bacon and the promotion of Bishop Williams to the great seal'; W. J. Jones, 'Due Process and Slow Process in the Elizabethan Chancery', *American Journal of Legal History*, VI (1962), 123, and *Elizabethan Court of Chancery*, 16, 306–8, 335–6.

[2] See D. E. C. Yale's introduction to *Lord Nottingham's Manual of Chancery Practice and Prolegomena of Chancery and Equity* (Cambridge, 1965), 51–2.

[3] Cf. below, pp. 161–2. Actions *in forma pauperis* could be brought if the petitioner was worth less than £5. Such a petitioner was not penalised in costs if he lost, but he might be whipped for his impertinence!: see Spence, *Equitable Jurisdiction*, I, 381; Monro, 690; Jones, *Elizabethan Court of Chancery*, 323–8.

[4] Cf. below, pp. 160–8, where the eighteenth-century evidence is discussed.

[5] 4th Report, 7; see below, pp. 53–6.

ensure the proper application of charitable endowments.[1] But in the Court of Chancery there was before 1597 no adequate procedure which enabled the Crown, the Ordinary's successor as the guardian angel of charity, to protect the charitable gift. Some judges have claimed that the Crown did attempt to do so from the reign of Elizabeth onwards through an information brought by the Attorney-General at the relation of a private individual.[2] This is not so. The Chancery records do not reveal a single example of a sixteenth-century information to enforce a charitable use or legacy.[3] In fact the lack of any suitable procedure which could ensure the efficient administration of charitable funds was to become a matter of grave concern to an Elizabethan Council anxious to utilise every economic asset for the relief of poverty. It is true that by statute (1571–2[4]) transfers of property for the use of the poor in any hospital were deemed to be valid even though the transfer would have been void at common law because the hospital's corporate name had been erroneously spelt out in the instrument of transfer; and there is an occasional example of the Crown enforcing a charitable gift through an information of intrusion in the Exchequer, where the legal title to the property held to the charitable use had been vested in the Crown.[5] But these were *ad hoc* solutions of particular problems. What was needed was a general procedure which would supplement the traditional Chancery procedure, which would manifest the Crown's concern

[1] See above, p. 4.

[2] For example, *Eyre* v. *Countess of Shaftesbury* (1722), 2 P. Wms. 103, 119, *per* Jekyll M.R. No authority is quoted for this assertion.

[3] The earliest information to enforce charitable uses dates from *c.* 1635 when the Attorney-General intervened to enforce a charitable use which was within neither the letter nor equity of the charity statute: see below, pp. 34–7.

There are extant informations, dating from the reign of James I, where the Crown sought to compel an individual to maintain a public highway or to perform other public works. But these were *sui generis*, even though the individual's duties might arise from his position as a feoffee under a charitable trust: see, for example, C. 8/24/15 (1610). And see below, pp. 34–7.

[4] 14 Eliz. I. c. 14; and cf. 39 Eliz. I. c. 5.

[5] E.g. *Porter*'s case (1592), 1 Co. 22b. It has been suggested that *Porter*'s case is evidence that the Chancellor's jurisdiction over charities was suspended in 1592, and that the parties had to make out their case as best they could at law: see *Att.-Gen.* v. *Bowyer* (1798), 3 Ves. 714, 726, *per* Lord Loughborough; Spence, *Equitable Jurisdiction* I, 589; cf. J. Story, *Commentaries on Equity Jurisprudence*, 14th ed. (Boston, 1918), §§ 1581–3. This interpretation is not supported by any evidence and is conclusively refuted by the Chancery records cited in appendix A, below, pp. 184–201, and by the *Entry Books*.

to protect charity and which would ensure the application, in accordance with the intent of the donors, of those charitable uses whose endowments could alleviate the sufferings of the 'Godly and honest sort of the poor Subjects of this realm.'[1]

The statutes of charitable uses

'The extream and miserable estate of the Godly and honest sort of the poor Subjects of this realm'[2] became more desperate in the last decade of the sixteenth century with a series of disastrous harvests and the increasing strain of the Spanish War. When Parliament met in 1597 members anxiously drew attention to their suffering and to the danger of violent upheaval if their misery was not immediately relieved. The result of this momentous session was a series of statutes which gave to the English system of poor relief a moulding which it preserved for centuries.[3] This legislation confirmed that the relief of poverty was a local as well as a national responsibility, and that the burden of assisting the poor should be borne by the parish and the county and financed by a compulsory rate levied on householders. At the same time it recognised that private philanthropy could materially contribute to the relief of poverty and that the conduct of feoffees to charitable uses had hitherto been inadequately supervised, so that existing charitable funds were being diverted into uncharitable pockets. Charitable funds

> have bene and are still like to be most unlawfully and uncharitably converted to the lucre and gayne of some fewe greedy and covetous persons, contrary to the true intente and meaning of the givers and disposers thereof.[4]

The traditional Chancery method of supervision was a wholly inadequate means of controlling the administration of charitable endowments, and could not have failed to discourage the hesitant philanthropist. It was essential, therefore, to establish a procedure which would enable the Crown to initiate and sustain a thorough

[1] Simond D'Ewes, *The Journals of all the Parliaments during the Reign of Queen Elizabeth* (London, 1682), 552, attributes this remark to Henry Finch, the member for the city of Canterbury in the 1597 Parliament.

[2] See above, n. 1.

[3] Beatrice and Sidney Webb, *English Local Government: English Poor Law History* (London, 1927–9), part I, 61.

[4] 39 Eliz. I c. 6, preamble.

investigation of charitable uses that their endowments might be 'duly and faithfully employed' in accordance with the intent of the donors. From these needs was born the statute 39 Elizabeth I c. 6, being 'An Acte to reforme Deceits and Breaches of Trust, touching Lands given to Charitable Uses', which was re-enacted four years later, with amendments, in the Charitable Uses Act, 1601, 43 Elizabeth I c. 4.[1]

Simond D'Ewes described the 1597 Act as of 'no great moment'.[2] Though it formed an integral part of the Elizabethan poor relief legislation, its role, in comparison with that of the major statutes such as the Poor Relief Act (39 Elizabeth I c. 3), was indeed a minor one. It was not referred to the principal committee of the House of Commons which was considering the major statutes, but to a smaller committee composed largely of lawyers.[3] Its first reading was on 12 January 1597, and by 26 January 1597, it had passed through all its stages in both Houses of Parliament.[4] The Act provided for commissioners to investigate breaches of trust within the county specified in the commission. Parishioners were invited to furnish evidence of breaches known to them, and the commissioners, on the inquisition of a jury, would then make their decree correcting any breach. An appeal from that decree could subsequently be made to the Chancellor. This procedure, which will be discussed in detail later in this book,[5] was a method of inquiry much employed by Tudor Councils.[6] In comparison with the ancient Chancery procedure of bill and answer it was, in many ways, better adapted for the conduct of a highly inquisitorial investigation, and it had been successfully used to ferret out superstitious uses. It was initially an equally successful method of detecting breaches of charitable trusts,[7] although there were

[1] Tudor monarchs knew full well the value of private philanthropy; but the 1597 and 1601 statutes were hardly, as Professor Jordan has claimed (*Philanthropy in England*, 114), great gathering Acts, 'bringing under codification a long development and a fruitful national experience in the growth of charitable trusts as instruments of social betterment': see below, pp. 52 ff.

[2] *Journals*, pp. 579–80. The text of the statute is to be found below, pp. 221–3.

[3] Its members included Serjeants Harris, Lewkenor, and Warburton; the knights and burgesses of London; Miles Sands; Sir Robert Wroth; and others.

[4] D'Ewes, *Journals*, 541–2, 543, 579, 589.

[5] See below, pp. 39–47.

[6] 'With modifications, some commissions issued from the Exchequer. Cf. the activities of the commissioners of sewers, described by T. G. Barnes, *Somerset 1625–1640* (London, 1961), 146 ff.

[7] See below, pp. 52–6.

some aspects of the procedure which invited adverse comment. In the debate in 1601 on the 'continuance' of 39 Elizabeth I c. 6, Francis Tate, the member for Northampton Borough, criticised that statute on the ground that:[1]

That could be no Law, which was contrary to the Great CHARTER of England. And this was, because it gave Power against the Great CHARTER which giveth Challenges to Jurors, which this law alloweth not.

Therefore he wished that there might be Commitment, to consider, whether it were fit to be continued, or repealed.

The committee which was appointed to consider this question[2] was given authority to 'put in the Bill of Repeal or in the Bill of Continuance of Statutes, the statute 39 Elizabeth I c. 6.' Hayward Townshend narrates that on 4 December 1601, three days after the committee's first meeting, a Mr Philips, who was most probably Edward Philips (or Phelips), later to be Speaker and Master of the Rolls, then member for Somerset and a lawyer of standing,[3] presented to the House of Commons the report of the Committee. It reads as follows:[4]

The Committee met, and entered into three Considerations: First, whether the Act of 39 *Reginae* Intituled, *An Act to Reform Deceipts and Breaches of Trusts touching Lands given to Charitable Uses* should stand in force or no, as now it is? And all generally agreed it should not.

The second was, whether Reformation thereof should be by Explanation or Abrogation? And in the end it was concluded, it should be by Abrogation.

The Third was, whether it should be abrogated by the general Repeal of Statutes, or that there should be a particular Statute for that purpose: And 'twas agreed that it should be done by a particular Statute.

[1] Hayward Townshend, *Proceedings of the last Four Parliaments of Queen Elizabeth* (London, 1680), 259.

[2] Its members were Sir Edward Stafford, Sir Robert Wroth, Sir Edward Hobbie, Sir Francis Hastings, Sir George Moore, Mr Philips, Sergeant Harris, all members of the Commons who were counsel learned in the law, the Master of Requests, and 'divers others': see D'Ewes, *Journals*, 626, 657, 669. Sir Francis Moore, who is reputed to have drafted the 1601 statute, is not mentioned by name.

I do not think the available evidence supports the traditional claim that Moore was the statute's 'penner'. Philips, according to Townshend, claimed that honour. Most probably, however, the bill was a corporate enterprise. See appendix E, below, pp. 232 ff. where there is also a brief sketch of Moore's life and an evaluation of his importance as a common lawyer.

[3] *Dictionary of National Biography* (London, 1896), XLV, 143; E. Foss, *The Judges of England* (London, 1870), 513.

[4] Townshend, *Proceedings*, 285. See also D'Ewes, *Journals*, 685.

And for that purpose, being so commanded by the Committee, I have drawn a Bill referring it to the Wisdome of the House to be considered of; The Title is, *An Act for the good Execution of Charitable Uses in this Statute particularly mentioned.*

The debates on the proposed Act appear to have been completed by 16 December 1601.[1]

In the preamble to the new Charitable Uses Act, 1601, were set out the 'good, godly and charitable' uses over which the commissioners were to have jurisdiction, a remarkably comprehensive statement of those charitable uses whose endowments, properly employed, could assist in combating the social evils of vagrancy.[2] This preamble was later to be claimed as the quintessence of the statute's sense and reason and was to have the greatest influence on the English law of charity. Not only was it to provide a new rationalisation for many of the privileges anciently awarded to charity[3] but it helped to draw definitively the outlines of 'legal' charity,[4] outlines which were to remain authoritative long after the procedure of investigation established under the Act's substantive provisions had fallen into decay.[5]

The 1601 Act adopted and perfected the commission procedure established by the 1597 Act. It was a better drafted and more sophisticated document than its predecessor, adding new provisos and making significant amendments.[6] Under its provisions, commissions in the county were appointed to inquire into 'any breach of trust, falsity, non-employment, concealment, misgovernment or conversion' of charitable funds. The success of this procedure was immediate, and the years before the Civil War were distinguished by a thorough investigation of the administration of charitable trusts. That conflict, however, helped to erode the effectiveness of the commission. Without the support of strong parish government, the commission was revealed as a dilatory and expensive procedure, draining the energy and patience of all

[1] D'Ewes, *Journals*, 615, 669, 685; Townshend, *Proceedings*, 288, 289. Francis Bacon appeared to have been active in the debates on the Bill: see *ibid.* 298.

[2] In 'Illustrations of the Origin of *Cy-près*', *Harvard Law Review*, VIII (1894), 69, 70, Joseph Willard commented upon the similarity between the catalogue of charitable uses set out in the preamble (see below, p. 26) and that contained in Langland's *Vision of Piers Plowman*. Cf. the language of the preamble of the Irish statute of 1634 (10 Car. I, sess. 3, c. 1); on which see V. T. H. Delany, *The Law Relating to Charities in Ireland* (Dublin, 1962), 10, 18.

[3] See below, pp. 61–2.

[4] See below, pp. 57–8, 120–7.

[5] See below, pp. 54–6, 160.

[6] See appendix D below, pp. 224 ff. for the text.

concerned in its administration. There is evidence of an attempt to resurrect it after the Restoration. But by that time petitioners were already seeking other ways to enforce charitable trusts, particularly through the information (brought in the name of the Attorney-General at the relation of a private individual), which was essentially a variant of the bill procedure. Indeed the information proved so successful that by the end of the seventeenth century it had supplanted the commission as the primary method of enforcing charitable trusts.[1]

(i) *The jurisdiction of the commissioners*

Not every 'good, godly and charitable' use was subject to the jurisdiction of the commissioners, and the preamble of the 1601 Act set out in detail those which the commissioners were authorised to investigate. The preamble read:

Whereas lands tenements, rents annuities, profits, hereditaments, goods, chattels, money, and stocks of money, have been heretofore given, limited, appointed, and assigned as well by the Queen's most excellent majesty, and her most noble progenitors, as by sundry other well disposed persons: some for relief of aged, impotent, and poor people, some for maintenance of sick and maimed soldiers and mariners, schools of learning, free schools, and scholars in universities: some for repair of bridges, ports, havens, causeways, churches, seabanks and highways; some for education and preferment of orphans; some for or towards the relief, stock, or maintenance for houses of correction; some for marriages of poor maids; some for supportation, aid, and help of young tradesmen, handicraftsmen, and persons decayed; and others for relief or redemption of prisoners or captives, and for aid or ease of any poor inhabitants concerning payment of fifteens, setting out of soldiers, and other taxes; which lands, tenements, rents, annuities, profits, hereditaments, goods, chattels, money, and stocks of money, nevertheless, have not been employed according to the charitable intent of the givers and founders thereof, by reason of frauds, breaches of trust, and negligence in those that should pay, deliver and employ the same.

Here is an elaborate catalogue of uses the support of which would relieve poverty and at the same time reduce the parish's financial responsibility to succour the vagrant. This catalogue was never regarded as exclusive,[2] but as typical of the kind of charity which

[1] See below, pp. 52–6 for a full discussion of these themes.

[2] See, e.g. Moore's remarks in his *Reading* (on which see below, p. 27, n. 1), C.U.L. MS. Hh. III 2(c), fo. 11: 'le charitable uses sont touts trois destre meynteyne; mes le chapleine per le common ley de chauncery. Et le pulpitt

the State wished to encourage. In his *Reading*[1] Francis Moore consistently emphasised that the statute was *beneficiall ley* enacted to redress wrongs and frauds against charity and charitable gifts,[2] and urged that the preamble should be generously construed to protect those uses whose endowments could be applied for the public benefit. Public benefit was the key to the statute, and the relief of poverty its principal manifestation.[3] So, Moore concluded that the following uses[4] were within the equity of the statute:

(*a*) To find bows and arrows for children between the age of seven and seventeen; for many of the parents and masters who are statutorily bound to supply these weapons are poor and not able to meet that charge.[5]

(*b*) To build a causeway to a mill, even though the mill is in private hands and does not grind 'toll free'; for the causeway is within the letter of the statute and the passage is a public passage.[6]

et Bell per cest statute.' See also fo. 31^{v}: 'lannuitie *pro consilio* in divinitie nest deins lestatute pur les commissioners de faire decree, uncore nest void done. . . .' And see below, pp. 33 ff.

[1] There are two sources of the *Reading*, one in MS. and one in print. The MS. source, which is preserved in the Cambridge University Library, is in Moore's own hand. It is C.U.L. MS. Hh. III 2(c) (cited hereafter as Moore). For a bibliographical discussion, see appendix E below, pp. 234 ff.

The other source is in print, and is to be found in George Duke's *Law of Charitable Uses* (1676) (Duke (Moore)). Duke's book purports to contain collections from Moore's *Reading* based on Moore's own abridged MS. This MS. is now lost. See below, p. 233. For a bibliographical discussion, see appendix E, below, p. 232 ff.

[2] So, in his first case, fo. 9^{v}, he writes: 'le statute est beneficiall et fait de redresse wronge et frawde encountre le charitable dons et voluntes del people.'

[3] So, in *Fisher* v. *Hill* (1612), Duke, 82, it was held that 'where no use is mentioned or directed in a deed, it shall be decreed to the use of the poor'. And see below, p. 34, n. 2.

[4] These are examples taken from many, found in Moore's *Reading*.

[5] Fo. 9: 'car bowes et arrowes sont commaund per lestatute de 33 h. 8, pur chescun oustre 7 et deins 17 destre atchate per parents et masters, lou les parteis sont infants; des queux parents et masters ne poit estre mes que mult de de eux sont poore et nient able de supplie le chardge. Et pur ceo, de atchater pur lour children, est releif al eux quia toll le chardge de eux mesmes, et sic cest use est deins les parolls, *Releif of poore*.'

The duty was imposed by 33 Hen. VIII c. 9, § 1, being 'an Acte for Mayntenance of Artyllarie and debarringe of unlawful Games'.

[6] Fo. 40: 'car est cawsway deins le letter de lestatute, et le passage est publick, et ease le people in voy de passage pur chose de necessity. Sic semble de cawsway al watering place, etc.'

(*c*) To support bastards, orphaned on the death of their mothers; for charity does not respect birth, only need.[1]

(*d*) To relieve the inhabitants of taxes for bastards, for the parish is under an obligation to maintain them where their parents cannot do so. But a general gift to relieve bastards is not within the statute, for only the bastards of *disabled* parents are charged on the parish.[2]

(*e*) To maintain a public midwife within the parish, for it is for the benefit of poor women who cannot afford her services.[3]

(*f*) To instruct soldiers in surgery, for it is deemed to be within the words of the statute, *Relief of sick and maymhed soldiers*.[4]

(*g*) To pay the fees for decayed persons to go out of prizon to treat with their creditors, for the statute was designed to relieve persons decayed.[5]

(*h*) To buy stock to assist 'tradesmen', for the donor must intend this use to benefit only those who are 'young tradesmen or persons decayed'; and the commissioners can order the money for their support and no others.[6]

(*i*) To support poor women in childbirth, for it is for the relief of poverty.[7]

[1] Fo. 28v: 'Si bastard soit orphane puis mort sa mere, et semble que cy, car Charitie ne respect sa birth, mes sa nede, come prisoners malefactors sont deins cest statute.'

[2] Fo. 155v: 'de ease linhabitauntes de taxes pur bastard children est charitable use deins (*ease of other taxes*) quia plusors fois il aveigne que les parents ne sont able mes que le parishe doit de charity et necessity gard le children . . . Et done generall pur meynteynaunce de bastard children nest deins lestatute mes de ease linhabitaunts de eux est, quia nul de eux sont chardge sur le parishe; mes ceux quex ont disable parents.'

[3] Fo. 19: 'le meynteynaunce del publick midwyffe est charitable use deins lestatute, quia tend al releif del plusors poore femes quex ne sont able de payer le midwyffe.'

[4] Fo. 31: 'le doner de counsaile al soldiers in surgery est charitable use quia est pur lour releif deins les parolles *Releif of sick and maymhed soldiers*.' See also below, p. 32.

[5] Fo. 35: But not any other prisoner: 'de paier ffees pur bankrupt alant hors de prizon de treate ove lour creditors, est charitable use deins lestatute, quia est Releife al person decayed . . . il ne serra charitable use pur paier fees pur auters prisoners.'

[6] Fo. 64: 'lou statute est, *young tradesmen or persons decayed*, et cest volunt est, (tradesmen), uncore semble bone, quia est entend que le donor entend tiel tradesmen . . . Et les commissioners poient per decree order les stocks al ceux, et nul auters.'

[7] Fo. 75v: 'si soit ascun charitable use, et semble que sustenaunce de poore femes in childbirth est bone Releife de poore.' For similar reasons a trust to distribute money to the poor at the feoffor's funeral was charitable: see fo. 80.

(*j*) To gravel highways at Whitsuntide.[1]

(*k*) To find a herdsman within a town, for it relieves the inhabitants of taxes. Although no specific tax is imposed for that purpose, a contribution will inevitably be demanded from the inhabitants. The statute extends not only to taxes imposed by authority, but also to those extracted by practical necessity. Moreover, the use relieves the burden on the poor inhabitants.[2]

(*l*) To repair seabanks, even though the source of the obligation is a private agreement, for the private agreement concerns the public and makes the Commonwealth interested in the discharge of that duty.[3]

(*m*) To maintain sea works is within the words *repair of bridges and havens*, for these works are for the safety of people's ships in harbour.[4]

(*n*) To pay for the admission and induction of scholars presented to benefices by their university, for it is implied that a person so presented is poor and unable to pay these fees.[5]

As long as the use benefited the poor it was within the equity of the statute, even though it incidentally benefited the rich. In his very first case, Moore chose to emphasise this point; the trust was to provide bows and arrows for children between the ages of seven and seventeen:[6]

[1] Fols. 111–12.

[2] Fo. 136: 'si de garder heardsman soit charitable use deins le statute, Et semble que est deins les parolles and *Ease òf Inhabitaunts for other taxes* et coment que ne soit tax destre impose sur inhabitaunts pur trover heardsman, uncore est de necessity que publick contribucion soit ewe enter eux, et ceo est ease del chardge del contribucion, et lestatute entend si bien voluntary contribucions induce per necessity come taxes impose per authority et auxi il est ease al poore car nest possible mes ascun poore serra releive per trover del publick heardsman.'

[3] Fo. 160^{v}: 'Lou agrement private est ewe per entre Segnor et son tenant pur repaire les seabancks . . . les commissioners poient entermeddle [sic] de compell le performaunce de cest privat agrement . . . car cest private tend al publick, et le tenant ayant imprist sur luy ceux reparacions ad dischardg le segnor de eux, quex, aura sufficiement fait le Commonwealth ad interest.'

[4] Fo. 181^{v}: 'si seaworks soit charitable use deins lestatute, et semble cy deins les parolls repaire *de ports et havens*, car toute repaire sont fait pur safty del people ove lour ship al harboure.' See also fols. 159–60.

[5] Fo. 23: 'payment de fees dadmission et institucion et inducion de scholler prefer hors del universitie al benefice, est deins les parolls, maynteynaunce de schollers in universityes quia tanque il est institute et induct al benefice il est in le university, et ceo que est le cawse de luy advaunce hors del university est assets deins le statute, quia entendable que il est poore et nient able de paier tiels fees quex sont payable dent que il est de prender ascun fruits del benefice.'

[6] A duty imposed on parents by 33 Hen. VIII c. 9; see above, p. 27.

But it can be objected that . . . where the use expressed in the case is to all the inhabitants, which include rich as well as poor, accordingly the use in the case does not match the use in the statute, to which argument I reply: that if the use be in any part for the poor it is assets within our statute. And if the poor cannot be relieved without also benefiting the rich, the rich also in this unseverable case will benefit by being counted with the poor. And the construction of the statute in this situation is reasonable, because the statute is beneficial and seeks to redress a wrong and a fraud against the charitable gifts and wills of the people. Also, the commissioners in their decree can order the employment solely to the poor if they think fit, without any violation, and thereby rectify the intent of the gift and the statute.[1]

This is a recurring theme in Moore's *Reading*.[2] But he was careful to distinguish a trust which incidentally benefited the rich from one whose sole object was to benefit them, or was sumptuary, or was for the benefit of an individual or group of individuals as distinct from the public, distinctions which are, of course, well known to modern lawyers.[3] So a trust to erect a mill on private ground where the poor cannot grind their corn free, was not within the statute;[4] nor was a trust to provide wedding rings, which is a mere 'public token of friendship between them [the spouses] and cannot be construed as an advancement of the woman'; nor one to supply a wedding dinner which is a mere 'transitory thing not valuable for relief, but for ornamentation.'[5] The trust, moreover, had to concur with the law. A use 'to make seats for people to beg by the highways [was] no charitable use within this law,

[1] Fols. 9–9^{v}: 'mes poit estre object que . . . lou le use expresse in le case, est al touts inhabitaunts, inter quex sont rich sibien come poore, per que le use in le case ne match le use in lestatute, a ceo jeo respoigne, Que si le use soit in ascun part pur poore il est assets deins nostre statute. Et si le poore ne poient estre releif sans amesner auxi benefitt al Rich; le Rich auxi in cest case individable aura benefitt pur compulacion ove le poore. Et le construcion del statute in cest kynde est reasonable, quia lestatute est beneficiall et fait de redresse wronge et frawde encountre le charitable dons et volunts del people. Auxi, les commissioners in lour decree poient order lemployment solely al poore sils pense meete, sans ascun violacion, et issint Rectify lentent del done et de lestatute.'

[2] So, for example, a trust for a public midwife was within the equity of the statute; 'coment que le rich auxi prist benefitt per ceo, uncore quia le poore est in part releif, ceo est assets charitable use deins le statute, esteant publick, et est deins le parolls Releif del poore' (fo. 19). See also fo. 28^{v}.

[3] See, for example, *I.R.C.* v. *Baddeley* [1955], A.C. 572.

[4] Moore, fo. 40^{v}. Cf. above, p. 27, n. 6.

[5] Moore, fo. 145^{v}: Le diner semble nest deins lestatute, car est chose transitory nient valuable pur relief mes ad ornament.'

... the law prohibits begging, therefore it is no charity to maintain begging;[1] similarly a bequest of 'interest money' to charitable uses would have failed since it would have infringed the usury laws.[2]

Only a use for the repair of a church was within the letter of the statutes. The financial burden of repairing the church and of providing for the administration of divine service was imposed at common law on the parish,[3] and a trust for these purposes would release parish funds for more urgent needs.[4] So a trust to repair the pulpit or to provide bells or a communion table was within the statute; for 'these things are incidents to the church at all times and are common to every religion.'[5] But other religious uses, for example, to find a chaplain to celebrate communion[6] or to repair private pews and aisles[7] or to supply surplices, copes, and prayer books,[8] were outside the statute; for the efficient employment of their endowments could not in any way free parish funds for the relief of poverty. Moreover some of these uses might be deemed to be superstitious and infect the privileged status of those uses set out in the 1601 Act's preamble. For that very reason the general words of the 1597 Act ('and such like good lawfull and charitable uses') had been omitted.[9] Men were well aware of the potential threat of the chantry statute of 1547[10] and were justly sceptical of the religious constancy of Tudor sovereigns. Sir Francis Moore, who had been a member of both the Parliaments of 1597 and 1601, gave expression to the fears of a society which had scant respect for the authority of the Established Church,[11]

[1] Duke (Moore), 133.

[2] Moore, fo. 35.

[3] 2 Co. Inst. 489.

[4] Moore, fo. 108[v]: 'Repaire de Churches . . . entend tiels churches quex persons publick contribucions doient repaire, et le charity est entend in ease de tiel parishioners, mes Cathedrall esglises soit repayrable per Evesque deane et chapter, et issint hors de lestatute'.

[5] *Ibid.* fo. 18[v]: 'le pulpitt est deins reparacion del Esglise quia est chose de inseperable necessity quex parachioners sont tenus de trover comes walles, dores, font, stone, communion table, wyndowes, Belles, pewe pur le minister . . . Car ceux choses sont incidents al esglise in touts temps, et chescun religion ceo use.'

[6] *Ibid.*, fo. 18[v]: below, p. 32.

[7] *Ibid.* fo. 108[v]. But the parish had to repair the minister's pew: above, n. 5.

[8] *Ibid.* fo. 18[v].

[9] *Ibid.* 'il y ad in lestatute enumeracion des uses, sans ascun general parolls'.

[10] See above, pp. 13–14.

[11] See Christopher Hill, *Economic Problems of the Church* (Oxford, 1956), *passim.*

when he emphasised in his *Reading* that a gift to find a chaplain to celebrate divine service was not within the statute:

> because it is not to repair the church and was expressly excepted from [the preamble] for fear of future construction in superstitious times that the words *ad divina celebranda* will be taken [to include] massing priests as well as he who holds divine service.[1]

Similarly a trust to teach Divinity to maimed soldiers was outside the preamble; the statute was intended to relieve men's bodies not their souls:

> And note that Divinity is not on any view within the statute, nor the maintenance of preachers, nor the reading of lectures because the statute was cautiously penned in much particulars with the express purpose of avoiding all cowle of approval of superstitious uses, which can be gleaned by a liberal construction of Instruction in Divinity, Reading, lectures, preaching, etc.[2]

What uses would be deemed superstitious was a matter for conjecture. In 1601 it was still a debatable question whether a use to find a chaplain *ad divina celebranda* was or was not superstitious.

[1] Moore, fo. 18^{v}: 'le trover de chapleine nest deins lestatute, quia nest de repaire Lesglise. Et fuit expressment entend destre hors pur pavour de construction future in supersticious temps que les parolls *ad divina celebranda* serra prise massing preistes, sibien come est cesty que el divine service.'

In Duke (Moore), pp. 131–2, Moore appears to put the matter more bluntly: 'a Chaplain or Minister, to celebrate Divine Service, is neither within the Letter, nor meaning of this Statute; for it was of purpose omitted in the penning of the Act, lest the gifts intended to be imployed, upon purposes grounded upon charity, might, in change of times (contrary to the minds of the Givers) be confiscate into the King's Treasury. For Religion being variable, according to the pleasure of succeeding Princes, that which at one time is held for Orthodox, may at another, be accounted Superstitious, and then such lands are confiscate, as appears by the Statute of Chanteryes, 1 E. 6 cap. 14.' These plainer words, if written by Moore, would be more tactfully committed to paper than uttered in public.

[2] Moore, fo. 31: 'mes Consayle in Divinity al maymehed soldiers nest use deins lestatute; car lestatute entend releif de lour bodyes in lour maymes et sickness, come per surgery, meate, drink, apparell, Lodginge, et nemi a lour sowles. Et nota que Divinitie nest ascun voy deins lestatute, ne le maynteynaunce de preachers, ne Reading de Lectures pour le reason quia lestatute fuit cautiously penned al mult particulers ove expresse purpose de avoid tout cowle dapprobcion de supersticious uses, queux puissoient etre enduce per L iberall construction de Counsaile in Divinitie, Readinge, lectures, preachinge, etc.' But a Divinity Reader in a university was within the statute, being 'in the words, *scholars in universities*': see *ibid.* fo. 104^{v}. A trust to find a chaplain in a college or hall of either university was also within the statute for similar reasons: 'car les Halls esteant in les universetyes, le trover de chapleine pur eux est part de [lour] meynteynaunce' (fo. 185^{v}).

And it was not until 1606, just before Moore gave his *Reading* in Middle Temple Hall, that the Chancellor and the Justices of the King's Bench finally held[1] that a gift

> *cuidam Capellano ad Divina Celebranda*, in a certain church or chapel, is no superstitious use within the statute 1 Edward VI . . . and the reason is, because it is the general case of all parsons in England.[2]

Uses which were outside the statute could, as Moore accepted, be charitable in law.[3] The preamble was not an exclusive definition of legal charity. Exclusion of a use from the equity of the statute did mean, however, that a petitioner who sought to enforce it would have to proceed, as he would have to have done before 1597, by simple bill, which was a 'tedious and chargeable'[4] procedure. Conversely the charitable commissioners could not intervene to enforce the use however much they might wish to do so.[5] Whether the commissioners did or did not have jurisdiction over a particular charitable use was a question which appeared to arise relatively frequently after the enactment of the Charitable Uses Act, 1601. In the case just mentioned the commissioners had taken jurisdiction over a use to find a chaplain to celebrate divine service. 'But . . . this decree was made void by the Lord Chancellor, because the use . . . was no use within the statute inquirable, but the Chancellor by his Chancery authority, may, and did decree the land' to that purpose.[6] Similarly, the Chancellor (by his Chancery authority) and not the commissioners had jurisdiction over uses to establish

[1] Duke (Moore), 156. This case may well have been *William Rycardes, on behalf of the Inhabitants of Rodboroughe* v. *Richard Payne*, C. 2/Eliz./R. 12/48, which had been presented to Sir Christopher Hatton. The Bill and Replication are transcribed in appendix B. It is referred to, *sub nom. Payne et Ricards Case Banck le roy et Chauncery*, in Moore, fo. 18v. Cf. F. H. Newark, 'Public Benefit and Religious Trusts', *Law Quarterly Review*, LXII (1946), 234, 234–5.

[2] Cf. Moore's similar language at fo. 18v, above, p. 32.

[3] Moore, fo. 11, quoted above, p. 26 n. 2; and cf. *ibid.* fo. 32 quoted below, n. 5.

[4] *Hynshaw* v. *Morpeth Corporation* (1629) Duke, 69.

[5] Cf. *Pember* v. *Inhabitants of Kington*; discussed below, p. 34. In other cases, the use was within the statute, yet the charity commissioners were deemed not to have jurisdiction, the trust property having vested in the King because of the attaint of the feoffee. So in fols. 31–2, Moore discusses this case: an annuity is charged on leasehold land, *inter alia*, to a feoffee to teach surgery to soldiers arriving at Dover. The feoffee is convicted of treason. The term is vested in the Crown—'per que nest subject al decree des commissioners, uncore le use nest determine tielment mesque per peticion al roy il poit doner licence daver commission pur faire decree. Et issint le conclusion meynteyne pur le Annuitie, que est charitable use et uncore nul decree poit estre fait per Commissioners' (fo. 32).

[6] Duke (Moore), 156.

schools of catechising, 'because Religion is variable, and not within this Statute.'[1]

Until 1639 it was accepted that uses for the support of preaching ministers were religious uses over which the commissioners had no jurisdiction.[2] It was important, therefore, to establish a procedure which would effectively enforce them, for uses for preaching ministers, properly supervised, could help to secure the stability of the Erastian Settlement.[3] 'People are governed by the pulpit more than the sword in times of peace',[4] and it was the Crown's duty, as Supreme Head of the Church to ensure that its people were instructed in 'true and sound religion'. So between 1635 and 1638 there is a small crop of informations brought in the name of the Attorney-General and directed to recalcitrant churchwardens and parishioners, who had refused or neglected to apply funds for the proper maintenance of those preaching ministers who would 'teache and instructe his Majestie's people . . . in the grounds and principles of true and sound religion, and to celebrate divine service and minister the holy sacraments and do and execute all other rites duties and mynysteriall offices there . . . according to the laws of God and the constitutions of the Church of England.'[5] In *Pember* v. *Inhabitants of Kington*,[6] there was an attempt to break with former practice, apparently inspired by a desire to support preaching ministers. The commissioners decreed that some of the money bequeathed for charitable purposes

[1] Duke (Moore), 134.

[2] Moore, above, p. 32. See also *Fisher* v. *Hill* (1612), not fully reported in Duke, 82. A more complete account of that litigation is to be found in the Chancery *Entry Books of Decrees and Orders*: see C. 33/124/238. The Chancellor, in that case, acting under his Chancery authority, decreed that the terms of the will be carried out and that part of the profits of the land be 'paied for the maintenance of a preacher'.

[3] Christopher Hill, *Society and Puritanism in Pre-Revolutionary England* (London, 1964), chap. 2; and see Jordan, *Charities of London*, 286–8.

[4] Charles I to his son, the future Charles II; quoted by Hill, *Society and Puritanism*, 38.

[5] See, e.g. C. 5/558/61 (1637); C. 8/634/16 (1637); C. 10/35/7 (1639). There is a significant increase in the number of bequests for religious purposes between 1604 and 1640: see W. K. Jordan, *The Charities of London, 1480–1660* (London, 1961), 268, 269.

[6] The decision is erroneously reported in Duke, 82, *sub nom. Inhabitants of Knighton*; below p. 35. n. 3. The account in the text is based, however, on the fuller report in the *Entry Books*: see C. 33/176/62, 281, 433, 453, 623; C. 33/178/63, 177, 207. In some of the records and in Duke, the Inhabitants are wrongly described as the *Inhabitants of Knighton*, which is in Radnorshire. This litigation originated in Kington in Herefordshire.

under Sir Francis Pember's will should be applied 'for and towardes the mayntheninge of a preachinge.'[1] The decree was attacked before Lord Keeper Coventry[2] on the ground that a 'donacion for the maintenance of a preacher is not within the statute of charitable uses', a demurrer which Coventry considered 'most materiall'. He therefore remitted the case to Jones, Croke and Berkeley, Justices, for their opinion on this question of law. On 6 July they reported to him that they were all

clearlie of opinion that the circumstances of the case considered the maintenaunce of a preacher in the said case is not within the meaninge of the statute of 43 Elizabeth as upon readinge of the said certificate appeareth.

Coventry accepted the judges' advice and held that the commissioners had acted wrongly in applying the money to the support 'of a preachinge'. Consequently he reversed that part of the commissioners' decree, and ordered that the £200 must be bestowed upon a school.[3]

[1] Pember had left in his will money for this purpose and for 'teachinge of schoole or trayninge of schollers' in certain parishes.

[2] In argument before Coventry L. K., Herbert, the Queen's Attorney who was seeking to uphold the commissioners' decree, hinted that the judges' conclusion of law might have been influenced by improper considerations. For he pointed out that Jones J., when he had been on the Hereford circuit, had inquired of the Dean of Hereford and the local gentry whether the legacy should be employed 'for finding a preachinge minister'. But the gentry 'certified under their handes that if it should have been employed for the maintenaunce of a preachinge minister it would have beene a disturbaunce in that place both to the Church and the Commonwealth': see C. 33/178/83.

[3] He refused to make any allowance for the sums which Pember's executors had already paid for the support of a preaching minister.

The report in the *Entry Book* conflicts therefore with the well known report in Duke, 82, which reads: 'Money was given to maintain a Preaching Minister; this is no Charitable Use named in the Statute, yet by the Lord Keeper and two Judges, it was decreed to be good, and the Use a Charitable Use, within the equity of that Statute: and the Executor was ordered to pay that Money to the Charitable Use, for maintenance of it.'

Duke's account of the case appears to be based on Tothill's report: see Tothill, 34. Tothill's reputation as a reporter is abysmal. Chancellor Kent of New York, for example, thought that Tothill was 'altogether unfit to serve as a guide and unworthy to be cited as an authority': see *King* v. *Baldwin*, 2 Johnson's Ch. 556. The Duke/Tothill report should therefore be discounted. Coventry's judgment, as set out in the *Entry Book*, was later confirmed by Nottingham: see the text above, at p. 36.

A third report of *Pember*'s case is to be found in 1 Eq. Cas. Abr. 95, which also follows Tothill.

Cf. Tothill's report (p. 34) of *Penstred* v. *Pavier* (1639), where a devise of £20 per annum to a preaching minister was upheld by the Chancellor. But there is no indication that the charity commissioners had first taken jurisdiction.

The principle of *Pember*'s case was confirmed by Lord Nottingham. On two separate occasions he decreed that money bequeathed to 'ministers for their lectures'[1] and a devise to the 'ministers of the service of God placed to serve the cure in Crowland at their own charge'[2] were not charitable uses 'within the statute and so out of the commission'. The charity ought, therefore, to have been 'prosecuted by information at common law in the name of the Attorney-General'[3] or by original bill.[4] But by 1676, when Nottingham's decisions were given, the commission was ceasing to be the efficient instrument of investigation and control of its earlier years, and petitioners were once more anxious to appeal to the ordinary jurisdiction of the Chancellor.[5] It was the procedure by commission which was now 'tedious and chargeable'; and in each information, formally brought in the name of the Attorney-General,[6] relators set out reasons why the particular charity was not 'within the remedye of the statute . . . and soo [was] properly and in noe other way relievable but by this Honourable Court as all good and charitable uses which are not within the provicion of the said statute are.'[7] From the middle of the seventeenth century onwards ingeniously successful attempts were made to escape from the Charitable Uses Act, 1601, and the jurisdiction of its commissioners. One relator prays that the commissioners have no jurisdiction and that only an information can lie to enforce the trust, because the gift was void at law for uncertainty;[8] another, that the statutory procedure was ousted because the devise to the charity was voidable 'according to the strictness of the statutes touchinge Mortmain'[9]; a third, that the 'persons themselves—to whome and to whose benefitt in the said yearly rentes or summes by the said will soe charitably given and appointed were not of capacity by the strict rules of the common lawe to sue to be relieved therein nor weare . . . within the remedye of the statute',[10] in which

[1] *Harding and Edge* (1675), Selden Society, LXXIII, case 346.

[2] *Cudrington* v. *Stokes* (1673–1674), Selden Society, LXXIII, case 62.

[3] *Harding and Edge* (1676), Selden Society, LXXIII, case 346.

[4] *Cudrington* v. *Stokes* (1673–1674), Selden Society, LXXIII, case 62.

[5] See below, pp. 54–6 for a further discussion.

[6] The Crown's interest was emphasised thus: 'Wherefore and for as much as the preservacion and performance of all charitable uses of this nature were of publique interest which concerned his Highness to take care might be preserved and performed . . .'

[7] C. 5/588/71 (1656); see also C. 7/14/80 (1655).

[8] C. 6/171/79 (1662).

[9] C. 8/166/1 (1669).

[10] C. 5/588/71 (1656).

case the devise was imperfect and 'the commissioners had no jurisdiction to cure it'.[1]

Other charities were excluded from the jurisdiction of the charity commissioners by express provisions in the 1601 Act:

Provided alwaies, That neither this Acte, nor any thinge therein conteined, shall in any wise extende to any Landes Tenements Rents Annuities Profits Goods Chattels Money or Stockes of Money, given limitted appointed or assigned, or which shalbe given limitted appointed or assigned, to any Colledge Hall or Howse of Learninge within the Universities of Oxforde or Cambridge, or to the Colledges of Westmynster Eaton or Winchester, or any of them, or to any Cathedrall or Collegiate Churche within this Realme.

And provided alsoe, That neither this Acte nor any thinge therein shall extende to any Citie or Towne Corporate, or to any the Landes or Tenements given to the uses aforesaide within any suche Citie or Towne Corporate, where there is a speciall Governor or Governors, appointed to governe or directe suche Landes Tenements or Things disposed to any the uses aforesaide; neither to any Colledge Hospitall or Free Schoole whiche have speciall Visitors of Governours or Overseers appointed them by their Founders.

These provisos which exempted favoured charities from the scope of the commissioners' inquiry were strictly construed. As Moore said:

The proviso which abridges the public good of a beneficial statute will not be construed against the letter[2] . . . The proviso is not to be extended by equity, as is the body of the act [which is] beneficial.[3]

Consequently a gift had to be made to the 'Citie or Towne Corporate' under its corporate name; it was not sufficient if it was made to one of its members, even if it was to its principal member.[4] 'Lands or tenements' within the meaning of the second proviso

[1] See also *Att.-Gen.* v. *Townsend* (1670?), Duke, 34 where it appears that the question relating to the application of surplus charitable funds (below, pp. 91–3) was determined on 'an information in Chancery'. These devices to avoid the commission procedure were novel as well as ingenious. The evidence suggests that before the Civil War the charity commissioners would have taken jurisdiction over gifts which would have failed at law for failure to vest the legal title in feoffees: see below, pp. 67 ff.

[2] Fo. 190: 'quia le proviso que abridge publick bone de beneficiall statute ne serra construe ouster les Letter.'

[3] *Ibid.* fo. 202: 'le proviso nest destre prise per equity, come est corps del act esteant beneficiall.' And see also fo. 201v.

[4] *Ibid.* fo. 185v. Thus a gift had to be made to the Dean and Chapter, and not to the Dean alone. But cf. below, p. 39, n. 2.

set out above did not include, in Moore's opinion, either rents of land[1] or marriage money, even though a lease of land secured the payment of the marriage money.[2] The special governors of the particular city or town had to reside within its boundaries; if they resided outside its boundaries the city or town could not claim that it was exempt.[3] Only corporations *in esse* at the time of the making of the statute could claim to be free from the commissioners' jurisdiction, 'and [the provisos were] not to be stretched to such as shall be made after.'[4] Nor did the benefit of the provisos extend to lands given after the making of the statute, though the corporation was in existence when the statute was enacted.[5] Moreover, a corporation, whether it was a college, a city, a town or a hospital, could only claim the benefit of a proviso if both the property given to it and the employment of the trust were vested in the corporation.[6] Moore elaborated this principle in the following words:[7]

[1] *Ibid.* fo. 220, *semble*; and see also fo. 190. However in an earlier passage (at fo. 174^{v}) Moore seems to reach a contrary conclusion, saying that rents were within the words 'or Thinges disposed to any the uses aforesaid'. But he clearly did so with great hesitation. His original conclusion, which he deleted, was that the proviso could not embrace rents devoted to charitable uses.

[2] *Ibid.* fo. 190.

[3] *Ibid.*, fo. 190^{v}. But it did not matter that the land charged or the charitable use (though not both) was outside the city or town: see fols. 174^{v}, 190^{v}.

[4] Duke (Moore), p. 171. See also *Hynshaw* v. *Morpeth Corporation* (1629), Duke, 69; cf. *Phillips* v. *Bury*, *Case of Exeter College, Oxford* (1694), 4 Mod. 106, Shower, P.C. 35. Moreover an Oxbridge hall which was not incorporated could not claim to be within the proviso: Moore, fo. 186.

[5] Duke (Moore), 171.

[6] Moore, fo. 172: 'Si les Corporacions, ou Supervisors, nont in eux le property del chose done, Et auxi le trust de ceo imployer, il ne serra exempt.'

[7] *Ibid.* fo. 168: 'lexempcion est ordeigne solement in cases lou ceo que est per lestatute appoint al commissioners de faire appert per le volunt del donor al College de faire, cest de premier order que les choses done serra faithfully et trewley imploy a tiels uses pur quex ils sont done per les foundors, issint Limployment est ceo que lestatute entend et limployment est loffice des Commissioners, Et Lentent del proviso est, lou le trust del imployment est appoint al City, college, etc. la le trust ne serra toll de eux per lestatute et mise in Commissioners, dont ensuist que lou le imployment nest appoint al college, le College nest exempt del commission, come feoffment ou leas al College ove reservacion, condicion ou agreement express que ils payera Annuel somme al maior de Dale destre per luy distribute ou loane al Tradesmen ou pur ease inhabitants de taxes, ici limployment est appoint al maior, nemi al college, per que le college nest exempt pur cest done, car sils paya al maior et le maior ne ceo imploy, le commissioners ont de order le maior et nemi le college, per que le college ne poit estre exempt pur cest matter.'

For other examples, see *ibid.* fols. 172, 174^{v}, 179^{v}, 182, 189^{v}–90. See also Duke (Moore), 172.

The exemption only applies in cases where what is by statute the commissioners duty, the donor's will appoints the College[1] to do. It is of first importance that the things given will be faithfully and truly employed to the uses for which they are given by the founders. Thus the employment is that which the statute intends and the employment is the office of the Commissioners. And the intent of the proviso is, where the trust of the employment is appointed to the City, College etc., there the trust will not be taken from them by Statute and given to the Commissioners, from which it follows that where the employment is not given to the College, the College is not exempted from the Commission, as where a feoffment or lease to a College, with reservation, condition or express agreement that they will pay annually a sum to the Mayor of Dale to be distributed or loaned by him to tradesmen or [to be used] for the ease of the inhabitants' taxes. [H]ere the employment is given to the mayor, not to the College, from which the College is not exempt for this gift, for if they pay the mayor and the mayor does not employ [the gift], the commissioners must order the mayor and not the college, thereby the college cannot be exempt on this matter.

It was exceptional,[2] therefore, for these provisos to be construed with any generosity; to have done so would have defeated the equity of the statute.

(ii) *The commission and the hearing*

The commission issued by the Chancellor[3] under the authority

[1] In this particular case, the corporation was Winchester College.

[2] For such a case, see Moore, fo. 171, and his conclusion that 'hospital' could include an unincorporated body: but cf. above, p. 66, n. 7. But his example concerned the 'poor Knights of Windsor', who were a 'hospitall in foundacion car hospitall in foundacion est lou ordinaunce et graunt est fait, que poore aura meason, et meynteynaunce a touts jours'.

For other examples, see Moore, fols. 181^{v}–2; Duke (Moore), 171–2.

[3] The commission was generally awarded under the Great Seal of England, but was granted by the chancellor of the county palatine for lands within the duchy; see Duke (Moore), 144–5. Moore writes, fols. 59^{v}–60: 'les parolls de lestatute sont, and for the Chauncelor of the Countey Palentine of Lancaster for lands within the Countey Palentine, Issint que si ne sont terres deins le Countey Palentine destre order per les commissioners, le Chauncelor del Duchy ne poit agard Commission. Et voit estre object que ici nest ascun Land deins le Countey Palentine, mes est Annuitie que ne issuist hors dascun terre, Et pur ceo lagarder del Commission per le Chauncelor del Duchy est ousterment void, et le Joininge nient bone. A que destre respoigne que le paroll (Land) conteyne chescun chose hors de ter, ou chargde sur le ter, come. Rents, Commons, advowsons, estovers et similia . . . mes semble clere que pur Annuitie ou sommes del argent done de performe charitable use deins le Countey Palentine, le Chauncelor dengleter sole poit agarder le commission et nemi le Chauncelor del Duchy.' *Semble* the commissioners of the Great Seal did not have power to issue the commission: *ibid.* fo. 68.

of the Charitable Uses Act, 1601, named at least five commissioners to conduct an inquiry within a particular county, four of whom had to have capacity to execute and did in fact execute the commission.[1] One of the commissioners had to be the Bishop of the diocese and his Chancellor;[2] the others, 'persons of good and sound behaviour'[3] who, if not Justices of the Peace, were invariably gentlemen of the county.[4] A person could not receive the commission if he was an excommunicate, an outlaw, a felon or had been fined 'for acquitting a felon against the evidence given'.[5]

Equally no person could be a commissioner if he pretended title to property alleged to be held to a charitable use; 'whosoever may have any finger in the Interest, or Titles, shall be excluded.'[6] In his *Reading* Moore was much concerned with this question. He emphasised that it was immaterial 'if they have title or not if they [the Dean and Chapter] pretend probable title as here, for although the Commission is to them in their personal capacity, and the title [is] in their body politic, yet semble such title is pretended within the statute.'[7] Moore gives other examples of commissioners who were

[1] *Ibid.* 83^{v}: 'si le parson soit disable pur pretence de title, uncore le commission est agard al 5 persons in tout, dont sont 4 nient disable et le nosmer de disable parson ne sont void le commission, si sont autres nosme nient disable et taunt in nombre que poient execute le commission.' See also *ibid.* fo. 56^{v} and *Anon* (1602), Duke, 62, 63.

[2] Moore, fo. 83^{v}: 'si le omission del Chauncelor, la esteant Bishop al temps ne fait le Commission void, et semble nemi, car quant le Evesque est spare, le Chauncelor poit estre spare, les parolls esteant to the Bishop of the Diocese and his Chauncelor in Case there shalbe any Bishop in that tyme. Issint si ne soit evesque, et uncore est Chauncelor (come poit estre per patent) uncore le Chauncelor ne besoigne destre nosme, et per consequence lou le Bishop est disable per le proviso, le Chauncelor auxi est.' This was a recognition of the ancient position of the Bishop, *qua* Ordinary, as the guardian of charity: see above p. 4.

[3] Moore, fo. 84: for example, a person could not be a commissioner if he was guilty of simony. But the statute did not require the Bishop and his Chancellor to be of good and sound behaviour: see Moore, f. 80^{v}. Consequently, 'though a Bishop be notoriously criminous, yet unless he be deposed, he ought to be named in the Commission' (Duke (Moore), 145).

[4] Cf. Barnes, *Somerset, 1625–1640*, 147, 149.

[5] Duke (Moore), 145–6. But an outlaw or felon whose conviction was reversed before he executed the commission, was a person of good and sound behaviour. An excommunicate was always disabled, even if afterwards absolved: see *ibid.* 146.

[6] *Ibid.* 145.

[7] Moore, fo. 53: 'Et nest materiall sils ont title ou nemi, si ils pretend title probable come icy ils sont . . . car coment que le commission est al eux come singuler persons, Et le title in lour corps politick, Uncore semble tiel title est pretence deins lestatute.'

disqualified from sitting on this ground.[1] One such case was if[2]

goods be given to one in trust, to a charitable use, and he defrauds the use, and dies intestate, because the goods are presently in the hands of the bishop, until administration be committed, he [the Bishop] cannot be named a commissioner, for the pretence of title he hath to the goods, unless the defrauders died in a peculiar parish in the diocess, exempt from the jurisdiction of that bishop.

A person could serve as commissioner if his 'possibility is too remote to make him pretend title'.[3] If there was a trust to use income of a fund to buy stock for tradesmen who had fallen on evil times, a tradesman could be a commissioner even though he might one day benefit from the trust. Moore concluded that this[4]

possibility is too remote and is not material to the commissioner, for he is of good and sound behaviour, as is required by the body of the statute, and he has not in his hands or possession any of the things nor pretends title, as those to whom the proviso extends.

Generally, however, the proviso that 'no person doth or may pretend title'[5] was generously construed, 'being made to corroborate a beneficial law'.[6]

After the issue of the commission, the commissioners gave notice to the churchwardens and overseers for the poor of the parishes of the county, that they were authorised to inquire, by the oaths of twelve men[7] of the county,[8] whether property devoted to charitable uses had been employed according to the intent of the donors. This notice encouraged parishioners to make known to the commissioners breaches of trust of which they were aware and urged them to appear with all the necessary documents substantiating their allegations. It read:[9]

It is this day ordered by the said Commissioners, that notice be given to all Parishes and places within the said County of . . . the Commission

[1] See Moore, fo. 60 (the grantor's heir); fols. 56^{v}, 75^{v} and 93 (the grantor's executor); fo. 83^{v} (the Bishop). [2] Duke (Moore), 146. See also Moore, fo. 67.

[3] *Ibid.* fo. 56^{v}: 'uncore son possibility est trope remote de faire luy pretender del title.'

[4] *Ibid.* fo. 64: 'le quel possibility est trope remote et est nient materiall al commissioner, car il est de good et sound behaviour come est require per le corps del act, et il nad in ses maynes ou possession ascun des choses, ne pretend title come ceux que le proviso exclude.'

[5] Duke (Moore), 145. [6] *Ibid.* 145. Cf. above, p. 39.

[7] If sixteen were empanelled and twelve agreed to serve, 'this is a good inquisition' (Duke (Moore), 150).

[8] Moore, fo. 56^{v}: 'si le towne ewst estre exempt del countey, lexecucion ewst estre made per 6 del towne.' [9] Duke, 9–10.

aforesaid, and the power thereby given to the said Commissioners, that so all persons that have occasion, may take the benefit of the said Commission, and have remedy and redress thereby; and withal, that Directions be given, that such persons as do come to the said Commissioners, for relief in the premises, do bring with them the *Wills*, *Evidences*, *Charters*, and *Writings*, whereby the *Charitable Uses* do appear to be given, created, limited, assigned and appointed, and sufficient Witness to prove the Breaches of Trust, not imploying or misimploying of such things as shall be so abused, not imployed or misimployed, as aforesaid. *By T. W. Clerk, attending the said Commissioners.*

A warrant was then issued to the sheriff of the county, requiring him to summon on the day stated and appointed in the commission a jury of twelve 'honest and lawful' men of the county who did not pretend title and made no claim to the property devoted to the trust, and to return the jury on the day stated and appointed in the commission. But the presence of such an interested juror on the jury did not vitiate an inquisition which 'found' a charitable use:

The reason [is] because the proviso was made in favour of the charitable use, and for fear that interested jurors will not wish to make [their verdict] according to the truth, and for that when the inquisition finds for the charitable use, the cause is taken out of the proviso which disables jurors, but if the inquisition be held or finds against the charitable use, there is a good exception.[1]

The Sheriff was also charged to summon[2] the church-wardens and officers of the parishes and all other 'interested' parties. Moore described an '*interested party*'[3] as anyone who would be

[1] Moore, fo. 93: 'Le reason quia le proviso fuit fait in favoure del charitable use, et pur feare que jurors interested ne voile faire accoret al veritie, et pur ceo quant linquisicion est trove pur le Charitable use, le cawse est toll del proviso que disable jurors, mes si inquisicion soit tende ou trove encountre le charitable use, il est bone excepcion.' The Chancellor would then issue a new commission and a new panel would be sworn. Commissioners who knowingly empanelled a juror who pretended title could be fined in Star Chamber.

[2] The summons was by precept under the seals of the commissioners; the precept was sent to the sheriff who gave notice to the interested parties.

[3] Moore also discusses at some length how an interested party was given notice of the hearing. It was enough, for example, that he was present at church when the precept was read; indeed it was sufficient that the precept 'was generally published in [his parish] Church, at Prayer' (see Duke (Moore), 152). Joint tenants could cause problems. If one was summoned and the other gave evidence, that summons would be sufficient to bind both 'sur presumpcion que lauter ad done luy notice'. But if the one who had no notice did not give evidence he was not bound by the commissioners' decree: see Moore, fo. 92v.

affected either directly or indirectly[1] by the commissioners' decree. The class could include the donor; the donor's heirs, feoffees[2] or executors;[3] a grantee of land charged with the charitable use, or his heirs;[4] a person who had the power to nominate charitable uses under the trust;[5] and the Ordinary if he who 'hath goods to a charitable use, dies intestate.'[6] It was not sufficient notice to summon an interested party as a juryman, for the summons was given him that he might bring documents and witnesses to meet any allegation that he had broken his trust, or had participated in a breach of trust.[7]

An interested party was not only entitled to give evidence before the commissioners but could 'challenge' the commissioners and the jurors. This right of challenge was particularly valued, and it was because the Charitable Uses Act, 1597, had not expressly provided for any challenge to the jurors that Francis Tate had opposed its simple re-enactment in debate in the House of Commons.[8] Consequently the commissioners' decree could be attacked before the Chancellor if an interested party who should have been summoned was not summoned.[9] Moore was of the opinion that failure to summon him avoided their decree.[10] But in the *East Greensted* case[11] in 1633, the Lord Keeper, Thomas Coventry, resolved that:

If the parties upon their appeal do take exception, that they had not any notice of the time of the executing of the commission from the commissioners, that shall not avoid the decree, unless they shew withall, in their exception, that for lack of such notice, they lost the benefit of such an exception, to the commissioners or some of them, or of such a challenge to a juror, expressing the cause in certain . . .

[1] Moore, fo. 116^{v}; if he is not interested 'in droit mes in cowle, les commissioners poient deny le chaleng'.

[2] *Ibid.* fo. 96^{v}.

[3] *Ibid.* fols. 92^{v}, 100.

[4] *Ibid.* fo. 120.

[5] Duke (Moore), 152: 'he which hath the nomination of the persons, upon whom the alms ought to be imployed, is a party interested to be called.' Consequently he had to be summoned to the inquisition although he has 'no property': see Moore, fo. 100.

[6] Duke (Moore), 152. For other examples, see *ibid.* 151.

[7] Moore, fo. 93.

[8] See above, p. 24.

[9] If a party was summoned he was bound by the commissioners' decree even though he was absent from the inquiry. The 'calling' was sufficient notice of the inquiry, and of its time and place (see Duke (Moore), 152).

[10] Moore, fo. 92^{v}, even though he was present at the hearing and gave evidence: see *Vinar*'s case (date unknown). If 'un interested [party] . . . ne soit summon, mes il veigne et done evidence, si ceo inquisicion soit sufficient, et sil ewst estre summon, et semble nemi, per *Vinars* case.'

[11] Duke, 64.

At the hearing, which was often at the home of one of the commissioners, the commission would be read, the sheriff would return his writ summoning the jury, the jury would be called, the interested parties would make their challenges to the jury,[1] and the jury would be sworn to inquire[2] what property had been devoted to the charitable uses enumerated in the preamble to the statute and what breaches of trust ('fraud inquirable') had been committed. The jury, having heard the evidence,[3] found in the inquisition 'the gift and [any] negligence or misemployment'.[4] And it was upon this inquisition that the commissioners who made the inquiry based their decree, which was returned, under their seals, into the Court of Chancery[5] within the time specified in the original commission.[6] No decree could be made, therefore, without a complete inquisition.

Yet if the inquisition finds the matter in substance, namely that there was a gift of a rent to the charitable use and that is not employed, this inquisition is good to the common intent, and other details can be supplied by writings, depositions or otherwise, the commissioners having power to enquire by other means as well as by Inquisition.[7]

[1] Generally a challenge was either a principal challenge or a challenge for favour (or cause). Principal challenges had to be allowed by the commissioners. But challenges for favour, which had to be proved by 'parolls ou autrement' (Moore, fo. 120), were in the 'discrecion des Commissioners dallowe ou disallowe, per que lour disallowaunce ne viciat linquisicion' (Moore, fo. 104^{v}; see *ibid.* fo. 112). In his *Reading*, Moore gives examples of these various forms of challenge. Criminosity was a principal challenge; as was the challenge that a commissioner or a member of the jury (other than a jury of the half-tongue) was an alien: see Moore, fo. 93 and Duke (Moore), 153. However, the charge that the jury-man was an interested party or that the juror was related by blood or affinity to an interested party was a challenge for favour: see Moore, fols. 100, 108^{v}, 120.

[2] At one time it was thought that two inquisitions were necessary: 'the first, as an indictment to accuse the parties, the other before the parties being present' (Duke (Moore), 146). But this view was later abandoned.

[3] The evidence which might persuade a jury that a charitable use had been created could be varied; for example, an inscription on a tomb-stone in Brattlington, Sussex, was found in one case to be sufficient evidence of a charitable use: see *Anon.* (date unknown), Duke, 33.

[4] Moore, fo. 100. It was enough that the jury found the substance of the gift, 'though they miss in the particular': see below, pp. 49–50.

[5] The commission was returned into the Court of Chancery from which the commission originated: see above, p. 39, n. 3.

[6] E.g. 'with all convenient speed or, at the furthest, *in Crastino Sancto die Trinitatis* next coming'; and see below, p. 52.

[7] Moore, fo. 96: 'uncore si inquisicion trove matter in substaunce cest que la fuit done de rent al charitable use et ceo nest imploy, cest inquisicion est bone al common entent, et lauters circumstaunces poient estre supplie per escripts, deposicions ou autrement, les commissioners ayant powre dinquire per auters meanes sibien come per Inquisicion.' See also a similar statement at fo. 100.

So if the inquisition found 'a gift for the relief of the poor, which is one of the uses in the statute, and entitles the commissioners to jurisdiction, then they must by other inquiries, witnesses, accounts, records etc., inform themselves of the residue of the gift, and decree accordingly'.[1]

Parties who were aggrieved by the finding could appeal by bill to the Chancellor, excepting in writing to the commissioners' order and decree. To these exceptions the other party or parties could furnish written answers. An aggrieved party was one:[2]

> whosoever hath *bonum omissum*, or *malorum commissum* by the decree. Whosoever is interested, and hath a property and ownership of goods and lands to his own use, whosoever by the decree hath prejudice, either in law or equity is *pars gravata*, and may complain by bill [to the Chancellor].[3]
>
> But where the prejudice is common or general, there every man may complain as a *amicus curiae*, not as a party grieved, as where lands given to repair bridges or highways, which are publick easements, there any man may complain, if the decree limit the use to any other purpose . . . Everyone which hath a title, paramount the decree, is a party grieved . . . If a decree is made against one that is bankrupt, at the time for goods, every creditor is *pars gravata*, but not for lands.
> If a decree is made against an ancestor, a testator, or one that dies intestate, the heir, the executor, or administrator, is a party grieved; so is every one that claims, by estoppel, during the time of the estoppel.

If any aggrieved party failed to except after he had been served with a writ of execution,[4] 'it seems reasonable they should be concluded thereby, and not be admitted to exceptions after.'[5] For that reason the *Poor of the Parish of St Dunstan*[6] need not have sought the Chancellor's protection to combat the threat of *Beauchamp*, the defendant, who had stated that he was going to except to the commissioners' decree as soon as all the petitioners' witnesses were dead.

[1] Moore, fo. 111^{v}: 'il trove le done pur releif de poore, quel est un des uses deins lestatute, et entitle les commissioners al jurisdicion, et donques ils doient per auters inquieryes et testmoignes accomptes, Records et similia informe eux mesmes del residue del done et faire decree accordant.'

[2] Duke (Moore), 167–8. See also Moore, fols. 132^{v}–3.

[3] See Moore, fo. 140.

[4] The commissioners' decree having been returned into the Petty Bag.

[5] *Poor of the Parish of St Dunstan* v. *Beauchamp* (1671), 1 Cas in Chan. 193, 194, *per* Orlando Bridgman L.K.

[6] *Ibid.* 193.

On the hearing of the exceptions, which 'could allege new matters' and when new evidence could be introduced, the Chancellor could annul ('which rarely is done'),[1] confirm, or reform the decrees of the commissioners, in a manner 'which concurs with the intent of the donor for the execution of the charitable use'.[2] Accordingly,

> where the donor has appointed the executors to pay the mortgage money to the mortgagee, which the heir has payed, the Chancellor by way of addition can order the executors to repay the heir notwithstanding the default of the heir.[3]

Once the decree had been annulled, modified or confirmed by the Chancellor, there could be no further proceedings by bill of review; for the decree took 'its authority by the Act of Parliament, which mentions but one examination; and it is not as where a decree is made by the Chancellor by his ordinary authority'.[4] A party could, however, petition the King in Parliament where 'the decree [could] be confirmed, altered ar annulled, which [was] to be final'.[5]

There was some uncertainty surrounding the commissioners and the Chancellor's power to award costs. The commissioners could order feoffees to pay costs to the person who successfully prosecuted the reform of the charitable trust;[6] and the Chancellor,

[1] 2 Co. Inst. 712.

[2] Moore, fo. 127v. And see fo. 133v.

[3] Moore, fo. 137: 'lou le donor ad appoint lexecutors de paier le mortgage money al mortgagee, quel le heir ad paye, le Chauncelor per voy de addicion poit appoint lexecutors de repay al heire, nient obstant le default le heire.' For other examples, see *ibid.* fols. 140, 148, 152v. And see below pp. 51–2 for a further discussion.

[4] *Windsor* v. *Hilton and other Inhabitants of Farnham* (1626), Duke, 62, Cro. Car. 40 (a less full report); and see below p. 225.

[5] *Poor of Eastham* v. *Kemp* (1623?). Duke gives the date as 1643, which must be erroneous for it is cited in *Windsor* v. *Inhabitants of Farnham* (1626), Duke, 62; see also *Coleman* and *Coleman*'s case (1673), Finch, 30, Selden Society, LXXIII, case 8; *Saul* v. *Wilson* (1684), 2 Vern. 118. These decisions were subsequently criticised by Blackstone, citing Duke's text and *Burford Corporation* v. *Lenthall* (1743), 2 Atk. 551 (below, p. 47), which was, however, concerned with the question of costs: see William Blackstone, *Commentaries on the Laws of England* (London, 1783), III, 428. Cf. *Warner* v. *North* (1695), Shower, P.C. 110.

[6] *Inhabitants of Eltham in Kent* v. *Warreyn* (1634), Duke, 67; *East* v. *Ryal* (1725), 2 P. Wms. 284; but cf. *Wharton* v. *Charles* (1673), Finch, 81; *Rockley* v. *Keyly* (1700), 1 Eq. Cas. Abr. 126, pl. 12; *Aylet* v. *Dodd* (1741), 2 Atk. 238.

so it was held in *Inhabitants of Eltham in Kent* v. *Warreyn*[1] in 1634, could increase these costs if the feoffees or any other aggrieved party appealed without cause. At one time it was doubtful, however, whether a successful exceptant to the commissioners' decree in favour of charity could be granted costs. Coke thought that he could not. The Charitable Uses Act, 1601, did not give either the commissioners or the Chancellor any such power, for the Act only gave them authority to award costs *against* those who had complained 'without just and sufficient cause of the orders, judgments, and decrees before mentioned'.[2] But from the mid-seventeenth century, costs were awarded to successful exceptants,[3] and this practice was confirmed by Lord Hardwicke in *Burford Corporation* v. *Lenthall*[4] in 1743. The Chancellor's power to award costs in this and similar cases was deemed to be a personal one, independent of any statutory authority, arising 'from conscience, and *arbitrio boni viri*, as to the satisfaction on one side or other, on account of vexation'.[5]

(iii) *The powers of the commissioners and the Chancellor*

The powers of the commissioners were extensive and were directed to ensuring that property devoted to the charitable uses set out in the preamble was employed in accordance with the intention of the donors. The commissioners were empowered to

> set downe suche orders, judgments and decrees, as the saide landes tenements rents annuities profits goods chattels money, and stockes of money may be duly and faithfullie imployed, to and for suche of the charitable uses and intents before rehearsed . . .[6]

Consequently, a feoffee or purchaser with notice could be ordered to transfer property or repay money wrongfully withheld from

[1] Duke, 67. This was not a novel decision. Moore (fo. 156) reached a similar conclusion and quoted authority for his view: 'Coment que lestatute parle que il donera good costes, uncore ne luy restreines de doner damages . . . le Chauncelor poit ad reasonable et construable choses al decree des commissioners et ouster per le delaye dexecucion per lour complaint sans cawse, come plusors fois in corts dequity decree poit estre fait encountre le plaintiff come *Brokes et Savages* case, le cawse esteant oye, mes sur default le plaintiff nul decree poit estre fait vers luy.'

[2] 2 Co. Inst. 712, below, p. 228.

[3] *Burford Corporation* v. *Lenthall* (1743), 2 Atk. 551, 569.

[4] (1743), 2 Atk. 551.

[5] (1743), 2 Atk. 551, 552.

[6] 43 Eliz. I c. 4; see below, p. 225.

charitable uses, and be charged with interest, often at a rate of 8 per cent per annum;[1] and any lease or conveyance made by fraudulent feoffees to third parties, other than *bona fide* purchasers, could be declared 'void in interest and estate'.[2] The commissioners could also order feoffees to maintain in repair property held to charitable uses, even though the feoffees had already distributed the rents to the charitable uses;[3] and require executors, administrators and heirs of fraudulent or negligent feoffees to contribute to the maintenance of the charitable use, in so far as they have 'assets in law or equity'.[4] They could decree that land devised to dishonest or negligent feoffees, be transferred to other persons to hold to the same use;[5] and that land be conveyed to a corporation *in esse* without danger of infringing the statute of mortmain.[6] A rent charge originally devised to a charitable use could be revived,[7] and a sale of land ordered even though the testator 'doth not appoint by whom the sale shall be made'.[8]

In fact, the commissioners' powers were generally as extensive as the evil demanded. So, they could examine whether the consideration for a particular conveyance of lands devoted to charitable

[1] *The Case of the Poor of Walthamstow* (1628), Duke, 65, 67; *Seymour* v. *Poor of Twyford* (1634), Duke, 79. See also Moore, fo. 156 and Duke (Moore), 156. The defendant could not escape responsibility by pleading the fraud of his servant: see *Middleton* v. *Masters and Mariners of the Royal Navy* (1618), Cases *temp.* Bacon, Ritchie, 90, where the defendant was required to pay 10 per cent interest.

[2] *Anon.* (1602), Duke, 62, 63. These questions were resolved by Egerton, L.K.; Popham C.J.K.B.; Anderson C.J.C.P.; and Coke A.G.

[3] *Anon.* (1602), Duke, 62, 63.

[4] Moore, fo. 136: 'si le pere devie sans faire ascun provision ou direcion pur le charitable use, donques hors de quex choses que il relinguishe decree poit order le performaunce. Et semble a ceo que les biens et chattels in maynes lexecutors ou administrators, ayant assetts in ley ou equity, et les terres ou auters assets in equity in maynes, le heire serra auxi chardgable al charitable use, le quel est prove per le darreign clause de lestatute que ordeign recompense decreeable vers executors ou administrators, ou heires de ceux quex defrawde Charitable uses, ayant assets in ley ou equity. . . . Et issint negligence aura tiel recompense come frawde, quia in le premisses de lestatute ils sont accowple ambodeux ensemble.' For the distinction between assets at law and assets in equity, see below, p. 96.

[5] *Bernard Hide*'s case (1628), Duke, 76, 77. See also Moore, fols. 133–133^{v}.

[6] Duke (Moore), 158; cf. below, pp. 109 ff. The commissioners could not, however, create a new corporation although they could 'decree lands . . . to a corporation already incorporate, to be trustees': see *Anon.* (1602), Duke, 62; Moore, fo. 133^{v}; and below pp. 70–1.

[7] *The Poor of East Greensted* v. *Howard* (1633), Duke, 64; *Inhabitants of Woodford* v. *Parkhurst* (1638), Duke, 70.

[8] *Steward* v. *Germyn* (1599), Duke, 79.

use was truly stated,[1] order the lord of copyhold land[2] to admit a feoffee to charitable uses as his tenant,[3] and apportion the liability to make recompense among the 'guilty' parties, as they in their discretion thought fit.[4]

The commissioners had to exercise their powers with the utmost good faith. If they 'reduce[d] the donor's intent to an unconscionable or unlawful act, the decree [was] not good'.[5] Nor could they rewrite the trusts appointed by the donor, or alter the purpose and quality of the original gift. As Moore said:[6]

> if the donor limit the imployment of the profits to persons of one sex, quality, nation, trade, or profession, the commissioners cannot decree the imployment to persons of another sex, quality, nation, trade, or profession.
>
> So if the imployment be appointed to be upon the poor of one parish, or the parishioners of one parish, or the prizoners of one prizon; or the scholars of one grammar school; in certain, the commissioners' power cannot decree it to the poor of another parish, to the prizoners of another gaol, nor to the scholars of another school, for that were contrary to the intent of the donor.

But the commissioners could limit the charitable use if that limitation carried out the donor's intention.[7] If there was a gift for the 'relief of the poor', the commissioners could 'ordain that it shall be [employed on] a stock of money to provide hemp, iron, etc., to set the poor in work upon'.[8] Similarly if there were a gift 'to marry poor maids', they could decree how much money each was to receive or impose conditions, for example, that no payment be made to any maid 'gotten with child before marriage'.[9] The commissioners could not however interfere with or vary the discretion

[1] Duke (Moore), 178; see below, pp. 49, 98–9.

[2] Copyhold land could be charged to a charitable use: see *Kenson*'s case (1599), Duke, 80; Moore, fo. 240[v].

[3] *Ranshaw(e)* and *Robottom*'s case (1601), Moore, fo. 164, Duke (Moore), 140; see below, p. 72, n. 6. *Aliter* if the feoffee was a corporation: see below pp. 71 ff. for a further discussion.

[4] Moore, fo. 206. For a further example, see *ibid.* fo. 221[v], discussed below, p. 101, n. 2.

[5] Moore, fo. 152: 'si les commissioners ayant generall done de faire decree, reduce le entent del donor al act unconscionable ou unlawfull, le decree nest bone.' So if they leased at an under-value to their friends or 'ordain[ed] that their own servants be the poor', their decree could be avoided: see Duke (Moore), 156.

[6] *Ibid.* 157–8.

[7] Their decrees could be modified or annulled by the Chancellor; see above, p. 46, and below, p. 51.

[8] Duke (Moore), 158; see also Moore, fo. 80[v].

[9] Duke (Moore), 159.

of feoffees, if the feoffees had acted responsibly, deliberately and in accordance with the donor's will.[1] Nor could they perfect an unlawful devise and appoint to a valid use. Thus,

> if a man devise that his heir, as often as such a church shall become void, shall present a poor scholar of such a college; and that the clerk presented, shall have a certain sum of money to the repair of highways, and the commissioners decree accordingly: this decree is to be annulled, and made void, although it be according to the intent of the donor, because the use for highways, depends upon symony.[2]

Perhaps the most radical power enjoyed by the commissioners was a power to supply and cure defects in conveyances and assurances to charitable uses. A donor might attempt to transfer property to charitable uses but would omit to enrol the deed so that the transfer would have been imperfect at law; or he might devise land to a corporation to hold to a charitable use, which devise would have been void under the Wills Act, 1540. Nevertheless in these, and similar cases, which will be discussed more fully in a later chapter,[3] it was consistently held that the commissioners could uphold the defective gift or devise as a valid declaration or appointment *inter vivos*. Charity was to be encouraged, and no charitable gift should be allowed to fail simply because of a defect of form. The powers of the commissioners enabled them therefore not only to correct breaches of trust but to perfect imperfect charitable gifts.

[1] See the examples given in Moore, fols. 144–5, 152 and 253. One example will suffice (fo. 152): 'quant le testator appoint le terme destre vend pur releive captives generalment, le quel done choice al executor sur quex captives il voit imployer, si ore les commissioners poient prender le trust et choice hors del executor et appoint le redempcion al captives in certeynes. Et semble que ils poient in cest case quia la sont captives releivable, et la est negligence de sale que amount al non-employment per lexecutor, issint le default del executor done jurisdicion al commissioners, quex un fois ayant jurisducion, poient proced accoret a lestatute, quel est de faire tiels decrees que les choses dones serra trewly and faithfully imployed al tiels des uses que le donor ad appoint, le quel ils ont fait in nostre case, car le donor in son generall done pur releive captives, ad monstre luy mesme indifferent quel captive, si soit captive, et le commissioners ordaynant ceux captives, nont digrest del volunt le donor, mes il est clere si lexecutor ewst vend le terme dent le decree, et ewst imploy largent sur auters captives, le commissioners ne puissoient aver fait ascun decree ne aver reforme le fait del executor coment que il avoit fait pluis indiscrement que ils pense[nt] que il doit aver fait in le choice des captives. Auxi si la ne fuissent captives al temps del commission, les commissioners ne puissoient entermedle quia nul non imployment ne negligence in lexecutor.'

[2] Duke (Moore), 168. See also Moore, fols. 23^{v}–4, 152.

[3] See below, pp. 60 ff.

The commissioners did not have jurisdiction to investigate charitable uses which did not fall within the equity of the statute.[1] Equally the commissioners' decree could not touch the Crown, so that the commissioners could not make a decree which bound property held by the King to a charitable use.[2] Moreover, they could neither bind by decree any *bona fide* purchaser for money or money's worth of property held to the charitable use, nor 'those which have rights, titles, estate and interest paramount. . . . But all those whom the donor might have bound by his own act, or conveyance, shall be bound by the decree of the commissioners.'[3]

The commissioners were constantly subjected to the supervisory jurisdiction of the Chancellor. It was he, with the advice of the common law judges, who determined whether the commissioners could perfect imperfect charitable gifts[4] and ensured that they did not exceed or improperly exercise their lawful powers. The Chancellor could vary their decree in order to carry out more perfectly the intention of the donor. Thus, in particular cases, he changed 'the employment [of the use] from a causeway, to make a bridge' because 'the passage was the principal';[5] and where the commissioners' decree charged the overseers for the poor with the use, he could alter it and 'lay it upon the churchwardens, *Et è converso*, or may divide it between them at his pleasure'.[6]

But if a gift be made general, *ad pios usus*, and the decree limits the employment for repair of highways, etc. this decree is not alterable to another use, because the commissioners have lawfully first reduced, the generality to a certainty.[7]

The Chancellor, but not the commissioners, could commit for contempt a party who failed to observe the decree, and order judgment to be levied on his lands and goods if he refused to support the charitable uses which he ought to have supported.

[1] See above, pp. 31–7.

[2] Moore, fols. 32^{v}, 71^{v}. 'If a feoffee to a charitable use convey the land to one for life, the remainder to the King, the King shall be bound by the decree of the commissioners, because the use was limited before the titles of the King' (Duke (Moore), 162).

[3] *Ibid.* 161. And see below, pp. 97 ff. for a discussion of the defence of *bona fide* purchase.

[4] See below, pp. 60–72.

[5] Duke (Moore), 169.

[6] *Ibid.* 169. See also Moore, fo. 137, where he points out that the commissioners could also exercise this power.

[7] Duke (Moore), 169–70.

Yet, though 'the manner of execution is deferred to the Lord Chancellor . . . his discretion should be limited and confined in awarding process of execution, unto the usual course of justice, in courts of justice and equity.'[1]

(iv) *The achievement of the commissioners*

The initial success of the commissioners' investigations can be measured by the fact that in the twenty-four years from the enactment of the first charity statute in 1597 to the death of James I over one thousand decrees were sealed,[2] each one of which concerned the administration of a particular charitable trust; whereas in the two hundred years between 1400 and 1601 not more than one or two decrees affecting charitable trusts could have been made by the Chancellor annually.[3] Moreover, the commissioners, who were charged in their commission to complete their investigations within a certain time, were speedy and efficient in the execution of their duties;[4] and the Chancellor, to whom an aggrieved party could appeal, did all he could (particularly by refusing successful exceptants their costs,[5] by holding that no bill of review would lie to challenge the commissioners' decrees[6] and by a generous and sympathetic interpretation of the preamble and the substantive provisions of the statute)[7] to ensure that their work was not frustrated.[8] The efficiency of the commissioners' investigation partly depended upon the fact that they came into the county and parish. The hearing was intimate and took place not in distant London but locally, perhaps in the home of one of the local

[1] Duke (Moore), 166. Moore then discusses (*ibid.* 166–7) the circumstances in which execution could be levied on a variety of recalcitrant defendants, including executors, bankrupts, recusants, King's accountants and husbands.

[2] See appendix I below, pp. 255–6.

[3] See above, pp. (18–19.)

[4] See above, p. 44. A few examples may be helpful:

1. C. 93/4/16: Commission, 20 February 1611; Decree, 3 October 1611.
2. C. 93/11/13: Commission, 3 December 1627; Decree, 25 April 1627.
3. C. 93/11/7: Commission, 20 July 1627; Decree, 5 March 1628.
4. C. 93/11/2: Commission, 24 October 1626; Decree, 30 November 1627.

[5] See above, p. 46.

[6] See above, p. 46.

[7] See above, p. 51.

[8] The petition on behalf of the charity enjoyed other procedural privileges. For example, 'to avoyde charge there shall need no bill but onely exceptions to the decree, and answer forthwith to bee made thereunto' (see Francis Bacon's Orders, dated 29 January 1618–19, Ord. 93, quoted in G. W. Sanders' *Orders of the High Court of Chancery*, I (London 1845), 121).

gentry, who might be a member of the commission; and the clear and peremptory notice,[1] sent to parish officers and prominently displayed and disseminated in the parish, encouraged vicar and churchwardens, parish officers and parishioners, to disclose to the commissioners breaches of trust of which they were aware. The Council at Westminster and the individual parishioner, upon whom the burden of supporting the vagrant fell, were united in their desire to fulfil the aspirations of the poor relief legislators, and it was this spirit of co-operation and interested dedication which vitalised the commission procedure and ensured its original triumph.[2]

Certainly the success of the commission in the county was not due to the magical quality of the legal procedure embodied in the Charitable Uses Act, 1601. The commission was a potentially ponderous instrument of investigation and supervision: commissioners and jurors had to be found to serve and give freely of their time; parish administration had to remain efficient and parishioners enthusiastic; and the Chancellor had to continue to hear speedily and sympathetically exceptions which, if encouraged, could cripple the commissioners' investigations. As long as society appreciated the urgency of the charity commissioners' task, the statutory procedure would flourish. However, once men become indifferent to the need to sustain 'good godly and charitable uses', the procedure would be revealed as cumbersome rather than summary, dilatory rather than speedy, costly rather than cheap in execution. The method of investigation established under the Charitable Uses Act, 1601, could not efficiently function in a society whose gentry served with reluctance as commissioners,[3] whose jurors resented their jury service, whose parish officers were lax and inefficient, whose central government was apathetic, and whose Chancellor would not 'oppress any man for the sake of a charity'[4] and bitterly regretted the privileges which his predecessors had afforded the charitable trust.

[1] See above, p. 41.

[2] See, generally, Jordan, *Philanthropy in England, 1480–1660*, 116–17. And cf. Barnes, *Somerset, 1625–1640*, 150, who points out that in that county some complaints concerning charitable trusts were summarily (and illegally) dealt with in Quarter Sessions.

[3] Cf. Christopher Hill, *The Century of Revolution, 1603–1714* (Edinburgh, 1961), 102–3.

[4] *Att.-Gen.* v. *Lord Gower* (1736), 2 Eq. Cas. Abr. 195, *per* Lord Hardwicke L.C., below, p. 106.

The seeds of the effective demise of the charity commission were sown in the Civil War, and between 1640 and the Restoration there is a sharp decline in the number of charity commissions.[1] 'The late distractions', wrote Henry Twyford, George Duke's publisher, in 1676, 'have tempted so many to imbezel what was given to pious uses, that if this book [on Charitable Uses] seemed requisite before, 'tis absolutely necessary now.'[2] Men no longer cared whether the commission procedure worked efficiently and effectively, and John Herne, in the preface to his treatise on *Charitable Uses*, published sixteen years earlier, commented that:[3]

being frequently present at Commissions grounded on this Statute of Charitable Uses, I have found the Gentlemen of the Countrey, Commissioners, Jurors, and parties prosecuting (by want of experience in Clerks attending such Commissioners) forced to unnecessary attendance and charge; Whereupon grown almost weary of well doing with ill direction, they never cheerfully embraced the Commissions; Nay, many Inquisitions and Decrees, which have been returned, miscarried, and were rendered ineffectual through the unskilfulnesse of those that drew them.

The publication of such books reflected some awareness of the problem of enforcement and a modicum of concern to secure the smooth functioning of the statutory procedure. There is evidence too of a considerable revival of national and local interest, particularly between 1670 and 1688.[4] But the commissions' renewed popularity was not only short lived, but somewhat deceptive.[5] For contemporaneously efforts are being made, through the information, to secure an alternative and less demanding method of enforcing charitable trusts.

The information had been used before the Restoration to enforce charitable trusts over which the charity commissioners had no jurisdiction;[6] for such uses were not 'within the remedy of the statute . . . and so were properly and noe other way relievable but by this Honorable Court as all good and charitable uses which are not within the provicions of the said statute are.'[7] Each

[1] See appendixes H and I below, pp. 251–6.

[2] From the publishers' advertisement to G. Duke's *Law of Charitable Uses.*

[3] *The Law of Charitable Uses* (London, 1660). For a bibliographical note, see appendix E, p. 233.

[4] See appendixes H and I below, pp. 251–6, particularly, pp. 255–6. And cf. *Parliamentary Debates* (Hansard), XXXVIII, 606–7 (1818).

[5] See below, p. 160.

[6] See above, p. 36.

[7] From an information, dated 11 November 1656: C. 5/588/71.

information set out elaborately why the relator had to proceed by information and why the charity commissioners lacked jurisdiction. For example, informations were brought to enforce charitable uses which would have failed for uncertainty[1] or which ran foul of the mortmain statutes.[2] In all probability these were elaborate devices to circumvent, and to replace a dilatory procedure, for there seems little doubt that the charity commissioners had taken jurisdiction over such uses before the Civil War. The information was now thought to be a speedier procedure, and its attractions were enhanced by a series of decisions between 1670 and 1680,[3] in which Lord Nottingham confirmed that the Court of Chancery could cure defective charitable uses and uphold them as valid appointments *inter vivos*, even though the matter had come before the Court by way of information.[4] For

> the King as *Pater patriae* may and ought to be the great protector of all charities which were not within the regulation of the statute of 43 Eliz., for he was so at Common Law before that statute. . . .[5]

At the same time there are attempts to extend the scope of the information. In 1674 the Attorney-General, at the relation of the vicar of Hartwell in Northampton, proceeded to establish a gift to the vicar of Hartwell for the time being for 'puttinge oute ffower poore boyes apprentices',[6] a charitable object within the preamble and consequently within the jurisdiction of the commissioners. By 1680 such informations were not uncommon, and by the end of the seventeenth century quite frequent.[7] The information could by that time be used to establish or to investigate any charitable trust.

Before any conclusion is drawn, therefore, from statistics based on the number of commissions issued between 1660 and 1668, it

[1] C. 6/171/79 (1662); *Att.-Gen.* v. *Peacock* (1675), Finch, 245, 2 Lev. 167, Selden Society, LXXIII, cases 300, 440; see above, p. 36 and below pp. 69–70.

[2] C. 8/166/1 (1669); see above, pp. 36–7.

[3] *Coleman* and *Coleman*'s case (1673), Finch, 30, Selden Society, LXXIII, case 8; *Att.-Gen.* v. *Peacock* (1675), Rep. *temp.* Finch, 245, 2 Lev. 167, Selden Society, LXXIII, cases 300, 440; *Att.-Gen.* v. *Platt* (1675), Selden Society, LXXIII, case 225, below, p. 62; *Queens' College, Cambridge* v. *Fabian* (1680), Selden Society, LXXIX, case 1027. See also *R.* v. *Newman* (1670), 1 Lev. 284.

[4] See below, p. 88.

[5] *Att.-Gen.* v. *Peacock* (1675), Selden Society, LXXIII, case 300, p. 209. And see below, p. 88.

[6] C. 5/585/14: see also C. 5/585/12 (1673); C. 5/441/106 (1678); C. 5/441/108 (1677); C. 5/441/112 (1679).

[7] This is evident from a random sampling of MS. Public Record Office Lists and Indexes for the period. And see *Att.-Gen.* v. *Hewer* (1700), 2 Vern. 387.

must be remembered that it was not until 1680 that an alternative and suitable method of enforcing *all* charitable trusts was firmly established. The acceptance of that role for the information foreshadowed the effective demise of the commission procedure. It is no accident that there is a very sharp decline in the number of charity commissions after the Glorious Revolution.[1] The demands made on the private individual by the statutory procedure (in particular the time and sacrifice demanded from gentry and parishioner), combined with the indifference of the Council, ensured the popularity of the information—even though it, too, in its turn, failed to provide an effective means of controlling the administration of charitable trusts.[2] In the eighteenth century commissions to investigate charitable trusts rarely issued, and those that did led 'him who pursue[d] it sooner or later into the Court of Chancery'[3] and possible financial ruin. The last commission was issued in 1787.[4] By this time the statutory procedure was a creaking anachronism.

[1] See appendixes H and I below, pp. 251–6.

[2] See below, p. 160.

[3] The words are Henry Brougham's: *Parliamentary Debates* (Hansard), XXXVIII, 606–7; and see below, pp. 162–4.

[4] See below, p. 160.

CHAPTER IV

THE DEVELOPMENT OF THE LAW OF CHARITY, 1545–1700: A DEFINITION OF CHARITY

BEFORE the Reformation pious causes honouring God and his Church constituted a coherent and measurable class which was accepted by the Chancellor as setting the limits of legal charity.[1] After the breach with Rome, however, piety and charity ceased to be synonymous. Gifts for popish purposes were avoided by the courts, and the valid charitable use was sharply distinguished from the void superstitious use.[2] Though the distinction between the charity and the superstition was a real one, the conception of superstition was fluid and amorphous; 'that which at one time is held for orthodox, may at another, be accounted superstitious.'[3] Indeed, the fear that the religious use might infect by association other charitable uses, whose endowments the Crown could then appropriate, encouraged the draftsmen of the Charitable Uses Act, 1601, to exclude it[4] from the list of good and godly uses over which the charity commissioners had jurisdiction.

The preamble to the Charitable Uses Act, 1601, did not attempt to mark out the limits of legal charity or condemn as non-charitable those uses which were outside its letter and equity. The object of that Act, like its predecessor of 1597, was simply to secure the proper application of the endowments of those charitable trusts which could alleviate poverty and relieve the parish of the financial responsibility of supporting the vagrant. The preamble contained a most comprehensive catalogue of secular charitable objects, which the Chancellor generously extended.[5] There were other uses which were recognised to be charitable but which fell outside the letter and equity of the preamble. These included many religious uses, such as for a chaplain to celebrate divine service or for the support of a preaching minister and,

[1] See above, pp. 7 ff. This short chapter draws together conclusions reached in chapter III.

[2] See above, pp. 10 ff.

[3] Duke (Moore), 132; quoted above, p. 32, n. 1.

[4] Other than the use for the repair of churches: see above, p. 31.

[5] See above, pp. 27 ff.

after the Civil War, gifts for general charitable purposes which would have failed at common law for uncertainty or some other reason.[1] Any parishioner who sought to enforce trusts for objects within the preamble could appear before the commissioners and substantiate his allegations; but if he wished to establish trusts for the support of charitable objects outside the preamble he had to proceed by simple bill or, in later years, by information.[2] When it was established, however, as it was in the late seventeenth century, that *all* charitable uses 'are taken to be within the extensiveness of this proceeding [the information] in the name of the Attorney-General'[3] and as soon as the information had supplanted the commission procedure as the only practical method of enforcing charitable trusts, the distinction between charities within and outside the preamble could and did disappear.[4]

During the period 1532 to 1700 the task of defining charity arose, therefore, in two contexts: the superstitious use was to be distinguished from the charitable use, and charities within the preamble were to be distinguished from those outside the preamble. These questions apart, the seventeenth-century judge was never troubled by the problems of definition. The class of charitable clauses was otherwise well defined, and the character and quality of men's bounty did not significantly change in the two hundred and fifty years after the Reformation.[5] The energies of the contemporary judge were primarily directed into determining the nature and extent of the privileges of charity rather than in marking out its boundaries.

[1] See above, pp. 33 ff.

[2] See above, pp. 36 ff.

[3] *Att.-Gen.* v. *Brereton* (1752), 2 Ves. Sen. 425, 426, *per* Lord Hardwicke; see below, p. 120.

[4] See below, pp. 120 ff.

[5] David Owen, *English Philanthropy, 1660–1960* (London, 1965), 71.

CHAPTER V

THE DEVELOPMENT OF THE LAW OF CHARITY, 1545–1700: THE PRIVILEGES OF CHARITY

THE privileges granted to the charitable use were varied and extensive and, during this period, were sympathetically interpreted by the Chancellor. '*Le Commonwealth et le majesty divine, pur quel honor charitie est fait et commaund*',[1] were anxious to ensure that philanthropy should be encouraged and that the objects of charitable trusts should not be frustrated by the formalism and rigidity of the common law.

The most influential of these privileges were the Chancellor's refusal to allow charitable trusts to fail because of a defect of form or the incapacity of the particular feoffees and his willingness to apply *cy-près*, to similar purposes, property held for a charitable object, which it was impossible or illegal to perform, or which would have failed at law for uncertainty. But there were other privileges, which equally vividly if more modestly, illustrate the Chancellor's concern to protect the endowment of godly and charitable uses. For example, no statute of limitation was allowed to bar any action to enforce a charitable use; charitable legacies were preferred on a marshalling of assets; and no charitable use was allowed to be destroyed by a tortious feoffment in fraud of the use.

Some of the privileges which will be described in this chapter find their origin in civil or canon law. The records suggest, however, that the Chancellor had adopted many of them as his own before the enactment of the Charitable Uses Act, 1601, although it was that statute, which was to lead to the confirmation and extension of the nascent Chancery development. As Francis Moore emphasised in the first case he posited in the Middle Temple:[2]

[1] Moore, fo. 47^{v}.

[2] Moore, fo. 10: 'le defect in nostre case est, quia le disseissee nad graunt ouster le rent . . . per que in extremity del ley le rent nest bone, a que jeo respoign. Que leffect et fruite de mon statute est daver decree fait per Commissioners, le quel decree nest restreine al suire principales del ley, mes poient estre fait sur equity, Et pur ceo lestatute appoint le decree destre examinable et corrigible per Chauncelor sur English bill, le quel est judge de Equity, et nemi tie al ley. Et pur ceo si soit equity pur le charitable use, ceo est assets sufficient, comment que ne soit ley. Et ceo est prove per les ample parolls de lestatute, cest (Given, appointed, Limited and assigned) to the uses etc.'

The defect in our case is, because the deseisee has not granted over the rent [to the charitable use] . . . so in law the rent is not good, to which I respond. That the effect and fruit of my statute is to have a decree made by the commissioners, which decree is not restrained to follow the principles of law but can be made on equity. And for that, the statute appoints the decree to be examinable and correctable by the Chancellor on an English bill, who is judge of equity, and not tied to law. And for that, if it be equity for the charitable use, that is sufficient assets, although [it] be not law. And that is proved by the generous words of the statute, that is (Given, appointed, Limited and assigned) to the uses etc.

The perfection of imperfect instruments

(i) *Defect of form*

The Chancellor would not allow any charitable trust to fail for a defect of form. If the settlor could have made a perfect transfer by another instrument, the Chancellor would intervene, cure the formal defect, and enforce the use. The settlor was not obliged 'to the observance of any form or ceremony either of lease or release, or common recovery or fine,' etc.[1]

albeit there be defect in the deed, or in the will, by which they were first created and raised; either in the party trusted with the use, where he is misnamed, or the like; or in the parties for whose use, or that are to have the benefit of the use, as where they are not well named, or the like; or in the execution of the estate, as where livery of seisin, or attornment is wanting or the like.[2]

There are many examples in the records of the Chancellor's concern to sustain 'good, godly and charitable uses' by upholding a defective transfer. Even before the Charitable Uses Act, 1601, he had dismissed demurrers that a feoffment to a charitable use was void because the conveyance by bargain and sale had not been enrolled within six months as required by the 'Enrolmentes of Bargaines and Contractes of Landes' Act, 1535.[3] In a case decided in 1582 and cited by Moore:[4]

[1] *Att.-Gen.* v. *Rye and Warwick* (1702), 2 Vern. 453, *per* Nathan Wright, L.K.

[2] Duke, 109.

[3] 27 Hen. VIII c. 16.

[4] Duke (Moore), 162–3. This case is not mentioned by Moore in the C.U.L. MS.; but cf. fo. 11^{v}, where the tenant agrees to convey the frank tenement to another, to suffer a recovery and to pay a rent to maintain a chaplain: 'In nostre case le tenant est le bargainee et le recovery est suffer dent inrolment, sur que le question est, si bargainee dent inrolment soit bone tenant al precipe pur recovery. Et semble que cy . . .'

One Symons, an Alderman of Winchester, [had] sold certain land to Sir Thomas Flemming, now Lord Chief Justice,[1] then Recorder of that Town, and this was upon confidence to perform a charitable use, which the said Symons declared by his last will; that Sir Thomas Flemming should perform the bargain, was never inrolled; and yet the Lord Chancellor decreed, that the heir should sell the land, to be disposed according to the limitation of the use; and this decree was made the 24 of Queen Elizabeth before the Statute of Charitable Uses, and this decree was made upon ordinary and judicial Equity in the Chancery.

This principle appears to have been confirmed two years later, in 1584, in an action brought by William ffrenche and other inhabitants of Laystoft against Edmund Tetter. In this case the Chancellor decreed property to a charitable use notwithstanding a plea by Serjeant Rodes[2] that the feoffment was void because it had not been enrolled.[3]

After the Charitable Uses Act, 1601, these and other defective transfers were consistently perfected and upheld by the Chancellor, often with the advice of the common law judges, as valid declarations, limitations or appointments *inter vivos*. The novelty of the *post*-statute decisions was not that relief was given where it had hitherto been denied, but the emphasis on the statute's preamble, which commenced with a declaration that property had 'been heretofore given, limited, appointed and assigned' to the charitable uses enumerated therein, as the source of the courts' power to perfect charitable gifts. Though a transfer of property to feoffees to charitable uses was void at law because of a defect of form, yet it would stand as a declaration upon the statute of charitable uses.[4] As Chief Justice Wilmot was to say:[5]

The judges . . . could not say the devises were good at law; and therefore they left the legal estate to follow the course of the law, but considered the devise as an equitable declaration of the trust of the estate, and as a valid limitation and appointment of the *utile dominium* . . .

[1] Flemming (or Fleming) was made Lord Chief Justice on 25 June 1607, barely six weeks before Moore began his *Reading*: see *Dictionary of National Biography*, VII (London, 1889), 286.

[2] On whom, see the entry in William Dugdale, *Origines Juridiciales, Chronica Series* (London, 1680), 97.

[3] The history of this dispute will be found in the Chancery *Entry Book of Decrees and Orders* for 1584: C. 33/68/34, 73, 209. The demurrer appears to have been abandoned early in the proceedings. See below, p. 92 for a further discussion of this case. Laystoft is now known as Lowestoft.

[4] Cf. *Pennyman* v. *Jenny* (1626), Duke, 82.

[5] In *Att.-Gen.* v. *Lady Downing* (1767), 1 Wilm. 1, 12.

'The intent of the [statute] was to make the disposition of the party as free and easy as his [the transferor's] mind; and not to oblige him to the observance of any form or ceremony.'[1] A tenant in tail who had devised his entail, without having levied a fine or recovery, for the maintenance of a schoolmaster, could nevertheless bar not only his heirs but the remainderman, and thereby appoint the property to the charitable use.[2] Again in *Platt* v. *St John's College, Cambridge*,[3] Platt had settled a copyhold estate[4] on his wife for life with remainder to St John's College for the maintenance of scholars in the college. The settlement had been made in pursuance of a recovery, purporting to bar Platt's entail, which proved to be void because no judgment had been given in the manorial court against the vouchee. The Lord Keeper, Thomas Coventry, held that though the wife could be evicted at law

> yet the remainder to the college shall stand good, and be a remainder without a particular estate, which by rules of law cannot be; but these defects in cases of charitable uses, are made good by that statute [of Charitable Uses], by a benigne, and favourable interpretation thereupon for maintenance of charity; as it is in other cases upon statutes for piety and charity.[5]

There are many examples too in Francis Moore's *Reading* of the Chancellor's readiness to disregard the common law of conveyancing if he could thereby save the charitable use. Charitable uses could be limited on both a covenant to stand seised (the confidence reposed in the feoffee was 'sufficient ground for decreeing [to] the charitable use');[6] on a bargain and sale, even without

[1] *Att.-Gen.* v. *Rye and Warwick* (1703), 2 Vern. 453, *per* Nathan Wright L.K.

[2] *Tay* v. *Slaughter* (1690), Prec. Ch. 16; *Att.-Gen.* v. *Rye and Warwick* (1703), 2 Vern. 453.

[3] (1638), Duke, 77; see below, p. 69, for a further discussion of the history of this particular litigation. In the records, quoted below, the plaintiff's name is consistently given as Platt. In Duke, he is, wrongly, called Plate.

[4] Copyhold land was within the equity of the statute: see above, p. 49.

[5] Duke, 77, 78.

[6] Moore, fo. 119^v. At common law no use to a stranger could be raised on a covenant to stand seised. Moore equates the confidence reposed in the feoffee to charitable uses with natural love and affection and marriage consideration, which could normally support the use. 'Ceo est imposicion in equity sur le party que ad le use raised et confidence est sufficient ground pur decree charitable use': see also fo. 19. *Semble* the charitable use had to be declared in writing: see fols. 19 and 133.

enrolment;[1] on the grant of a reversion without attornment;[2] upon a feoffment without livery;[3] upon an estate by estoppel;[4] and sometimes, on a jointure to bar dower [5]—even though in all these cases to limit uses on such feoffments would generally have been impossible at law.

Moore devoted considerable time to the consideration of these questions, and consistently emphasised how beneficent were the statute's preamble and provisions. A declaration and appointment to charitable uses would be gleaned from an abortive attempt to grant over a rent charge to charity;[6] or from the mere *grant* of an 'annuitie *pro consilio* al soldiors'.[7] Equally such expressions as 'in the hope that',[8] 'in confidence that'[9] or 'on condition that'[10] could support a charitable use, 'because all words of trust are words of

[1] Moore, fols. 11v, 71, 71v. A bargain and sale had to be enrolled: see above, p. 60. *Sed quaere* whether at law *any* active use could be limited on a bargain and sale. Moore does not suggest this; but cf. *Moyl Finch*'s case (1600), 4 Co. Inst. 86, D. E. C. Yale, 'The Revival of Equitable Estates in the Seventeenth Century', *Cambridge Law Journal* (1957), 72, 77.

[2] Duke (Moore), 140. See also Moore, fo. 47, where he upholds the grant of a seignory, without an attornment, to a charitable use. This case is transcribed in appendix G, below, p. 247.

[3] Duke (Moore), 140.

[4] Moore, fo. 87v: 'car le charitable use nest que confidence chardg sur cesty que ad le chose, cesty le ter, et estate per estoppell poit estre chardg ove tiel confidence, mes nemi ove use que executera per 27 h. 8 [Statute of Uses]. Le reason quia le charitable use est le consideracion del recovery [by estoppel].'

[5] *Ibid.* fo. 28v: 'si Jointure que barr dowre poit estre al charitable use, Et semble nemi generalment, quia adonque, nul advauncement al feme, mes moderate allowance poit estre chardg sur ceo, quia la est remayne al feme, quel el accept, uncore doit estre expresse in le fait, car ne poit estre averr per paroll.' The charitable use had to be averred by deed. 'Where things cannot pass without a deed, there charitable uses cannot be averred, without a deed, proving the use': see Duke (Moore), 141.

[6] Moore, fo. 10. For analogous cases, see fols. 127v and 245.

[7] *Ibid.* fo. 31.

[8] *Ibid.* fo. 19: 'les parolls sur hope sont assets sufficient de declare le use come ils sont in tout confidences sur termes bargains et sales . . ., quex ne poient estre al use transfferable per lestatute in possession.'

[9] Moore, fo. 28v, citing *Adams* and *Lambert*'s case (1602), 4 Co. 104b, and *18 Eliz. Dyer,* which is a possible reference to *Anon.* (1576), Dyer, 348a: 'sub condicion prist pur declaracion nemi condicion. Ici est condicion et auxi limitacion al charitable use.' See Moore, also for further examples, fols. 18, 47v, 83, 136 and 147. The last example (fo. 147) is worthy of note; a lessee's covenant to repair a bridge was construed to be a 'declaracion de confidence' and an appointment within the statute. 'Le leas del ter est fait al charitable use . . . car le covenant est le consideracion del leas.'

[10] Moore, fo. 136. See also fol. 91v: 'mesme in cases lou le ter mesme passe per mesme le instrument in quel le condicion est Conteyne.'

limitation and appointment and thus within the letter of the statute'.[1]

Many other examples may be found in the pages of Moore's *Reading* and in the printed reports.[2] Perhaps the most influential line of authority concerned the fate of those charitable uses declared in a will which failed at law. This problem frequently arose. In a case posited by Moore, there was a surrender of copyhold land to the uses declared in the will. The will, however, was void at law. Nevertheless, it operated as a

> direction in equity to the lord to admit, and thus the will is a declaration of the use of the copyhold in equity which use is not executed in possession by 27 Hen. 8 [the Statute of Uses] but endures all the time. Trusts and confidences are not bound by common law rules of possession and [of] freehold estates, and consequently it is not necessary for the party to be in being at the time of the limitation of the use of copyhold . . .[3]

Moore's audience would not have been deeply shocked by this statement of law for any feoffment to uses could avoid the common law 'rules of possession'.[4] Charitable uses were, however, particularly favoured. In *Stoddard*'s case,[5] in 1622, property had been charged in a nuncupative will with the maintenance of two scholars in Oxford and Cambridge. Bishop Williams, Lord Keeper, decreed that, although

> by law, a rent cannot be created or granted without deed, or will in writing; yet this nuncupative will was good to create the rent to a

[1] Moore, fo. 136: 'quia touts parolls de trust sont parolls de limitacion et appointment, et issint deins le letter del statute.'

[2] See, for example, the cases selected in Duke (Moore), 139–43.

[3] Moore, fo. 52: 'quia coppihold que ad resemblaunce al frehold est governe per mesme le principals ale al raiser de estates. Uncore ceo nient obstant, semble le remainder al premier fils bone in le principall case, car le Surrender esteant al use de son volunt le volunt apres fait nest done ou graunt in possession del coppihold, mes est direcion in equity al Segnor de faire admittaunce, et issint le volunt est declaracion del use del coppihold in equity le quel use ne execute al possession per lestatute de 27 H.8, mes demurt tout temps. Trusts et Confidences nient lie al rules in possessions et estates de francktenements al common ley, et pur ceo nest de necessitie que le party soit in esse al temps del limitacion del use del coppihold.'

[4] *Hussey*'s case (1604–5), Moo. K.B. 789, Moore, fo. 240. See also *Lady Dacres*' case (date unknown), Moore, fo. 240v.

[5] (1622) Duke, 81. This decision had been anticipated by Moore. In a case, discussed at fols. 35–35v, he had declared that a use imposed in a nuncupative will 'de paier ffees pur bankrupts alant hors del prizon de treate ove lour creditors' was a valid charitable use.

charitable use, by the words of the statute, or limitation or appointment; for although it be not a good gift, yet it is a good limitation or appointment.[1]

For similar reasons a devise to a corporation to hold to a charitable use was upheld as an appointment *inter vivos* though the Wills Act, 1540,[2] prohibited devises to a corporation.[3] And in *Rolt*'s or *Collison*'s case,[4] in 1617, the two Chief Justices, Montague, King's Bench, and Hobart, Common Pleas, advised the Lord Keeper, Francis Bacon, that even a devise to charitable uses made before the Wills Act 'is a limitation or appointment . . . to be relieved by the statute'. Acting on this advice Bacon confirmed the commissioners' decree which had applied the property to the charitable use set out in the will.

A void devise at law was, therefore, capable of being a 'good limitation within the statute.'[5]

The Statute of Wills binds not this Statute; [so] if Tenant by Knight service dispose of two parts of his lands, for the advancement of his wife and children, etc., and after devise by his will, that his heir shall perform a charitable use with the third part; the heir shall be charged with the use, because he is in by descent.[6]

(ii) *Incapacity at law*

The Chancellor was frequently asked to perfect a feoffment, a devise, or bequest which had been made to one who lacked capacity at common law to hold the property transferred to him.[7] The common law rule was a strict one. If there was no person who had *capacitie à prendre*, the transfer was void.[8] For this reason a devise to a chantry would fail if at the time of the devise 'y n'avoit

[1] Similarly a devise to charitable uses of a *chose in action*, for example, a debt, though void at law, served as a declaration upon the statute of charitable uses: see *Damus*' case (1614), Duke, 72.

[2] 32 Hen. VIII c. 1.

[3] *Hellam*'s case (1629), Duke, 80; *Mayor of Bristol* v. *Whitton* (1633), Duke, 81; and see below, p. 136.

[4] (1617), Duke, 73, Moo. K.B., case 1251, Hobart, 136. (This decision was to puzzle Lord Eldon in *Att.-Gen.* v. *Master etc. of the Skinners' Company* (1827), 2 Russ. 407, 418–19: see below pp. 135, 154.) In *Griffith Flood*'s case (1615), Hobart, 136, a devise to a corporation to charitable uses contained in a will executed *before* the charity statute of 1601 was upheld as a valid declaration of trust under that statute. And see above, p. 72, n. 1.

[5] Moore, fo. 40; see also for further examples, fols. 10^v and 104^v.

[6] Duke (Moore), 142. See also Moore,fols. 67 and 225–6 for analogous cases.

[7] See above, p. 36, for a discussion of the cases where there was a direct gift to general charitable objects.

[8] H. Rolle, *Abridgment*, 1 (London, 1668), 614.

nulle persone en estre nomez en les ditz testamentz.'[1] As Chief Justice of the Common Pleas Babington said in a case in 1429:[2]

Come si home devise teres a les prestes de un Chaunterie, ou dun college en l'Eglise de A et devie, acel temps, il ny ad nul Chaunterie ne nul College, ceo devise est void, non obstant que ceo devise est per lycence le Roy, et si apres un Chaunterie ou un College est fait en mesme le lieu, uncore ils naueront ceo terre pour ceo que al temps del devise ils ny aueront null corporacion en quel le devise purre prendre effect.

Because 'at common law . . . a charitable use has no capacity to "take" as other persons have',[3] a testator or settlor had to exercise some care to ensure that the legal title did vest in feoffees so that the charitable use could be supported.[4] For rarely did common law incorporate representative bodies,[5] and the conception of the corporation sole was even at the end of the medieval period a very limited one.[6] Occasionally, and very exceptionally, common lawyers jettisoned its fundamental rules,[7] but generally it was left to the Chancellor to intervene to save the defective charitable gift.

There are a number of instances in the early records of bills

[1] From the petition of the House of Commons in 1394, quoted by Miss Wood-Legh in her article on 'Chantries and Corporations Sole', *Law Quarterly Review*, LCCIV (1958), 272, 273–4. [2] Y.B. 9 Hen. VI, fo. 24b.

[3] Moore, fo. 276^{v}: 'et al common ley . . . charitable use nad capacity de prender come auters persons ad.'

[4] Common law was not generally concerned to determine whether the *cestui que* use, as distinct from the feoffee, had '*capacitie à prendre*'. In exceptional cases, however, for example in proceedings under the statute 1 Rich. III c. 1, which gave the *cestui que use* power to deal with the land as if he were a feoffee, common law did inquire whether the *cestui que use* was a person who had capacity to hold land at law: see Y.B. 12 Hen. VII fo. 27, pl. 7.

[5] In certain circumstances inhabitants of a town might be incorporated if the Crown granted lands to them: see *Anon.* (1553), Dyer, 100a; Rolle, *Abridgment*, I, 513. Also 'in London parson et churchwardens sont corps politick' (Moore, fo. 39^{v}).

[6] F. W. Maitland, 'The Corporation Sole', *Collected Papers*, III (Cambridge, 1911), 210.

[7] See, for example, *Anon.* (1571), Owen, 35, where a devise to a corporate body was upheld although 'they were incorporate by another name'. This decision may have been regarded as of doubtful authority, for the statute 14 Eliz. I c. 14 (above, p. 21) immediately validated all transfers of property for the use of the poor in any hospital or almshouse, despite the misnaming of the hospital or almshouse in the deed of transfer. Moore does not mention this statute in his discussion of the fate of a gift 'to the poor knights of Windsor' (fo. 171). He concluded, however, that 'coment que ils ne sont de eux mesmes incorporate, uncore ils sont hospitall in foundacion'.

See also *Welkden* v. *Elkington* (1578?), abstracted by Viner, Abr., 439. And cf. 39 Eliz. I c. 5 and 21 Jac. I c. 1.

brought by unincorporated bodies to enforce charitable uses.[1] Churchwardens were at common law a corporation only for limited purposes; the personalty which belonged to the parish was vested in them,[2] but they had no capacity to hold the church's realty which was vested in the parson for the time being.[3] Nevertheless the number of bills brought by churchwardens to enforce feoffments of realty to the use of their church suggests that the Chancellor was perfecting such feoffments many years before the enactment of the first charity statute in 1597;[4] and this surmise is confirmed by the evidence of the *Entry Books of Decrees and Orders*. In 1580 the Chancellor rejected the demurrer of *John Crooke* and *William Plowman* to the bill of the *Churchwardens of Ibberton in Dorset* that they need not answer because the churchwardens lacked capacity to take this gift, so that the feoffment of realty to them failed. For the lands and tenements were made[5]

> by reason of a gayft made thereof to there predecessors beinge churchewardens of Oberton aforesaid who were not any corporacion. And so not capable. And for that yt was thought by this courte That albeit they were not Incorporate yet the same churchwardens may be capable to some purposes. It ys ordered that a subpoena be awarded against the defendants to make an answere to the plaintiffs bill of complaint . . .

Nevertheless the defendants 'brought an accion of *ejectionae firmae* at the common law' against the churchwardens, who petitioned the Chancellor for an injunction to restrain the defendants from proceeding with their suit at law.[6] The injunction was granted on 8 June 1580, after the defendants' refusal to discontinue their suit at law.

> For that the plaintiffs (beinge no lawfull or suffycyent corporacion in lawe) could not make any defence against the same at the common lawe. As also for that the plaintiffs and there predecessors and there tennants have beene in possession thereof and ymployed the same to good and godly uses above the space of cccc yers . . .[7]

It was sufficient that the petitioners, the churchwardens, had *some*

[1] Appendix A, below, pp. 189–201.
[2] Y.B. 37 Hen. VI fo. 30, pl. 11.
[3] See, generally, Maitland 'The Corporation Sole', *Collected Papers*, III, 210. But see above, p. 66, n. 5.
[4] Appendix A, above pp. 189–201.
[5] C. 33/61/220. I have not been able to trace the bill. The spelling of the village's name in the records is not consistent. In some entries it is Oberton, in others Iberton. Today it is known as Ibberton.
[6] C. 33/61/485. The date of these proceedings is given as 31 May 1580.
[7] C. 33/61/524. And there, apart from one subsequent application for the discharge of an attachment with proclamation (C. 33/61/546), made on 13 June 1580, the story ends.

capacity at law, for example, capacity to take personalty; this was enough to justify the Chancellor's intervention and the issue of the injunction.

An analogous principle may underly the tersely reported decision of Lord Keeper Egerton in *Mayor and Burgesses of Reading* v. *Lane* in 1601.[1] In that case, a

> devise was made to poor people, maintained in the hospital of St. Lawrence in Reading for ever; exception was taken, that the poor were not capable by that name, for that they were no corporation, yet because the Mayor and Burgesses were capable to take lands in mortmain, and they did govern the hospital: It was decreed, that the defendant Lane should assure the land to the Mayor and Burgesses for the maintenance of the said hospital.

Apparently Egerton did not invoke the preamble to the Charitable Uses Act, 1601, to uphold the devise as a declaration or as an appointment *inter vivos*. His language suggests that the devise was saved because the mayor and burgesses were *in fact* capable of holding lands in mortmain to the particular charitable use, so that the reasoning appears to follow that of the earlier authorities, like the *Churchwardens of Ibberton*'s case.[2]

Thereafter, however, feoffments which failed at law because the legal title had not been vested in the charity or in feoffees were constantly upheld as declarations or appointments *inter vivos*. The preamble was claimed as the source of the Chancellor's power to perfect the defective instrument and to sustain the devise or feoffment; the defect was cured 'for that charity's sake by the construction of the statute'. So, in a case posited by Moore,[3] he concluded that the words in a will

> yielding £10 annually to a midwife [were] a sufficient appointment in equity of £10 for the midwife . . . although there be no certain person who can bring an action for debt or distrain for that, the words of the statute being liberal.

[1] Duke, 81.

[2] For a similar case, of uncertain date, where a corporation, which had ceased to have capacity to take property, was 'continued' for the preservation of the charitable use; see Duke (Moore), 139. And see *Champion* v. *Smith* (1605), Duke, 81; *Mayor of London*'s case (or case of *St Bartholomew's Hospital*) (1639), Duke, 83, where the facts were akin to *Mayor of Reading* v. *Lane* (1601), Duke, 81, above.

[3] Moore, fo. 19: 'les parolls yelding l 10 anualment al mydwyffe, sont sufficient appointment del l 10 pur le mydwyffe in equity . . . coment que nul person certeyne poit porter accion de dett ou distreyne pur ceo, les parolls de lestatute esteant liberall.' For another case, see *ibid.* fols. 39–40.

Moore was also of the opinion that a settlor could select as feoffees to charitable uses those who could not be 'feoffees to other uses', so that 'if a feoffment be made to a Dean and Chapter, upon condition to perform a Charitable Use, it is good, though they cannot be seised to another man's use'.[1]

So great was the emphasis on the beneficent qualities of the preamble that judges began to doubt whether the Court of Chancery could cure an imperfect charitable gift if the petitioner had sought to enforce it by simple bill or information. In 1641 the *Master and Fellows of St John's College, Cambridge*, petitioned the Chancellor by simple bill to compel *Robert Platt and others* to convey to them land which had been devised to the college by Platt's father.[2] The defendant's pleaded that the devise was 'voyd in Lawe in that the name of the said corporacion was not fully expressed in the said will', and that the devise could not be construed as a valid declaration or appointment *inter vivos* because the petitioners had proceeded by bill and not under the charity statute. The Chancellor ordered the question to be 'put into a Case Stated' to the judges, 'to certify their opinions whether the said will did amount to a good disposition in equity of the premises to the said College—within the meaning of the statute for Charitable Uses'. But before their opinion could be delivered 'the late troubles and confusions [the Civil War]' broke forth. Not until 30 January 1657 was the question again referred to the judges, who held that the devise to the college was void at law but was a good appointment in equity.[3] *Platt*'s case was not immediately accepted, and it was not until Lord Nottingham's Chancellorship that the principle of this decision was conclusively confirmed.[4] Thereafter

[1] Duke (Moore), 138. Equally a bankrupt or a recusant could be a feoffee to charitable uses, although he could not hold to non-charitable uses. But an idiot or a married woman could never be a feoffee.

[2] The account in the text is based on an information brought by the Attorney-General at the relation of the college, on 18 February 1672. The information contains the whole history of the suit: see C. 5/588/62.

[3] This fact is also to be gleaned from *West* v. *Knight* (1669), 1 Cas. in Chan. 135. The decree made in 1657 did not defeat the defendants' ingenuity and the litigation dragged on: see C. 5/588/62.

[4] *Coleman* and *Coleman*'s case (1673), Rep. *temp.* Finch, 30, Selden Society, LXXIII, case 8, p. 4; *Att.-Gen.* v. *Peacock* (1675), Finch, 245, 2 Lev. 167, Selden Society, LXXIII, cases 300, 440, pp. 209, 304; *Att.-Gen.* v. *Platt* (1675), Selden Society, LXXIII, case 225, p. 160; *Lilburn* v. *Turner* (1675–6), Selden Society, LXXIII, case 416, p. 288; *Queens' College, Cambridge* v. *Fabian* (1680), Selden Society, LXXIX, case 1027, p. 820. See also *R.* v. *Newman* (1670), 1. Lev. 284.

no one doubted that feoffments, devises or bequests to charitable uses, which would fail at law because the transferee lacked capacity, could be perfected in chancery, even though proceedings had been initiated by bill or information.[1]

(iii) *The limits of the Chancellor's indulgence*

The cases, which have just been discussed, graphically portray the Chancellor's anxiety to perfect the charitable gift, even at the expense of ancient common law rules and even in the teeth of statutory provision. But there were limits to the Chancellor's indulgence, some inspired by inherited legalism, others by considerations of higher social policy.

Certain common law principles appeared to be sacrosanct; 'the statute enables no devise where the testator had no power to do that by act executed which he hath done by his will'.[2] For example, a joint tenant could not grant (though he could release), 'his part to the other [joint tenant] to a charitable use; that is void, for one joint tenant cannot grant to the other'.[3] 'Where things [which could not] pass without deed, there charitable uses [could not] be averred, without a deed, proving the use';[4] and 'a charitable use [could not] be limited upon an estate in dower, nor upon a gift in frank marriage; nor upon exchange made of lands'.[5] Remote possibilities,[6] bare conditions,[7] 'things that yield no profit',[8] and 'things that are incident to others and unseparable'[9] likewise could

[1] But see below, p. 88 and *Att.-Gen.* v. *Peacock*, above, where Lord Nottingham upheld a gift to general, indefinite purposes on other grounds.

[2] *Gwyn* v. *Parker* (1678–9), Selden Society, LXXIX, case 875, p. 703.

[3] Duke (Moore), 140. Cf. *ibid.* 142: 'an advowson in gross, a way, or passage, matters of pleasure, as licence to hunt in a park, a signory *pro* fealty only, etc., cannot be granted . . . but they may be released to a charitable use.'

[4] *Ibid.* 141, cf. above, pp. 60 ff. However where no deed was necessary, 'a charitable use may be averred by witnesses' (Duke (Moore), 141). 'Coment que obligacion esteant chose in accion, charitable use ne poit estre declare de ceo sans Escript, uncore quia le propertie del obligacion va al executor in privitie per le volunt nuncupative le direcion per mesme le volunt al executor dimploier ceo est assets sufficient sans escript' (Moore, fo. 35).

[5] Duke (Moore), 139. But see above p. 65 n. 1.

[6] Moore, fo. 144: such as escheats and forfeitures. In this same passage, however, he distinguishes remote possibilities from those which were 'pregnant et apparent', 'quant le chose happa'. As an example of the latter, he gives the case of a lease to a widow as long as she remained unmarried, followed by her grant, with revocation, to charitable uses.

[7] Duke (Moore), 142.

[8] *Ibid.*

[9] *Ibid.*

not be granted[1] to charitable uses. A tenant in fee simple[2] could destroy the use by re-entry[3] for breach of condition, provided his entry was in good faith[4] and not made with the single intention of destroying the charitable use. His title was paramount, and 'it is seemingly reasonable that the use will determine, because *cuius est dare eius est disponere*'.[5] Again, a feoffor to charitable uses was required to have capacity to make a feoffment, a rule which excluded from the class of potential philanthropists infants, married women and lunatics.[6]

The Chancellor considered that these and other common law principles were so fundamental that he could not waive them. Some of them embodied a deliberate expression of social policy, which transcended that of the Charitable Uses Act, 1601. In *Gwyn* v. *Parker*,[7] Lord Nottingham refused to uphold as a valid declaration or appointment *inter vivos* a remainder to a charity which followed a devise in tail. 'The remainder [is] void as much as a remainder after a fee', he declared. '[T]he mischief of perpetuity is still the same and greater, for all men would so settle their lands if they might.'[8] A more obvious conflict of policies arose when a testator devised all his land held by knight service for the support of charitable uses. If such a devise had been upheld as an appointment, despite the Wills Act, 1540, the Crown would have lost its rights of wardship and *primer seisin*, which before 1660 were important items of royal revenue.[9] In these circumstances the

[1] Although some of them might be released: see above, p. 70, n. 3.

[2] But not his heir. 'Semble le heire ne poit per entry defeate [le use]' (Moore fo. 18ᵛ). 'Nient pluis que lou le done est fait sur condicion expresse coment que le condicion soit infrint' (*ibid.* fo. 31). See also *ibid.* fols. 47ᵛ and 83; and for an analogous case, fo. 40.

[3] *Semble* the tenant could not defeat the charitable use by release. 'Et si donor release le condicion uncore decree poit estre fait' (Moore fo. 18ᵛ; but cf. fo. 47ᵛ).

[4] *Ibid.* fo. 18ᵛ.

[5] Moore, fo. 47ᵛ: 'il semble reasonable que le use serra determine quia *cuius est dare eius est disponere.*' And cf. below, p. 98, where Moore discusses the case of a lessor who had leased land for a charitable use and reentered for breach of condition.

[6] *Jesus College* case (1615), Duke, 78; *Bramble* v. *Poor of Havering* (1639), Duke, 83. Cf. above, p. 5.

[7] (1678–9), Selden Society, LXXIX, case 875, p. 703.

[8] For analogous cases, see *Mayor and Commonalty of London* v. *Alford* (1640), Cro. Car. 576; *Company of Pewterers* v. *Governors of Christ's Hospital* (1683), 1 Vern. 161.

[9] H. E. Bell, *An Introduction to the History and Records of The Court of Wards and Liveries* (Cambridge, 1953), table A. Under the 1540 Act, a testator could divise only two thirds of land held by knight service.

Chancellor, on the advice of the common law judges, held that the devise was void as to a third part and not 'aided by the statute of 43 Eliz.'[1] It was not until after the Tenures Abolition Act, 1660,[2] that a devise to charitable uses of the whole of the testator's land held by knight service was sustained as a valid appointment.[3] As Lord Nottingham frankly admitted in *Company of Vintners* v. *Simonds*:[4]

> [i]t seems that all these resolutions [in the previous cases] were strained by the judges for advancement of the King's profit and prerogative in wardships and primer seisins. For ever since [military] tenures were abolished and [turned into socage]—the Judges have conceived themselves at more liberty to speak plainly in this matter.

The Chancellor was just as tender of the interests of the mesne lord. So, for example, he would only uphold a surrender of copyhold land to charitable uses if this would not prejudice 'the fines . . . and other customary dues'[5] owed to the lord of the manor. For similar reasons he would not allow a surrender to be made to a corporation 'for then the lord should have been prejudiced in his services'.[6]

The application of charitable funds cy-près

Neither the Chancellor, the commissioners, nor the trustees could vary the terms of a charitable gift merely because they deemed it desirable so to do.[7] Money for the relief of the poor could not be spent to support grammar school scholars;[8] 'if the use be to ease a parish of fifteens', it could not be extended to relieve the parish of its obligation to support bastards born within parish boundaries;[9]

[1] *Lord Edward Mountague*'s case (1619), Duke, 78; *Ascough* v. *Phillips* (1639), Wm. Jones, 428. But see *Griffith Flood*'s case (1615), Hobart, 136, which had (*semble*) decided to the contrary: see above, p. 65, n. 4.

[2] 12 Car. II c. 24.

[3] *Higgins* v. *Town of Southampton* (1670–1), Nelson, 146 ('after a long argument').

[4] *Company of Vintners* v. *Simonds* (1677), Selden Society, LXXIX, case 714, pp. 536, 538.

[5] Moore, fo. 163^{v}.

[6] Duke (Moore), 140. And cf. *Ranshaw(e)* and *Robottom*'s case (1604–5), Moore, fo. 164 (above, p. 49, n. 3), where a surrender to the use of the school at St Albans was upheld, the Chancellor ordering the lord to admit two tenants to hold to that use. The report of the case in Duke (Moore), 140, is incomplete.

[7] See above, pp. 49, 51–2; and see *Christ's Hospital* v. *Hawes* (1620), Duke, 84.

[8] Cf. Duke (Moore), 158.

[9] *Ibid.* 158; Duke, 115.

if 'monies given to the relief of the poor [were] paid out to build a conduite, [this was] a mis-employment'.[1] To have allowed the provisions of the trust to be summarily altered would be to take 'a great step towards destroying all charities'. In *Man* v. *Ballet*,[2] where Lord Nottingham made this observation, a testator had left in his will a bequest for the relief of poverty, the repair of highways and the repair of the testator's parish church. In fact no money had ever been spent on the church. The trustees of the charity pleaded, however, that they had made amends by the 'greatness and excess' they had shown to other charities, particularly to preaching ministers and lecturers. Lord Nottingham dismissed this plea:

> [A]t this rate we should have all persons' charities given away to preaching ministers and lecturers; but they should not thus think *to rob Peter to pay Paul*: however, for as much as this money for a long time had been thus promiscuously applied for the time past, they should not be punished for that mis-employment in anything, saving as to what was paid to the parson, for which they should not be allowed one farthing.[3]

Not even if the application was unopposed would the Chancellor vary the terms of the trust; the heir-at-law and next-of-kin had no more power than the trustees to alter their ancestor's disposition.[4]

To the general rule that the courts would not vary the terms of a charitable trust there was one important exception, the so-called *cy-près* doctrine: namely, where a charitable trust failed because its objects were uncertain, impossible to achieve or illegal, the court would apply the property to similar charitable uses, provided that this was in accordance with the settlor's intention. Its origins are obscure. *Cy-près* was known to the Romans.[5] Modestinus[6] was of the opinion that where money was given to commemorate a deceased person in an unlawful way, the elders of the city should commemorate him in a lawful manner. But it is conjectural

[1] Case of *Wivelescom in Somersetshire* (1629), Duke, 94.

[2] (1682), 1 Vern. 43. See also *Att.-Gen.* v. *Platt* (1675), Finch, 221; above, p. 69.

[3] (1682), 1 Vern. 43, 44. The Attorney-General in his argument had much 'harped' on the fact that the particular lecturer was a Presbyterian. But Lord Nottingham refused 'to be led or harangued with prejudice into cause', and declared that 'he minded the matter only and not the man'.

[4] *Att.-Gen.* v. *Lady Margaret and Regius Professors in Cambridge* (1682), 1 Vern, 55, below, p. 75.

[5] H. F. Jolowicz, *Roman Foundations of Modern Law* (Oxford, 1957), 138–9.

[6] D. 33.2.16.

whether equitable *cy-près* is entirely civilian in inspiration.[1] Canon law may have had some influence on its development[2] for it is known that the ecclesiastical courts did apply property *cy-près* where particular charitable purposes could not be accomplished.

Whatever the origins of equitable *cy-près*, by the beginning of the seventeenth century it is a sophisticated and mature doctrine. This is apparent from Sir Francis Bacon's decision in *Emmanuel College, Cambridge* v. *English*.[3] A testator had bequeathed £1,000 to his executors to buy lands to the yearly value of £50 *per annum*, the profits from the land to be applied for the maintenance at Emmanuel College of two fellows and six scholars. £10 *per annum* was to be spent on each fellow and £5 *per annum* on each scholar. The college found that £10 was, even in 1617, too little to maintain a fellowship, and prayed that the testator's bequest be altered and the money for fellowships applied for the foundation of additional scholarships. In their defence the executors pleaded that they had no power to do this. Nevertheless Lord Keeper Bacon varied the terms of the bequest, increasing the number of scholarships to nine and increasing the stipend of each scholar to £5 6s. 8d. *per annum*. He is reported to have said:

> That he did not intend to alter anything concerning the disposition of the legacy contrary to the will, except it were in that which was impossible to be performed, which might prove a hindrance and inconvenience to the college; and also that, in that which was necessary to be altered in respect of impossibility and inconvenience as aforesaid, he desired to tie himself to come as near as might be to the will and meaning of the testator in the ordering and disposing thereof.

The terms of a charitable trust would be altered if it was 'impossible'

[1] Cf. Joseph Willard, 'Illustrations of the Origin of Cy-Près,' *Harvard Law Review*, VIII (1894), 65. (The evidence does not, in my view, wholly support Willard's thesis.) And see *Att.-Gen.* v. *Platt* (1675), Finch, 221, where the Chancellor was prepared to accept some of the Roman rules of construction: cf. *Att.-Gen.* v. *City of Rochester* (1674), Selden Society, LXXIII, case 186, p. 135.

[2] Cf. Wilmot C.J.'s speculations in *Att.-Gen.* v. *Downing* (1767), 1 Wilm. 1, 32. H. Swinburne, *A Treatise of Testaments and Last Wills*, 6th ed. (London, 1793), 67–70.

[3] (1617), cases *temp.* Bacon, 27, 28; see also *Grant* v. *Huish* (1621), *ibid.* 28. (The authority of Ritchie's edition of Bacon's *Cases* was evaluated by Sir William Holdsworth in *Law Quarterly Review*, XLIX (1933), 61.) See also Moore, fo. 9^{v}.

to perform them; but the testator's intention must, as closely as possible (*cy-près*), be followed.[1]

Bacon's interpretation of 'impossibility' was undoubtedly generous and there is no other recorded example in the seventeenth-century reports of a successful prayer to vary a trust on similar grounds.[2] In *Attorney-General at the relation of Peterhouse, College in Cambridge* v. *The Lady Margaret and Regius Professors of Divinity in the University of Cambridge*[3] an unsuccessful attempt was made to alter the terms of a trust for the election of a lecturer in polemical or casuistical divinity. The lecturer was required to be a bachelor or doctor in divinity, at least fifty years old; he had to deliver five lectures each term and to deliver fair copies of each lecture at the end of each term to the University. There was a gift over to an Oxford college if no lecturer were appointed. The University, with the consent of the heir-at-law, sought to vary these onerous conditions and to appoint a lecturer who need only be forty years of age, give three lectures a term and deliver fair copies of his lectures once a year to the University. Lord Nottingham rejected their prayer; 'they [the University] should be held to the letter of the charity.'

The remaining seventeenth-century decisions helped to formulate what is now termed *prerogative* (as distinct from *judicial*) *cy-près*, whereby property devoted for the support of an illegal charity or given directly to indefinite charitable objects can be applied *cy-près*, not by the Court but by the Crown under the sign manual. This doctrine, formulated on the Equity Side of the Exchequer and subsequently adopted by the Chancellor, was the product of the bitter religious controversies of the seventeenth century and of the disputes surrounding the fate of funds devoted to the support of schismatic sects.

[1] Cf. Moore's example at fo. 9^{v}: 'si appointment dargent destre distribute al 20 porest de son kynde soit deins lestatute, quia ne appere que il ad ascun poore de son kynde ou al menis que il nad 20 poore. Et semble clere que il est deins lestatute, car le presumpcion est que il ne voile aver fait tiel limitacion sil navoit conus que ils fueront poore de son kynd, Et si serroit poore in verity et uncore cest graunt revert hors de lestatute per negative presumpcion encountre lexpresse mencion del donor, ceo serroit tort al donor et al fesors de lestatute.'

[2] But see *Att.-Gen.* v. *Guise* (1692), 2 Vern. 266, where money had been bequeathed for the maintenance of Scotsmen in the University of Oxford, who were to be sent to Scotland to propogate the doctrines of the Church of England. It was held (*semble*) that since 'Presbyters are settled in Scotland . . . the charity cannot now take place according to the letter and express direction of the will'. The money was then applied *cy-près*. The report is imperfect.

[3] (1682), 1 Vern. 55.

(i) *Illegal charitable objects*

Prerogative *cy-près* first makes its appearance in a dispute surrounding the will of Sara Venables, who died in 1607, bequeathing the residue of her estate 'for the releif and mayntenance of such ministers as then were or after should be putt from their places within this realme of England'.[1] After Sara's death, her will was published

> at the Gyld Hall in London with much ostentacion before divers Aldermen and manie strangers . . . whereby it came to my Lord of Canterbury his Graces knowledge And of the Judges ecclesiasticall who made the late Lord Tresurer and some othere of the lords of the counsell acquaynted withall who in there honorable wisdomes thought it not fit that a legacie of that nature should take place, Whereupon the probate of the will was stayed. And order was gyven unto Mr. Attornie generall to exhibit the bill dependinge in the Exchequer Chamber.

An information was duly filed in the Exchequer, where Sir Henry Montague, the Recorder of the City of London, argued that the legacy should be forfeit to the Crown:

> 'For when a thing is disposed, to maintain contempt and disobedience in any, this ought to be ordered and disposed by the court to a contrary end and use;' Since the King is offended by the contempt, 'he ought to have means to punish it, and so he prayed that it may be decreed for the King.'

Edward Buckland and Anthony Wotton 'being ministers non conformable were ordered not to intermeddle in the execution of the will'. And the remaining executors, Robert Bateman and John Slaney, 'submitted themselves to the order and direction of this courte', which required them on 9 June 1607, to 'paye deliver and dispose of the sayd money by five hundred poundes a yeare to such persons and in such manner as by such order and direcion of this courte shalbe appointed and not otherwise nor in other manner', that the will of the testatrix might (as near as conveniently possible) be performed.

The unfortunate publicity which had surrounded Sara's will and James I's distrust of schismatic sects, particularly inflamed after the abortive Hampton Court Conference of 1604,[2] must have

[1] The account in the text is based on the records contained in S.P. Dom. 14/37/113. There is a very brief and imperfect account in Lane's report of *R.* v. *Earl of Nottingham* (1610), Lane, 42, 44.

[2] See, generally, W. K. Jordan, *The Development of Religious Toleration in England, 1603–1640* (London, 1936), chap. I.

contributed to the decision to exhibit the information. Certainly there appeared to be no precedent for this high-handed appropriation, and Sara's brothers and sisters had been advised that it was the 'civile law' which demanded that 'the goods so gyven by reason of the invaliditie of the gyfte was due unto the Kinge'. Yet the King, being the father of his country, 'hath interest chiefly in all publique works of charity', a responsibility which had been recognised in Henry VIII's speech to the Parliament of 1545, and in the preamble to the chantry statute of 1547.[1] Just as it had been the Crown's intention, as *pater patriae*, to distribute the chantry revenues to good and godly lawful uses, so it was hoped, if not anticipated, that James I would distribute Sara's legacy for lawful charitable objects in accordance with the Exchequer decree.[2] Lord Exeter, however, had heard that Thomas Sackville, when he was Lord High Treasurer, 'sought otherwise to have intytled his Majestie unto'.[3] These rumours were apparently to prove false and in 1609 a distribution[4] was made by Sackville's successor, Robert Cecil, to 'such preachinge conformable ministers as stood in need thereof and to the wives and children of such deprived and silenced inconformable ministers as were dead'.[5]

No more is heard of prerogative *cy-près* until 1632 when a dispute arose over the application of the endowments of the feoffees to impropriations.[6] The feoffees to impropriations were a

[1] See above, pp. 12–13.

[2] Cf. Moore, fo. 31^{v}: 'le divine esteant disable per son recusancy de doner counsayle, le surgeon aura tout et il esteant attaint ou convict de treason, le roy aura tout le Annuitie in propertie, per que les commissioners ne fairent decree de lier le propertie le roy, et uncore le use demurt quia le roy nest deins le statute lie per decrees, mes suite per peticion de grace est destre exhibite al roy.' He does not mention *Venables*' case which was decided only two months before his *Reading*.

[3] S.P. Dom. 14/45/147. Exeter, writing to his brother, Robert Cecil, Earl of Salisbury, is pleading on behalf of some poor ministers, who had heard there was to be a distribution of the money bequeathed by Sara Venables to conformable clergy. The letter is dated 25 June 1609.

[4] But it is not clear from the records whether the whole of Sara's residue was distributed in this way.

[5] The decree is cited in argument in the *Feoffees to Impropriations*' case: see I. M. Calder, *Activities of the Puritan Faction of the Church of England, 1625–1633* (London, 1957), 63; see below, p. 78. It is not among the S.P. Dom. papers.

[6] The records have been transcribed by Miss Calder in her *Activities of the Puritan Faction of the Church of England* (hereinafter cited as Calder). This book contains a brief historical introduction to the dispute, but there is no discussion of the legal significance of the Exchequer's decision. Two other accounts of the

group of Puritan churchmen who had established a trust fund for the purchase of impropriations, to fill livings with men of their choice and theological persuasion.[1] They were active for some seven years, from 1625 to 1632, and in this short period were supported by a substantial body of sympathisers who contributed over £6,361 to their trust fund. Their aims and very existence were an anathema to Laud and Charles I, who, like his father, thought that dissent and the 'Bishop of Geneva' were as great a threat to political and religious stability as superstition and the Bishop of Rome. Steps were taken to secure the suppression of the movement and appropriate their endowments. In the Easter Term 1632 the Attorney-General, William Noy, exhibited an information against the feoffees in the Equity Side of the Exchequer. The cause was heard on 31 January, 7 February, and 11 February 1633, before the Lord High Treasurer (Lord Weston), the Chancellor of the Exchequer (Lord Cottington), Lord Chief Baron Sir Humphrey Davenport and the Barons of the Exchequer.

The information charged,[2]

That since the tenth year of the reign of the late King, these *Feoffees*, to the intent to procure into their hands divers Manours, Lands, and Tenements, Rectories, Tythes, Oblations, and Sums of Money, which well-disposed People should give to the sustaining and endowment of Perpetual *Vicars*, having Cure of Souls, and other Charitable Uses; did of their own Authority erect and make themselves into a *Society*, or Body Corporate, called sometime by the name of the *Collectors of St. Antholins*; and used to hold Assemblies and Councils, and make Ordinances, appoint Registers and Actuaries for their doings: and have gotten into their hands Sums of Money, intended by the Donors for the foresaid Pious Uses. With part whereof they had purchased divers *Rectories*, *Tithes*, *Prebendaries*, *Lands and Tenements*, the Remonstrances whereof are registered in a Book, and had not imploied the same as was intended by the Givers, as by Law they ought.

Feoffees to Impropriations' case have proved valuable. The first is in the Hale MS. LXXXII, no. 8, at Lincoln's Inn; the second, contained in John Rushworth's *Historical Collections*, part II (London, 1680), 150–2, gives a convenient summary.

[1] See, generally, Christopher Hill, *Economic Problems of the Church* (Oxford, 1956), pp. 252ff.; I. M. Calder, 'A Seventeenth Century Attempt to Purify the Anglican Church', *American Historical Review*, LIII (1947–8), 760.

[2] Rushworth, *Historical Collections*, part II, 150; see Calder, 3–7, for a fuller statement of the charges.

Noy argued that as the feoffees had unlawfully incorporated themselves and had attempted to encourage schism in the Church the property they held as feoffees was forfeit to the Crown, which, however, would *in its grace* apply it to lawful uses. The concept of the King, the father of his country, whose duty it was to secure the performance of good uses in a lawful manner, figured prominently in his argument; for 'it perteyneth to his Majesty to take care ffor such publique works of charitye, And that nothing given to soe good uses and purposes be withdrawn or misemployed.'[1] Noy attempted to buttress the claim that the property was forfeit to the Crown by a profusion of medieval authorities, most of which were irrelevant, but not, significantly, by any reference to the chantry statute of 1 Edward VI c. 14.[2] He also asked that the decree in *Venables*' case,[3] 'touching pious uses made by will might be read for a president to shew what this Court had formerly done in the like case, and it was read.'[4]

The feoffees in their answers and at the hearing denied the Crown's contention that they had acted as a corporation and that, like Sara Venables, they had supported an 'unlawful end'. Indeed, they maintained that the opposite was true; for they had always endeavoured to maintain services and preaching according to the canons of the Church of England, a truly pious work.[5]

Charles I took a considerable interest in the fate of these arguments and forcibly made known his views to the judges. Before the opinions of the Barons were delivered on 13 February 1633, the Lord High Treasurer reminded the court that:[6]

> [Y]ou were present (my lord cheife Baron) and the rest of the Barons together with his majesties Judges and others of his learned Counsell, when a report of this Cause being espetially required by his Majesty, being a Carefull father of the Church, was given unto the kings Majesty, where (my lord cheife Baron[)] you truly reported the state of this cause, and opened the Circumstances of it which being heard, His Majesty gave order, that we should in our sentence consider how the good uses might be continewed, and not destroyed.

It is not therefore surprising that the Exchequer was persuaded by Noy's arguments and concluded: that the defendants had in fact

[1] Calder, 45–6, *per* counsel, Robert Mason, *arguendo*.
[2] *Ibid.* 56–9.
[3] See above, pp. 76–7.
[4] Calder, 63.
[5] *Ibid.* 97–98.
[6] *Ibid.* 105.

encroached on the royal prerogative by assuming themselves to be incorporated; that their proceedings were against the laws of the realm, drawing upon themselves the dependency of the clergy and introducing many novelties into the Church and Commonwealth; and that they had not properly exercised the trust reposed in them by their supporters, to buy advowsons and to support lecturers and school-masters.[1] Some of the Exchequer Barons were concerned, however, by the implications of Noy's submission that the King did have the power, if he so wished, 'to take all such lands and gufts into his owne hands for misimployment made of them'.[2] They emphasised that the purchase of the impropriations was merely a misemployment of a *lawful* use, contrary to the wills and minds of the donors, and that the 'good uses' remained. It was only the manner of performance of those good uses—the feoffees forming themselves into a corporation—that was unlawful; 'the manner of doing this is not good though the use be good'.[3] In his speech the Lord High Treasurer sought to allay the anxieties of his more legalistic brethren by expressly and publicly renouncing any intention on behalf of the King to appropriate the charitable funds 'to his own uses'.[4]

For his Majestys intention, whereas some things opened by Mr. Attorney have offended some mens eares, as that if a misemployment should bee found to be made by them, then his Majesty may take all the monyes and estates into his owne hands, to his owne uses, as forfeited; His Majesty hath declared his resolucion And pious intention, that hee would use it according to the intent of the Donors as nigh as might be And to use his owne words, That he would not poyson his treasure with anything so ill gotten, And for that there may be a Channell to receive mens Charityes this way; He purposes to appoint Comissioners to enquire of things, And theis men or some of them . . . may bee with others: a Corporation for this purpose, for ought I knowe.

The Equity Side of the Exchequer then decreed that it was his Majesty's 'good pleasure and his gracious intencion . . . that whatsoever hath been given and bestowed as aforesaide [on the buying of impropriations] should bee ymployed wholly to the

[1] Calder, 125 ff., where the decree is transcribed.

[2] *Ibid.* 59.

[3] *Ibid.* 118, *per* Davenport C.B., citing *Porter*'s case (1592), 1 Co. 22b, above p. 14; see also Calder, 110 (*per* Weston B), 111 (*per* Trevor B). It was on this ground that Baron Trevor (*ibid.* 113) explained *Venables*' case, above, p. 76.

[4] *Ibid.* 124.

good of the Church, and the maintenance of good and conformable preachers and ministers of the Church in the right and best way, and as neere as may stand with conveniencie accordinge to the true intentes of the donors and benefactors there[of].'[1]

The principles embodied in the *Feoffees to Impropriations*' case were to survive both the annulment of the decree in 1648[2] and the Interregnum, although the case is never mentioned by name in any later report. Their application is next illustrated in a cluster of *post*-Restoration decisions. One of these cases was *Attorney General* v. *Baxter*,[3] decided in 1684. The testator had left £600 to Richard Baxter, the Protestant divine, to be distributed among sixty pious ejected ministers. In his will he stated that he did not want his 'charity misunderstood'; he gave because he knew many of them to be pious and good men in great want, and not because of their non-conformity. The Attorney-General exhibited an information claiming the charity was against the law; if the ministers were allowed to take the gift, the court would 'almost . . . make a corporation of them.' Moreover schism in the Church would be encouraged. The endowment should therefore be forfeited to the Crown, who would then apply it as of grace *cy-près*. Lord Keeper North accepted this submission and the distinction between the charity and the mode of its performance. In this case only the mode of performance was illegal and void; the charity 'subsisted.' The Lord Keeper, having taken steps to inquire what was the royal pleasure, decreed that the £600 should be applied under the sign manual for the maintenance of a chaplain in Chelsea Hospital.[4]

North's reasoning in *Baxter*'s case is identical with that of the Equity Side of the Exchequer in the *Feoffees to Impropriations*' case. The significance of *Baxter*'s case in the history of prerogative *cy-près* is simply that it is one of the first recorded examples of an information brought in the Court of Chancery for the *cy-près*

[1] Calder, 141. [2] *Ibid.* viii.

[3] (1684), 1 Vern. 248; see also *Att.-Gen.* v. *Combes* (or *Combe*) (1678), 2 Freeman, Ch. 40, Selden Society, LXXIX, case 879, c. 33/251/727; *Att.-Gen.* v. *Guise* (1692), 2 Vern. 266.

[4] After the enactment of the Toleration Act, 1688 (1 Wm. and M. c. 18, below p. 141), the decree was reversed by the Lords Commissioners, and the estate was ordered to be distributed according to the terms of the will: see *Att.-Gen.* v. *Hughes* (1689), 2 Vern. 105. *Semble* it was construed as a bequest to sixty ejected ministers *eo nomine*: *Moggridge* v. *Thackwell* (1803), 7 Ves. 36, 76, *per* Lord Eldon.

application of endowments devoted to the support of schismatic bodies. Because of the Crown's consistent admission that it would apply such funds *cy-près*, to lawful charitable objects, the Court of Chancery, not the Court of Exchequer, was now the appropriate forum for exhibiting the information.

Gifts for the support of Rome and papist purposes could hardly expect a better fate. Yet in two cases decided immediately before *Venables*' case,[1] *Croft* v. *Evetts*[2] and *Lady Egerton*'s[3] case, the Crown made no claim to property held on a secret trust to relieve poor recusants and Jesuits and Seminary Priests, respectively. Nevertheless, Lord Chancellor Egerton, with the concurrence of the Chief Justices, refused to uphold the trusts. They were too pernicious and dangerous an example to be tolerated in the 'Commonwealth of this Land', and were 'unlawful and merely void.'[4] Accordingly the feoffees were ordered to hold to the use of the feoffor's heir-at-law who, in both cases, happened to be a Protestant.

These were the last recorded occasions, during the period of this study, on which an heir-at-law or next-of-kin successfully claimed funds devoted to superstitious purposes. But it is not easy to tell from the extant records what was the *precise* fate of property devoted to the support of popish, as distinct from dissenting, objects. After the Restoration endowments for the support of dissenting sects were always applied *cy-près*. In contrast funds devoted for popish objects were not consistently applied *cy-près*.

Gifts for popish purposes inevitably sheltered behind a secret trust and only appeared before the courts through accident or misfortune. From the language of the informations and petitions presented to the Crown it is certain that any endowment for popish purposes was forfeit to the Crown.[5] But it is uncertain whether the

[1] See above, pp. 76 ff.

[2] (1605), Moo. K.B. 784.

[3] Duke (Moore), 133.

[4] Moo. K.B. 784, 785, 786.

[5] Each information brought by the Attorney-General to secure property devoted to superstitious purposes ended thus: the property 'is alleged to have been heretofore given towardes superstitious uses and therefore belonginge to the Kinges' Majestie': see the entry in the Exchequer *Entry Book of Decrees and Orders* relating to the dispute between *Att.-Gen.* v. *Giles Churchill* (1636), E. 126/4/206. See also *Att.-Gen.* v. *Yate* (1682–3), E. 126/14/26, and the Special Commissions C. 205/19/1, 2, 3A, 3B, 4, 5, 6A and 6B. (Cf. Duke, 87–95; all the cases cited by Duke fall within the letter of the Chantry statute of 1 Edw. VI c. 14, and are not therefore *in pari materia*.)

This is also evident from the petitions to the Crown of relatives of testators who had devised land to superstitious uses, cited below, p. 83, n. 3; and *Gaynor Jones*' case (1686–90), discussed below, p. 84.

crown based its claim on the 'equity' of the Edwardian chantry statute, for the Exchequer informations, simply if dogmatically, state that, 'whereas by the Lawes and Statutes of this Realme' property is 'alleged to have been heretofore given towardes superstitious uses and therefore belonginge to the Kinges' Majestie'.[1] It is equally uncertain whether the Crown appropriated the property beneficially to its own use, as it would have been entitled to do if the devise had been made before 1547,[2] or whether it felt compelled to apply it to like charitable objects. There may well have been no consistent practice.[3] Each succeeding prince may have applied his endowments in an individual and capricious fashion. Indeed there is evidence that the Catholic James II enforced the very terms of trusts for popish purposes, even though such a trust was still illegal at common law.

Contemporaries were equally at a loss to explain the basis of the Crown's claim to forfeit property devoted to superstitious uses, and in all probability did not know, as Francis Moore had not known seventy years earlier, what was its scope and extent. Their dilemma and confusion is reflected in judgments of the various courts in *Gaynor Jones*' case, decided between 1686 and 1690. That case did, however, ultimately clarify and settle the law.

[1] Perhaps lawyers also had in mind statutes such as 23 Eliz. I c. 1, which declared that secret conveyances, made by recusants to evade penalties imposed upon them by law, were void; or statutes such as 3 Car. I c. 2, which forfeited to the Crown the property of recusants who sent their children abroad to be 'popishly bred'.

[2] See above, p. 13. Informations to secure the endowments of trusts for popish purposes were still brought in the Exchequer: see, for example, *Gaynor Jones*' case.

[3] Not uncommonly the Crown granted property devoted to superstitious purposes to the donor's Protestant relations who had 'discovered' the superstitious trust. On 26 May 1682, Sir Thomas Preston petitioned the Crown, which had applied lands 'towardes a charitable use for providing for wounded and disabled soldiers in an hospitall intended to be built at Chelsea', 'to bestow upon him the ancient estate settled on him and his family . . . which would have been settled on his father, but for his constant adherence to the Church of England'. 'His Majestie . . . taking withall into consideration the services of the Petitioner . . . in making proof of the forfeiture of the said landes' was 'graciously pleased to refer this petition' to the Lords Commissioners of the Treasury to report to his Majesty who later leased the lands to Preston. The history of Preston's petition is to be found in S.P. Dom. 44/57/157, 200.

There are a number of similar petitions to be found in the State Papers, Domestic: see also S.P. Dom. 44/55/388 (1684); 44/71/22 (1684); 44/238/101 (1697).

If before *Gaynor Jones'* case the Crown could appropriate superstitious endowments into its own Treasury, thereafter it was publicly recognised that it should devote such funds to lawful charitable objects. The principles embodied in the *Feoffees to Impropriations'* case were adopted and extended to govern the distribution of all endowments sustaining any religious use which conflicted with the teachings and tenets of the Established Church.

In *Gaynor Jones'* case[1] land had been granted by one Robert Charnock, a Roman priest, to the use of Grace Bold, a papist, 'in [secret] trust for the support and maintenance of the priests of the secular clergy of the Roman religion in the county of Lancaster'. Grace entered, levied a fine, and devised the land to Gaynor Jones, her sister, a protestant, for life with remainders over, 'better to secure the land' from forfeiture 'for concealing'. Gaynor entered, enjoyed the profits of the land, and destroyed, so it was alleged, the writings declaring the secret trust. In an information brought in the Exchequer in 1686, the Attorney-General claimed that Grace Bold had exercised a 'great influence' over her sister and persuaded her to carry out the secret trust. Accordingly the grant and devise, 'by the statutes of this realme, [should be] declared to be superstitious and unlawfull and thereby [the endowment] would become forfeited for concealing'. During the reign of James II, in Trinity Term 1688, the Exchequer held that the land was forfeited to the Crown 'for concealing'[2] and that it should be delivered up to the Crown or to such persons as His Majesty should nominate under the sign manual.

Gaynor, who had throughout denied the secret trust, after the accession of William and Mary, brought a bill of review in the Exchequer[3] to set aside the decree on the gound that the original information had been brought at the relation of a Roman priest,

[1] Exchequer *Entry Book*, E. 126/15/93, 207.

[2] The Exchequer had remitted to the Lancaster Assizes the question whether the property had been conveyed for the support and maintenance of secular Roman priests. And on 23 June 1687, a jury had 'found' the secret, superstitious trust.

These simplified facts, and the subsequent history, also emerge from the defendant's petition to the House of Lords, which will be found in the Lincoln's Inn collection, part in MS., of *Cases in the House of Lords*, I, 175. There is said to be a report of the case in Serjeant Hill's MS. Collection, which is reproduced in a note to *Re White* [1893], 2 Ch. 49. This is not so. The note in *Re White* is taken verbatim from *Cases in the House of Lords*.

Gooden,[1] 'who had some promise the same should be granted to the use of the priests in Lancashire' and that eleven of the original jury which had 'found' the secret trust were papists, 'not quallifi'd by the Law of the Land to be Jury-men; and the Witnesses were also Papists'. In fact the relator was alleged to have brought the action to deprive the Protestant defendant of the devised land, knowing that an indulgent Catholic monarch would apply the profits of the land so forfeited, or part of them, for the express popish purposes of the secret trust. Her argument was unsuccessful. In Easter Term, 1690, the Exchequer confirmed the original decree, 'with this Explanation or Addition, That the Premises are to be disposed of to such Charitable and Pious uses as their Majesties, their Heirs and Successors shall think fit'. The property was forfeit to the Crown, but the Crown had to dispose of it to lawful (non-popish) uses.

Gaynor Jones was nothing if not indefatigable. The amended decree of the Exchequer could not have given her any greater satisfaction, and in the following Trinity Term she petitioned the House of Lords, by writ of error, for the reversal of the Exchequer decree. She argued that there was no ground for the original decree; that no secret trust had been sufficiently proved and that the decree ought not to have been made without further trial of the issue. Further, the Exchequer had no power to amend its original decree; it could only 'confirm or reverse it'.

For that if the same was to a Superstitious Use, it either ought to descend or be given to the next of Relation, or the Court ought to appoint a charity agreeable with the Protestant religion: For which reason the first Decree was also void, it being absolutely Decreed to King James without any direction of the Charity, and the Warrant pretended to be granted by his now Majesty to Trustees; For the benefit of the Vicar of Leyland in Lancashire, and his Successors, will not, its hoped, make any Alteration in the Case, and take away the Petitioners Right by bestowing the Estate upon a Charity.[2]

The House of Lords, however, 'affirmed the decree and dismissed the Appeale'. No report of their lordships' speeches has survived.

[1] By Statute, 25 Car. II c. 2 (1672), popish recusants were declared incapable of prosecuting any suit at Law or in Equity. It is doubtful how far this provision was ever enforced. Cases such as *Gaynor Jones*' suggest that it was certainly a dead-letter in the reign of James II.

[2] *Cases in the House of Lords*.

Gaynor Jones' case is of interest for at least two reasons. First, it confirms that the Crown did appropriate endowments for popish purposes, and, at least during James II's reign, was ready to apply them for the very popish purposes which the law deemed to be illegal. Secondly, it shows that from the accession of William and Mary onwards the courts, while rejecting the Crown's beneficial claim, still upheld its right to apply property, devoted to superstitious purposes, *cy-près* to lawful (non-popish) uses, even in the face of a petition by members of the testator's family.

Two years later in 1692 a further attempt was made to challenge the Crown's right to apply funds devoted to superstitious uses *cy-près*. In *R.* v. *Lady Portington*,[1] a jury, on an inquisition *post mortem*, had 'found' that certain lands had been devised to the defendants, who were Roman Catholics, for superstitious purposes. The testator's heir-at-law then brought an action of ejectment in the King's Bench against the devisees. The Court of King's Bench dismissed the suit; the devise was absolute, no trust was declared or appeared in the will and no averment could be made to 'defeat or supply' the will, 'both from the Statute of Frauds and from the nature of the thing'.[2] Chief Justice Holt, however, in a vigorous judgment went on to suggest that the Crown's claim to appropriate the land was without foundation:

> The statute 23 Hen. VIII [c. 10] makes such uses void, but doth not give them to the King, and the statute 1 Edward VI [c. 14] gives them to the King, but doth not extend to future uses made after that statute.[3]

Therefore, continued Holt, 'it might be convenient for the heir-at-law to seek his remedy in Parliament, according to the case in Moore',[4] *Croft* v. *Evetts*.[5]

Holt's judgment in *Lady Portington*'s case shows how far the wind of change had blown through the realm, and it is refreshing to see an independent and fearless mind not only attacking the basis of the royal claim to forfeit superstitious endowments but also inciting the heir-at-law to challenge in Parliament the succession of Exchequer and Chancery decisions which had formulated the Crown's claim to the property. The heir-at-law did not, as far as is known, seek to resolve the issue in the High Court of Parliament, perhaps he may have learnt of *Gaynor Jones*' case and

[1] 3 Salk. 334. Cf. *Addlington* v. *Cann* (1741), 3 Atk. 141; below, p. 116.
[2] 1 Salk. 162.
[3] 3 Salk. 334.
[4] *Ibid.* 334.
[5] See above, p. 82.

the fate of her writ of error to the House of Lords, and on 26 May 1693, the Attorney-General exhibited an information in the Exchequer for 'the application of the devise to an use truly charitable'.[1]

> And it was held, 1st., that the Statute of Frauds did not bind the King, but took place only between party and party. 2dly, That the King, as head of the Commonwealth, is obliged by the common law, and for that purpose entrusted and empowered to see that nothing be done to the disherision of the Crown, or the propagation of a false religion, and to that end entitled to pray a discovery of a trust to a superstitious use. 3rdly., This use being superstitious, is merely void, and for that reason the King cannot have it: yet however it is not so void as that it shall result to the heir, and therefore the King shall order it to be applied to a proper use.

The Exchequer's judgment in *Lady Portington*'s case was yet another attempt to justify the Crown's claim to apply property devoted to popish uses to lawful charitable purposes. The Crown's claim to this property was ostensibly based upon the 'statutes of the realm'; but, as Holt pointed out in the King's Bench, no statute did in fact support it. The Exchequer was not prepared, however, to abandon the principles which the court believed to underly Francis North's judgment in *Baxter*'s case even though that decision had been annulled in 1690, just as North had followed the *Feoffee to Impropriations*' case despite the annulment of that decree in 1648. The courts would not uphold any trust for the support of any religion or any religious organisation which was not tolerated by the State. Public policy demanded that their funds be used to maintain the only good and lawful religious purpose, the Established Church.

The judges of the next century were to be as puzzled as Holt by the origins of prerogative *cy-près* and by the rejection of the heir-at-law and the next-of-kin's claims. They viewed the cases divorced from their historical context, ignored the broad principle of religious policy which was their justification, and vainly sought for a statutory origin for the Crown's claim to apply *cy-près* property devoted to the use of 'false' religion. Nevertheless the chains of precedent were to ensure the survival of this series of Exchequer and Chancery decisions and, in consequence, of this particular application of prerogative *cy-près*.[2]

[1] 1 Salk. 162, 162–3. [2] See below, pp. 144–53.

(ii) *Indefinite charitable objects*

During the Chancellorship of Lord Nottingham the doctrine of prerogative *cy-près* was extended to enable the Crown to apply under the sign manual property directly devoted to indefinite charitable objects. Gifts, such as to 'the poor of Dale', had always been upheld by the charity commissioners.[1] But from about 1656 onwards, gifts to indefinite charitable uses came to be enforced only by information, and, it was subsequently established, were still valid as declarations or appointments even though no longer enforceable by the commissioners.[2] There is no suggestion in the records, however, that at this time the Crown (as distinct from the Court) disposed of the property, under the sign manual.

In *Attorney General* v. *Peacock*[3] in 1675, Lord Nottingham broke new ground and upheld a bequest to a general use on grounds similar to those underlying *Venables*' case and the *Feoffee to Impropriations*' case, namely that the 'King by his prerogative could cure the uncertainty and apply the property *cy-près* to like charitable objects under the sign manual.'[4] In *Peacock*'s case Henry Fryer had given the residue of his estate 'to charitable uses for the good of the poor forever'. His heir challenged the will, arguing that it failed for uncertainty. The will was referred to Charles I who, on the advice of Laud and Coventry, awarded £100 *per annum* to the three parishes mentioned in the will; £80 for the repair of St Paul's; and the residue to Fryer's heir, which he enjoyed for forty years. On the advice of counsel, all the parties formally agreed to this division. The heir died and devised his estate to the defendant. On an information, dated 26 May 1673, which reopened the whole question, and sought to set aside the agreement and apply the whole of Fryer's estate to

[1] See above, pp. 49–50 and see *Wingfield*'s case (1628), Duke, 80, where money given for 'the good of the church of Dulk' was resolved 'to be a good gift, notwithstanding these general words.'

[2] See above, pp. 36 and 54.

[3] Finch, 245, 2 Lev. 167 (*sub. nom. Att.-Gen.* v. *Matthews*), Selden Society, LXXIII, cases 300 and 440, which is the fuller report. The account in the text is based primarily on the Selden Society material.

[4] There was no plea in the original information that the property devoted to general charitable uses vested in the Crown: see C. 9/403/105. The Attorney-General was Lord Nottingham himself, then Heneage Finch.

It is true that the will had been originally referred to Charles I. But it does not appear that it was thought necessary to do so in order to save the residuary gift.

charity, the defendant demurred that the original devise was void for uncertainty. Lord Nottingham, who had set aside the charity commissioners' decree because general charitable objects were not within the equity of the Charitable Uses Act, 1601, dismissed the demurrer and ruled:

For a general and indefinite charity may be so applied by the King as to become certain and particular, but then the application must ever be to a charity *ejusdem generis* and not an application of that which is given to the poor to repair churches or bridges, for when a charity is certain and particular at first but the uses to which it is designed are illegal and void, it becomes at last a charity at large, that is, general and indefinite. But then the King may make it certain and particular again by applying it to good uses *ejusdem generis*, as in 4 Jac., *Venables' case*: a widow gave great sums of money to be paid by her executors to poor ministers silenced for not subscribing etc., adjudged the charity should be applied to poor ministers that were conformable: cited Lane's reports, 44. *A fortiori*, when the charity is general and incertain at the first. And therefore the award and the conveyances so much insisted on are not to be regarded, for the case had been never the better though the award had been decreed. For 'tis not in the power of this Court either to divert the charity or straighten the remedy of it. Nevertheless what hath been well settled by the award pursuant to the will shall stand and be confirmed by the decree of this Court now. As for example where the will gave 100 *l.* to three parishes, Aldersgate, Chiswick, and Harleton, viz. 100 *l.* a year forever without saying how much to each, the proportions which have been ascertained by the award shall continue, but the 80 *l.* a year given to the repair of Paul's and the dispositions of the residue cannot stand.

And yet I am not ripe for a decree at this time, for though the judicial declaration of the King's pleasure in the application of the surplusage is to be by me, yet before I proceed to such declaration I will be first attended with the particular of the estate and acquaint his Majesty with the nature and circumstances of this case and know his private pleasure in it.

His Majesty's declared pleasure was that the money should be applied, subject to the charge for the poor of these named parishes, for the benefit of the 'poor children of his new royal foundation in Christ's Hospital, who were to be taught arithmetic and the art of navigation.'[1]

[1] Nottingham left open the question whether the executors of Fryer's heir should account for the profits he received during his life 'under the colour of that award and in breach of the charity . . . These things will make many busy suits and references to Masters. Wherefore as to most of these points I incline not to look very narrowly into what's past'.

In Lord Nottingham's judgment, because the bequest would have failed but for the Crown's intervention, the Crown should be allowed to control the disposition of the funds left to charitable purposes. 'The King as *Pater patriae* may and ought to be the great protector of all charities which were not within the regulation of the statute of 43 Eliz., for he was so at common law before that statute.'[1] Such reasoning, the analogy of *Venables*' case, and the fact that the will had been originally referred to Charles I, made Nottingham seek the Crown's pleasure as to the disposal of the money.

Charles II's known interest in the welfare of social and educational charities, such as Christ's and Chelsea Hospitals, may have been particularly influential in persuading Nottingham to establish this exercise of royal prerogative.[2] Stuart kings were not unconscious of the political importance of social patronage, and realised full well that the Crown's reputation as *pater patriae* could not fail to be enhanced by acts of charity with the money of others.[3] Moreover royal courtiers, even Chancellors, knew that they might influence the Crown in favour of a charity dear to them.[4]

Throughout Charles II's reign the Chancellor consistently consulted the Crown about the disposal of property devoted to general charitable uses.[5] One such case was *Attorney-General* v. *Syderfin*.[6] The testator had declared in his will that money should be applied for such charitable uses as he had formally directed in writing. No writing could be found. 'It being cleere it was his

[1] Selden Society, LXXIII, p. 209.

[2] See generally G. N. Clark, *The Later Stuarts, 1660–1714* (Oxford, 1934), chap. XIV. It is known that 'that greate worke' Chelsea Hospital had been built 'without the helpe of the Treasury who indeed never gave the least countenance towards it. For it was carried on by his Majesties giving out of his Privy Purse' (Wren Society, XIX (Oxford, 1942), 65).

There is also evidence that property devoted to superstitious, popish purposes was also applied for the support of the royal hospitals: see for example S.P. Dom. 44/57/157; above, p. 83, n. 3.

[3] In *Moggridge* v. *Thackwell* (1803), 7 Ves. 36, 71, Lord Eldon suggested that in *Att.-Gen.* v. *Syderfin* (1683), 1 Vern. 224 (below) the information of the Attorney-General had originated from the initiative of Christ's Hospital which had 'found out, that there was such a will', in which case the 'ordinary rule upon an escheast' was that the Crown gave 'as good a lease as it can give'. This explanation is not implausible; cf. above, p. 83, n. 2.

[4] So £80 had been originally devoted for the repair of St Paul's, a cause very close to Laud's heart.

[5] With the possible exception of the badly reported case of *Anon* (1678), 2 Freeman, Ch. 40.

[6] (1683), 1 Vern. 224, which is less full than the *Entry Book* record, C. 33/261/340, upon which the account in the text is based.

intention and design that the same should be paid out of his estate and applyed to charitable uses, That the defendants contriving to defeat the said charitable gift doe detayne and conceale the said deed and writing whereby the said charitable uses are lymitted and directed by the testator.' Accordingly Lord Keeper North held that the money 'ought to go to such charitable uses as the Corte persuant to his Majestie's gracious pleasure, would direct.

Property devoted to charitable purposes could, therefore, be applied *cy-près* under the sign manual if the property had been given directly to 'indefinite' or 'general' charitable purposes; the Crown would 'cure' the uncertainty and enforce the gift. But if the property was conveyed to trustees[1] for general charitable purposes, the transfer was perfect; there was no 'legal' uncertainty for the Crown to cure and consequently the doctrine of prerogative *cy-près* had no application. In such a case the court would 'take the administration of the trust' and settle its own *cy-près* scheme. This fine distinction was to lead to confusion in the next century.[2]

Yet whatever agency distributed the funds, property devoted to illegal or general charitable uses was consistently applied *cy-près* to lawful and certain charitable uses. Judges distinguished between the 'good' use and the 'improper' manner of its employment; but they never doubted that the donor's real intention was to benefit charity, even though that intention had been imperfectly expressed and executed.[3] From the mid-eighteenth century onwards, however, the courts changed their attitude, refused to presume that every donor, whose gift to charity had failed, had a 'general charitable intention' and sought to formulate rigid, analytical rules of construction which would enable them to distinguish his specific from his general charitable intention.[4]

The application of surplus funds

Suppose a testator had charged land with the sum of £100 (being the annual value of the land at the time of the devise), payable to

[1] *Semble* even if the trustees lacked capacity to be trustees; see below, pp. 149–51; but cf. above, pp. 67–70.

[2] See below, pp. 151–3.

[3] See above, pp. 79–80. See also *Goffe* v. *Webb* (1602), Duke, 80; *Lilburn* v. *Turner* (1676–7), Selden Society, LXXIX, case 698.

[4] See below, p. 144 ff.

charitable uses. Many years later it is found that the land had increased in value. Who is to get the increased rents: the charity, the feoffees or the testator's heir-at-law?

The late sixteenth century was a period of rapid inflation and this problem often arose for decision. To solve it, the courts established a principle of deceptive simplicity: namely, did the testator intend when he made his will to devise the whole of the land's rents at any one time to charity; or was his intention merely to devise to charity a fixed sum of money, which happened to be the annual value of the land at his death? Rules of construction were gradually formulated 'to discover' his intention and many of them were 'weighted' in favour of charity. It is not insignificant that in every reported case before the beginning of the eighteenth century, the charity was given the benefit of the increase in value.

So, in the earliest known case, *William Frenche and other inhabitants of Laystoft in Suffolk* v. *Tetter*[1] in 1584, feoffees claimed the surplus rents, over and above the sums expressly devoted to charity. Lord Chancellor Bromley ordered that two of the Masters, Carew and Awberry should have:

> the said will and feoffment or trewe copies thereof brought unto them and then they upon the consideracion thereof . . . make reporte to this courte whether yt was the meaninge of the said testator that the said feoffees shoulde take the benefit of the overplus of the premisses to their own use or otherwise that the same should be imployed to the use of the poor . . .

The Masters reported that the intention of the testator was to convey all his property 'to the performance of the will'.

Feoffees who sought to appropriate surplus rents found the common law judges as unsympathetic as the Chancellor. In the well-known *Thetford School* case[2] in 1607, land, at the testator's death worth £35 in value, was devised to charitable uses in such a way that the whole of the annual value was expended. The land then increased in value. The House of Lords sought the opinion of Chief Justice Flemming, King's Bench, Chief Justice Coke, Common Pleas, and Justice Walmesley, whether the feoffees were beneficially entitled to the increase. The judges advised the House that:[3]

[1] C. 33/68/73 (1584); and see above, p. 61 for the other proceedings concerning this case. See also the similar facts of *Reade* v. *Silles*, C. 33/85/591 (1593).

[2] (1607), 8 Co. 130b.

[3] *Ibid.* 131a.

it appears by his [the testator's] distribution of the profits, that he intended that the whole should be employed in works of piety and charity, and nothing should be converted to the private use of the executors or their heirs. And this resolution is grounded on evident and apparent reason; for, as if the lands had decreased in value, the preacher, schoolmaster etc. and poor people, should lose; so when the lands increase in value, *pari ratione* they shall gain.

If the testator had devoted the whole of the annual value of the land at a particular time to charity, it was presumed that he intended the whole income of the land, whatever it might be at any one time, should go to charitable uses. And, consistently, it was held in a case decided four years later, in 1611,[1] that a devise of all the rents was a devise of the land itself; and 'that when one deviseth the rent of his land to a charitable use, it shall be taken largely for a devise of the rent then reserved, or afterwards to be reserved upon an improved value'.[2]

In *Attorney-General* v. *Arnold*[3] in 1698 the claim to the surplus was not by the feoffees but by the heir who had been given a mere forty shillings. His counsel urged the House of Lords not to extend 'the general words of a will to enlarge a charity beyond the intent expressed, especially against a near relation and heir', and pointed out that the testator had not devised the whole income of the land at his death to charity. Nevertheless the House of Lords awarded the surplus funds to the charitable use. To have upheld the heir's claim would have contradicted the testator's plain intention, derived from the terms of the preamble to the will, to devote all his property to charity.[4]

Limitation

Moore was of opinion[5] that neither statutes of limitation[6] nor the equitable doctrine of laches[7] prevented the enforcement of a

[1] *Kennington Hastings Almshouse* (1611), Duke, 71; see also *Att.-Gen.* v. *City of Rochester* (1675), Selden Society, LXXIII, case 186.

[2] Duke, 71. See also the *Sutton Coalfield* case (1635), *ibid.* 68.

[3] (1698), Shower, P.C. 22. By this time it had been held that the proper procedure to determine the fate of surplus funds was by information in Chancery, in the name of the Attorney-General at the relation of an individual: see *Att.-Gen.* v. *Townsend* (1670?), Duke, 34, above, p. 37.

[4] This decision was to puzzle later judges: see below, p. 155.

[5] Duke (Moore), 161. Duke's text must be here interpolated, for he quotes Moore as citing 21 Jac. (1623–4), enacted some years after Moore's death.

[6] The relevant statutes of limitation would be 4 Hen. VII c. 24 (1488–9), 32 Hen. VIII c. 2 (1540–1) and 21 Jac. I c. 16 (1623–4).

[7] This doctrine defeats stale claims, when a party has slept on his rights.

charitable use. If the heir of a disseisor 'be in by descent of lands given to a charitable use, yet he shall be bound by the decree',[1] however long he was in possession of those lands.

And

> if a tenant for land given to charitable use levy a fine, and five years pass, yet the decree shall bind the tenants of the land, because the use is no interest in the lands, and this Statute of Uses was made after these statutes, which bind rights.[2]

This privilege was never challenged during this period, and was confirmed by Lord Shaftesbury in 1672.[3]

The Chancellor would hear charity suits even though the value of the property was under forty shillings

Before 1596 the Chancellor would not deign to hear petitions touching land, the annual income of which was less than forty shillings.[4] That charitable endowments were exempt from this order was established at an early date.

On 1 June 1579, in the dispute between *Lawrence Parrott* (*on behalf of the inhabitants of Drayton*) and *Richard Pawlinge*,[5] the question whether the Chancellor could hear a petition to enforce a charitable use, though 'the lands mencioned in the plaintiff's bill are under the valewe of xl^{s} by yere', came before Lord Chancellor Bromley. At a previous hearing the defendant had secured an order that if the value of the land was indeed less than forty shillings then it should be dismissed. However Bromley now ordered

> that where the plaintiffs for and in the behalf of the inhabitants of Drayton in the county of Oxon were . . . to have assurance to them made of the said landes to the use of the poore of the said towne he the said

[1] Duke (Moore), 161.

[2] *Ibid.* 161. By 4 Henry VII c. 24 (1488–9), a person with a 'righte, title, clayme and *interesse*' had to 'pursewe their title' within five years of the proclamation of the fine (my italics).

[3] *Richard, Earl of Dorset* v. *Governor of Bridewell*, cited by Lord Nottingham in his *Prolegomena of Chancery and Equity*, ed. D. E. C. Yale (Cambridge, 1965), 335: 'if land be given to corporation to charitable use, a fine and non-claim bar the entry at law, but will [not] bar the remedy by commission for charitable uses.'

[4] After 1596 'all suits touching land under the value of £10 shall be 'dismissed this Court': see G. W. Sanders' *Orders of the High Court of Chancery* (London, 1845), I, 27, 69. Charity suits remained an exception.

[5] C. 33/57/187. And see C. 1/70/89 (? early fifteenth century).

defendant usinge the name of the plaintiffs . . . did take an assurance to himself of the said landes for the which the poore are lyke to be defrawded and the plaintiffs without remedy by lawe. It ys therefore ordered that yf that be the matter of the bill then the sayd cause ys here still retayned the sayd former order notwithstandinge.

Suits to enforce legacies to charities were not remitted to the ecclesiastical courts

It has already been seen[1] that the Chancellor would not compel a petitioner, who sought to enforce a legacy to charity, to incur the further expense and delay of a suit in the ecclesiastical courts.

Priority over creditors of a bankrupt feoffee to charitable uses

The Court of Chancery did not generally interfere with the jurisdiction of the commissioners in bankruptcy,[2] and by statute[3] the courts were required to construe all laws for the benefit of a bankrupt's creditors. Identifiable property (land or chattels) held to charitable uses by the bankrupt as feoffee was not an asset available for distribution amongst his creditors 'quia nest part de lour estate'. But if money given to a charitable use were lent to one who became bankrupt, the charitable use would rank with other creditors.[4] The property in the money had passed from the charity to the bankrupt, so that the charity could have no

[1] See above, p. 17.

[2] Commissioners in bankruptcy were first appointed by statute in 1542–3 (34 & 35 Hen. VIII c. 4), to protect creditors against the wiles of dishonest debtors. This statute was subsequently re-enacted with amendments: see 13 Eliz. I c. 7 (1570–1); 1 Jac. I c. 15 (1603–4); 21 Jac. I. c. 19 (1623–4).

[3] See, for example, 21 Jac. I c. 19, § 1.

[4] Moore touches upon this question obliquely in a case posited at fo. 35^{v}, where he was considering the implications of a trust to lend money to bankrupt prisoners (above, p. 28): 'Mes si lexecutor prist bond pur largent, le propertie del argent est in le bankrupt quia ore le banckrupt est dettor; nota le difference per entre argent et auters biens loans, car argent loane de uses le propertie est dispose, mes chivall ou auter chose loane, le propertie demurt in le lendor. . . . Ceo que est appoint pur releif des prisoners et banckrupts pur necessitie de viver . . . nest orderable per les commissioners de Banckrupts quia nest part de lour estate, ne est approprie al eux per ascun done, graunt ou autrement mes come almes pur supplie extreme necessitie, in quel case cest statute de charitable uses esteant fait puis le statute de Banckrupts, est destre prefer. Si done est fait al Bankrupts, al charitable use, les commissioners sur cest statute poient order le charitable use destre performe coment que commissioners de banckrupts voile order pur les creditors.'

Moore reiterates this point at fo. 128. See also Duke (Moore), 183–4.

preferential claim.[1] But if the bankruptcy commissioners sold land, with knowledge that it was held to a charitable use, to a creditor, the charity commissioners could enforce the charitable use against the creditor even though he took without notice, at least where the bankrupt died without an heir. A charitable use should not be barred without recompense, so that the creditor was deemed in this case to have had notice of the charitable use.[2]

The commissioners for charitable uses were allowed to decree land to a corporation in esse *without danger of infringing the mortmain statutes*[3]

Marshalling of assets in favour of charity

It was frequently necessary to decide what assets of a testator's estate should be primarily liable for the payment of his debts. In equity, as at law, the general rule was that debts had to be paid before legacies.[4] A limited but important exception was made at this time in favour of charity, if the deceased died leaving assets in equity as distinct from assets at law. There was no question that legal assets, which were those assets 'an executor or administrator [took] as executor or administrator'[5] and which could be reached by an action at law against him, satisfied debts before legacies to charity. But this was not true of the application of equitable assets; these were assets chargeable in equity, which could only be reached with the aid of a court of equity.[6] In Moore's words:[7]

[1] Moore, fo. 35^{v}; quoted above, p. 95 n. 4. [2] *Ibid.*, fo. 264; see below, p. 100.

[3] *R.* v. *Newman* (1670), 1 Lev. 284. See above, p. 55.

[4] *Wray* v. *Sapcote* (1579), Cary, 86; Holdsworth, *A History of English Law*, v (London, 1924), 318–19.

[5] J. Story, *Commentaries on Equity Jurisprudence*, 14th ed. (Boston, 1918), §§ 750–2, *Lord Nottingham's Prolegomena of Chancery and Equity*, ed. Yale, 247.

[6] Story, *Equity Jurisprudence*, §§ 751–2. Equitable assets were generally of two kinds: 'the first is, where assets are created such by the intent of the party; the second is where they result from the nature of the estate made chargeable'; see Story, *Equity Jurisprudence*, § 751. Moore, in his *Reading*, discusses at some length which assets were deemed to be equitable; see fols. 233, 241.

[7] *Ibid.* fo. 241: 'coment que executor ayant assets in ley, doit preferr detts de record dent torts ou legacies. Uncore quant il nad assets in ley, il est hors de cest rule, et ad son elecion. Mes in nostre case lestatute ad specialment appoint recompense pur defrawding charitable use destre satisfy hors del assets in equity, per que le elecion est toll. Et cest recompense est destre preferr ayant equity dobble, cesty, chauncery equity et Statute equity, quel statute equity est superior al Chauncery equity.'

For a similar statement, see *ibid.* fo. 233.

Although the executor having assets in law must prefer debts of record before wrongs or legacies, Yet when he has no assets in law, this rule does not apply, and [he] has his election. But in our case the statute has especially appointed recompense for defrauding the charitable use to be satisfied out of assets in equity, by which [law] the election is destroyed And it is recompense [that] is to be preferred, having a double equity, namely, Chancery equity and statute equity, which statute equity is superior to Chancery equity.

Disputes could also arise as between private legatees and a charity. It had been held even before the Charitable Uses Act, 1601, that legacies to charity must be paid before any others. In the action between the *Mayor and Communalty of Salisbury* and *Thomas Oldefylde, and others, executors of William Chambers*, in 1583,[1] the defendants pleaded that they had insufficient assets to pay in full both a legacy to the poor of the town and other private legacies. They admitted, however, that they still had certain sums in their hands which had belonged to the testator. Lord Chancellor Bromley ordered a subpoena *duces tecum* to be awarded against them: 'because this legacy given to the poore would be first paide in equity and conscience.'

This privilege was confirmed by Lord Ellesmere in *Damus*' case[2] in 1614, and by Sir Francis Bacon in *Rolt* v. *Smith*[3] three years later; but, as will be seen,[4] it was to be severely limited in the eighteenth century.

The restriction of the defence of bona fide *purchase*

The Charitable Uses Act, 1601, expressly protected those

persons which hath purchased or obtained, or shall purchase or obtain, upon valuable consideration of money or land, any estate in, or interest of, in, to, or out of any lands, tenements, rents, annuities, hereditaments, goods or chattels that have been or shall be given, limited or appointed to any of the charitable uses above mentioned, without fraud or covin, (having no notice of the same charitable use).

Just as the Chancellor restricted the scope of the proviso exempting special charities from the commissioners' jurisdiction, so he limited the proviso which protected the *bona fide* purchaser 'quia le clause de notice est exempcion hors del ley beneficiall.'[5] The burden was

[1] C. 33/68/448 (1583).
[2] (1614), Duke, 72, Moo. K.B. 822.
[3] (1617), Cases *temp*. Bacon, 53.
[4] See below, p. 156.
[5] Moore, fo. 249.

on the purchaser to show affirmatively that he had bought his estate, without notice of the use,[1] for consideration of money or land. The following principles,[2] which are gleaned from Moore's *Reading* and contemporary cases, illustrate how restrictively the proviso was interpreted so as to protect the charitable use.

(a) A lessor, who had leased land for a charitable use, reentered and forfeited the lease for breach of a condition. Not only was he bound by the use but so was his heir, who had no notice, for the 'descent is accompanied with notice'.[3] The heir and next of kin, if they came in by descent, were always charged with notice of the use. So too were the issue in tail, if the tenant in tail had acquired notice. The notice 'charged the entire estate'.[4]

(b) The consideration had to be land or money. A conveyance made 'de save harmless de dett' was not such consideration.[5] Again, neither good nor marriage consideration[6] protected the purchaser, even if it was 'mixt' with land or money.[7]

And if such mixed consideration will avail, the statute will be utterly defrauded, for heirs will convey charity land for a small sum and in consideration of blood to their sons and kindred in defraud of the statute.[8]

More remarkably, money did not include all forms of money's worth. Thus, plate of a known weight[9] and jewels[10] were not consideration within the meaning of the proviso. Indeed, there is a hint in Moore's *Reading* of a doctrine of *laesio enormis* and a

[1] Moore, fo. 249.

[2] Some, though not all, of these principles applied to purchasers of land bound by uses other than charitable uses.

[3] Moore, fo. 260: 'si un que conus de Charitable use enter per forfeture fait puis le use declare, il serra subject al use. Et si le pere [the lessor] que avoit le title denter per le forfeture avoit notice, et le title discend de cesty pere a son fils, cest discent est accompany ove notice . . . Ceo est entend lou le fils nad actuall notice.' But cf. above, p. 71.

[4] *Ibid.* fo. 249.

[5] *Ibid.* fo. 245.

[6] *Ibid.* fo. 269^v. Cf. above, p. 62, where Moore states that such consideration is sufficient to raise a charitable use.

[7] *Ibid.* fo. 268: 'payment de argent et naturall affecion conjoyne ensemble sont la consideracion del purchase mixt; per que nest consideracion de argent ou ter, mes dargent et sanck.'

[8] *Ibid.* fo. 269^v: 'et si tiels mixt consideracions availera, lestatute vail estre outrement defrawde, car heirs vail pur petite argent et pur sanck a lour fils et kyndred convey charitable ter in defrawding de lestatute.'

[9] Duke (Moore), 177.

[10] Moore, fo. 276^v.

suggestion that courts might inquire into the adequacy of consideration given by a purchaser.[1]

> Whether the rateable part is much less than the true value, be consideration of money within the statute. And seemingly that [it is] not . . . For where it is presumed that the money is not the value of the land as here the rateable part due out of the mortgage, which is not the true value, cannot be presumed [to be] the true value. So a contract for a small sum, where the fraud is apparent, is not valuable consideration of money. But a bona fide bargain for money, although in fact the money is not the full value, is good and valuable consideration of money within the statute.

Moore's statement appears to be a startling innovation. It is significant, however, that there is no reported case of a conveyance being set aside on the express ground that the consideration was inadequate, and it may well be that here Moore was merely expressing the view that where the consideration was less than half the true value, fraud shall be presumed unless the contrary was proved.

(*c*) The consideration had to be partly executed. A wholly executory consideration was not, in Moore's view, enough.[2]

(*d*) Notice acquired by a purchaser while an infant bound him on attaining majority.[3]

(*e*) There was authority that 'if a purchasor of land given to charitable use, for consideration of money, hath legal notice of the use, and afterwards selleth the land to another for money, who hath no notice of the use, this second purchasor shall hold the land chargeable with the charitable use'.[4]

[1] Moore, fo. 264^{v}: 'si ratable part est pluis moynes que le trewe value soit consideracion dargent deins lestatute. Et semble que nemi . . . Car lou in presumpcion largent nest le value del ter come ici ratable part dewe hors de mortgage que nest le trewe value, ne poit estre presume le trewe value. Sic contract pur petit somme, lou frawde est apparent, nest valuable consideracion dargent. Mes bargayne bona fide pur argent, coment que in verity largent ne fait del full value, est bone et valuable consideracion dargent deins lestatute.' Cf. Duke (Moore), 180 and Moore, fo. 264: 'But if one purchase lands or goods under halfe the value, and sell them to another, upon good consideration, bona fide, the fraud is purged.'

Moore distinguishes this case from one where the consideration was non-existent or worthless: 'si riens passe per release, le release nest consideracion deins lestatute' (fo. 245^{v}).

[2] *Ibid.* fo. 264. And see fo. 260^{v}; Duke (Moore), 178.

[3] Moore, fo. 249.

[4] *East Greensted*'s case (1633), Duke, 64, 65. See generally E. Sugden, *Law of Vendors and Purchasers*, 14th ed. (London, 1862), 722.

(*f*) It was held[1] that a purchaser, without notice, of land charged with a rent to a charitable use did not take free of the charge.

Yet the rent remains, because it is collateral to the land, and another thing; and the notice required by the statute is to be given, as well of the land, as of the charitable use.[2]

(*g*) Constructive notice was fatal. For example, all the tenants and suitors of the manor were deemed to have notice of a surrender of land within the manor to a charitable use; as were all the parishioners if the terms of the charitable use was read out in the parish church. A scrivener, who wrote the will of a man devising land for the repair of highways, was deemed to have notice of the charitable use, even though the testator subsequently changed his mind, without the scrivener's knowledge, and left the land for the repair of churches;[3] yet a 'counsellor', who gave legal advice, was not so bound if he had only construed a document at his client's request.[4]

(*h*) Notice could also be imputed to the purchaser. The attorney was the 'servaunt substitute et quasi agent pur luy in le prisell del estate'.[5] The lord of the manor was deemed to have notice of charitable uses known to his tenant,[6] and the executor of those uses known to his testator.[7] A remarkable instance of the application of the doctrine of imputed notice was Moore's conclusion that the knowledge of the commissioners in bankruptcy could be imputed to a purchaser for valuable consideration, at least if the bankrupt had no heir against whom recompense could be ordered.[8]

[1] *Bernard Hide*'s case (1628), Duke, 76, 77; see also *The Poor of East Greensted*'s case (1633), as reported in Duke, 64, (but cf. the report of the same case in Tothill, *sub nom. Maynard* v. *Paupers de East Greensted*, 160, where it is dated 1630–1); *Peacock* v. *Thewer* (1638), Duke, 82; *Inhabitants of Woodford* v. *Parkhurst* (1639), *ibid.* 70.

[2] *Bernard Hide*'s case (1628), *ibid.* 76, 77, *per* Coventry L.K. And cf. Moore, fo. 127.

[3] Duke (Moore), 181.

[4] *Ibid.* 181.

[5] Moore, fo. 260^{v}. But the attorney's authority was limited. If he had no notice 'al temp del conclusion el contract pur estate, ad notice apres dent execucion ceo nest sufficient'. *Aliter* if he who had notice was the purchaser's servant.

[6] *Ibid.* fo. 269.

[7] *Ibid.* fo. 269.

[8] *Ibid.* fo. 264: 'les commissioners ayant notice encore ne poient faire recompense, quia ils execute que authority per lestatute, et nont benefitt, per que ils ne lours executors, administrators ne heirs faira recompense. Et semble sur ambodeux clauses del Proviso que le charitable use continuera sinoque soit ascun party vers que recompense est recoverable. Et pur ceo le notice des commissioners continuera le use in le vende.'

(*i*) Notice given to a purchaser of land charged with a charitable use between 'his agreement, and sealing of the writings, before the perfecting of the settling of the estate in him, by attornment, livery, or inrollment of the deed of conveyance' was sufficient notice of the use.[1]

(*j*) If land was purchased in the name of another and he who had supplied the consideration had notice of the charitable use; the named purchaser was bound, 'whether he [had] notice or not, because he [had] not give[n] consideration'.[2] Conversely, in Moore's view, the named purchaser who had notice was bound, even though the person who gave the consideration had no notice of the charitable use.[3]

[1] *Inhabitants of Woodford* v. *Parkhurst* (1639), Duke, 70, *per* Coventry L.K. Moore had anticipated Coventry's conclusion: 'Que le notice al bargainee dent le fine et apres le bargane et sale et auxi dent le bargane et sale inroll luy chardgera pur tout lestate que il prist per le fine' (fo. 249).

[2] *Ibid.* fo. 221^{v}: 'car le fils [the feoffee] est chardg ove le use soit que il ad notice ou nemi, quia il ne done consideracion.'

[3] *Ibid.* fo. 236: 'si le charitable use soit continewe in le frere que ad notice coment que laccomptaunt que pay largent et fait le purchase navoit notice. Et semble que cy.'

THE DEVELOPMENT OF THE LAW OF CHARITY

1700-1827

CHAPTER VI

INTRODUCTION

THE charity statutes had been inspired by a national concern to encourage charitable giving and to protect from peculation and maladministration the funds of charity. With the cooperation of common law judges, the Chancellor bent the law to perfect the imperfect charitable gift[1] and generously applied the *cy-près* doctrine to prevent endowments from reverting into the uncharitable hands of the testator's heir or next-of-kin. After the Civil War, however, the commission procedure functioned less effectively. Men no longer warmly endorsed the aims of the Elizabethan legislature, and petitioners on behalf of charities turned for assistance to other procedures, such as the information, whose efficacy was less dependent upon the energy and enthusiasm of their neighbours.

This change of temper does not affect the substantive law until the beginning of the eighteenth century. It was traditional at one time to represent the years 1680 to 1760 as the dark age of English philanthropy. Lecky's[2] England was an England where the poor were depicted as contentedly wallowing in their own, self-imposed degradation and where the charitable impulse was dismissed as unworthy of any responsible *pater familias*. This highly coloured representation ignored the presence of virile philanthropic forces operating through mechanisms and techniques different from those of a century earlier.[3] Only a detailed statistical analysis,

[1] See above, pp. 59–72.

[2] *A History of England in the Eighteenth Century*, II (London, 1898), 126 ff.

[3] There is as yet no satisfactory, general account of philanthropy and philanthropic movements in the eighteenth and early nineteenth centuries, akin to W. K. Jordan, *Philanthropy in England, 1480–1660* (London, 1959). The most comprehensive analysis is David Owen, *English Philanthropy, 1660–1960* (Cambridge, Mass. and London, 1965) which is primarily concerned with nineteenth-century philanthropy; although somewhat dated, B. Kirkman Gray, *A History of English Philanthropy, from the Dissolution of the Monasteries to the taking of the First Census* (London, 1905) is also of considerable value. For more specific and limited studies, see: M. G. Jones *The Charity School Movement* (Cambridge, 1938); Betsy Rodgers, *Cloak of Charity* (London, 1949); E. M. Hampson, *Treatment of Poverty in Cambridgeshire, 1597–1834* (Cambridge, 1934); T. F. Reddaway, *The Rebuilding of London after the Great Fire* (London,

comparable to that undertaken by Professor Jordan in his *Philanthropy in England, 1480–1660*, can show how representative were such enlightened souls as Richard Taunton[1] and Hannah Moore.[2] The legal evidence, at least, suggests that an influential segment of the community, the judiciary and legal profession, remained suspicious of the worth of charity and resentful of the death-bed gift which disinherited the testator's heir-at-law and next-of-kin. Lord Harcourt's remark in 1721[3] that he liked 'charity well' but he would 'not steal leather to make poor men shoes' was not untypical. If these sentiments were less vigorously expressed in the last decades of the eighteenth century, Sir Richard Pepper Arden, Master of the Rolls,[4] and Lord Eldon, Lord Chancellor,[5] would have readily accepted Lord Hardwicke's appraisal of the judge's role in charity cases, that he should sit there 'to do justice to all, and not to oppress any man for the sake of a charity'.[6]

It was inevitable, therefore, that many of the privileges which judges had granted to charity should be closely scrutinised. Many regrets were expressed that the preamble to the charity statute of 1601 should have been so freely construed so as to uphold defective testamentary instruments as valid appointments *inter vivos*.[7] The 'old precedents' were thought strange and contrary to every principle,[8] and if 'now originally to be considered, courts of law

1946); Beatrice and Sidney Webb, *English Poor Law History* (London, 1927–9); A. S. Turberville, *Englishmen and Manners in the Eighteenth Century* (Oxford, 1926); W. S. Lewis and R. M. Williams, *Private Charity in England, 1745–1757* (New Haven, 1938); A. W. Coats, 'Economic Thought and Poor Law Policy in the Eighteenth Century', *Economic History Review*, Second Series, XIII (1960), 39.

[1] Philanthropist, 1694–1752; on whom, see Owen, *English Philanthropy, 1660–1960*, 80–1.

[2] Philanthropist, 1745–1833; on whom see, M. G. Jones, *Hannah Moore* (Cambridge, 1952).

[3] In *Att.-Gen.* v. *Sutton* (1721), 1 P. Wms. 754, 765–6, quoting, in part, Twisden J. in an unreported case. See also *Earl of Plymouth* v. *Hickman* (1690), 2 Vern, 167.

[4] Arden, later to become Lord Alvanley, was Master of the Rolls from 1788–1801.

[5] Eldon was Lord Chancellor from 1801–6 and 1807–27.

[6] In *Att.-Gen.* v. *Lord Gower* (1736), 2 Eq. Cas. Abr. 195. Cf. these observations with those of Sir Richard Pepper Arden M.R. in *Pickering* v. *Lord Stamford* (1795), 2 Ves. 581, 584 and of Lord Eldon L.C. in *Legge* v. *Asgill* (1818?), Turn. and R. 265 n.; cf. below, pp. 146 ff.

[7] For a full discussion, see below, pp. 135–8.

[8] See, for example, Lord Cowper's remarks in *Att.-Gen.* v. *Bains* (or Barnes), (1708), Prec. Ch. 270, 272, 2 Vern. 597 (a less full report).

and equity would not have gone so far'.[1] A more critical analysis of the principles underlying the doctrine of *cy-près* is further evidence of the eighteenth-century lawyer's concern to protect the heir and next-of-kin from the charitable caprices of their ancestor.[2] The Chancellor would no longer lightly assume that a testator had a general charitable intention merely because he had bequeathed money to a particular charitable object which had failed for one reason or another. But, again, the authorities were 'too many, and too strong to contend with.'[3] The consistency of the case law, stretching back as it did over a hundred years, had transformed mere precedent into the 'established doctrine of this Court',[4] which withstood the individual prejudices of successive Chancellors. It was a principle of overriding importance that 'settled rules of construction . . . must not be disturbed.'[5]

But the most vivid legal example of contemporary dislike and distrust of charity is a statute, the Mortmain Act, 1736,[6] which avoided devises of land to charity and vested the property so devised in the testator's heir-at-law or (exceptionally) his next-of-kin.[7] This statute was inspired by a fear and hatred of the Church and ecclesiastical charities, by a contempt for the 'vainglorious' ambitions of charitably minded testators and by a desire to ensure that the heir-at-law should enjoy 'some sort of natural right to succeed after his [ancestor's] death, at least to his [ancestor's] land-estate.'[8] Yet, paradoxically, it was the existence of the Mortmain Act, 1736, which preserved from serious questioning the inherited, generous conception of legal charity; for by classifying an object as charitable, the judges, who interpreted the statute 'to repel the mischief, and advance the remedy,'[9] ensured that the

[1] *Att.-Gen.* v. *Andrews* (1748–9), 1 Ves. Sen. 225, 226, *per* Lord Hardwicke L.C.; Ves. Sen. Supp. 116.

[2] For a full discussion, see below, pp. 138–53.

[3] *Att.-Gen.* v. *Herrick* (1772), Ambl. 712, *per* Earl Bathurst L.C.

[4] *Moggridge* v. *Thackwell* (1803), 7 Ves. 36, 68, *per* Lord Eldon. See also *Wagstaff* v. *Wagstaff* (1724), 2 P. Wms. 258, 259, *per* Earl of Macclesfield L.C.

[5] *Att.-Gen.* v. *Mayor of Bristol* (1820), 2 J. and W. 294, 318, *per* Lord Eldon.

[6] 9 Geo. II c. 36; below, pp. 257 ff.

[7] For example a bequest of leasehold property to charitable uses was within the Act and, not being realty, would revert at law to the next-of-kin: below, pp. 118–19.

[8] William Cobbett, *Parliamentary History of England*, IX (London, 1811), 1126; and see below, p. 110.

[9] *Att.-Gen.* v. *Meyrick* (1754), 2 Ves. Sen. 44, 47, *per* Sir John Strange M.R.; below, pp. 118–19.

devise to charity would be avoided and that the land would result to the heir-at-law or next-of-kin. Consequently, there was little concern to restrict the class of objects which the law deemed to be charitable. It is true that if a testator had bequeathed pure personalty, his next-of-kin could generally benefit only if the object of the bequest was characterised as non-charitable. But land was still the prime source of wealth, and the value of bequests of pure personalty was relatively trivial. Moreover, it is significant that only when confronted with a bequest to charity of pure personalty[1] did the courts show any readiness to defeat the gift by characterising the object of the testator's bounty as non-charitable.[2]

[1] But see below, pp. 118, 130.

[2] For a full discussion, see below, pp. 128–33.

CHAPTER VII

THE MORTMAIN ACT, 1736

The background to the Act

THE years between 1730 and 1750 have been said to mark a 'low ebb of public decency, order and principle'.[1] They saw the climax of an anti-clerical movement which had been gathering momentum since the Hanoverian succession and which manifested itself in public insult of the Church and calumny of the clergy. 'Since the days of the Lollards', wrote Mark Pattison, 'there had never been a time when the established ministers of religion were held in so much contempt as in the Hanoverian period, or when satire upon churchmen was so congenial to general feeling'.[2] The laity feared the wealth of the Church; they feared that great ecclesiastical charities, like Queen Anne's Bounty, whose constitution allowed it to receive any amount of property, 'the statute of mortmain . . . notwithstanding', would garner in all the land of the kingdom; they feared the power of prelates, like Edmund Gibson; and they feared that the clergy would emulate what they thought to be the example of their medieval predecessors and terrorise them into making death-bed devises *ad pias causas* to the ruin of their heirs.

These deep-seated apprehensions inspired the Mortmain Bill,[3]

[1] G. F. A. Best, *Temporal Pillars* (Cambridge, 1964), 94.

[2] 'Tendencies of Religious Thought in England, 1688–1750', in *Essays and Reviews* (London, 1860), 315. See also Norman Sykes, *Edmund Gibson, Bishop of London, 1699–1748* (London, 1926), 183; Alan Savidge, *The Foundation and Early Years of Queen Anne's Bounty* (London, 1955), *passim*.

[3] There is, however, a mystery surrounding the events which were the immediate cause of its enactment. There is some suggestion in contemporary pamphlets that it was prompted by an increasing number of 'vainglorious', 'foolish' charitable devises such as Thomas Guy's munificent endowment of the hospital bearing his name, which, rumour falsely said, had impoverished his heirs. In William Cobbett, *The Parliamentary History of England*, IX (London, 1811), 1110, it is noted that the Mortmain Bill arose because of several incidents by which heirs had suffered considerably by injudicious charitable gifts, particularly by one Mr Mitchell. This may be a reference to the will of John Michel, who had left a considerable estate to The Queen's College, Oxford: see Courtney Kenny, *The True Principles of Legislation with regard to Property given for Charitable or other Public Uses* (London, 1880), 60–1. But Francis Palgrave, giving evidence before the 1844 *Committee on Mortmain*, 16, thought that the allusion related in some way to Guy's benefaction. Certainly there were Parliamentary jibes against those misguided spirits who had lately erected and endowed hospitals. Palgrave's explanation seems, therefore, more plausible.

which the Master of the Rolls, Sir Joseph Jekyll, introduced in the House of Commons on 5 March 1735.[1] It was proposed that after a stated day no land or any sum of money for the purchase of land should be given to any person or body corporate in trust for, or for the benefit of any charitable purpose, unless it was made by deed executed in the presence of two or more witnesses twelve calendar months before the grantor's death. Any devise made to charity should be void and the land should revert to the testator's heir-at-law.[2] Large majorities in both Houses welcomed the introduction of the Bill and, as the following extracts from the *Debates* show, expressed their distrust of all charity, particularly ecclesiastical charity, and their concern to safeguard the financial interest of the testator's family.[3]

[I]t has always been reckoned a most necessary and a fundamental maxim of our constitution, not to allow any great share of our landed-interest to be vested in societies or bodies politic, either sacred or profane . . .

[B]ut, my Lords, there is an evil lately grown up; an evil not founded upon our ancient constitution, but an evil which took its rise from our having departed, about two centuries ago, from the common law of this kingdom. I mean the liberty of granting or devising all sorts of land estates by will, and even upon death-bed, not only to the disappointment and disherison of a man's natural and lawful heirs, but to the prejudice of the common good of this kingdom, and in contradiction to that ancient maxim, which forbids the granting or alienating any lands in Mortmain . . .

I am very far, my Lords, from disapproving of all charitable foundations, or of all donations to charitable uses, either by will or deed; but I am convinced that our charitable foundations may become too numerous, and that some of those we have already established, may become too rich and extensive, especially if the unlimited power of granting licences, first vested in the Crown, by the statute of the 7th and 8th of the late King William, be not cautiously and moderately used . . . for, by the specious pretence of charity, the solicitations of those who are interested in charitable foundations, and the pride and vanity of donors, it is to me highly probable, that too great a part of the lands in this kingdom may soon come to be in Mortmain, to the prejudice of the nation in general, and to the ruin or unjust disappointment of many a

[1] See generally Abel Boyer, *The Political State of Great Britain*, LII (London, 1736), 506 ff.; Cobbett, *Parliamentary History*, IX, 1110 ff.

[2] For the full text, see appendix J.

[3] Cobbett, *Parliamentary History*, IX, 1122, 1123, 1125–6, 1144–5.

man's poor relations, for I cannot but think that a man's heirs-at-law have some sort of natural right to succeed after his death, at least to his land estate. . . . The giving of any such charity I shall always look on rather as an act of injustice towards the heir-at-law, than as an act of charity in the donor . . .

To assist the widow and fatherless, to nourish the tender infant, and succour the helpless old; in short, to relieve the poor distressed, who cannot provide for themselves, is a duty incumbent upon every society, as well as upon every private man: but, my Lords, this duty is to be discharged with great caution, and with great circumspection; for if we mistake the objects of our charity, if by giving what we call charity we encourage laziness, idleness, and extravagance, in the persons to whom we give it, or in others, the action is so far from being pious, charitable, or commendable, that it becomes impious, ridiculous and injurious, to our native country. . . . The funds for relief of deserving poor are sufficient. There is a . . . new gulf opened, under the name of charitable uses, which may be said to be without either bottom or bounds, and which will certainly swallow up that remnant which may be left by the others . . . The representative of the most ancient house in England may . . . utterly ruin his family by such a devise . . . Our clergymen will soon begin to watch the last moments of every dying person, as insidiously as ever the others did.

Numerous amendments were tabled after the Bill had been read a second time. Petitions for exemption were presented from the universities and colleges of Oxford and Cambridge, and from Eton, Westminster and Winchester; these were subsequently granted. These petitioners were said to be the only public foundations 'either useful or necessary in this Kingdom'.[1] A petition to exempt Queen Anne's Bounty was, in contrast, coolly received and was ordered to lie on the table of the House of Commons, a decision which roused the Church of England to attack the Bill even more vehemently. The Church's protagonists argued that the Bill was ill-conceived, that it was riddled with illogicalities and that the ambition of its proposers could best be satisfied by the re-introduction of a *legitim*. The prevailing temper of both Houses ensured that such arguments, however logical, would never prevail, and a virulent attack in the House of Lords by Lord Hervey[2] on the Bounty sealed its fate and that of ecclesiastical charities.

[1] Cobbett, *Parliamentary History*, IX, 1156. And see, W. R. Ward, *Georgian Oxford* (Oxford, 1958), 157–61.

[2] John, Lord Hervey, *Some Materials towards Memoirs of the reign of George II*, ed. Romney Sedgwick, II (London, 1931), 535–6. For an analysis of Hervey's motives, see Best, *Temporal Pillars*, 106–8.

Vain attempts were also made to exempt 'those charitable foundations which had been lately established, none of which', hoped the Earl of S . . . d, 'their lordships would look on as a public mischief . . . but this Amendment was disagreed to; because some of the late Dispositions made to such Foundations seemed to be a little extravagant, and even the Foundations themselves, if they had not already, might very soon become a public Mischief.'[1] Even a motion to protect the *bona fide* purchaser was opposed on the ground that it would be easy for a charity to give the testator 'reasonable money' in consideration of the devise, arranging that the consideration should be repaid to it by way of pecuniary legacy. '[B]ut it being the general Opinion that such a Conveyance and Bequest would be interpreted as made by Fraud or Collusion, in order to evade the law', the motion was defeated.[2]

On 20 May 1736, the Mortmain Bill received the royal assent. It was not mortmain legislation in the traditional sense. The analogy, invoked in its preamble, of 'Magna Carta, and divers other wholesome laws' was misleading, for statutes, such as Magna Carta,[3] *De Viris Religiosis*,[4] 15 Richard II c. 5 (1391–2)[5] and 23 Henry VIII c. 10 (1531–2)[6], though enacted to meet the evil of land falling into the dead hand, were designed to protect the feudal rights of mesne lords rather than to nurture the selfish aspirations of the heir-at-law. In Lord Hardwicke's view, 'the reasoning producing this Act [was] more like the political reasoning relating to the statute of Westminster, 2, of intails'.[7] Moreover it appeared to be, at least through the eyes of later commentators,[8] an ill drafted statute, curiously arbitrary in its operation and easy

[1] Boyer, *The Political State of Great Britain*, LII, 515. The Earl of S . . . d may have been the Earl of Stamford, who had married the daughter of Nathan Wright L.K. See also Lord Hardwicke's remarks in *Att.-Gen.* v. *Day* (1749), 1 Ves. 218, 222–3.

[2] Boyer, *The Political State of Great Britain*, LII, 516.

[3] (1215), 17 John, §§ 39 and 43.

[4] 7 Edw. I, stat. 2, c. 3 (1279), which forbade gifts or sales of land to religious houses without royal licence.

[5] This statute struck at conveyances in mortmain by way of use, as well as conveyances to temporal and spiritual corporate bodies.

[6] This statute, it will be remembered, sought to prevent conveyances in mortmain to chantry priests or other unincorporated bodies: see above p. 11.

[7] *Att.-Gen.* v. *Day* (1749), 1 Ves. Sen. 218, 223. In his report, Vesey gives the statute as Westminster, 3, an obvious error.

[8] See, for example, Kenny's comments in his *True Principles of Legislation*, 67–8.

to evade: it caught devises of land but not bequests of pure personalty (unless they were to be laid out in the purchase of land), and it neither restricted significantly a donor's power of *inter vivos* disposition nor a charity's power to acquire land *inter vivos*. In retrospect it is puzzling to find such lacunae. Yet lawyers as able as Jekyll and Hardwicke must have been aware of them, but equally have been persuaded that the value of bequests of pure personalty would be insignificant and that only rarely would a testator act with munificent generosity in his own lifetime.[1] Moreover there was a latent reluctance on the part of most members of Parliament to restrict even further a person's power of testamentary disposition.[2]

To what extent the statute effectively discouraged philanthropy in its life span of over one hundred and fifty years is a question which has not yet been answered. What is known is that the Mortmain Act, 1736, did lead to 'doubt, expense, uncertainty and litigation . . .; while from the existing facilities for evasion' the statute failed to secure 'the heir from the unexpected alienation of property to which he might reasonably have hoped to succeed'.[3]

The interpretation of the Act

The provisions of the Mortmain Act, 1736, were the source of much litigation. The task of interpreting them first fell to Philip Yorke, 1st Earl of Hardwicke, 'whose profound learning and enlightened judgment', said Anthony Highmore, 'enabled him to elucidate it with liberal precision, and whose determinations alone form the best-reading of almost every clause it contains'.[4] This encomium has not been universally echoed. Sir Francis Palgrave, for example, thought that Hardwicke's narrow, 'bigotted' views 'have caused . . . much mischief to charitable uses'.[5]

[1] See Lord Hardwicke's remarks in *Att.-Gen.* v. *Day* (1749), 1 Ves. Sen. 218, 222: 'And it is plain, that the legislature did not intend absolutely to forbid all kind of purchases of land for the benefit of charity; but has put them under some restrictions . . . [T]hat this was not intended to prevent the execution of charities already established; in several of which the funds are vested in trustees with intent to lay out in lands: . . . but to leave them open, restraining the increase of such donations *in futuro*; that it should not be in the power of any person, or of a court of equity, to direct subsequent gifts of money to a charity to be laid out in land. . . .'

[2] *Att.-Gen.* v. *Tancred* (1757), 1 Eden, 10, 15, *per* Henley L.K. ('a point of the utmost importance in a trading country').

[3] *Report from the Select Committee on Mortmain* (London, 1844), viii.

[4] *A Succinct View of the History of Mortmain* (London, 1809), 90.

[5] In his evidence before *The Select Committee on Mortmain* (1844), 13.

Hardwicke did indeed have a deep suspicion of deathbed charity. He believed that much public mischief had been caused by 'many large and improvident alienations, or dispositions, made by languishing or dying persons . . . to uses called charitable',[1] and he was anxious to avoid any devise or bequest to charity which fell within the equity of the statute.[2] Nevertheless, Hardwicke's interpretation of the Act does not support Palgrave's violent denunciation. It was more liberal than that of his immediate successor, Lord Northington, and sought to keep the statute within the bounds intended by its sponsors. 'The general intention of the statute', he declared in *Attorney-General* v. *Bowles* in 1754,[3] 'is not to restrain charity, but to prevent the disposition of real estate, and unwarrantably or by surprise disinheriting the heir at law.' Earlier in *Sorresby* v. *Hollins* in 1740[4] he had resisted counsel's invitation to extend the equity of the statute so as to avoid bequests of pure personalty to charities. The Act was not

> at all aimed against perpetual charities merely as such, or to prevent the establishment or creation of them, but is designed against the cases of perpetual charities in lands, and, as the title imports, to restrain the disposition of lands whereby the same become unalienable.

He also refused to interpret the Act to avoid charitable devises which had been made before 1736:

> All the cases arising before, must be left on the same rules of law and equity; otherwise it would cause great confusion, if those wills and settle-

[1] *Att.-Gen.* v. *Lord Weymouth* (1743), Ambl. 20, 23.

[2] The following is an extract from the MS. note of the speech on the Mortmain Bill, which was apparently never delivered. It is reproduced in George Harris, *The Life of Lord Chancellor Hardwicke*, I (London, 1847), 308–13 (it is not reprinted in the more comprehensive biography of P. C. Yorke, *Life of Lord Chancellor Hardwicke* (Cambridge, 1913)).

'At present [has] no bounds . . . Stat. 43 Eliz. c. 4 lets in all kinds of imaginary charities, not so much as a *licence in mortmain* wanting—may give to the poor—church—dissenters . . . *Obj. Bill prohibits—stops up ye channels of charity Ans.* Charity—a noble, a necessary duty—not consist entirely in *alms giving*—much less *in perpetual alms.* Church of Rome flourished in y^t species of charity—w^n she had almost banished ye very notion of y^t virtue out of her system of Xtianity.
Duty of ye present case—ye end best attained by present benefactions.
Death-bed charity—death-bed repentance.
Vanity—superstition—abuses—*faction.*
Sufficient room left for useful charities—money—stocks—distributed.
Will nothing satisfy but ye lands of ye kingdom?'

[3] (1754), 3 Atk. 806, 808. (The case is less fully reported in 2 Ves. Sen. 547.) See also Hardwicke's observations in *Att.-Gen.* v. *Day* (1749), I Ves. Sen. 218, 222.

[4] (1740), 9 Mod. 221, 222.

ments made before, should be construed in a different way by reason of the statute, though not affected by the statute.[1]

These principles were to be important landmarks in the statute's history, and the cases establishing them were never to be seriously challenged.[2] But other decisions, which interpreted the Act in favour of charity and against the heir, met a less fortunate fate. In *Vaughan* v. *Farrer*[3] and *Attorney-General* v. *Bowles*,[4] Hardwicke had distinguished a valid bequest of money to be used for the erection of a building from an invalid bequest to buy land on which a building was to be erected; a bequest to erect a building did not compel trustees to buy land for they could spend the money on building on land already in their ownership. It is true that Hardwicke thought this distinction unfortunate. The plaintiff, the heir and next-of-kin, was 'as much or more perhaps, an object of charity, than any of these people, who may come into this hospital. . . . But yet [the court] must go according to such rules, as will hold in other cases.'[5] Later judges were not so embarrassed, and were to reject Hardwicke's reasoning as a bewildering and perplexing subtlety. Lord Northington in *Attorney-General* v. *Tyndall*,[6] for example, thought it was a simple and objectionable means of avoiding the statute, by doing '*per obliquum, quod non potuit facere per directum*', merely perpetuating the memory and gratifying the vanity of testators.[7]

Hardwicke also refused to 'break in' on the Statute of Frauds and to permit the introduction of extrinsic evidence to prove a secret trust for charity.[8] To have done so would 'open a door to

[1] *Att.-Gen.* v. *Andrews* (1749), 1 Ves. Sen. 225; see also *Ashburnham* v. *Bradshaw* (1740), 2 Atk. 36. *Aliter* if a will made before the Mortmain Act, 1736, was confirmed by a codicil made after the Act: see *Willet* v. *Sandford* (1748), 1 Ves. Sen. 178.

[2] But see below, p. 116.

[3] (1751), 2 Ves. Sen. 182.

[4] (1754), 3 Atk. 806; see also *Glubb* v. *Att.-Gen.* (1759), Ambl. 373.

[5] *Vaughan* v. *Farrer* (1751), 2 Ves. Sen. 182, 189.

[6] (1764), 2 Eden, 207.

[7] (1764), 2 Eden, 207, 210; and Ambl. 614. See also *Att.-Gen.* v. *Hyde* (1775), Ambl. 751 (Earl Bathurst L.C.); *Att.-Gen.* v. *Nash* (1791), 3 Bro. C. C. 588 (Lord Thurlow L.C.); *Chapman* v. *Brown* (1801), 6 Ves. 404, 1 Ves. Jun. Supp. 606 (Sir William Grant M.R.); *Att.-Gen.* v. *Davies* (1804), 9 Ves. 535, 2 Ves. Jun. Supp. 189 (Lord Eldon L.C.); *Pritchard* v. *Arbouin* (1827), 3 Russ. 456 (Sir John Leach M.R.). But cf. below, p. 117, n. 4.

[8] Such a trust would, of course, be then caught by the statute, and the land would revert to the heir. But if no extrinsic evidence was allowed, the testator would have had to rely completely on the integrity of his devisee, who could safely appropriate the land to his own use or later carry out his 'moral' obligation.

infinite inconvenience . . . which would considerably overbalance the mischief that can arise by leaving a loop-hole whereby to elude the statute of mortmain'.[1] These observations were to share the same fate as the distinction he drew in *Vaughan* v. *Farrer*[2] and *Attorney-General* v. *Bowles*.[3] Not to prove the secret trust would be, said Northington, to adopt instruments which are full of craft and evasion of law. The Statute of Frauds was enacted merely to regulate the proof of trust estates not 'to prevent persons taking trust estates'. But the statute of mortmain was

> meant to prevent a particular species of trust, i.e. trusts for charities. The one struck at imposture, the other at weakness and superstition. The statute of mortmain meant to prevent honorary trusts, or devises for charities, *quacunque arte vel ingenio*; and the honorary trust infects the will as much as if it were declared in the most solemn manner.[4]

Other examples will be found in the reports to support the view that Hardwicke's interpretation of the Mortmain Act was a balanced one.[5] Certainly it was more objective and less splenetic than that of his immediate successor, Northington, who frequently expressed his happiness that he was in a position to prevent

[1] *Addlington* v. *Cann* (1744), 3 Atk. 141, 150. Moreover, he thought (*ibid.* 153) that the mischief was slight, 'because the instances of trustees abusing the trust of charity are so frequent, that they are a sufficient warning to reasonable men, not to leave their estates under such uncertainty, as to put them absolutely under a person's power, and then trust to his generosity for the disposing of them in charity'.

Although Hardwicke refused to 'break in' on the Statute of Frauds, he encouraged the plaintiff to bring an action of ejectment at law and retained the bill to enable her to do so. '[F]or the plaintiff's is undoubtedly an hard case, as she is an only child, and heir-at-law; but this is all the relief I can give her' (p. 155).

[2] (1751), 2 Ves. Sen. 182; above, p. 115.

[3] (1754), 3 Atk. 806; above, p. 115.

[4] *Boson* v. *Statham* (1760), 1 Eden, 508, 514. See also *Muckleston* v. *Brown* (1801), 6 Ves. 52, 69, *per* Lord Eldon.

Northington was, however, able to distinguish *Addlington* v. *Cann* (1744), 3 Atk. 141 in *Boson* v. *Statham* on the ground that in the former case there was 'nothing in the will attaching a trust' (1 Eden, 508, 513). See also *Stickland* v. *Aldridge* (1804), 9 Ves. 516, 519, *per* Lord Eldon.

[5] See, for example, *Grimmett* v. *Grimmett* (1754), Ambl. 210, where a testator desired his executors, within twelve months of his death, to settle by purchase of land, *or otherwise as they should be advised*, an annuity of £50 among certain poor. Hardwicke upheld the gift. The testator's wishes could be carried out in a lawful way. The executors were not *directed* to buy land.

foolish or, as he called them, superstitious devises to charity.[1] Northington would have avoided *any* testamentary gift, even of pure personalty, to charity and would have rejected many of the decisions of Hardwicke which had favoured charity at the expense of the heir.[2] If Northington, who was 'bent by [his] judgment against all chicanery to avoid the statute',[3] had been Chancellor in 1736, the equity of the statute might well have been extended to avoid bequests of personalty and devises of realty made before the enactment of the Act.[4]

Few judges of the period shared Northington's concern to extend so indiscriminately the equity of the Mortmain Act, 1736.[5] Yet they remained, even at the end of the eighteenth century when the passionate anti-clericalism of Walpole's England had given way to an alliance of Church and State, broadly in sympathy with the legislature's desire to strike down the death-bed charitable devise which deprived the heir of land deemed to be his natural

[1] See his *dicta* in *Att.-Gen.* v. *Heartwell* (1764), 2 Eden, 234, 235. The decision is also reported by Ambler, 451.

[2] See above, p. 114.

[3] *Att.-Gen.* v. *Tyndall* (1764), 2 Eden, 207, 212.

[4] Thus in *Att.-Gen.* v. *Heartwell* (1764), 2 Eden, 234, 235, counsel on both sides were prepared to accept the authority of *Ashburnham* v. *Bradshaw* (1740), 2 Atk. 36 and *Willet* v. *Sandford* (1748), 1 Ves. Sen. 178, above, p. 115, n. 1, where Hardwicke had held that the Mortmain Act, 1736, did not catch devises of realty made before it was enacted:

'The *Lord Chancellor*, however, stated a distinction between those cases on that part of the present case which related to the devise of the residue of the personal estate to be laid out in land; in those cases the devise was of real estate, here of personal, and a will speaks at different times with respect to the different estates...'

After argument, the Lord Chancellor continued:

'The distinction in *Ashburnham* v. *Bradshaw* is not now to be disputed. It was founded upon the certificate of eleven judges, though I think a great deal might be said against the determination.'

Northington was so vehement in his dislike of all charity that, in *Att.-Gen.* v. *Tyndall* (1764), 2 Eden, 207, 213, he said that money bequeathed to improve *existing* buildings was within the mischief of the Mortmain Act, 1736, and was, therefore, a void bequest. 'If these precedents were to prevail, we should see alms-houses turned into palaces, and small spots of ground covered with immense buildings.' But subsequent cases rejected this ground of the decision: see *Harris* v. *Barnes* (1767), Ambl. 651; *Att.-Gen.* v. *Bishop of Chester* (1785), 1 Bro. C. C. 444; *Corbyn* v. *French* (1799), 4 Ves. Jun. 418, 427–8, *per* Pepper Arden M.R.

[5] See, for example, *Att.-Gen.* v. *Hartley* (1793), 4 Bro. C.C. 412; *Att.-Gen.* v. *Williams* (1794), 4 Bro. C.C. 526; *Att.-Gen.* v. *Whitchurch* (1796), 3 Ves. 141; *Moggridge* v. *Thackwell* (1803), 7 Ves. 36; *Att.-Gen.* v. *Davies* (1802), 9 Ves. 535, 539–40, *per* Romilly, *arguendo*; *Att.-Gen.* v. *Goddard* (1823), Turn. and Russ. 348.

right.[1] The statute was remedial law, and should be construed 'as is most effectual to repel the mischief, and advance the remedy'.[2] Every known artifice to avoid the equity of the statute was exposed and defeated. Thus in *Attorney-General* v. *Lord Weymouth* in 1743[3] a testator had directed his lands to be sold and the proceeds given to charity. Lord Hardwicke refused to be bound by the words of the short title, which described the Act's aim as restraining 'dispositions of land', and held that the Act avoided not only devises of land but bequests of money produced from the sale of land. Otherwise

> the person entitled to the residue might have come, and prayed to have land in this Court, instead of the money, and might have retained it as land.[4]

A bequest of money to be laid out in the purchase of land was also within the mischief of the Act, not only if the purchase was expressly or impliedly directed[5] but also when it followed from the charter or constitution of the charity, to which the bequest was made, that land had to be bought with the money.[6]

In *Attorney-General* v. *Graves*[7] Hardwicke also rejected the argument that the Act did not catch a bequest of leasehold property

[1] Although during this period judges did not reject the ideals of the Mortmain Act, 1736, there is evidence that in the early decades of the nineteenth century, if not earlier, some members of the laity were beginning once again to applaud and encourage the philanthropic impulse: see generally David Owen, *English Philanthropy, 1660–1960* (Cambridge, Mass. and London, 1965), *passim*; B. Kirkman Gray, *A History of English Philanthropy* (London, 1905) *passim*; A. V. Dicey, *Law and Opinion in England*, 2nd ed. (London, 1962), lxiii; E. C. P. Lascelles's essay on 'Charity' in *Early Victorian England, 1830–1865*, ed. G. M. Young, 2 vols. (London, 1934), II, 315.

[2] *Att.-Gen.* v. *Meyrick* (1750), 2 Ves. Sen. 44, 47, *per* Sir John Strange M.R.

[3] (1743), Ambl. 20.

[4] *Ibid.* 24. For 'if the entire equitable interest in property is vested absolutely and indefeasibly in a person *sui juris*, that person can elect to take the property in its actual state' (P. H. Pettit, *Equity and the Law of Trusts* (London, 1966), 431.)

[5] *Att.-Gen.* v. *Day* (1749), 1 Ves. Sen. 219; *Att.-Gen.* v. *Heartwell* (1764), 2 Eden, 234; *Grieves* v. *Case* (1792), 1 Ves. Jun. 548; *Pritchard* v. *Arbouin* (1827), 3 Russ. 456; see also *Att.-Gen.* v. *Davies* (1804), 9 Ves. 535. But cf. *Oliphant* v. *Hendrie* (1784), 1 Bro. C.C. 571 and *Campbell* v. *Earl of Radnor* (1783), 1 Bro. C.C. 271.

[6] Queen Anne's Bounty particularly suffered from this strict construction, for by its charter it was bound to invest any bequest it received in the purchase of land: see *Widmore* v. *Woodroffe* (1766), Ambl. 636, 1 Bro. C.C. 13 n.; *Middleton* v. *Clitherow* (1798), 3 Ves. 734. Hatred of the Bounty was one of the principal reasons which inspired the Mortmain Act, 1736 (above, p. 111), and it was not until 1803 that the Bounty was again allowed to hold land in mortmain: see 43 Geo. III c. 107.

[7] (1752), Ambl. 155; see also *Att.-Gen.* v. *Tomkins* (1754), Ambl. 216.

to charity since it would, if avoided, revert to the next-of-kin and not the heir; 'it takes in money to be laid out in land',[1] which disinherits not heirs but next-of-kin, for the Act speaks of 'any estate or interest whatsoever'. Devises of copyholds, of the rents and profits of land and of mixed funds of realty and personalty, and bequests of money secured by mortgages of land were also deemed to be within the mischief of the statute.[2] The Act was even extended to catch mortgages of turnpike tolls devised to charity,[3] for in this case a mortgagee had the right to have the tolls applied in discharge of his mortgage. This reasoning is hardly convincing, and Lord Loughborough admitted in *Knapp* v. *Williams*[4] that such a devise 'is not all within the mischief: but the consequences would open a much larger field for charitable donations'.

A final example, from among many, may be given of the judicial concern to interpret the Mortmain Act, 1736, in such a way as to defeat the charitable devise. In a long line of cases, the judges held that a bequest of pure personalty, dependent upon a devise of land to charity, failed with the void devise and could not be applied *cy-près*. In the same way as the courts refused to marshall assets to circumvent the Mortmain Act,[5] so they refused to bend the *cy-près* doctrine and to find that, in such a case, the testator had a general charitable intention.[6] Thus in *Attorney-General* v. *Whitchurch*[7] the testator devised four houses to the churchwardens and vestrymen of a certain parish to be used as almshouses. He also bequeathed £2000 to them, the interest to be used to maintain the inhabitants of the almshouses. The Master of the Rolls, Sir Richard Pepper Arden, held that the intention of the testator was to provide an endowment for the almshouses; but 'there is no general intention beyond that; and therefore the bequest . . . must fail, with the object, to which it was attached'.[8]

[1] (1752), Ambl. 155, 156.

[2] *Att.-Gen.* v. *Meyrick* (1750), 2 Ves. Sen. 44: *Att.-Gen.* v. *Caldwell* (1766), Ambl. 636; *White* v. *Evans* (1798), 4 Ves. 21; *Att.-Gen.* v. *Hurst* (1790), 2 Cox, 364.

[3] (1798), 4 Ves. 435 n. For similar reasons a bequest of shares in a company possessing land, the use of which was not merely incidental to the company's principal undertaking, was to be held void: see *Morris* v. *Glynn* (1859), 27 Beav. 218.

[4] (1798), 4 Ves. 435 n.

[5] See below, pp. 157–9.

[6] See below, pp. 144–51, for a full discussion of the importance of general charitable intention in the history of the *cy-près* doctrine.

[7] (1796), 3 Ves. 141; see also *Att.-Gen.* v. *Goulding* (1788), 2 Bro. C.C. 428; *Chapman* v. *Brown* (1801), 6 Ves. 404, 1 Ves. Jun. Supp. 606; *Att.-Gen.* v. *Davies* (1804), 9 Ves. 535; *Finch* v. *Squire* (1804), 10 Ves. 41, 2 Ves. Jun. Supp. 200; *Att.-Gen.* v. *Hinxman* (1820), 2 J. and W. 270.

[8] (1796), 3 Ves. 141, 146.

CHAPTER VIII

THE PREAMBLE TO THE CHARITABLE USES ACT, 1601, AND THE DEFINITION OF CHARITY

THE preamble to the Charitable Uses Act, 1601, did not seek to describe the objects which were charitable in law. The uses which were deemed to be within the equity of the statute were those whose endowments could materially contribute to the relief of poverty. Other charitable uses, such as those for the support of religious purposes, were outside the statute and had been enforced not by the charity commissioners but by an information brought by the Attorney-General at the relation of a private individual. The information, however, proved to be such an attractive procedure that by the end of the seventeenth century it had come to be used to enforce *all* charitable trusts.[1] It was no longer

> confined to cases considered as charities before the statute of charitable uses, but all others are taken to be within the extensiveness of this proceeding in the name of the *Attorney-General*.[2]

Thereafter the antithesis between charities enforceable by commission on the one hand and by information on the other gradually disappeared. No obstacle now remained to the formulation of a definition of legal charity which was not bedevilled by procedural distinctions. Not until 1804, in *Morice* v. *The Bishop of Durham*,[3] however, was this step taken and the preamble to the Charitable Uses Act, 1601, equated with the legal definition of charity.

Before the enactment of the Mortmain Act, 1736, English judges were rarely called upon to consider whether a particular use was or was not charitable.[4] Even after 1736, there is in the cases little discussion of the general question, 'what is charity?' The pattern and quality of English philanthropy changed but little during the eighteenth century. 'New charitable dispositions and bequests tended, by and large, to follow paths already explored

[1] See above, pp. 57–8.

[2] *Att.-Gen.* v. *Brereton* (1752), 2 Ves. Sen. 425, 426 *per* Lord Hardwicke. See also *Att.-Gen.* v. *Hewer* (1700), 2 Vern. 387.

[3] (1804), 9 Ves. 399; (1805), 10 Ves. 522; below, pp. 122–5.

[4] See above, p. 58.

and made familiar by donors of an earlier age.'[1] In most cases, therefore, a judge could confidently and peremptorily categorise objects as charitable or non-charitable. But occasionally he was compelled to look beyond the immediate facts of the case and formulate a definition or description of legal charity. When this proved necessary, there was universal agreement that any object enumerated in the preamble to the Charitable Uses Act, 1601, was charitable. In *Attorney-General* v. *Ruper*,[2] for example, the Master of the Rolls, Sir Joseph Jekyll, was content to uphold as charitable a use for the repair of a church on the ground that it is 'one of the charities mentioned, preserved, and established, by the statute'; and in *Attorney-General* v. *Whorwood*,[3] Lord Hardwicke accepted that the 'establishment of learning is a charity; and so considered on the statute of Elizabeth'.[4] At the same time it was recognised that, though 'in statute 43 Eliz. there is a great enumeration of charitable uses . . . the statute does not affect to mention all'.[5] There were charitable uses which were deemed to be within the equity of the statute but outside its letter. But there were also uses, admittedly charitable, which were neither within the statute's letter nor its equity.[6] Their existence consequently led some judges to seek elsewhere than the Elizabethan preamble for a comprehensive definition of legal charity. Indeed if there is any thread linking these crude judicial attempts to define charity, it is in the conception of charity as a *public use*. This was not a novel idea. Sir Francis Moore in 1607 had emphasised in his *Reading* that all charitable uses were 'publique' uses. Over a hundred years later, in *Attorney-General* v. *Pearce*,[7] Lord Hardwicke was to echo Moore's view; the epithet *publick* 'was meant only by way of

[1] David Owen, *English Philanthropy, 1660–1960* (Cambridge, Mass. and London, 1965), 71.

[2] (1722), 2 P. Wms. 125, 126. See too 29 Car. II c. 8, § 7, being an Act confirming and perpetuating 'Augmentations made by Ecclesiastical persons to small Vicarages and Curacies'. § 7 reads: 'and if any question shall hereafter arise concerning the validity of such grants . . . such favourable constructions, and such further remedy, if need be, shall be had and made for the benefit of the Vicars and Curates, as heretofore hath been had and made, or may be had *for other Charitable uses, upon the Statutes for Charitable Uses*' (my italics).

[3] (1750), 1 Ves. Sen. 534, Ves. Sen. Supp. 236. The case is badly reported. See also *Att.-Gen.* v. *Downing* (1767), 1 Wilm. 1.

[4] *Ibid.* 537.

[5] In *Turner* v. *Ogden* (1787), 1 Cox, 316, 317, *per* Sir Lloyd Kenyon M.R.

[6] See above, pp. 33 ff.

[7] (1740), 2 Atk. 87, 88.

description' of charity, 'and not by way of distinguishing one charity from another. . . . It is the extensiveness which will constitute it a public [use]'. And in 1767 Lord Camden defined a charitable gift as:[1]

a gift to a general public use, which extends to the poor as well as the rich, [of which there are] many instances in the statute of 43 *Eliz.* carrying this idea, as for building bridges.

The element of public benefit was also the basis of the Lords Commissioners' opinion in *Grieves* v. *Case*[2] that the use was charitable because 'of the benefit the congregations were meant to derive from the preaching of their teachers'; and in *Townley* v. *Bedwell*[3] in 1801 a devise of land to establish a perpetual Botanical Garden was declared void, being within the Mortmain Act, 1736, 'upon the expression of the testator, that he trusted it would be a public benefit'.[4]

It is true that the reports of eighteenth-century charity cases are not, on the whole, characterised by comprehensiveness or lucidity; but the available evidence does lead to a tentative conclusion that uses which benefited the public were *ipso facto* deemed charitable. Moreover, there is nothing to suggest that the Chancellor regarded the preamble as an exclusive touchstone of legal charity as distinct from a valuable and historical catalogue of charitable uses. It was not until the decision of the Master of the Rolls, Sir William Grant, and the Lord Chancellor, Lord Eldon, in *Morice* v. *Bishop of Durham*[5] in 1805 that the decisive step was taken to enshrine the preamble as the *fons et origo* of all charity, and the argument that 'upon the authorities almost everything, from which the public derive benefit, may be considered a charity'[6] was conclusively rejected.

In *Morice* v. *Bishop of Durham* the testatrix had bequeathed her residuary personalty for 'such objects of benevolence and liberality as [her executor] the Bishop of Durham in his own discretion, should most approve of'. At the Rolls, the arguments of Sir

[1] In *Jones* v. *Williams* (1767), Ambl. 651, 652. See also *Turner* v. *Ogden* (1787), 1 Cox, 316, 317, *per* Kenyon M.R.

[2] (1792), 4 Bro. C.C. 67, 70.

[3] (1801), 6 Ves. 194.

[4] *Ibid.* 198, *per* Lord Eldon. But cf. his judgment in *Morice* v. *Bishop of Durham* (1805), 10 Ves. 522; discussed below, pp. 125 ff.

[5] (1804), 9 Ves. 399; (1805), 10 Ves. 522. The decision is very fully reported.

[6] (1805), 10 Ves. 522, 523, *per* Richards *arguendo*. 'Mr Richards' was probably Richard Richards, who was later to become Lord Chief Baron.

Samuel Romilly[1] for the next-of-kin, Mr Richards[2] for the Bishop, and Mr Mitford for the Attorney-General,[3] are significant for one, albeit negative, reason; no counsel chose to cite the preamble to the Charitable Uses Act, 1601. Romilly argued that 'benevolence and liberality' could not possibly be equated with 'charity'. 'Benevolence' might connote charity but 'liberality' could not, since it did not suggest anything 'from which the public is to derive any benefit'.[4] In fact the intention of the testatrix was expressed in so vague a way that the court could not execute it, and even if 'benevolent' could be equated with 'charitable,' the good (benevolence) could not be separated from the bad (liberality), so that the whole gift failed.[5] In reply, Richards asserted that it was 'very difficult to define to the satisfaction of anyone, what is an object of charity'.[6] The facts of the case were, in his view, no different from *Attorney-General* v. *Peacock*,[7] where the court had enforced an indefinite trust 'for the good of the poor forever'; or *Moggridge* v. *Thackwell*,[8] where the objects were 'as loose as can be described'.[9] The testator intended to benefit only charitable objects.

The Master of the Rolls, Sir William Grant, held that the bequest was void for uncertainty. His judgment is couched in wider terms than Romilly's argument for the next-of-kin. It rejected the absolute equation of public benefit and charity, and concluded that no object had been held to be charitable which did not fall within the letter or equity of the Elizabethan preamble or which had not been expressly described by the testator as a 'charitable purpose'.

Then is this a trust for charity? Do purposes of liberality and benevolence mean the same as objects of charity? That word in its widest sense denotes all the good affections, men ought to bear towards each other; in its most restricted and common sense, relief of the poor. In neither of these senses is it employed in this Court. Here its signification is

[1] (1804), 9 Ves. 399, 400. [2] *Ibid.* 401–2.

[3] *Ibid.* Mr Mitford was to become Lord Redesdale and Lord Chancellor of Ireland. [4] (1804), 9 Ves. 399, 400.

[5] Romilly cited, *inter alia*, in support of his argument *Browne* v. *Yeall* (1791), 7 Ves. 50 n., below, pp. 125, 131; *Att.-Gen.* v. *Whorwood* (1750), 1 Ves. Sen. 534, below, p. 130; *Gwynn* v. *Cardon* (*c.* 1800?), unreported but cited in (1805), 10 Ves. 522, 533, below, p. 132. [6] Ves. 399, 402.

[7] (1675), Finch, 234, Selden Society, LXXIII, cases 300 and 440; above, pp. 88–90.

[8] (1803), 7 Ves. 36; below, p. 149. [9] (1804), 9 Ves. 399, 402.

derived chiefly from the Statute of *Elizabeth* (Stat. 43 *Eliz.* c. 4). Those purposes are considered charitable, which that Statute enumerates, or which by analogies are deemed within its spirit and intendment; and to some such purpose every bequest to charity generally shall be applied. But it is clear liberality and benevolence can find numberless objects, not included in that statute in the largest construction of it . . .[1]

The trust could be lawfully executed by bestowing the residue on objects which were not strictly charitable; it was, therefore, void for uncertainty.

On appeal before Lord Eldon, Richards, for the Bishop of Durham, attempted to meet Grant's reasoning by arguing that there were many charitable objects which were 'not within' the preamble, and that there were other objects within the preamble, such as uses for the repair of bridges and ports, which did not properly come within the meaning of the word 'charity' but fell within the description of 'liberality'. Moreover, ' "benevolence" is that sort of goodwill, peculiarly intended by "charity": especially if it is collected from the statute of *Elizabeth*.'[2] Spencer Perceval, the Attorney-General, also attacked Grant's judgment but on different grounds. He equated 'benevolence' with 'charity'; and submitted that, even if 'liberality' could include objects which were not charitable, a benevolent (i.e. charitable) object should not be defeated merely because it was coupled with one which was not charitable.

Romilly claimed that since there was no precedent governing the case, the meaning of charity should be a question of philology rather than of law. Having contrasted Dr Johnson's definition of 'liberality' with Cicero's, he concluded that its meaning was so extensive as to defy definition![3] He then formulated a description of charity, which was later to be adopted and adapted (without attribution) by Lord Macnaghten in *Pemsel*'s case.[4] Romilly said:[5]

There are four objects, within one of which all charity, to be administered in this court, must fall. First, relief of the indigent; in various ways: money: provisions: education: medical assistance; etc.; Secondly, the advancement of learning: Thirdly, the advancement of religion; and Fourthly, which is the most difficult, the advancement of objects of general public utility.

[1] (1804), 9 Ves. 399, 405.

[2] (1805), 10 Ves. 522, 524.

[3] *Ibid.* 528–9.

[4] In *Commissioners of Income Tax* v. *Pemsel* [1891], A.C. 531, 583.

[5] (1805), 10 Ves. 522, 532.

Although 'benevolence' might be synonymous with 'charity' in some contexts, it assumed a wider meaning when coupled with 'liberality':

There are various instances of liberality, that cannot be described as charity: the establishment of a Cabinet of Natural History, Anatomical Exhibitions, Galleries of Pictures, to be open to the Public: a legacy to the African Society, for acquiring information in the interior of Africa to contribute to raise the degraded state of society in that part of the world: all these are instances of liberality; but not charity.[1]

The objects of the trust were, therefore, too vague to be enforced.[2]

Lord Eldon affirmed the judgment of Grant. He thought that (with the single exception of *Browne* v. *Yeall*[3]) this was a 'new case', and agreed with the Master of the Rolls that the Court of Chancery had never executed 'a charitable purpose, unless the will contains a description of that, which the law acknowledges to be a charitable purpose; or devotes the property to purposes of charity in general'.[4] In law charity meant

either such charitable purposes as are expressed in the Statute or to purposes having analogy to those. I believe, the expression 'charitable purposes,' as used in this Court, has been applied to many acts described in that Statute, and analogous to those, not because they can with propriety be called charitable, but as that denomination is by the Statute given to all the purposes described.[5]

[1] (1805), 10 Ves. 531.

[2] Citing *inter alia, Gwynn* v. *Cardon*, an unreported Exchequer decision (*c.* 1800), 10 Ves. 522, 533, below, p. 132.

[3] (1791), 7 Ves. 50 n. In this case the testator, a Mr Bradley, bequeathed his personal estate 'to accumulate for many years; and meaning, that it should be disposed of to charitable purposes [namely, "the purchasing of such books, as by a proper disposition of them under the following directions, may have a tendency to promote the interests of virtue and religion and the happiness of mankind"], constituted a fund; expressly stating that his purpose was a charitable purpose; and confirming that by directing that charitable purpose to be carried on, as to the mode of executing it, by that Court, which according to the constitution of the country ordinarily administers property, given to charitable uses': for this statement of facts see 10 Ves. 539, *per* Lord Eldon. Nevertheless, Lord Thurlow held that the bequest was void for uncertainty, on grounds which are not clear from this report. In *Moggridge* v. *Thackwell* (1803), 7 Ves. 36, 50–1, Lord Eldon had doubted whether *Browne* v. *Yeall* was correctly decided, and had lamented the fact that no accurate account existed of that case. He was to give further expression to these hesitations in *Morice* v. *Bishop of Durham* (1805), 10 Ves. 522, 534, 539.

[4] (1805), 10 Ves. 522, 540.

[5] *Ibid.* 541.

The preamble to the Charitable Uses Act, 1601, was the quintessence of legal charity. Benevolent and liberal objects were neither within the letter nor equity of the preamble; therefore they were not charitable objects, and the trust failed for uncertainty.

After the decision in *Morice* v. *Bishop of Durham* the preamble to the Elizabethan statute figures more prominently and authoritatively in argument and judgment in charity cases. The full logic of Grant and Eldon's pronouncements gradually led to the acceptance of the view that there could be no synonym for 'charitable' and no substitute for the preamble as the source of the definition of legal charity.[1] In *James* v. *Allen*[2] a bequest to such 'benevolent' purposes 'as the trustees in their integrity and discretion may unanimously agree on', failed for uncertainty, despite Romilly's admission in *Morice* v. *Bishop of Durham*[3] that 'benevolent' and 'charitable' might be synonyms. Sir William Grant[4]

> certainly did not conceive, that, in the case of *Morice* v. *Bishop of Durham*, it was merely by the addition of the word 'liberality' that the trust was rendered uncertain, and therefore incapable of being carried into execution. . . . Nor . . . how the required concurrence of three persons in the selection of the objects does, by any necessity, exclude the appropriation of the property to purposes very different from any that are specified in the Statute of Queen Elizabeth, or that have been held to be within the analogies of that statute.

And in *Ommanney* v. *Butcher*,[5] in 1823, the Master of the Rolls, Sir Thomas Plumer, held that a residuary bequest to 'private charity' was not charitable and failed for uncertainty; the phrase 'private charity' was no more certain than 'benevolent purpose'. For

> the charities recognised by this Court are public in their nature . . . In all cases the general principle is, that the trust must be of such a tangible

[1] It was not uncommon, however, even after *Morice* v. *Bishop of Durham*, for Chancery judges to describe 'legal' charity in terms which did not exclusively rely on the preamble: see *Mellick* v. *President and Guardians of the Asylum* (1821), Jac. 180, 184, *per* Plumer M.R. ('now what are charitable uses, have been enumerated in the statute of *Elizabeth* and in *Duke*'). And in *Att.-Gen.* v. *Fowler* (1808), 15 Ves. 85, 86–7, Sir Samuel Romilly, *arguendo*, still sought to describe charity independently of the preamble: 'to the description of a charity, in the enlarged sense of this Court, two qualities are attached: 1st, it must be a public benefit; 2dly, it must be gratuitous'. See also *Doe. d. Thompson* v. *Pitcher* (1815), 6 Taunt. 359, 366–7, *per* counsel.

[2] (1817), 3 Mer. 17.

[3] (1804), 9 Ves. 399, 400, 401–2; above p. 123.

[4] (1817), 3 Mer. 17, 18–19.

[5] (1823), Turn. and Russ. 260.

nature as that the Court can deal with it; when it is mixed up with general moral duty it is not the subject of the jurisdiction of a Court of Justice.[1]

Ommanney v. *Butcher* is an extreme case, which is not easy to justify in principle or precedent.[2] *Vezey* v. *Jamson*,[3] where the Vice Chancellor, Sir John Leach, held that a trust for 'charitable or public purposes' was not charitable and must fail as being 'so general and undefined'[4] that it could not be executed by the Court of Chancery, is more significant in the history of the law of charity; for it confirmed the fundamental distinction drawn in *Morice* v. *Bishop of Durham* between the trust which is charitable and for the public benefit, and the trust which merely benefits the public.[5]

[1] (1823), Turn. and Russ. 260, 273.

[2] Cf. the earlier cases of *Waldo* v. *Caley* (1809), 16 Ves. 206 ('charitable purposes, as well of a public as a private nature'); *Johnston* v. *Swann* (1818), 3 Madd. 457 (for 'public and private charities as the executors may think fit'). *Waldo* v. *Caley* was cited in argument but not in Plumer's judgment in *Ommanney* v. *Butcher*. And see the later cases of *Jemmit* v. *Verril* (1826), Ambl. (Blunt ed.) 585 n.; *Horde* v. *Earl of Suffolk* (1833), 2 Myl. and K. 59; *Ellis* v. *Selby* (1836), 1 Myl. and Cr. 286.

See generally, W. R. A. Boyle, *Law of Charities* (London, 1837), 295–7.

[3] (1822), 1 Sim. and Stu. 69.

[4] (1822), 1 Sim. and Stu. 69, 71.

[5] On which, see below, pp. 129 ff.

CHAPTER IX

THE INFLUENCE OF THE MORTMAIN ACT, 1736, ON THE DEFINITION OF CHARITY

THE judiciary initiated and welcomed the Georgian mortmain statute. Yet they made little attempt to limit the class of objects which the law had hitherto deemed to be charitable, for the terms of the Mortmain Act, 1736, enabled them to protect the interests of the family by characterising the object of the testator's bounty as charitable. This had the immediate effect of avoiding the devise and causing the property to result to the heir or the next-of-kin.[1] Thus, in *Jones* v. *Williams*,[2] in 1767, Lord Camden was asked to consider whether a bequest of £1,000, to be paid from the sale of land,[3] for bringing spring water from St Arvans or elsewhere to the town of Chepstow for the use of the inhabitants for ever, was charitable. He held that it was, and that consequently it was void. Again in *Turner* v. *Odgen*[4] a legacy payable out of land, for preaching a sermon on Ascension Day, for keeping the chimes of the church in repair, for the playing of certain psalms and for paying choristers was categorised as charitable and struck down; and in *Townley* v. *Bedwell*[5] a devise of a mixed fund of realty and personalty to establish a perpetual botanical garden was avoided as being a devise to charity. Conversely, there is no reported case of a devise being saved from the Mortmain Act, 1736, by a finding that the particular public object was not charitable.

It was not surprising, therefore, that objects which were in danger of being stigmatised as charitable often sought to divest themselves of this unwelcome status. An argument that the devise was not charitable but was to individuals *eo nomine* was not uncommon, although generally it only succeeded if the devisees

[1] Cf. *Townley* v. *Bedwell* (1801), 6 Ves. 194; and Samuel Romilly's comment *arguendo*, in *Morice* v. *Bishop of Durham* (1805), 10 Ves. 522, 533. And see the comment, below, p. 132, n. 3.

[2] (1767), Ambl. 651; above, p. 122.

[3] And, therefore, within the mischief of the Mortmain Act; above, p. 118.

[4] (1787), 1 Cox, 316; see also *Howse* v. *Chapman* (1799), 4 Ves. 542, 1 Ves. Jun. Supp. 456.

[5] (1801), 6 Ves. 194.

chanced to be the testator's poor relations[1] whose interests the judges were content to protect. So, in *Grieves* v. *Case*[2] the court refused to accept that the testator, who had devised land to poor dissenting ministers of certain chapels, intended to benefit personally those ministers alive at the date of his death; the devise was charitable, and the land accordingly passed to the heir-at-law. A similar plea was more successful in *Blandford* v. *Fackerell*,[3] where the objects of the testator's bounty included members of his family. A testator had devised a mixed fund to trustees to take 'a proper and commodious house' in Bridgewater for the reception and education of specific children and grandchildren and also to admit and take into the school a number of other boys and girls who were in need. The heir-at-law argued, citing *Grieves* v. *Case*, that this was nothing 'more than a public charity, with a particular benefit to such of the founder's kin whose situation makes them the objects of a public charity'.[4] Lord Loughborough held that, though the devise was void in so far as it was for the general purpose of establishing a charity, the testator's children and grandchildren 'were entitled to the benefit of the dispositions made in their favour by the said will, so far as the objects thereof were not too remote . . .'.[5]

After *Morice* v. *Bishop of Durham*, other potential charities sought to escape from the coils of the Mortmain Act, 1736, by claiming that they were public as distinct from charitable bodies. The British Museum, argued Sir Charles Wetherell, the Solicitor-General, in *Trustees of the British Museum* v. *White*,[6] was 'founded by the munificence of the State for the benefit of the public. Every gift for the use of the public is not, necessarily, a charity. There must be something in the nature of relief to constitute a charity',[7] and the British Museum did not relieve anyone or anybody! The Master of the Rolls, Sir John Leach, in characteristically cavalier fashion, dismissed this argument on the unsupportable ground that 'every gift for a public purpose, whether local or

[1] See appendix K, pp. 260–2 for a discussion of these cases.

[2] (1792), 4 Bro. C.C. 67, 1 Ves. Jun. 548, 2 Cox, 301.

[3] (1793), 4 Bro. C.C. 394; also reported in 2 Ves. 238 (where the defendant is called *Thackerell*).

[4] *Ibid.* 396–7, *per* John Mitford, *arguendo.*

[5] *Ibid.* 397 n.

[6] (1826), 2 Sim. and Stu. 594.

[7] *Ibid.* 594.

general, is within the 9th Geo. 2nd, although not a charitable use within the common and narrow sense of those words.'[1]

The attitude of the courts was markedly different, however, when confronted with a bequest of pure personalty (as in *Morice* v. *Bishop of Durham*) or a devise of realty which was exempt from the Mortmain Act, 1736 (such as a devise to an Oxbridge college). The interests of the heir or next-of-kin could only be protected by declaring the object to be non-charitable; the transfer would then fail and the property would result to them. In these circumstances Chancery judges were prepared to restrict, when precedent permitted, the class of charitable objects.[2] If the number of such cases is not large, the attitude of the courts appears to be consistent.

An early example is *Attorney-General* v. *Whorwood*[3] in 1750. A testator had devised[4] the residue of his real and personal estate, including his house in the village of Denton, to University College, Oxford, to enable the senior fellow, who had to be a divine aged at least forty, to live there, and while there, to distribute cordials

[1] (1826), 2 Sim. and Stu. 594, 596.

[2] A curious group of cases is that in which the testator devised or bequeathed property for the erection and maintenance of a monument. Early authority (see 3 Inst. 202) suggested that such devises and bequests were *sui generis*, akin to funeral expenses, which were allowable before 'any debt or duty whatsoever, for that is *opus pium* or *charitativum*', and which did not abate with charitable and private bequests (see *Masters* v. *Masters* (1718), 1 P. Wms. 421, below, p. 156.) After the Mortmain Act, 1736, however, judges described devises to erect and maintain monuments as vainglorious, given to perpetuate the testator's memory, and generally refused to characterise them as charitable. 'It would be very unfortunate', said Lord Hardwicke in *Durour* v. *Motteux* (1749), 1 Ves. Sen. 320, 321–2, 'if that part [for charity], which is really good, were it not for the above-mentioned inconvenience [the Mortmain Act, 1736], should be set aside as void; and at the same time it should happen, that the worst, such as tends only to perpetuate the vanity of the testator, should be established.'

However, the courts contrived to find other reasons for refusing to uphold such a devise or bequest; for example, that a devise to keep up a tomb was inextricably intermingled with a void devise for charitable uses; see *Durour* v. *Motteux* (1749), 1 Ves. Sen. 320, *semble* (note that Lord Hardwicke's observations at pp. 321–2 must be read with counsel's argument); *Gravenor* v. *Hallum* (1767), Ambl. 643; *Mellick* v. *President of the Asylum* (1821), Jac. 180; but cf. *Doe. d. Thompson* v. *Pitcher* 3 M. and S. 407, 410–11, *per* Lord Ellenborough C.J., 6 Taunt. 359, 370, *per* Gibbs C.J.

[3] (1750), 1 Ves. Sen. 534; Ves. Sen. Suppl. 236.

[4] The dates of the will and later codicil do not appear. But it is apparent, from the argument and judgment, that there was never any question of the application of the Mortmain Act, 1736; so that the will must either have been made before the Act or it was thought that this must be a devise to an exempt charity.

and pamphlets of good morals and piety to the poor. He was also required to provide annual entertainments for fellows in the house, which the college was enjoined not to sell. The college argued that the devise was for academic purposes, and that although the regulations surrounding it were absurd, the absurdity should not render the devise void. Counsel for the defendants, the testator's heir-at-law and next-of-kin, while admitting that a devise to a college for the encouragement of learning was charitable, argued that this was a trust which should not be established by a court of equity:[1]

When a man will settle his estate in this odd, whimsical way, the court ought not to establish it: it is locking up property, which is against the policy of the law of England. The court has refused carrying into execution a particular turn of mind, though it was not a superstitious or illegal, but an indifferent use; as to feed sparrows etc., especially as this is for ever. It would be a reproach to a court of justice and policy of the nation to suffer keeping up for ever a trust for such a purpose as that or as this, which is only a charity *ad bibendum et edendum.*

Lord Hardwicke accepted that the devise could only be upheld if the objects were charitable, but he expressed grave doubts whether a gift to enable a fellow to live comfortably in a house which the college could not alienate was any 'good to the college or to the public'. He left open the question whether the endowment could be applied *cy-près* under the sign manual. But on a rehearing in 1756, Lord Northington, then Henley Lord Keeper, held that 'the regulations endorsed on the codicil were inconsistent with the constitutions of the College',[2] and that consequently the trust was wholly void.

In all other cases where the trust was found to be non-charitable the disputed disposition fell outside the Mortmain Act, 1736. Such were *Morice* v. *Bishop of Durham*,[3] *James* v. *Allen*[4] and *Vezey* v. *Jamson*.[5] And in *Browne* v. *Yeall*,[6] in 1791, where a testator had bequeathed personal estate to trustees for the purchase

[1] (1750), 1 Ves. Sen. 534, 536. Counsel then cited *Att.-Gen.* v. *Oakover* (1736), unreported, where the court refused to establish a stipend to maintain choristers 'as the choristers never were allowed in parochial churches'. The analogy is not a close one as the trust in *Att.-Gen.* v. *Oakover* may well have been illegal or impossible to execute; but there was no *cy-près* application.

[2] (1756), Ves. Sen. Supp. 236, 240. And see Lord Eldon's observations in *Morice* v. *Bishop of Durham* (1805), 10 Ves. 522, 538.

[3] (1805), 10 Ves. 522; above, pp. 125 ff.

[4] (1817), 3 Mer. 17; above, p. 126.

[5] (1822), 1 Sim. and Stu. 69; above, p. 127.

[6] (1791), 7 Ves. 50 n.; above p. 125, n. 3.

of such books as might promote the interests of virtue, religion and the happiness of mankind, Lord Thurlow said that he did not know what books did promote the happiness of mankind, and held that the bequest failed for uncertainty. Similarly, in *Gwynn* v. *Cardon*[1] the Court of Exchequer held that a sum of money 'given by will, to be employed in giving prizes by the President of the Royal Academy for the best examples of the fine arts, sculpture and painting, or one of them, . . . was expressed in so vague a way, that . . . it could not be executed, and was void'; as was 'a legacy to the African Society, for acquiring information in the interior of Africa to contribute to raise the degraded state of society in that part of the world'.[2]

It is paradoxical that the Mortmain Act, 1736, should have persuaded the courts to preserve for posterity a liberal definition of legal charity. But the general desire to protect the interests of the heir and the next-of-kin from the claims of rapacious charities could generally best be fulfilled by categorising the object of the testator's bounty as charitable.[3] Consequently there was little judicial enthusiasm for any attempt to restrict the class of charitable objects which had been established in an age whose social aspirations and ideals were far removed from those of Hanoverian England. Only when the charity could be defeated were such attempts made. *Morice* v. *Bishop of Durham*,[4] for example, drove a wedge between the charitable and public trust and thereby restricted the legal definition of charity, but its immediate result was to benefit the testator's next-of-kin at the expense of charity. In the long term, the legal consequences of that decision were subtle and far-reaching. Whether Grant and Eldon's restrictive definition of charity was inspired by their desire to defeat the particular bequest must be speculative. What is certain is that their reliance on the preamble of the Charitable Uses Act, 1601,

[1] Unreported, but cited by Romilly, *arguendo*, in *Morice* v. *Bishop of Durham* (1805), 10 Ves. 522, 533. *Gwynn* v. *Cardon* was decided only 'a few years ago' (*c*. 1800?).

[2] Cited by Samuel Romilly, *arguendo*, in *Morice* v. *Bishop of Durham* (1805), 10 Ves. 522, 531. The name and date of the case is not known.

[3] This was, of course, not the only way to have protected their interests. If the courts had held the devise to be non-charitable, they could have also held that the devise nevertheless failed because the objects of the trust were too uncertain. Cf. *Morice* v. *Bishop of Durham*, above, and *Re Endacott* [1960], Ch. 232.

[4] (1804), 9 Ves. 399; (1805), 10 Ves. 522; above, p. 122.

set the fashion for their successors. The equity, or 'spirit' of the preamble, as it was to be called, was elevated into the Delphic oracle of legal charity. Cases such as *Morice* v. *Bishop of Durham* and *Vezey* v. *Jamson*[1] helped to persuade even those Victorian judges who were lukewarm in their admiration for the ideals of the legislators of the Mortmain Act, 1736,[2] that 'the limits assigned to the statute of Elizabeth are sufficiently extensive to take in almost every act, purpose, or object which can be considered as having any legitimate connection with charity'.[3] The spirit of the preamble could, it was thought, unerringly distinguish the charitable from the public trust.

It has not been my task in this book to trace the development of the law after the final retirement of Lord Eldon from the woolsack. But a cursory study of the later cases, including those of very recent years, will reveal how tantalising the legacy of *Morice* v. *Bishop of Durham* has been.[4] That case, and its successors, have bequeathed to future lawyers the thankless, often impossible, task of distinguishing the charitable gift (which must be *pro bono publico*) from the gift which is merely for the public benefit. This antithesis would have puzzled Francis Moore, Nottingham and Hardwicke, as it still puzzles contemporary judges.

[1] (1822), 1 Sim. and Stu. 69; above, p. 127.

[2] Including W. Page Wood V.C. and Lord Romilly M.R.: see *Marsh* v. *Att.-Gen.* (1860), 2 J. and H. 61; *Sewell* v. *Crewe-Read* (1866), L.R. 3 Eq. 60.

[3] W. R. A. Boyle, *A Practical Treatise on the Law of Charities* (London, 1857), 60.

[4] The Mortmain and Charitable Uses Act, 1888 (51 and 52 Vict. c. 42), repealed the Charitable Uses Act, 1601; but s. 13(2) apparently preserved the preamble. The 1888 Act was, however, in turn repealed by the Charities Act, 1960 (8 and 9 Eliz. II c. 58). By s. 38(4) of the 1960 Act: 'Any reference in any enactment or document to a charity within the meaning, purview and interpretation of the Charitable Uses Act, 1601, or of the preamble to it, shall be construed as a reference to a charity within the meaning which the word bears as a legal term according to the law of England and Wales.' But, although the preamble is repealed, 'the somewhat ossifactory classification [of the preamble]... survives in the decided cases': see *Re Hopkins* [1965], Ch. 669, 678, *per* Wilberforce J.; and *Tudor on Charities*, ed. the late Douglas H. McMullen, Spencer G. Maurice and David B. Parker, 6th ed. (London, 1967), 5–8.

CHAPTER X

THE DEVELOPMENT OF THE LAW OF CHARITY, 1700–1827: THE PRIVILEGES OF CHARITY

THROUGHOUT this period vigorous attempts were made to restrict the scope of the privileges anciently awarded to charity. But precedent enabled the majority of them to survive. Even Lord Northington, the most zealous of the supporters of the Mortmain Act, 1736, was uncomfortably aware that the principle that settled rules of construction should not be disturbed was of paramount importance; he would not 'shake foundations' and overturn the 'old cases,' or the most disastrous consequences would ensue.[1] And Lord Eldon considered[2]

> this principle is of so much importance in administering the justice of the country, that according to my notion, if there has been not merely a variety of cases, but even only one ancient case, and there has been practice and experience in favour of it, it ought to be adhered to.

Some privileges, because they were so well established, escaped the faintest murmur of criticism. So, for example, there was never any question that the Chancellor would hear any charitable suit even though the amount in dispute was less than forty shillings, and no decision suggested that the analogy of any statute of limitations or the doctrine of laches should bar a claim by a charity.[3] In contrast, many of the 'old' *cy-près* cases were closely scrutinised and criticised; but, though characterised as incomprehensible, they were reluctantly followed.[4]

Exceptionally, however, the courts were able to restrict the ambit of a privilege: oral wills devising land to charity were not upheld as valid appointments *inter vivos* after the enactment of the Statute of Frauds in 1677;[5] debts were to be paid before

[1] See, for example, *Att.-Gen.* v. *Tancred* (1757), 1 Eden, 10; *Att.-Gen.* v. *Bradley* (1760), 1 Eden, 482; above, p. 106, below, p. 135.

[2] In *Att.-Gen.* v. *Mayor of Bristol* (1820), 2 Jac. and W. 294, 318.

[3] See Lord Cranworth L.C.'s comments on the 'old law' in *St Mary Magdalen, Oxford* v. *Att.-Gen.* (1857), 6 H.L.C. 189, 207.

[4] See below, p. 144.

[5] See below, p. 136.

charitable legacies, which were also required to abate in proportion with private legacies on a deficiency of assets;[1] and some of the restrictions on the defence of *bona fide* purchase,[2] whose origin may simply have been the pages of Francis Moore's *Reading*, are never mentioned in any report during this period and passed into decent oblivion.

The perfection of imperfect instruments

The Chancellor would not allow any transfer to charitable uses to fail simply because it was formally defective,[3] and he continued to rely on the language of the Elizabethan charity statute, 43 Elizabeth I c. 4, in order to perfect imperfect *inter vivos* and testamentary instruments. So, in *Attorney-General* v. *Tancred*,[4] the court upheld as a declaration or appointment *inter vivos* a conveyance which was defective in that the land had been 'limited to certain officers of the corporation and not to the corporate body.'[5] No 'form or ceremony' should defeat a charitable trust.

The seventeenth-century cases, establishing this principle, were unpopular; but most of them stood firm despite protestation and complaint. Lord Northington admitted in 1760 that:[6]

> It is true, and I am sorry for it, that there are old precedents in this court, where, by a perverse and mistaken construction of the statute of *Elizabeth*, this Court enabled persons to give to charities, who had no power to do so by [common] law; and it is as true that these precedents not only injured private families, but became a public nuisance, which called upon the legislature to interpose and stop them . . . But I found the equity of this Court liberal and impartial, and no respecter of persons; and, please God, I will leave it so.

In some cases, however, the Chancellor was able to cut back

[1] See below, p. 156.

[2] See above, pp. 97 ff.

[3] See above, pp. 60 ff.

[4] (1757), 1 Eden, 10. See also *Att.-Gen.* v. *Hickman* (1732), 2 Eq. Cas. Abr. 193; *Doyley* v. *Att.-Gen.* (1735), *ibid.* 194, 4 Viner Abr. 485, pl. 16.

[5] (1757), 1 Eden, 10, 14. For other cases, see *Piggot* v. *Prentice* (1717), Gilb. Rep. 137; *Att.-Gen.* v. *Burdet* (1717), 2 Vern. 755; *Att.-Gen.* v. *Hickman* (1732), 2 Eq. Cas. Abr. 193; *Lloyd* v. *Spillet* (1734), 3 P. Wms. 346, 2 Eq. Cas. Abr. 241; *Att.-Gen.* v. *Tancred* (1757), 1 Eden, 10.

[6] In *Att.-Gen.* v. *Bradley* (1760), 1 Eden, 482, 487. See also his observations in *Att.-Gen.* v. *Tancred* (1757), 1 Eden, 10, 14–15. For statements in a similar vein, see *Att.-Gen.* v. *Master and Wardens of the Skinners' Co.* (1820), 5 Madd. 173, 200, *per* Leach V.C.; (1827), 2 Russ. 407, 420, *per* Lord Eldon L.C.

the old law. Such was *Attorney-General* v. *Barnes* (or *Bains*) in 1708.[1] It will be remembered that a series of seventeenth-century decisions had upheld a void will as a valid appointment *inter vivos*, even though that will had been made before the enactment of the Wills Act, 1540.[2] In *Attorney-General* v. *Barnes*, a Dr Johnson had devised freeholds to Sidney Sussex College, Cambridge, 'to maintain two scholars, to augment vicarages, and to buy presentations, and to maintain widows'. The will was void since it had not been attested in the presence of three witnesses, although it had been confirmed by a codicil duly executed and attested.[3] Lord Cowper refused to uphold the void will as a valid appointment *inter vivos*, for the testator 'intended to dispose by will; that the writing imported a will, and being void as a will, could not operate as an appointment'.[4] There was a conflict between the Charitable Uses Act, 1601, and the Statute of Frauds, 1677; and the former being an earlier statute, must give way. Lord Cowper, who had little understanding of the earlier cases, would not[5]

> break in upon the Statute of Frauds and Perjuries in this case, as there are no instances where men are so easily imposed upon as at the time of their dying, under the pretence of charity . . .
>
> It is true, the charity of judges have carried several cases on the 43 Eliz. great lengths, and this occasioned the distinction between operating by will and appointment, which surely the makers of that statute never thought of.

Barnes was followed in *Jenner* v. *Harper*[6] in 1714, where a tenant in tail had devised rent payable out of land to a charity. The will was void, not being attested by three witnesses. Lord Harcourt would not uphold the will as an appointment, even though it was made and the testator had died before the Statute of Frauds. 'It would', he considered, 'be very dangerous to allow of nuncupative wills of lands',[7] especially if a rent was charged to a charity since a rent could only pass by deed.[8]

In contrast an unattested, or improperly attested, will devising

[1] (1708), 2 Vern. 597, Prec. Ch. 270, Eq. Cas. Abr. 97, pl. 7.

[2] See above, p. 65.

[3] Statute of Frauds (29 Car. II c. 3), § 19, as interpreted in *Lee* v. *Libb* (1689), Carthew. 35.

[4] (1708), 2 Vern. 597, 598.

[5] (1708), Prec. Ch. 270, 272.

[6] (1714), 1 P. Wms. 247.

[7] *Ibid.* 248.

[8] See above, p. 70.

unsurrendered copyholds[1] to charity was still upheld as an appointment *inter vivos*.[2] The Statute of Frauds, 1677, did not extend to copyhold lands.[3] Yet, mused Lord Hardwicke in *Attorney-General* v. *Andrews*,[4] if the old cases were 'now originally to be considered, courts of law and equity would not have gone so far; and it may be wished it was altered, as it is subject to the same inconvenience as a devise of freehold lands'.

This desire 'to alter' the cases is also evident from a study of *Attorney-General* v. *Sutton*[5] and *Attorney-General* v. *Lady Downing*.[6] In *Sutton*'s case, the testator had devised certain legal and equitable entail estates in Suffolk to his nephew, with remainder to charity. The nephew suffered a recovery and consequently, it was alleged, barred the charity. If the charity was not barred, argued Peere Williams, 'the greatest inconvenience would follow . . . [and] a perpetuity would be created, since none would buy if the charity could not be barred'.[7] The House of Lords unanimously accepted his argument that the recovery barred the legal estate. But the fate of the equitable estate was not so easily decided. Lord Harcourt, for example, considered that the recovery would defeat the charity,[8] but on the vote the Bishops 'made a majority' for the charity.[9] After a retrial in the Exchequer,[10] the Barons held that the recovery was void and did not bar the equitable estate, 'being contrary to the [charitable] trust created by the will'.

Attorney-General v. *Lady Downing*[11] had a less happy outcome

[1] 'The method by which copyhold lands were conveyed was peculiar. The copyholder surrendered his lands into the hands of his lord who then admitted the grantee. . . . Copyhold lands were devisable by the testator's making a surrender to the lord to the use of his will.' (See A. W. B. Simpson, *An Introduction to the History of the Land Law* (Oxford, 1961), 160.) The need for a surrender was abolished by 55 Geo. III c. 192 (1815.)

[2] See *Att.-Gen.* v. *Barnes* (1708), 2 Vern. 597, 598, *per* Lord Cowper; *Tuffnell* v. *Page* (1740), 2 Atk. 37, 38, *per* Lord Hardwicke; *Att.-Gen.* v. *Sawtell* (1742), *ibid.* 497.

[3] *Tuffnell* v. *Page* (1740), *ibid.* 37.

[4] (1748), 1 Ves. Sen. 225, 226, Ves. Sen. Supp. 116. See also *Wagstaff* v. *Wagstaff* (1724), 2 P. Wms. 258, 259, *per* Lord Macclesfield; *Habergham* v. *Vincent* (1793), 2 Ves. Jun. 204, 232, *per* Buller J., giving an opinion to the Lord Chancellor.

[5] (1721), 1 P. Wms. 754.

[6] (1769), Ambl. 571.

[7] (1721), 1 P. Wms. 754, 761–2.

[8] *Ibid.* 765–6.

[9] *Ibid.* 766 n.

[10] An information had originally been brought in the Exchequer to establish the charitable gift.

[11] (1769), Ambl. 571.

for the charities. In that case the testator had devised unsurrendered copyholds to persons in tail, with an ultimate remainder over to Downing College, a charity which was not yet in existence, not having received its charter of incorporation.[1] Lord Camden adopted the opinion of the Master of the Rolls, Sir Thomas Sewell, and Chief Justice Wilmot, and accepted that this imperfect testamentary instrument could not be upheld as a valid appointment *inter vivos*. Otherwise the court would be placed in an impossible situation; it could either 'supply the surrender *in toto*', or wait 'till the charity takes place, which might never have happened, for the preceding tenant in tail might have barred the charity'.[2] It would do neither, so that the remainder failed.

The application of charitable funds cy-près

During this period the doctrine of *cy-près* was subjected to close judicial analysis.[3] There are a few examples of what modern lawyers would call *supervening impossibility* (where the objects of the trust subsequently failed), and here the courts appeared ready to accept a *cy-près* application of charitable funds without any further question.[4] In the great majority of cases, however, the objects of the charitable trust *initially* failed, in some cases because of illegality, in others because of indefiniteness or impossibility. And in these cases the courts appeared to apply different principles.[5] The years between 1790 and 1805 were particularly influential in this area of the law. Sir Richard Pepper Arden, Master of the Rolls, and Lord Eldon, Lord Chancellor, reformulated the principles underlying the ancient doctrine and established the rule that the endowments of a charitable trust, whose objects initially failed, would be applied *cy-près* only if the donor had a general intention to benefit charity. Reformulated in this way, these

[1] It was not until 22 September 1800 that the Great Seal was affixed to the College's charter.

[2] (1769), Ambl. 571, 573.

[3] Many lawyers considered *cy-près* to be the most important part of the law of charities: see W. R. A. Boyle's preface to his *Law of Charities*, 1st ed. (London, 1837).

[4] And without inquiring whether the testator had any general charitable intention: see *Att.-Gen.* v. *Green* (1789), 2 Bro. C.C. 492; *Att.-Gen.* v. *Boultbee* (1794), 2 Ves. 380, 3 Ves. 220; *Att.-Gen.* v. *Hicks* (1809–1810), 3 Bro. C.C. 166 n.; *Hayter* v. *Trego* (1830), 5 Russ. 113.

[5] See below, pp. 144 ff.

principles appeared to be novel. Indeed many lawyers were led to conclude, quite prematurely, that the doctrine of *cy-près* had been 'much restrained', even substantially modified;[1] no longer, it was thought, would the interests of the donor's family be subordinated to the interests of charity. But precedent proved too strong, and the 'old cases' were once again followed.[2]

The seventeenth-century cases were puzzling. The eighteenth-century judge had no account of cases like the *Feoffees to Impropriations*' case,[3] and other important decisions were reported in a cursory and incomplete fashion.[4] It is not surprising that he did not appreciate that Davenport[5] and North's[6] decisions were inspired by a different philosophy. Davenport and North were anxious to apply funds *cy-près* if the '*good uses*' still subsisted, despite the '*improper manner*' of their employment. Through these phrases, they were seeking to express their view that if the particular donor intended to benefit a charity (for example the Established Church) that was enough—even though that donor had foolishly chosen an illegal or improper method of doing so (for example, by establishing feoffees as a corporation.)[7] They were determined to 'find' a general charitable intention, and were not concerned to nurture the selfish ambitions of the heir and next-of-kin. Chief Justice Wilmot, in *Attorney-General* v. *Downing*,[8] expressed the bewilderment of his contemporaries, whose sentiments were quite the opposite, when he said of their decisions:

The right of the heir at law seems to arise as naturally in this case as in any other; but instead of favouring him as in all other cases, the testator is made to disinherit him for a charity he never thought of; perhaps for a charity repugnant to the testator's intention, and which directly opposes and encounters the charity he meant to establish. But the doctrine is now so fully settled, that it cannot be departed from.

[1] See, for example, *Att.-Gen.* v. *Minshull* (1798), 4 Ves. 11; below p. 155.

[2] See below, pp. 144–51.

[3] See above, p. 77. And in *Mills* v. *Farmer* (1815), 1 Mer. 55, 101, Lord Eldon thought that the report of the case of 'one Jones', a reference to *Att.-Gen.* v. *Gaynor Jones* (above, p. 83), 'is not now to be found'.

[4] Such as *Venables*' case, above, p. 76; *Att.-Gen.* v. *Peacock*, above, p. 88; *Att.-Gen.* v. *Baxter*, above, p. 81.

[5] Davenport gave the leading judgment in the *Feoffees to Impropriations*' case, above, p. 77 ff.

[6] North decided *Att.-Gen.* v. *Baxter*, above p. 81.

[7] *Feoffees to Impropriations*' case, above, p. 77.

[8] (1767), 1 Wilm. 1, 32. See also *Att.-Gen.* v. *Herrick* (1772), Ambl. 712.

(i) *Initial failure of a charitable object*

It has been seen that a charitable trust could fail for a number of reasons. Francis Bacon had accepted that the terms of a charitable trust could be altered if it was *impossible* to carry them out.[1] His definition of impossibility was a generous one, but, during this period, that requirement was strictly construed. 'The court must despair of attaining the primary object, before it can enter into the question in what other way the fund is to be applied.'[2] As Lord Eldon said in *Attorney-General* v. *Whiteley*:[3]

> I do not apprehend, it is competent to this court, as long as it can find any means of applying the charitable fund to the charity, as created by the founder, upon any general notion, that any other application would be more beneficial to the inhabitants of the place, to change the nature of the charity.

Accordingly, he refused to order any part of the endowments of Leeds Grammar School, founded for teaching the learned languages, to be used to employ masters to teach French or German.[4]

The courts also held, as they had in the previous century, that funds might be applied *cy-près* if the objects of the trust were too indefinite to enforce,[5] although there was now considerable doubt whether a *cy-près* scheme should be settled by the court[6] or by the Crown under the sign manual.[7] Equally the principle of the *Feoffees to Impropriations*' case[8] that funds devoted for illegal religious purposes could be applied for the sustenance of the Established Church remained sacrosanct, though some Erastian judges were embarrassed by the conflicting claims of their religion and their family. During this period, however, the Toleration Act, 1688,[9] was to restrict significantly the class of illegal, religious charities.

[1] See above, p. 74.
[2] Boyle, *Law of Charities*, 168–9.
[3] (1805), 11 Ves. 241, 251. See also *Att.-Gen.* v. *Coopers' Co.* (1812), 19 Ves. 187, 2 Ves. Jun. Supp. 559; *Att.-Gen.* v. *Earl of Mansfield* (1827), 2 Russ. 501; and, cf. *Att.-Gen.* v. *Bishop of Chester* (1785), 1 Bro. C.C. 444; *Att.-Gen.* v. *Oglander* (1790), 3 Bro. C.C. 166.
[4] It was highly 'technical' decisions like these which led Brougham to inveigh against the supervisory jurisdiction of the Court of Chancery over charities.
[5] See below, p. 148.
[6] This was an application of *judicial cy-près*; above, pp. 72 ff. and below, p. 151.
[7] This was an application of *prerogative cy-près*; above, pp. 75 ff. and below, p. 151.
[8] See above, p. 77.
[9] 1 Will. & M. c. 18. See also 9 & 10 Will. III, c. 32.

The Toleration Act, 1688, exempted dissenters, but not Roman Catholics, from penalties imposed by earlier statutes and protected them from prosecution in the ecclesiastical courts on making a declaration of fidelity to the Crown and a profession of Christian belief. It did not specifically validate gifts to dissenting sects, and despite the reversal by the House of Lords of North's judgment in *Attorney-General* v. *Baxter*,[1] opinions were still expressed in the early decades of the eighteenth century that such gifts were not charitable. In *Attorney-General* v. *Eades*,[2] in 1713, Lord Harcourt 'did not incline to think' that a gift to poor Anabaptists could be a 'good charity'.

He was not satisfied to establish a charity of this kind, as it might be a means to draw people from the church; that it was one thing to tolerate dissenters, and another to establish a perpetual fund for their support.

Lord Harcourt's doubts did not prevail with his successors. Only twenty years later, in *Attorney-General* v. *Hickman*,[3] Lord King held that a bequest for the benefit of the work of non-conformist ministers among the poor 'and for encouraging the bringing up of some to the work of the ministry, who are designed to labour in God's Vineyard, among the dissenters', was charitable.[4] The legislature had, by statute, 'thought proper so far to countenance [non-conformists] as a denomination of Christians as to extend the toleration to them'.[5]

If after *Hickman*'s case trusts for the benefit of Presbyterians, Baptists and Congregationalists were characterised as charitable,[6] it was often with the mildest degree of enthusiasm. Lord Eldon was a particularly fervent champion of the Church of England's unique position, and his Erastianism and suspicion of dissenting sects are apparent in his judicial decisions. In *Attorney-General* v.

[1] *Sub nom. Att.-Gen.* v. *Hughes* (1689), 2 Vern. 105: 'the money then remaining in court ordered to be paid out to Mr Baxter, to be by him distributed according to the will.'

[2] Unreported; quoted by counsel in *Att.-Gen.* v. *Cock* (1751), 2 Ves. Sen. 273, 274.

[3] (1732), 2 Eq. Cas. Abr. 193, pl. 14.

[4] By this time it was so firmly established that a trust for dissenters was charitable that counsel could only attack the bequest on the ground that it purported to benefit 'all sorts of dissenters' (*ibid.* 194), and hence Jews and papists, who had been denied the benefits of the Toleration Act, 1688.

[5] *Att.-Gen.* v. *Cock* (1751), 2 Ves. Sen. 273, 276, *per* Sir John Strange M.R.

[6] *Att.-Gen.* v. *Cock* (1751), 2 Ves. Sen. 273; *Waller* v. *Childs* (1765), Ambl. 524; *Att.-Gen.* v. *Wansay* (1808), 15 Ves. 231, 2 Ves. Jun. Supp. 404.

Stepney[1] Eldon viewed with the deepest concern a bequest for the support of Welsh Circulating Schools; he was alarmed that a schoolmaster could be free of ecclesiastical licence and he warned counsel that 'a great deal is to be guarded against, before the Court can establish, and give its countenance to, the plan'.[2] But he conveniently concluded that the testator's general intention was to support religious purposes and that the Master would

> fail in executing the purpose of the Court, if he does not attend the circumstances, how far it is necessary to place checks upon such an institution, for the purpose of making it conformable to the establishments of the country... An unlicensed school would not be consistent with that view.[3]

Eldon's decision, in 1817, in *Attorney-General* v. *Pearson*[4] is an equally flagrant example of his Anglican prejudices. In that case he directed an inquiry whether a trust created in 1701 for the erection of a meeting house for the worship and service of God was established with the intention that the tenets of Unitarianism should be preached there. The Toleration Act, 1688, did not give any 'ease, benefit or advantage' to persons denying the Trinity, and excluded, therefore, Unitarians from its benefits.[5] The fact that Unitarianism was not 'tolerated' in 1701 suggested to the Lord Chancellor that the founders of the meeting house could not have intended it to be used for the maintenance of opinions impugning the Trinity. Indeed, if the intention of the founders had been to establish a meeting house for Unitarians, the trust would have been illegal and void. The Unitarian Relief Act, 1813,[6] which had repealed those parts of the Toleration Act, 1688, excluding from its benefits dissenters who denied the Trinity, 'left the common law exactly where it was'.[7]

Any trust for the support of the Jewish religion or Jewry was no less obnoxious, and Anglican judges were not averse to diverting their endowments for the sustenance of the Established Church.

[1] (1804), 10 Ves. 22.
[2] *Ibid.* 26.
[3] *Ibid.* 29.
[4] (1817), 3 Mer. 353.
[5] *Ibid.* 405–6, 411–12.
[6] 53 Geo. III c. 160.
[7] (1817), 3 Mer. 353, 408. Trusts for Unitarians created after 1813 were, however, held to be charitable: see *Shore* v. *Wilson* (1843), 9 Cl. and F. 355; cf. *Shrewsbury* v. *Hornby* (1846), 5 Hare, 406.

In the celebrated case of *Da Costa* v. *De Paz* in 1754,[1] a testator had bequeathed £1,200 for the support of a Jesuba and for the instruction of people in the Jewish religion. Lord Hardwicke enigmatically held that this was a charity which 'though not void by law, the Court could not tolerate'.[2] Accordingly, he applied the bequest *cy-près* under the sign manual[3] to an Anglican foundling hospital for the support of preachers, and the instruction of children under their care in the principles of the Christian religion.

Trusts for the maintenance of the Jewish religion, like trusts for Roman Catholic religious objects, were consequently compelled to lurk behind the anonymity of innocently absolute gifts. Despite such relieving statutes as 31 George III c. 32 in 1791,[4] trusts for the support of Rome and its religion were still deemed to be superstitious. Thus in *Cary* v. *Abbot*, in 1802,[5] a residuary bequest for the education and 'bringing-up' of poor children in the Roman Catholic faith was declared void. The 1791 Act had introduced no change in this branch of the law and had specifically declared that all uses and trusts which were illegal and superstitious before 1791 'shall continue to be so deemed'.[6] Yet the use, said the Master of the Rolls, Sir William Grant, 'is clearly charitable in its nature: viz. for poor orphan children. What vitiates it is, that they are to be educated in the Roman Catholic religion'.[7] The court therefore, as it had done in the past, directed that the fund 'must go to such use as the King shall direct. The Attorney General therefore will apply for a Sign Manual'.[8]

[1] (1754) 1 Dick. 258, Ambl. 228, 2 Swanst. 532 n. Cf. *Isaac* v. *Gompertz* (1786), cited in *Moggridge* v. *Thackwell* (1803), 7 Ves. 61, where a legacy for the support of a Jewish synagogue was applied *cy-près* under the sign manual. *Re Bedford Charity* (1819), 2 Swanst. 470, 487–8, *per* Romilly, *arguendo*. After the Jewish Relief Act, 1846 (9 & 10 Vict. c. 59) similar bequests were held to be charitable: see, for example, *Re Michel* (1860), 28 Beav. 39; and cf. *Straus.* v. *Goldsmid* (1837), 8 Sim. 614.

[2] 1 Dick. 258, 259. Cf. Lord Hardwicke's language with that of Sir Francis North in *Att.-Gen.* v. *Baxter*, above, p. 81.

[3] See below, p. 151.

[4] This statute relieved papists 'from certain penalties and disabilities to which [they] . . . are by law subject'.

[5] (1802), 7 Ves. 490.

[6] 31 Geo. III c. 32, § xvii.

[7] 7 Ves. 490, 497; see below, n. 8.

[8] 7 Ves. 490, 497. There is no indication in the report who were the eventual recipients of the royal bounty.

But cf. *De Themmines* v. *De Bonneval* (1828), 5 Russ. 288 and *West* v. *Shuttleworth* (1835), 2 Myl. and K. 684, where the Crown's claim failed and the next-of-kin succeeded; and *Bourne* v. *Keane* [1919], A.C. 815, 852, *per* Lord Birkenhead.

(ii) *The element of general charitable intention*

The cases of this period established principles of common law which stood for one hundred and fifty years, until they were recently modified by statute.[1] Judges, like Arden and Eldon, accepted that to settle a *cy-près* scheme it was no longer enough to prove the simple fact that the particular charitable object failed. They would no longer be willing *to presume* a general charitable intention; in each case it had to be shown that the donor intended to benefit charity generally and that the particular object which failed was a mere manifestation of that intention. Yet they were forced to admit that many of their predecessors' decisions, particularly those which settled a *cy-près* scheme where the charity failed because of illegality or indefiniteness, were 'strange', and seemed to conflict with these fundamental principles.

The renewed interest in the *cy-près* doctrine particularly dates from a group of cases in the last decades of the eighteenth century, which concerned the fate of charitable objects which had become impossible to execute.[2] These drew the attention of judges to the need to distinguish the testator's specific from his general charitable intention.[3] The most influential of them appears to have been *Attorney-General* v. *Bishop of Oxford* in 1786.[4] The testator had bequeathed the residue of his personalty to build a church at Wheatley, 'where the chapel now is, in such a manner as I shall hereafter direct' or for want of direction as my executors think best'. The Bishop of Oxford, as patron, opposed its erection (as did the chaplain of the church and the chapel wardens) but prayed that the money be used for the repair of the existing church and

[1] In the Charities Act, 1960, §§ 13 and 14, on which see P. H. Pettit, *Equity and the Law of Trusts* (London, 1966), 180–5; *Tudor on Charities*, 6th. ed., chap. 6.

[2] See above, p. 138.

[3] To Sir Richard Pepper Arden M.R. must be given credit for popularising the phrase *general charitable intention*. The analogy of the 'surplus' cases (below, pp. 153–6) persuaded him to distinguish a *specific charitable intention* (to benefit a particular object) from a *general charitable intention* (to give to general, indefinite charitable purposes even though the specific object failed): see, *inter alia*, *Att.-Gen.* v. *Hurst* (1790), 2 Cox, 364, 365, cited below, p. 146; *Att.-Gen.* v. *Earl of Winchelsea* (1791), 3 Bro. C.C. 373, 379; *Att.-Gen.* v. *Boultbee* (1794), 2 Ves. 380, 387–8. Cf. the more archaic language of Buller J. in *Att.-Gen.* v. *Goulding* (1788), 2 Bro. C.C. 428, 430, cited below, p. 145.

[4] Cited and discussed in *Corbyn* v. *French* (1799), 4 Ves. 418, 431–2. See also *Att.-Gen.* v. *Boultbee* (1794), 2 Ves. 380, 3 Ves. 220. Cf. *Att.-Gen.* v. *Montague* (1738), West, 587; *Brantham* v. *East Burgold* (1794), unreported, cited in 2 Ves. 388; *Att.-Gen.* v. *Mayor and City of London* (1790), 3 Bro. C.C. 171.

for the augmentation of the chaplain's stipend. The next-of-kin insisted that the testator's intention should be scrupulously followed and argued that, if the Bishop refused his permission for the erection of the church, the bequest should fail. The Master of the Rolls, Sir Lloyd Kenyon, referred the case to the Master to report, *inter alia*, whether the Bishop's consent was essential to the testator's purpose. The action was subsequently compromised: £3,000 was set aside for the new church; £1,000 was earmarked for the chaplain's stipend; and the remainder was given to the next-of-kin.

The authority of the case seems, therefore, to be slight.[1] But the Master of the Rolls, Pepper Arden, whose judgments on *cy-près* were to be particularly influential, regarded it as support for the proposition, that money given for the support of a specific charitable object which failed would only be applied *cy-près* if it could be shown that the testator had a general charitable intention. In *Corbyn* v. *French*,[2] Arden said of *Attorney-General* v. *Bishop of Oxford*:

This decree is completely decisive, that, the object not being capable of taking effect, the fund could not be applied to any other charitable purpose. The court could not have made the decree, unless they thought, the residue was not applicable to any other charitable purpose. I will not say, it could not have been applied for repairing or sustaining the chapel; and I doubt whether Lord Kenyon said so: but beyond that purpose, or after satisfying it, this is decisive, that it could be applied to no other purpose; for if it was applicable to any other general charitable purpose or any other purpose for the benefit of that parish, except of the nature pointed out, that decree could not have been justified.

The court would not now imply a general charitable intention from the mere fact that the testator intended to benefit a particular charity. As Mr. Justice Buller had observed in *Attorney-General* v. *Goulding* in 1788:[3]

The Court has certainly thought it could vary the use, but the rule may be drawn from the cases, that wherever the Court had directed the sum given to be applied to a different use, there has been proper ground for the Court to say the use to which it has been applied is consistent with the use declared in the will, but there have been subsequent cases which have varied the rule: where, according to the intention of the testatrix's

[1] There is a further puzzle about *Att.-Gen.* v. *Bishop of Oxford*. Why was the devise not caught by the Mortmain Act, 1736 (below, p. 118)? Perhaps the will was a pre-1736 will?

[2] (1799), 4 Ves. 418, 432–3.

[3] (1788), 2 Bro. C.C. 428, 430.

applying the fund otherwise than to the persons inhabiting the houses, would be contrary to that intention, the inhabitants of the houses being the principal objects of bounty: if they cannot be supported, it is not to be given to the poor in general.

Accordingly he refused to apply for the benefit of the poor a bequest of personalty which was attached to a devise of realty and which failed with it under the Mortmain Act, 1736.[1]

Cases such as *Attorney-General* v. *Bishop of Oxford* required judges to dissect in a rigorous fashion the principles underlying the *cy-près* doctrine. Arden reformulated them in *Attorney-General* v. *Hurst*, in 1790,[2] in the following manner:

> If there is one particular object to which a testator's mind applies, as the building of a church at Wheatley, and that purpose cannot be answered, the next of kin must take, there being, in that case, *no general charitable intention*; but where, as in the case of Thetford School, and other cases, the testator intends to give all generally to charitable purposes, the increase will go *cy près*.

Four years later in *Attorney-General* v. *Minshull*[3] he reiterated that in the old cases the *cy-près* doctrine had been 'pushed to a most extravagant length; but that is now much restrained',[4] and emphasised that 'if the charitable object is incapable of taking place at the time of the testator's death, the court is not to look out, and substitute another; as they did formerly'. Nowadays 'wherever the doctrine of *cy-près* has been pressed, the Courts have thought, they must find in the will a general intention for charity predominant over the particular charity'.[5] It was, said Lord Thurlow, 'very hard indeed, that the Court should give it to other charities, because those, which were mentioned, could not take'.[6]

Judges could not understand those decisions which held that the trust failed because of illegality. Lord Eldon, in *Moggridge* v. *Thackwell*,[7] admitted that it was the cases, and not his better

[1] See above, p. 119.

[2] (1790), 2 Cox 364, 365; the italics are the reporter's. See also *Att.-Gen.* v. *Earl of Winchelsea* (1791), 3 Bro. C.C. 373, 379, *per* Pepper Arden M.R.

[3] (1798), 4 Ves. 11.

[4] *Ibid.* 14, *per* Arden M.R.; see also *Att.-Gen.* v. *Boultbee* (1794), 2 Ves. 380, 3 Ves. 220.

[5] *Att.-Gen.* v. *Andrew* (1798), 3 Ves. 633, 644, *per* counsel.

[6] *Moggridge* v. *Thackwell* (1792), 1 Ves. 464, 469.

[7] (1803), 7 Ves. 36, 96–7, where Eldon criticised the report of *Da Costa* v. *De Paz*. See also his observations in *Mills* v. *Farmer* (1815), 1 Mer. 55, 100–1.

judgment, which called upon him to say that a testator who intended to benefit a superstitious object must be deemed to have a general charitable intention. They compelled him to conclude that[1]

> [T]he testator's intention of charity was the principal intention; that he meant at all event some charity; that his unlawful purpose was a mode of disappointing it; and the mode therefore was out of the question; and the intention should be carried into effect by another mode.

Lord Thurlow's prophecy[2] that *Attorney-General* v. *Baxter*[3] would not be followed in the future therefore proved false. Yet judges had the greatest difficulty in rationalising and justifying the principle that property devoted to superstitious purposes and forfeited to the Crown should be applied *cy-près*.[4] How could it be said that the testator had, in such a case, a paramount intention to benefit charity? And why were the interests of the heir and next-of-kin so summarily ignored? In *De Garcin* v. *Lawson*,[5] Lord Loughborough, a judge never distinguished by his knowledge of English law, thought that the source of the Crown's claim was some mortmain statute, perhaps the Act of 1532[6] or that of 1736,[7] although he admitted that it was remarkable that neither statute contained any forfeiture clause. On the other hand, in *Cary* v. *Abbot*,[8] the Master of the Rolls, Sir William Grant, accepted that the Edwardian chantry statute of 1547[9] was only retroactive and must, therefore, be irrelevant. At the same time, he declined counsel's invitation to dismiss the claim of the Crown and weakly concluded that the heir or next-of-kin would only be entitled to funds devoted to illegal charitable purposes if the devise was to a superstitious use which was 'made void by statute'. And 'there is no statute making superstitious uses void generally'.[10]

[1] (1803), 7 Ves. 36, 77.

[2] *Moggridge* v. *Thackwell* (1792), 1 Ves. 464, 469, *arguendo*. The date of the will is erroneously given in Vesey as 1799; it was in fact 1779: see 3 Bro. C.C. 517. See also *Corbyn* v. *French* (1799), 4 Ves. 418, 434, *per* Pepper Arden M.R.

[3] See above, p. 81.

[4] See above, p. 87.

[5] (1798), 4 Ves. 433 n. Cf. Wilmot C.J.'s observations in *Att.-Gen.* v. *Lady Downing* (1767), 1 Wilm. 1, 32.

[6] 23 Hen. VIII c. 10; above, p. 11.

[7] 9 Geo. II c. 36; above, pp. 109 ff.

[8] (1798), 7 Ves. 490.

[9] 1 Edw. VI c. 14; above, p. 11.

[10] 7 Ves. 490, 495 and 497, adopting in substance Mitford's argument for the Attorney-General.

The seventeenth-century cases, buttressed by the authority of Lord Hardwicke in *Da Costa* v. *De Paz*,[1] had permanently clothed the benefactor of the illegal religious object with a mantle of general piety. Cases like *Attorney-General* v. *Bishop of Oxford*[2] and *Attorney-General* v. *Goulding*[3] had merely encouraged false hopes that the doctrine 'ought never again to be mentioned in this Court',[4] or at least had been 'much shaken'.[5] The factual analogy of these 'impossibility' cases was deceptive; for the old cases had drawn a clear if irrational line between the lawful charitable use which failed for impossibility where a general charitable intention had to be specifically proved, and the gift which failed for illegality or indefiniteness where the court would presume that the testator had a general charitable intention.

Indeed the courts found the cases, where funds had been given to indefinite charitable objects, as difficult to justify as the 'illegality' cases. The most influential decision which persuaded judges to uphold their authority was an anonymous case, decided in 1702 and reported by Freeman.[6] His report read:

> It was said, and not denied, that if a man deviseth a sum of money to such charitable uses as he shall direct by a codicil to be annexed to his will, or by a note in writing; and afterwards leaves no direction, neither by note nor codicil, the Court of Chancery hath power to dispose of it to such charitable uses as the court shall think fit.

Eldon subjected this statement to trenchant criticism. He pointed out that its author was unknown, and that possibly it was a mere *dictum*.[7] Nevertheless he confirmed its authority on two separate occasions (in *Moggridge* v. *Thackwell*, in 1803,[8] and *Mills* v. *Farmer*[9] in 1815), although he considered that 'no other case goes the same length'[10] and would have been 'glad to meet with

[1] (1754), 1 Dick. 259, Ambl. 228, 2 Swanst. 532 n.; above, p. 143.

[2] (1786), 4 Ves. 431–2; above, p. 144.

[3] (1788), 2 Bro. C.C. 428; above, p. 145. See also *Att.-Gen.* v. *Boultbee* (1794), 2 Ves. 380, 3 Ves. 220.

[4] *Att.-Gen.* v. *Andrew* (1798), 3 Ves. 633, 649, *per* Lord Loughborough, who did, characteristically, add: 'I am not quite clear of that.'

[5] *Att.-Gen.* v. *Andrew* (1798), 3 Ves. 633, 645, *per* counsel. See also *Att.-Gen.* v. *Painter-Stainers' Co.* (1788), 2 Cox, 51, 55, *per* Lord Thurlow; *Att.-Gen.* v. *Whitchurch* (1796), 3 Ves. 141, 144, *per* Pepper Arden M.R.

[6] *Anon.* (1702), Freeman, Ch. 261.

[7] See *Mills* v. *Farmer* (1815), 1 Mer. 55, 80–1.

[8] (1803), 7 Ves. 36.

[9] (1815), 1 Mer. 55.

[10] *Ibid.* 55, 80.

sufficient ground to overrule it judicially'.[1] In such a case, Eldon ironically observed, the court must find that

> the general intention of this testatrix, who seems to have been saturated and satiated with the idea of charity, and yet not to have had mind enough herself to determine upon the particular objects, was to devote her property to charity.[2]

In *Moggridge* v. *Thackwell* in 1803,[3] a testatrix had bequeathed residuary personalty to her executor, Vaston, for such charities as he should think fit. Vaston predeceased her. Counsel for the next-of-kin argued that the testatrix had reposed in Vaston a personal and non-delegable confidence. Only he, not the court, could exercise the particular discretion; if the court or the Crown settled a *cy-près* scheme, a new charity would be created which 'never existed in the mind of the testatrix'. Counsel cited *Attorney-General* v. *Goulding*,[4] *Attorney-General* v. *Andrew*[5] and *Wheeler* v. *Sheer*[6] as support for the submission that the 'late inclination of the court has been not to dispose in general charity, where a particular one is pointed out';[7] attempted to distinguish *Attorney-General* v. *Syderfin*,[8] because it was decided 'when this court was in the habit of deciding monstrous propositions in favour of charity';[9] and invited Lord Eldon not to

[1] (1815) 1 Mer. 55, 59.

[2] *Moggridge* v. *Thackwell* (1803), 7 Ves. 36, 83. Only one eighteenth-century case, *Wheeler* v. *Sheer* (1730), Mos. 288, 301, appeared to doubt this proposition of law. In that case a testator had left the residue of his estate to his executors for such charitable purposes 'as by codicil I shall appoint'. Subsequently the testator executed a codicil directing his executors to apply the residue to such uses as he should by any other codicil appoint. No codicil was found. Lord King adjourned the case, and, unfortunately, no more is heard of it. But during the course of argument, he distinguished the facts before him from that of *Att.-Gen.* v. *Syderfin* (1683), 1 Vern. 224, above, p. 90, on the ground that in *Syderfin*'s case the testator must be presumed to have made an appointment, which had apparently been lost, while in *Wheeler* v. *Sheer* there was no evidence that he had made an appointment at all.

Whatever was the *ratio decidendi* of *Wheeler* v. *Sheer*, it had no influence on the development of the law. For attempts to explain the case, see *White* v. *White* (1778), 1 Bro. C.C. 12, 15, *per* Lord Thurlow; *Moggridge* v. *Thackwell* (1803), 7 Ves. 36, 79, and *Mills* v. *Farmer* (1815), 1 Mer. 55, 86, *per* Lord Eldon.

[3] (1803), 7 Ves. 36.

[4] (1788), 2 Bro. C.C. 428; above p. 145.

[5] (1798), 3 Ves. 633.

[6] (1730), Mos. 288; above n. 2.

[7] (1803), 7 Ves. 36, 46.

[8] (1683), 1 Vern. 224; above p. 90.

[9] (1803), 7 Ves. 36, 43.

strain this will to make it conform to the old cases. If Lord Northington and other judges had not stemmed the torrent, there would have been a vast number of charity cases of another kind.[1]

Eldon rejected these arguments and decided, 'entirely by the force of precedents,[2] much against my inclination',[3] that the residue should be applied *cy-près* by the court. He felt compelled to accept Lord King's observations in *Attorney-General* v. *Hickman*,[4] that:

The substance of the charity remains notwithstanding the death of the trustees before the testator; and though at law it is a lapsed legacy, yet in equity it is subsisting; and here is sufficient certainty of the testator's intention to revive it, the intention therefore of the party is sufficiently manifested that this charity should continue within 43 Eliz. c. 4.

Next-of-kin were nothing if not indefatigable. Eldon's doubts and hesitations[5] encouraged them, in *Paice* v. *Archbishop of Canterbury* in 1807[6] and *Mills* v. *Farmer* in 1815,[7] to challenge once more the 'old' cases, though the decree in *Moggridge* v. *Thackwell* had been affirmed by the House of Lords.[8] Their attacks again failed. If, said Eldon, they

should think proper to carry the question before the House of Lords; and if, in the further discussion before that tribunal, it shall be found practicable to mark any distinction between this case and those other cases upon the authority of which I have felt it necessary that this be now decided; I shall be glad to assist that distinction to the utmost point that it will bear. But I cannot say that I, at present, perceive any such distinction.[9]

[1] (1803), 7 Ves. 36, 65.

[2] The precedents, which Eldon found particularly persuasive, included *Att.-Gen.* v. *Hickman* (1732), 2 Eq. Cas. Abr. 193, pl. 14 and *Doyley* v. *Att.-Gen.* (1735), *ibid.* 194, 4 Viner Abr. 485. In *Att.-Gen.* v. *Hickman* the trustees had died before the testator; in *Doyley* v. *Att.-Gen.* the trustee had disclaimed. But in both cases the trust fund was applied *cy-près*. Lord Eldon considered these cases 'very strong' and the foundation of Wilmot C.J.'s observations in *Att.-Gen.* v. *Lady Downing* (1767), 1 Wilm. 1, which accepted that a testator who leaves property for general indefinite purposes must be deemed to have a charitable intention.

[3] As he subsequently admitted in *Mills* v. *Farmer* (1815), 1 Mer. 55, 99.

[4] (1732), 2 Eq. Cas. Abr. 193, 194, pl. 14.

[5] *Moggridge* v. *Thackwell* had originally been heard by Lord Thurlow in 1792, so that the dispute had dragged on over twenty-three years.

[6] (1807), 14 Ves. 364, 1 Russ. and Myl. 761 n.

[7] (1815), 1 Mer. 55.

[8] See (1807), 13 Ves. 416.

[9] *Mills* v. *Farmer* (1815), 1 Mer. 55, 103–4.

No further appeal was made; and the authority of this line of cases was never thereafter seriously questioned.[1]

Prerogative and judicial cy-près.[2] After the *Feoffees to Impropriations'* case in 1633[3] it became settled practice that funds devoted to 'illegal' charitable uses should be applied *cy-près* under the sign manual. In contrast, few eighteenth-century judges understood the principle which underlay *Attorney-General* v. *Peacock*,[4] and consequently did not know how large was the Crown's power to settle a *cy-près* scheme if property had been devoted to the support of indefinite charitable objects.[5] There are many examples in the contemporary cases of the ensuing procedural confusion. In *Baylis* and *Church* v. *Attorney-General*,[6] a Mr Church had bequeathed £200 to the ward of Bread Street, to be distributed in accordance with Mr . . .'s will. Lord Hardwicke refused to allow extrinsic evidence to discover the missing name, but nevertheless ordered a *cy-près* application to 'such charities as the alderman, for the time being, and the principal inhabitants, shall think the most beneficial to the ward'.[7] The similarity of these facts to those of *Attorney-General* v. *Syderfin*[8] is striking. In *Syderfin*'s case, however, Lord Keeper North had held that the funds should be applied *cy-près* to such objects as the Crown should appoint under the sign manual; while in *Baylis and Church* v. *Attorney-General*, the court ordered the Master to draw up a scheme. Again, *Attorney-General* v. *Herrick* (1772)[9] may be contrasted with *Attorney-General* v. *Clarke* (1762).[10] In *Herrick*'s case, property had been devised to 'charitable and pious' purposes; and in *Clarke*'s case, a legacy had been bequeathed to the poor inhabitants of St Leonard's, Shoreditch. The argument that the will was

[1] The appellants may have been disheartened by the House of Lords' decree in *Moggridge* v. *Thackwell*; see above, p. 150.

[2] For the earlier history, see above, pp. 72 ff.

[3] See above, p. 77.

[4] See above, p. 88.

[5] Confusion was multiplied by the fact that whether the appointment was the Crown's or the Court's, the decree was made by the Court. If the Crown appointed, the Court sought its pleasure and made its decree in accordance with that pleasure: see *Att.-Gen.* v. *Syderfin* (1683), 1 Vern. 224, above, p. 90; *Moggridge* v. *Thackwell* (1803), 7 Ves. 36, 71, *per* Lord Eldon.

[6] (1741), 2 Atk. 239.

[7] *Ibid.* 240.

[8] (1683), Vern. 224; above, p. 90.

[9] (1772), Ambl. 712.

[10] (1762), Ambl. 422.

void for uncertainty was rejected and the property was applied *cy-près* in each case. In *Herrick*'s case Lord Bathurst asked His Majesty to declare his pleasure under the sign manual, 'as Lord Nottingham did' in *Attorney-General* v. *Peacock*, while in *Clarke*'s case, Sir Thomas Clarke, Master of the Rolls, decreed that the legacy should be distributed to the poor inhabitants of St Leonard's Shoreditch, who were not receiving alms; and ordered a scheme to be laid before the Master to carry out such a distribution.[1]

The distinction between judicial and prerogative *cy-près* could be of more than academic interest. The Crown's power to distribute to 'similar' charitable objects was less constrained than the court's, and in *Moggridge* v. *Thackwell*[2] in 1803 counsel admitted that the poor relations of the testator 'will fare better under the Crown's disposition of this charity'. In that case, moreover, not only was the law clarified but a significant step was taken towards ensuring a uniform and consistent *cy-près* application no matter what body, Crown or court, settled the scheme. It will be remembered that a testatrix had bequeathed residuary personalty to one James Vaston, 'to dispose of the same in such charities as he shall think fit'. Vaston predeceased the testatrix. On the next-of-kin's petition for a re-hearing Lord Eldon, having held that the testatrix must be presumed to have had a general charitable intention,[3] went on to consider the basis of the doctrine of prerogative *cy-près*, 'a most difficult question'. He confessed that it was not easy[4]

> to raise a solid distinction between an original gift absolutely indefinite and without qualification, and a case, in which by matter *ex post facto*, the gift stands before the court in consequence of that accident, as if it had originally been given indefinitely, without any means for carrying it into execution prescribed. All I can say upon it is, I do not know, what doctrine could be laid down, that would not be met by some authority on this point; whether the proposition is, that the Crown is to dispose of it, or the Master by a scheme.

Having analysed the previous authorities, Eldon concluded that:[5]

[1] For another example, contrast *Cook* v. *Duckenfield* (1743), 2 Atk. 562 with *Att.-Gen.* v. *Berryman* (1753), Dickens, 168.

[2] (1803), 7 Ves. 36, 50; see also *Ware* v. *Att.-Gen.* (1824), and *Sanford* v. *Gibbons* (1829), both unreported, but cited by counsel in 3 Hare, 195 n.

[3] See above, p. 149.

[4] 7 Ves. 36, 83.

[5] *Ibid.* 86.

. . . [T]he general principle thought most reconcilable to the cases is, that, where there is a general indefinite purpose, not fixing itself upon any object, as this in a degree does, the disposition is in the King by the Sign Manual; but where the execution is to be by a trustee with general or some objects pointed out, there the Court will take the administration of the trust.

Lord Rosslyn's decree was therefore affirmed and the Master ordered to settle a scheme.

Eldon was determined that the court should supervise the trustee's discretion to distribute the property to charitable purposes. If Vaston had been alive, the court would undoubtedly have done so; what difference should it make if he were dead? The emphasis on the absence or presence of a trust provided him with a novel rationalisation of the old cases, which had suggested that only if the devise or bequest would have failed at law would the Crown cure the uncertainty and administer the trust fund *cy-près* under the sign manual. Nevertheless, his judgment, fully reported by the younger Vesey, did formulate a lucid and coherent principle to guide future judges, though there are a few later cases where a *cy-près* scheme was settled by the court when it should have been settled by the Crown, and vice versa.[1] Such procedural inconsistencies had henceforth less serious repercussions. Eldon's dictum that there ought not to be 'any difference in the execution', 'whether this Court, or the King by Sign Manual, executes it',[2] seems to have influenced future practice. Thereafter the discretion of the court and the Crown was generally, though not invariably, exercised in a similar way. The same charities benefited whichever body settled a *cy-près* scheme.[3]

The application of surplus funds

A testator devises an annuity to charitable uses, the annuity being charged on land and being its annual value at the testator's death. The annual value of the land increases over the years. Who is to get the benefit of the increase; the charity, the feoffees, or the

[1] Cf. *inter alia*, *Att.-Gen.* v. *Marchioness of Londonderry*, unreported, but quoted by L. Shelford in *A Practical Treatise on the Law of Mortmain* (London, 1836), 272–3, and *Att.-Gen.* v. *Fletcher* (1835), 5 L.J. (N.S.) Ch. 75 with *Bennett* v. *Hayter* (1839), 2 Beav. 81 and *Re Clergy Society* (1856), 2 K. and J. 615. See also *Hayter* v. *Trego* (1830), 5 Russ. 113, and cf. *Re Slevin* [1891], 2 Ch. 236.

[2] 7 Ves. 36, 87.

[3] Cf. Owen Tudor, *Charities*, 5th ed. (London, 1929), 131.

heir-at-law? In such a case the Chancellor had held, during the period 1532–1700,[1] that the charity would be entitled to the increased rents, if that 'accord[ed] to the true intent and meaning'[2] of the testator. One way of discovering the testator's intention was to inquire whether he had originally devoted the annual value of the land, or the whole of the rents from the land at the time of the devise, to charity.[3] Exceptionally, the court was able to find that a testator intended to devise the increased rents to a particular charity even though he had not given it the whole of that annual income.[4]

During this period, 1700–1827, the judges accepted the underlying principles of these 'old' cases.[5] As Lord Eldon said in *Attorney-General* v. *Master and Wardens of the Skinners' Co.*[6] in 1827:

> I apprehend that, when the cases ... are examined, it will be found that the rule is, that they depend entirely upon the intention of the testator.

But just as the seventeenth-century *cy-près* cases were accepted and followed with little enthusiasm, so it was thought that the 'surplus' cases were determined 'upon principles in the construction of deeds and wills, when charity was the object, which, if they could be reconsidered, would not now be adopted'.[7] Lord Hardwicke in *Attorney-General* v. *Johnson*[8] considered that the *Thetford School* case[9] would have been differently decided if the court had appreciated that it could have decreed that the surplus rents be held by the feoffees on trust for the heir-at-law. 'If the

[1] See above, pp. 91 ff.

[2] *Att.-Gen.* v. *Mayor of Bristol* (1802), 2 Jac. and W. 294, 315, *per* Lord Eldon.

[3] See above, p. 92.

[4] See *Arnold* v. *Att.-Gen.* (1698), Shower, P.C., 22; above, p. 93.

[5] *Att.-Gen.* v. *Johnson* (1753), Ambl. 190; *Att.-Gen.* v. *Sparks* (1753), *ibid.* 201; *Att.-Gen.* v. *Herrick* (1772), *ibid.* 712; *Att.-Gen.* v. *Earl of Winchelsea* (1791), 3 Bro. C.C. 373; *Att.-Gen.* v. *Master and Wardens of the Haberdashers' Company of the City of London* (1792), 4 Bro. C.C. 103; *Att.-Gen.* v. *Minshull* (1798), 4 Ves. 11; *Ex p. Jortin* (1802), 7 Ves. 340; *Att.-Gen.* v. *Coopers' Co.* (1812), 19 Ves. 187; *Att.-Gen.* v. *Mayor of Bristol* (1820), 2 Jac. and W. 294; *Att.-Gen.* v. *Skinners' Co.* (1827), 2 Russ. 407.

[6] (1827), 2 Russ. 407, 437. And see *Bishop of Hereford* v. *Adams* (1802), 7 Ves. 324; *Att.-Gen.* v. *Wansay* (1808), 15 Ves. 231; *Att.-Gen.* v. *Master and Fellows of Catherine Hall, Cambridge* (1820), Jac. 381.

[7] *Att.-Gen.* v. *Mayor of Bristol* (1820), 2 Jac. and W. 294, 307, *per* Lord Eldon.

[8] (1753), Ambl. 190.

[9] (1609), 8 Co. 130b; above, p. 92.

doctrine of resulting trusts had been then understood, the right of the heir-at-law would never, in all probability, have been got over';[1] and Lord Eldon further confessed[2] that if he had been the heir in *Arnold*'s case,[3] who had received a solatium of a mere forty shillings, he would have felt that he had been hardly treated. If the objects of these gifts had not been charity, the cases would have taken a different course.[4] But settled rules of construction could not be disturbed.[5]

Some judges appeared to treat the 'surplus' cases as examples of a *cy-près* application of charitable funds.[6] For example, Lord Thurlow in the *Painter-Stainers*' case[7] was influenced by the analogy of *White* v. *White*,[8] where the funds of a charitable trust which had failed for uncertainty were applied *cy-près*; and in *Attorney-General* v. *Earl of Winchelsea*[9] and *Attorney-General* v. *Minshull*,[10] the Master of the Rolls, Arden, having cited the *Bishop of Oxford*'s case,[11] took the opportunity of expressing the view that the doctrine of *cy-près* had hitherto been pushed to extravagant lengths.[12] Such observations expressed in this context were to confuse later judges and commentators and to lead them to treat all these cases as examples of the application of the equitable *cy-près* doctrine.[13]

[1] *Att.-Gen.* v. *Mayor of Bristol* (1820), 2 Jac. and W. 294, 307, *per* Lord Eldon.

[2] In *Att.-Gen.* v. *Skinners' Co.* (1827), 2 Russ. 407, 434.

[3] (1698), Shower P. C. 22; above, p. 93.

[4] In *Att.-Gen.* v. *Mayor of Bristol* (1820), 2 Jac. and W. 292, 318, *per* Lord Eldon.

[5] In the seventeenth century cases the judges had tended to distribute the surplus in proportion to the original amounts received by the charity. During this period, however, this practice was not invariably adopted. So, in *Att.-Gen.* v. *Johnson* (1753), Ambl. 190, 191, Lord Hardwicke refused to augment proportionally the charitable uses set out in the testator's will: 'ten shillings for an annual sermon, &c., need no greater allowance, unless, as the clergy in Wales are in general ill provided for, the augmentation to be considered as adding to his provision.' See also *Anon.* (*temp.* Hardwicke), cited 2 Jac. and W. 320; *Att.-Gen.* v. *Sparks* (1753), Ambl. 201; *Ex parte Jortin* (1802), 7 Ves. 340. Lord Eldon was subsequently to deny that the court had the jurisdiction to augment one charity at the expense of another; see *Att.-Gen.* v. *The Coopers' Co.* (1812), 19 Ves. 187, 190. But cf. *Att.-Gen.* v. *Marchant* (1866), L.R. 3 Eq. 424.

[6] See also the comment of a leading text-writer, W. R. A. Boyle, in his *A Practical Treatise on the Law of Charities* (London, 1857), 202.

[7] (1788), 2 Cox, 51, 55–6; above, p. 148.

[8] (1778), 1 Bro. C.C. 12; above, p. 149.

[9] (1791), 3 Bro. C.C. 373; above, p. 144.

[10] (1798), 4 Ves. 11; above, p. 146.

[11] (1786), 4 Ves. 431–2; above, p. 144.

[12] Cf. Lord Eldon's observations on *Arnold* v. *Att.-Gen.* (1698), Shower, P.C. 22, in *Att.-Gen.* v. *Mayor of Bristol* (1820), 2 Jac. and W. 294, 308.

[13] *Tudor on Charities*. 6th ed., chap. 6, § 5.

But the facts of *Painter-Stainers'* case, *Attorney-General* v. *Winchelsea* and *Attorney-General* v. *Minshull* were significantly different from those of *White* v. *White* and the *Bishop of Oxford*'s case. The former group of cases concerned the fate of 'surplus' funds; whereas in the latter group the trust had initially failed because of impossibility. In cases like *Painter-Stainers'* the courts were not attempting to perfect a trust which had failed but were merely inquiring whether it had been the testator's intention to apply surplus income for the benefit of existing, lawful, and certain charitable objects named by him in his will. As Lord Eldon once observed:[1]

> the court reserves to itself the disposition of such a surplus with the view of taking care, that it shall be applied under the control of the court *as nearly as possible* to the uses and purposes, to which the testator meant his property to be subservient.

Only in this limited sense can it be said that the 'surplus' cases are an example of the application of the ancient *cy-près* doctrine.

Marshalling of assets in favour of charity

In the seventeenth century the courts had been prepared to marshal assets in favour of charity: equitable assets had to satisfy charitable legacies before debts or private legacies.[2] The few cases which established these principles appear, however, to have been unknown to lawyers of this period, or if known, were peremptorily ignored. Debts were now ordered to be paid before charitable legacies,[3] and charitable and private legacies were required 'to abate in proportion, for they were but legacies'.[4] As Lord Chancellor Parker said in *Attorney-General* v. *Hudson*:[5]

> . . . and in a case of a deficiency of assets, let all the pecuniary legacies, as well that to the charity as others, abate in proportion; for though the Romans preferred a pious or charitable legacy to others, yet our law does not: they being all but legacies, and equally intended by the testator to be paid, it would be hard that one of them by being preferred should frustrate all the rest.

[1] *Att.-Gen.* v. *Coopers' Co.* (1812), 19 Ves. 187, 189 (my italics). Cf. *Tudor on Charities*, 6th ed., 289–301.

[2] See above, p. 96.

[3] *Tate* v. *Austin* (1714), 1 P. Wms. 264.

[4] *Masters* v. *Masters* (1717), 1 P. Wms. 421, 423, *per* Jekyll M.R.

[5] (1720), 1 P. Wms. 674, 675.

This reluctance to marshal assets to assist charity is particularly evident after the enactment of the Mortmain Act, 1736. This statute presented the courts with a new problem: if a testator had left his real and personal estate to trustees upon trust for sale to pay debts and private legacies and to apply the residue for charitable purposes, could the debts and private legacies be thrown onto the realty in order to give effect as far as possible to the residuary charitable bequest? The courts held that 'assets cannot be so marshalled to support a legacy contrary to law',[1] and refused to charge debts and non-charitable legacies exclusively on realty which could not be devoted to charity. This would accomplish *per obliquum* what could not be performed *per directum*,[2] namely, the devise of land for charitable purposes. The whole estate, real and personal, should bear the debts and legacies *pro rata*.

Lord Hardwicke,[3] however, while he would not 'set up a new rule for the benefit of charities', was prepared to give them 'the benefit of the old rule'.[4] This led him to make, in *Attorney-General* v. *Tomkins*,[5] a curious distinction. In that case a testator had devised his residuary realty and personalty to trustees, to apply the income for clothing the poor inhabitants of a hospital in Abingdon. He died possessed of leasehold but not freehold property. Lord Hardwicke held that even though leaseholds could not be devised to charitable uses,[6] the leaseholds should primarily bear the

> debts and legacies, as a real estate descending would be before that part that is devised; and there being more debts and [pecuniary] legacies than the leasehold estate would extend to pay, his Lordship ordered it to be sold, and the deficiency made up out of the other assets, and the rest to be applied to the charity.[7]

The leaseholds were considered 'as personal estate undisposed of, and to be first applied towards payment of the said testator's debts, funeral expenses, and pecuniary legacies'.

If the testator's estate had consisted of freeholds and pure personalty, Hardwicke would not have marshalled assets in favour

[1] *Mogg* v. *Hodges* (1750), 2 Ves. Sen. 52, 53, *per* Lord Hardwicke.

[2] *Att.-Gen.* v. *Tyndall* (1764), 2 Eden, 207, 210, *per* Lord Northington.

[3] Cf. above, pp. 113–16 for other instances of Hardwicke's interpretation of the Mortmain Act, 1736, in favour of charity.

[4] *Att.-Gen.* v. *Graves* (1752), Ambl. 155, 158; see also *Arnold* v. *Chapman* (1748), 1 Ves. Sen. 108.

[5] (1754), Ambl. 216.

[6] See above, p. 118.

[7] (1754), Ambl. 216, 218.

of the charity; for this would set up a 'new rule' and would 'support a legacy contrary to law'.[1]

Attorney-General v. *Tomkins*, although subsequently followed by Sir Thomas Clarke, Master of the Rolls[2], was impliedly rejected in *Attorney-General* v. *Tyndall*.[3] Lord Northington, who decided the latter case, would bend the language of the Mortmain Act, 1736, to the utmost in order to defeat charity.[4] He would not 'contradict the legislator'; and if he were to marshal assets so as to throw debts and non-charitable legacies solely on the leaseholds, he would enable the testator

> substantially, to give [his] lands to a charity, the devise of which I have decreed void . . . This seems to me a strange construction to put upon the statute . . .
>
> The old rule of marshalling assets respects *two* different funds, and *two* different sets of parties, where one set can resort to either fund, the other only to one: it is grounded on obvious equity; it does no prejudice to anybody, and it effectuates the testator's intent; but where there is no double fund, what is marshalling for the residue? . . .
>
> But I am now to suppose that the void devise of the leasehold dropped into the residue of the personal estate, and that it bore the proportion of debts and legacies in average, and augmented the residue for the charity. I am of opinion that this could not be done consistent with the statute of mortmain, and the intent of the testatrix: 1st, because the words of the statute are negative that no interest in land shall go to a charity; 2ndly, because it was the intent of the testatrix that the trustees should take this by specific devise, and not as part of the residue of the personal estate.[5]

These principles were thereafter accepted without challenge.[6] In *Attorney-General* v. *Earl of Winchelsea*[7] in 1791, Arden, Master of

[1] *Mogg* v. *Hodges* (1750), 2 Ves. Sen. 52, 53 (*semble*). See also *Arnold* v. *Chapman* (1748), 1 Ves. Sen. 108.

[2] *Negus* v. *Coulter* (1759), Ambl. (ed. Blunt), 367; *Att.-Gen.* v. *Caldwell* (1766), Ambl. 635. For a discussion of these cases, see 3 Bro. C.C. (ed. Belt), 380 n.

[3] (1764) 2 Eden, 207, which is to be preferred to Ambl. 614. *Att.-Gen.* v. *Tomkins* is not mentioned in the reports.

[4] See above, p. 116.

[5] (1764), 2 Eden, 207, 211–12.

[6] See, *inter alia*, *Waller* v. *Childs* (1765), Ambl. 524; *Foster* v. *Blagden* (1771), *ibid.* 704; *Hillyard* v. *Taylor* (1773), *ibid.* 713. *Middleton* v. *Spicer* (1783), 1 Bro. C.C. 201; *Makeham* v. *Hooper* (1792), 4 Bro. C.C. 153; *Howse* v. *Chapman* (1799), 4 Ves. 542; *Paice* v. *Archbishop of Canterbury* (1807), 14 Ves. 364, 1 Russ. and Myl. 761 n; *Curtis* v. *Hutton* (1808), 14 Ves. 537; *Currie* v. *Pye* (1811), 17 Ves. 462. See also *Ridges* v. *Morrison* (1785), 1 Cox 180; Boyle, *Law of Charities*, 352–3.

[7] (1797), 3 Bro. C.C. 373; and cases cited above, n. 6. See also *Att.-Gen.* v. *Meyrick* (1750), 2 Ves. Sen. 44.

the Rolls, applied them to throw debts and legacies on to a general residuary fund of pure personalty and mortgage securities; the pure personalty and securities should bear the debts and legacies *pro rata*, 'Nothing that in the least degree partakes of realty, can now pass under the Statute of Mortmain', so that the legacy failed to the extent it was payable out of the mortgage securities.

Lord Hardwicke's judgment in *Attorney-General* v. *Lord Weymouth* is also puzzling.[1] There a testator had bequeathed a legacy of £1,000 to charity. He directed his debts and funeral expenses to be paid out of his personal estate and, if it was insufficient, from his realty. Hardwicke ordered the legacy to be paid from the personalty, the debts from the remainder of the personalty and any deficiency from the realty, which, he said, was in this case an 'auxiliary fund' for payment of debts and legacies.[2] *Attorney-General* v. *Lord Weymouth* is an isolated case, impossible to justify in principle. After first providing for the payment of debts from the personalty, the charitable legacy should have been paid out of realty and personalty *pro rata*, and to the extent it was paid out of the realty it should have failed *pro tanto*.[3]

It is not easy to tell from the few reported cases whether the courts would allow a testator *expressly* to charge his real estate with all his debts and legacies (other than legacies to charity), in order to increase the proportion of his estate available for distribution to charity. In *Arnold* v. *Chapman*[4] Hardwicke thought that if the testator were allowed to do this, 'it would go a great way towards overturning this act: but as to that [he would] give no opinion: for there an intention appears in the testator; here no exoneration is intended by the will'. Although there is some suggestion in later cases that the testator could so relieve his pure personalty,[5] it is doubtful whether the courts did permit him to evade in such an obvious fashion the provisions of the Mortmain Act, 1736.[6]

[1] (1743), Ambl. 20.

[2] See Hardwicke's explanation of his own decision in *Mogg* v. *Hodges* (1750), 1 Cox, 9, 12.

[3] Cf. T. Jarman, *A Treatise on Wills* (London, 1844), 1, 208–9; see also *Williams* v. *Kershaw* (1835), 5 L.J. Ch. 84, 1 Keen, 274 n: *Hobson* v. *Blackburn* (1836), 1 Keen, 273. See generally, Boyle, *Law of Charities*, chap. VII.

[4] (1748), 1 Ves. Sen. 108, 110.

[5] See *Att.-Gen.* v. *Lord Mountmorris* (1765), 1 Dick. 379, which is reported in just five lines; and *Howse* v. *Chapman* (1799), 4 Ves. 542. Cf. Boyle's comment, *Law of Charities*, 357.

[6] See Boyle, *Law of Charities*, 356–9. For the later cases, see L. S. Bristowe, *A Treatise on the Mortmain and Charitable Uses Act*, 1891 (London, 1891), 53.

CHAPTER XI

THE ENFORCEMENT OF CHARITABLE TRUSTS: 1700–1827

CHARITY commissions under the statute 43 Elizabeth I c. 4 still issued in the eighteenth century, but with each year their number became fewer. The statutory procedure was cumbersome and intolerably slow.[1] Its demise was inevitable, and in 1787 the last commission under the statute 43 Elizabeth I c. 4 was sealed. In retrospect it is surprising that practitioners should have turned to the information as a more effective method of enforcing charitable trusts.[2] But it might have been thought that no procedure could be as unsatisfactory as the commission and it might have been hoped that the information would not inherit any of the simple bill's defects,[3] being injected with the authority of the Crown, acting through the Attorney-General, in whose name the information was presented:

... [T]hat the King is to be considered as the *parens patriae*, that he is the protector of every part of his subjects, and, that, therefore, it is the duty of his officer, the Attorney-General, to see that justice is done to every part of those subjects.[4]

Yet the information proved to be even more tardy, costly and frustrating than the commission-procedure it supplanted, so much so that in 1818 it could be asserted 'that it was impossible, through the Court of Chancery, to obtain redress for the abuses of charitable institutions'.[5] The interminable delays and crushing expense to which any eighteenth-century litigant in Chancery

[1] The history of the last commission, sealed in 1787, is not untypical. In 1804 the Chancellor was petitioned to confirm the commissioners' decree and in 1818, when Brougham mentioned the case in the House of Commons, Lord Eldon had still not disposed of the exceptions taken by indefatigable opponents: see *Parliamentary Debates* (Hansard), XXXVIII, 606–7; David Owen, *English Philanthropy 1660–1960* (London, 1965), 85.

[2] See above, p. 54.

[3] See above. p. 19.

[4] *Corporation of Ludlow* v. *Greenhouse* (1817), 1 Bli. N.S. 17, 48, *per* Lord Eldon. Cf. *Att.-Gen.* v. *Hewitt* (1804), 9 Ves. 232.

[5] *Parliamentary Debates* (Hansard), XXXVIII, 1230 (1818). The speaker was Sir Samuel Romilly.

were exposed are a matter of well known history. 'Many families were ruined with the very best cause before a decision could be given',[1] and a man who was foolish enough to initiate a suit in Chancery might well not live to see its determination. Hundreds and hundreds of litigants had been destroyed by a court, whose procedure was bedevilled with archaism and prolixity and whose administration was throttled with sinecure offices.[2]

There were many reasons why the information to enforce a charitable trust became, even by eighteenth-century standards, peculiarly 'tedious and chargeable'. The primary reason was that each information, although formally in the name of the Attorney-General, had to be brought at the relation of a private individual.[3] As Lord Eldon explained in *Corporation of Ludlow* v. *Greenhouse*:[4]

> It would be highly improper for the Attorney-General assisting in that character to press harder upon one party than another. It is his duty to see that justice is done, and it was for that purpose as I conceive that informations in the name of his Majesty's Attorney-General were permitted for the purpose of carrying into execution charitable dispositions, or for providing for the due distribution of charitable funds. Relators were required for this reason, because the Crown paid no costs. The Attorney-General, prosecuting as the officer of the crown, could not be liable for costs, and a complaint might be made against individuals highly oppressive to them unless there were some person responsible for the costs that might be incurred in consequence of that proceeding.

The Crown's role was now a muted one. Whereas charity trustees might well draw on the charitable funds for their expenses, it was generally the relator, who personally had to bear the defendants' costs if the information failed.[5] The relator was also liable in costs if the information was deemed 'improper';[6] or was

[1] *Parliamentary Debates* (Hansard) XXIII, 59 (1812). The speaker was Michael Angelo Taylor.

[2] *Ibid.* XVII (N.S.), 257 (1827), *per* Michael Angelo Taylor.

[3] *Semble* the Attorney-General could proceed without a relator: see *Re Bedford Charity* (1819), 2 Swanst. 470, 520, *per* Lord Eldon. In practice he did not do so.

[4] (1827) 1 Bli. N.S. P.C., 17, 48.

[5] The court did, of course, have a discretion how costs were to be awarded: see *Att.-Gen.* v. *Fishmongers' Co.* (1837), 1 Keen, 492; *Att.-Gen.* v. *Bolton* (1797), 3 Anst. 820. Cf. *Lloyd* v. *Spillet* (1734), 3 P. Wms. 344. If the relator was awarded costs, no costs could be given to the Attorney-General if he acted without a court order: see *Att.-Gen.* v. *Dove* (1823), Turn. and Russ. 328.

[6] See John Mitford, *Pleadings in Suits in the Court of Chancery*, 5th ed. (London, 1847), 24.

unnecessary and 'in contradiction to the right';[1] or was brought for insufficient or very improper cause, such as for a private motive of revenge[2]. It was little encouragement to him that the court would be reluctant to dismiss the information for a procedural defect,[3] that he possibly would be awarded solicitor and client costs if the suit was successful,[4] or that he would get costs, though the information was dismissed, if his conduct was beneficial to the charity.[5] The cost of litigation was burdensome even if the relator was awarded his costs, which anyway had to be exacted from the defendants. And failure might result in his financial ruin.[6] There were, not surprisingly, few altruistic enough to scatter hard-earned bread on Chancery waters. Because relators need have no 'interest in the result of the decision, it could not be expected', said Sir Samuel Romilly, 'that such a person would be disposed to put himself to great expense which this would occasion, for the public benefit. The delay and procrastination might occasion him to lie out of a great expense for a number of years. If a person hearing of any abuse, should think of having an information filed, he must lay his account with disbursing a great sum of costs, with the chance of recovering, if he gained the suit after a great number of years, strictly taxed costs. It would be difficult to find a man so public-spirited as to advance a great sum of money to carry on a cause in which he had no personal interest, imputing gross mis-conduct to a neighbour, with a chance of recovering a part of his expenses after so great a lapse of time.'[7]

Henry Brougham in his speech on the *Motion to Enquire into the Education of the Poor* eloquently dwelt on the inadequacy and expense of the information as a means of enforcing charitable

[1] *Att.-Gen.* v. *Smart* (1748), 1 Ves. Sen. 72, *per* Lord Hardwicke. See also *Att.-Gen.* v. *Gleg* (1738), 1 Atk. 356; *Att.-Gen.* v. *Newcombe* (1807), 14 Ves. 1, 2 Ves. Jun. Supp. 227, 356; *Att.-Gen.* v. *Hartley* (1820), 2 Jac. and W. 353; *Att.-Gen.* v. *Earl of Mansfield* (1827), 2 Russ. 501.

[2] *Att.-Gen.* v. *Middleton* (1751), 2 Ves. Sen. 327, 330, *per* Lord Hardwicke.

[3] *Att.-Gen.* v. *Smart* (1748), 1 Ves. Sen. 72.

[4] 'As otherwise, people would not come forward to file informations' (*Osborne* v. *Denne* (1802), 7 Ves. 424, *per* Samuel Romilly, *arguendo*). See also *Att.-Gen.* v. *Carte* (1746), 1 Dick. 113; *Currie* v. *Pye* (1811), 17 Ves. 462, 2 Ves. Jun. Supp. 491; *Att.-Gen.* v. *Goldsmiths' Co.* (1833), Coop. Ch., 292.

[5] *Att.-Gen.* v. *Brewers' Co.* (1717), 1 P. Wms. 376; *Att.-Gen.* v. *Bolton* (1797), 3 Anst. 820.

[6] The court had, however, no power to order the relator to give security for his costs: see *Att.-Gen.* v. *Knight* (1837), 3 Myl. and Cr. 154.

[7] *Parliamentary Debates* (Hansard), XXXVIII, 1230–1.

trusts and the consequent misery to the public-spirited relator. He confessed:[1]

that he himself had not much reliance on courts of law in that respect, especially with reference to expedition and cheapness. He allowed those courts the possession of learning without stint. He allowed them great copiousness, great power of drawing out written argument. The faculty of caring nothing for the time and patience of suitors and the hundreds of thousands of their clients money they enjoyed in a perfection which the wildest sallies of imagination could not go beyond. But as to expedition and cheapness, and attention to the comfort of those who were involved in the business of those courts, they were qualities by which they were certainly not distinguished. If he had previously doubted this fact, the evidence that had been produced before the committee only two days ago would have completely established it in his mind; for a more touching scene than was then exhibited, perhaps, had never been before witnessed. The committee had been inquiring into a charity that existed at Yeovil. He thought it was there, but he did not distinctly recollect the place; however the case was calculated most strongly to prove the existence of the evil which it was the object of the measure to remedy. It appeared from the testimony of three most respectable churchwardens who had devoted their time to the investigation of an enormous abuse in the parish, that of an income of £2,000, bequeathed to a charitable purpose, not above £30 or £40 were rendered available to it. Questions and answers to the following effect passed between the committee and those individuals. Q. Why did you not go into a court of law—there you would have found a remedy? A. We did. Q. Did you go to the court of Chancery? A. We instituted proceedings there eight years ago.—Q. How long did they continue? A. We are not out of the court yet. The first witness examined: 'I have paid £1,300 costs and have received only £300 of them from the town.' Q. Have you obtained no relief? A. Oh, it has ruined us.—Q. Have you found the other expenses heavy? A. Oh, good God, I have a thousand times wished myself out of the world; it has entirely ruined me; it had destroyed an excellent business of which I was possessed. The second witness examined: Q. What have you experienced with respect to this case? A. It has cost me £500 already and I fear I do not know the worst of it. The third witness examined: Q. Have you suffered any thing by this suit? A. My heart is almost broken; indeed, my nerves are so shaken by the losses which I have sustained in the prosecution of the affair, that I scarcely know what to do; it has been the most grievous thing I ever knew. I have a wife and several children; and I beg leave to add that unless the committee allow me to leave town to night, I do not know what will

[1] *Parliamentary Debates* (Hansard), XXXVIII, 1221 ff.

become of them. The whole appearance of the man bore ample testimony to the truth of the dreadful account he gave of his condition. So much for that instance of the advantage of resorting to a court of law. Sr. G. Paul a man of the most estimable character, who had devoted a long and useful life to the advancement of all that was calculated to benefit the poor, had, on the discovery of an abuse of a similar nature in a charity of £50 or £60 per annum, betaken himself to the same cheap and expeditious remedy. The House had already heard the general result of such steps, he would now show them a little of the mechanism by which a man's fortune and health and happiness were ruined. After the necessary preliminary steps, the cause was put on the paper in the court of Chancery in December, but was ordered to stand over. Again it was put on the paper, and again it was ordered to stand over for three days. On the 21st it was actually called on, but the court made up its mind that it would not make up its mind. On the 9th of April, for which it was fixed, the court with its usual promptitude determined that it would not determine. On the 13th of May it came on, and the court pronounced on one point, expressing its opinion that a certain lease was void, but reserved its judgment on other points. To elucidate those points the court took home the papers, and no more was heard of the cause for many months. The papers being taken home was a kind of respite and a suspension of proceeding, which relieved from expense during the time they were considering. The counsel both for the plaintiff and for the defendant however applied for judgment; but it was postponed to the 20th of January on which day it was not judged. Two days afterwards the same occurrence took place. It was then decided that it should not be decided until another day on which other day it was again decided that it should not be decided until another day on which other day it was again postponed. It was appointed positively for the 29th of February, there being but 28 days in that month. It was of course again deferred, and then again. On a subsequent day it was mentioned. This word 'mentioned' was a light and airy word in that House, but in the court of Chancery it was attended with fees to the counsel, fees to the agents, fees to the short-hand writer—in short, a 'mention' was not the most unexpensive and agreeable proceeding that could befal a suitor. Some days after the court acknowledged that it had mislaid the papers which so many months before it had taken home to peruse, and desired that a brief (attended with considerable expense) might be left with the court. On the 17th of March it was again called on, and at length it was—not decided, for decided it was not unto the present moment, but it was referred to the master.

Little effort had been made during the eighteenth century to find a new procedure which would secure the proper administration of charitable trusts, and it was not until the first decade of the next century that a concerted attempt was made to solve the problem. On 20 March 1811, Lockhart, member for the city of Oxford, introduced a bill for registering charitable donations for the benefit of poor persons in England.[1] During the debate Samuel Romilly intervened to point out that the

> continuance of these abuses did not proceed from ignorance of the nature of the charitable institutions, for the nature of the institutions and the abuses committed with respect to them, were notorious; but from the difficult and expensive nature of the remedy provided by the law . . . [T]he true remedy for this evil was to put an end to all this expense and delay, and to enable the Chancellor and the Master of the Rolls to act . . . in a summary way, upon petition and affidavits. If this mode of proceeding were adopted . . . these evils would soon be corrected.[2]

Lockhart[3] accepted Romilly's suggestion and invited him to draft a clause to his own Bill which would achieve that object. This scheme was later abandoned, but Romilly's clause eventually reached the statute book as a separate Act, 52 George III c. 101. It provided:

> That, from and after the passing of this Act, in every case of a Breach of any Trust or supposed Breach of any Trust created for charitable purposes, . . . it shall be lawful for any two or more persons to present a petition to the Lord Chancellor . . . or Master of the Rolls . . . stating such complaint, and praying such relief as the nature of the case may require . . ., and they are hereby required to hear such petition in a summary way, and upon affidavits or such other evidence as shall be produced upon such hearing to determine the same, and make such order therein.

The order was final and conclusive, although an appeal could be lodged within two years to the House of Lords.

Romilly's prophecy that this statute would correct the abuses which existed in the administration of charitable trusts was not, however, to be fulfilled. Hastily and loosely drafted, it was restrictively interpreted by the courts. In *Re Matter of Bedford*

[1] It was not the first time such a Bill had been introduced: see Returns of Charitable Donations Act, 1786 (26 Geo. III c. 58), (Gilbert's Act). Eventually Lockhart's own Bill reached the statute book as the Charitable Donations Registrations Act, 1812 (52 Geo. III c. 102).

[2] *Memoirs of the Life of Samuel Romilly*, edited by his son (London, 1840), II, 385–6.

[3] *Ibid.* III, 21. Lockhart had originally been in favour of sanctioning an action by a common informer against trustees of a charity, but had abandoned the idea: *Parliamentary Debates* (Hansard), XXI, 108.

Charity[1], for example, Eldon insisted that a petitioner under Romilly's Act should have a direct interest in the charity; and in *Attorney-General* v. *Green*[2] he refused to allow both an information and a petition, under the Act, to proceed together, for 'it is the duty of the Court, to take care that as little expense as possible should be incurred by the charity-estate.' The court would refer the question to the Attorney-General to determine which should proceed. Eldon also limited the scope of the Act to 'plain' breaches of trust committed by persons in their character of trustees,[3] and to actions between trustees and their beneficiaries. The Act would not apply if the breach of trust had been committed by a person not 'regularly invested with the character of a trustee'. [4] Indeed, even in cases which fell within the letter of the Act, the court refused to apply the Act when jurisdiction could not be exercised 'with justice to any parties or with benefit to the charity'.[5] And this discretion was in practice sparingly exercised. 'The intention of the legislature in framing the act, was to guard charitable trusts from abuse, and for that purpose, to prevent such proceedings from being instituted as are too frequently instituted for no other reason than because it is known that the costs will be payable out of the charity funds.'[6]

The Act did not then achieve the success which its sponsors originally anticipated. Lord Redesdale in his *Pleadings in Chancery*[7] condemned it in the following uncompromising terms:

> The loose mode of proceedings authorised by this act was probably intended to save expense in investigating abuses of charities: but in practice it unavoidably led to great inconvenience; the court not having before it any distinct record to which its judgment might be properly applied, and especially with respect to those against whom complaint might be made, or those against whom no such complaint could be made but whose interests might be affected by the judgment of the court. This inconvenience became apparent in a case which was made the subject of appeal to the House of Lords, who finally determined that a jurisdiction, so summary, and in which the proceedings

[1] (1819), 2 Swanst. 470.

[2] (1820), 1 Jac. and W. 303, 306.

[3] *Re Lawford Charity, ex p. Skinner* (1817), 2 Mer. 453.

[4] *Ibid.* 457, *per* Lord Eldon.

[5] *Att.-Gen.* v. *Bishop of Worcester* (1851), 9 Hare, 328, 357, *per* Turner V.C.

[6] *Re Lawford Charity, ex p. Skinner* (1817), 2 Mer. 453, 456, *per* Lord Eldon.

[7] 4th ed. (London, 1827), 20.

were so loose, ought, in just construction of the act, to be confined to the simple case of abuse of a clear trust, not involving any question beyond the question of such abuse, and particularly not involving the interests of persons to whom such abuse of trust could not be imputed.

Not surprisingly, reformers disenchanted with their experience in Chancery looked to Parliament rather than to the courts for a solution to the problem. Henry Brougham,[1] a passionate advocate of parliamentary intervention, constantly pressed for the appointment of a parliamentary commission to investigate breaches of charitable trusts. As a result of his campaign such a commission was set up in 1818 to conduct the necessary investigations. The statute[2] which established it was, however, a mere shadow of the Bill which Brougham had first introduced into the House of Commons. Brougham had originally proposed a commission to inquire into, and to investigate, the administration of all charities. But the House of Lords limited the Bill to educational charities, exempted many of the leading colleges and schools, excluded foundations which had special visitors and deprived the commission of any power to compel the attendance of witnesses and to institute legal proceedings. Though Brougham disliked these amendments,[3] he had little alternative but to accept them if he wished his Bill to survive at all. Public feeling was, however, with Brougham and may well have influenced the Government of the day to introduce a year later its own Charitable Foundations Act,[4] which amended the 1818 statute and adopted many of the provisions of Brougham's original Bill, though certain colleges and public schools and charities with special visitors were still exempted from the jurisdiction to the commissioners.

This is not the place to evaluate the work and achievement of the Brougham commissioners.[5] 'The history of successive Charity Commissions was to be long and complicated. Over the years many abuses were remedied, but for the crushing of all of them the mills ground slowly.'[6] Their reports vindicated Brougham's

[1] Chester New, *The Life of Henry Brougham* (Oxford, 1961), 217–18, 223–4; Owen, *English Philanthropy*, chap. VII.

[2] 58 Geo. III c. 91.

[3] See his *Letter to Sir Samuel Romilly M.P. Upon the Abuses of Charities*, 4th ed. (London, 1818), *passim.*

[4] 59 Geo III c. 81. On the background to this Bill, see New, *Henry Brougham*, 218–23.

[5] See Owen, *English Philanthropy*, chap. VII.

[6] New, *Henry Brougham*, 223.

prophecies, revealed a large number of abuses and led to a considerable increase in the number of charity causes before the Court of Chancery.[1] But the commissioners' work was essentially a 'fact-finding enterprise'.[2] Brougham had hoped that the inquiries and reports of the commissioners would in themselves check abuses.[3] But many dishonest trustees withstood with equanimity the glare of unfavourable publicity, and in the 1840's the search for a summary, expeditious and cheap Chancery remedy was wearily resumed.[4]

[1] W. F. Finlason, *The Act for the Better Regulation of Charitable Trusts, With Copious Notes and an Introductory Essay* (London, 1853), 81.

[2] Owen, *English Philanthropy*, 190.

[3] *Parliamentary Debates* (Hansard), XXXVIII, 1220–1; Brougham, *Letter to Romilly, passim.*

[4] A rather half-hearted and totally ineffectual attempt had been made in 1819 by statute (59 Geo. III c. 91) to enforce the findings of the commissioners. It provided, *inter alia*, that the commissioners could certify particulars of any breach of trust to the Attorney-General who could apply summarily or by information in Chancery to repair the breach.

Cf. the present Charities Act, 1960; and the Nathan Committee report, presented to Parliament in 1952: Cmnd. 8710.

APPENDIXES

APPENDIX A

BILLS AND ANSWERS IN CHANCERY RELATING TO CHARITY, 1350–1601

Bills and Answers: 1350–1558
P.R.O. citation: C. 1/6/21

6/21 *Parishioners of Kirkby in Kendal* v. *William Thornburgh*
Money entrusted to William Thornburgh for rebuilding the church.
Addressed to: Bishop of Winchester, 1413–26(?)

7/79 *Thomas Bernburgh* v. *Richard Parysh*
Bond given to celebrate masses for the soul of Richard Ogell.
Addressed to: Archbishop of York, 1391–1432(?)

7/118 *John Pomell et al. churchwardens of Great Linton Church* v. *John Wolf, parson of Hildersham*
£8 paid to defendant by a feoffee for the repair of Linton parish church.
Addressed to: Archbishop of York, 1391–1432(?)

7/264 *John Croxby et al.* v. *Thomas Rolf et al., chaplain, and feoffees*
Lands enfeoffed for foundation of a college in Oxford.
Addressed to: Archbishop of York, 1391–1432(?)

9/430 *John Petyt, parson* v. *Thomas Humphrey et al., executors*
Money due for repair of Woolpit church.
Addressed to: John, Bishop of Bath and Wells, 1432–43 (dated: 18 Hen. VI)

10/249 *Parson of Oxnead* v. *John Fode, priest*
Lands enfeoffed to be sold for the repair of Oxnead church.
Addressed to: John, Bishop of Bath and Wells, 1432–43

10/302 *Thomas Nicoll et al., churchwardens and parishioners of Hendon* v. *William Page et al., executors*
Land devised to find a priest to say mass for one year in the church.
Addressed to: John, Bishop of Bath and Wells, 1432–43

11/17 *Thomas Stanes* v. *Richard Dowe et al., executors*
Costs of building an aisle to Wytham Church, as directed by the testator.
Addressed to: John, Bishop of Bath and Wells, 1432–43

11/216 *Parishioners of St Dunstan* v. *John Neell et al., executors*
Money for foundation of a chantry in the church.
Addressed to: John, Bishop of Bath and Wells, 1432–43

12/83 *Henry Pygot et al., churchwardens of Ospring* v. *Seman at Sole, feoffees*
Land devised to be sold for the repair of Ospring Church.
Addressed to: John Frank, 1433

13/108 *Robert Kirkeham, parson, et al.*, v. *Thomas Boleyn, feoffee*
Detention of deed of feoffment of land devised for rebuilding church and steeple.
Addressed to: Archbishop of Canterbury, 1443–50 (dated: 27 Hen. VI)

13/114 *William Skyrmot, et al. proctors of the Fraternity of St Mary's Chapel on the bridge of Bristol* v. *Thomas Haleway et al., feoffees*
Land devised for the use of the chapel. Addressed to: Archbishop of Canterbury, 1443–50 (dated: 24 Hen. VI)

16/225 *Sir William Carlele, chaplain* v. *John Borough et al., executors of Symon Camps, esq.*
Legacy and fittings of a chapel.
Addressed to: Archbishop of Canterbury, 1407–56

16/522 *John Sturgeon et al.* v. *Richard Brune*
Lands enfeoffed to be sold, 100 marks to Wardens of Rochester Bridge and for work of 'pyte' in St Dunstan's parish in Fleet Street.
Addressed to: Archbishop of Canterbury, 1407–56

16/679 *Richard Porter et al., parishioners of Westham* v. *Adam Ywode et al., feoffees*
Lands for hospital of St John and works at Westham Church.
Addressed to: Archbishop of Canterbury, 1407–56

17/127 *John Barham et al., churchwardens of the church* v. *John Anabyll, feoffee*
Money charged on land bequeathed to church of St James Deeping.
Addressed to: Archbishop of Canterbury, 1407–56

18/19 *John Atte Wode et al., churchwardens of Pulborough* v. *John Snap*
Annuity charged on land to Pulborough Church.
Addressed to: John, Cardinal Archbishop of York, 1450–2 (dated: 29 Hen. VI)

19/266 *John Baron, master, and wardens of the Fraternity* v. *William Coton et al., feoffees*
Lands devised to the Fraternity
Addressed to: John, Cardinal Archbishop of York, 1450–2

19/428 *John, Abbot of Tewkesbury* v. *William Ingram, executor*
Foundation of a chantry in the abbey.
Addressed to: John, Cardinal Archbishop of York, 1450–2

20/43 *Robert Pathe et al., executors* v. *Geoffrey Devyll*
Land devised to provide a gilt cross for St Mary's Church in Hoo.
Addressed to: Archbishop of York, 1426–52

23/2 *John Walsshe* v. *John Walsshe, feoffee* (answer)
Lands to King's Walden church.
Addressed to: John, Cardinal Archbishop of Canterbury, 1453(?)

24/147 *John Hunt et al., churchwardens of St Margaret's Southwark* v. *Thomas Slyfeld, feoffee*
Lands to use of St Margaret's Church.
Addressed to: Earl of Salisbury, 1454–5 (dated: 32 Hen. VI)

25/183 *John Harry et al., churchwardens of Biddenden* v. *James Beghynden et al., sons of the original feoffees*
Money from land for purchase of a new church bell.
Addressed to: Thomas, Archbishop of Canterbury, 1455–6 (dated: 34 Hen. VI)

25/188 *Thomas Ive, on behalf of parishioners of St Pancras in the Field* v. *Robert Warner et al.*
Land for erection of a church.
Addressed to: Thomas, Archbishop of Canterbury, 1455–6 (dated: 34 Hen. VI)

28/146 *Richard Canon et al., churchwardens of St Mary, Stanwell* v. *Hugh Parker et al., feoffees*
Land bequeathed for repair of Stanwell Church.
Addressed to: Bishop of Exeter, 1460–5

28/430 *John Neell, master of Hospital of St Thomas, et al.* v. *Thomas Wombewell et al., executors*
Lands to be sold to establish a priest to sing in Botolph's Northfleet.
Addressed to: Bishop of Exeter, 1460–5

29/148 *Thomas Draper, feoffee and executor* v. *John Hexsalt*
Lands to be sold for making a highway, 'and other alms deeds'.
Addressed to: Bishop of Exeter, 1460–5

29/347 *Sir Stephen Brasier, vicar, and churchwardens* v. *John Hume, feoffee*
Lands for benefit of Rothwell chapel.
Addressed to: Bishop of Exeter, 1460–5

29/463 *John Hopton, executor* v. *Thomas Vavasour, co-executor*
Money bequeathed for providing a chantry priest for two years, to pray for testator's soul.
Addressed to: Bishop of Exeter, 1460–5

31/87 *Henry Virley, parson, and the churchwardens of Great Warley* v. *William Neweman, executor*
Money to parish church for a bell.
Addressed to: George, Archbishop of York, 1465, 1471

38/274 *John Ocley, churchwarden, and the parishioners of Ivychurch* v. *Stephen Harynden, feoffee*
Land bequeathed to a church.
Addressed to: Bishop of Bath and Wells, 1467–72

40/183 *John Nele, dean and canons of the College of St Mary, Norwich* v. *Simond Thornham*
Money granted to St Mary's College, Norwich.
Addressed to: Bishop of Bath and Wells, 1467–72

43/1 *Jamys Golbeter et al., churchreves of St Peter's Pormontergate, Norwich* v. *William Aubry, executor*
Debt bequeathed to a church.
Addressed to: Bishop of Bath and Wells, 1467–72

47/18 *Richard Raddenore, warden of the Friars Minors, Hereford* v. *Henry Collewall et al.*
Possession of bible promised by late Walter Peytewyn to the library of the Friars.
Addressed to: Bishop of Rochester, 1472–3, 1475

47/277 *Thomas Asshenden* v. *John Felde*
Money remitted out of a bond to find a priest to sing at St Magnus for soul of John Michell.
Addressed to: Bishop of Rochester, 1472–3, 1475

57/74 *Robert, prior of the church of Our Lady of Bilsington, Kent* v. *John Taillour, guardian in socage*
Money, charged on lands, to the church for saying of obits.
Addressed to: Bishop of Lincoln, 1475–80, 1483–5

61/559 *William Loveday, executor, and heir of testator* v. *William Freke et al., feoffees*
Rent of lands devised as an endowment for a chapel at Dunmow.
Addressed to: Archbishop of York, 1480–3

66/413 *John Medewall, administrator* v. *Richard Bracy et al., churchwardens*
Money advanced by deceased for church purposes at St Margaret's, Southwark.
Addressed to: Bishop of Lincoln, 1475–80, 1483–5

68/249 *The poor commons of the county of Middlesex* v. *John Davy et al., collectors of the pavage*
Detention of money collected for paving the high road in the parish.
Addressed to: Illegible

70/89 *Priest and churchwardens of St Nicholas, Lynn* v. *John Dekon, executor*
Bequest of 40s. to the church.
Addressed to: Illegible

98/17 *Richard Joy et al., executors* v. *John Hopton, vicar*
Breach of undertaking to provide a chrismatory for Southwold church from bequest of deceased.
Addressed to: John, Archbishop of Canterbury, 1486–93

109/48 *William Stanway, parson of parish church of Horton* v. *George Danyell, brother of late parson*
Refusal to dispose of late parson's goods towards the repair of the church.
Addressed to: John, Archbishop of Canterbury, 1486–93

114/43 *Thomas Assheman, and Isabel, executrix* v. *John Wylcokkis*

Goods by deceased to the use of a chantry in Welyngham.

Addressed to: Archbishop of Canterbury, 1486–93; 1504–15

116/6 *Thomas Bromwich and other inhabitants of parish* v. *Robert Bryan, executor*

Moneys left to inhabitants of Moche Levermere.

Addressed to: Archbishop of Canterbury, 1486–93; 1504–15

121/53 *John Berdefeld* v. *Thomas Wodeham et al., feoffees*

Lands to provide a priest's salary.

Addressed to: Archbishop of Canterbury, 1486–93; 1504–15

132/14 *Sir Thomas Downe, priest* v. *Lawrence Adams, feoffee*

Lands charged with an annuity for chantry of St Mary Magdelen, Taunton.

Addressed to: Archbishop of Canterbury, 1486–93; 1504–15

137/24 *Thomas Glyn et al., executors* v. *William Knappelocke*

Fraudulent conveyance, if daughters die without issue (*inter alia*), for masses, for a vestment, for poor maidens of good name on their marriage, for the lame and blind.

Addressed to: Archbishop of Canterbury, 1486–93; 1504–15

139/3 *William Homwode et al., wardens of Brotherhood of St Katherine in East Grinstead church* v. *Thomas or William Innyngfeld, feoffee*

Land bequeathed to find a priest at altar of the church.

Addressed to: Archbishop of Canterbury, 1486–93; 1504–15

150/80 *Richard Martyn et al., churchwardens of Sproughton* v. *William Sewall et al., executors*

Bequest for the repair of a church.

Addressed to: Archbishop of Canterbury, 1486–93; 1504–15

151/1 *The Friars Preachers of Norwich* v. *William Gibbes, executor* Bequest to rebuild complainant's church after fire.

Addressed to: Archbishop of Canterbury, 1486–93; 1504–15

152/52 *Robert Okynfold et al., executors* v. *William Hunkyn et al., feoffees*

Timber bequeathed to William Kete on condition of his presenting a chalice to Milstead church.

Addressed to: Archbishop of Canterbury, 1486–93; 1504–15

153/75 *Simon Playne and Alice his wife, executrix* v. *Nicholas Litelwode et al., feoffees*

Lands in remainder for acts of charity.

Addressed to: Archbishop of Canterbury, 1486–93; 1504–15

249/43 *William Kemp, parson of St Dunston's, Stephenhith* v. *Margaret Chadworth*

Bequests to the church.

Addressed to: Henry Dean, Archbishop of Canterbury, 1501–2

271/94 *John Smyth et al., churchwardens of church of Our Lady, Bury St Edmunds* v. *Thomas Mychell*

Debts bequeathed to the church.

Addressed to: William Warham, Bishop of London, 1502–3

279/55 *Elizabeth Barnardiston, executrix* v. *Thomas Barnardiston*

Refusal to convey land for maintaining a priest.

Addressed to: William Warham, Archbishop of Canterbury, 1504–15

293/53 *Thomas Cokshote et al., executors* v. *Godard Oxenbrige*

Debt bequeathed to charitable uses.

Addressed to: William Warham, Archbishop of Canterbury, 1504–15

299/52 *Mayor, bailiffs and burgesses of Cambridge* v. *Elizabeth Barbour et al., executors*

Refusal to construct a conduit in Cambridge Market Square.

Addressed to: William Warham, Archbishop of Canterbury, 1504–15

300/51 *Adam Langly et al., churchwardens of Collingham* v. *Nicholas Styrley, executor*

Money granted to the church and entrusted by complainants' predecessors to Alexander Meryng.

Addressed to: William Warham, Archbishop of Canterbury, 1504–15

309/56 *Vicar and churchwardens of Fressingfield* v. *John Tasburgh et al., executors*

Rents charged for church repair and charitable uses.

Addressed to: William Warham, Archbishop of Canterbury, 1504–15

311/13 *William Fyndern* v. *Prior of Thetford*

Neglect to find chantry priests, notwithstanding grants by complainant's ancestors of divers churches for that purpose.

Addressed to: William Warham, Archbishop of Canterbury, 1504–15

312/12 *John Grene et al., executors* v. *William Lee, executor*

Land willed to charitable uses, but sold.

Addressed to: William Warham, Archbishop of Canterbury, 1504–15

321/54 *Geoffrey Howys et al., executors* v. *John Pynnys et al., executors.*

Detention of deeds relating to lands devised to charitable uses.

Addressed to: William Warham, Archbishop of Canterbury, 1504–15

323/60 *Brian Hall, executor* v. *Thomas Sawier, chaplain*

Refusal to state where are the goods bequeathed to charitable uses.

Addressed to: William Warham, Archbishop of Canterbury, 1504–15

328/77 *Richard Ketells and other inhabitants of Shoreham* v. *Richard Wodde, and Edmund Page, feoffee's heir*

Lands for maintenance of almshouse, sold by feoffee's heir to Wodde.

Addressed to: William Warham, Archbishop of Canterbury, 1504–15

331/23 *Master and wardens of Merchant Taylors of London* v. *Isabel Howden et al., executors*

Money promised at a meeting of complainants in common hall to found a chantry in St Mary Abchurch and to distribute coals to parishioners there, never received because of his sudden death.

Addressed to: William Warham, Archbishop of Canterbury, 1504–15

331/81 *John Lilly et al., executors* v. *Hugh Wombwell*

Lands and rents to found a chantry in the college of Rotherham.

Addressed to: William Warham, Archbishop of Canterbury, 1504–15

331/88 *John Palmer, mayor of Lynn* v. *Katherine Nokkard, executrix*

Refusal to perfect a cistern in Lynn.

Addressed to William Warham, Archbishop of Canterbury, 1504–15

335/87 *Master and wardens of Merchant Taylors of London* v. *Isabel Howden, executrix*

Money promised to found a chantry in (St Mary) Abchurch; yearly distribution of coals in parish.

Addressed to: William Warham, Archbishop of Canterbury, 1504–15

335/89 *Churchwardens of Melksham* v. *Thomas Holwey, executor*

Bequest to repair the church.

Addressed to: William Warham, Archbishop of Canterbury, 1504–15

337/65 *John Mannyng* v. *William Sendell et al., feoffees*
Refusal to complete sale of land to charitable uses.
Addressed to: William Warham, Archbishop of Canterbury, 1504–15

351/9 *Thomas Bregge and other, churchwardens of parish church of Rawreth* v. *John Fuller et al., executors*
Land for support of a chantry priest and to keep church in repair.
Addressed to: William Warham, Archbishop of Canterbury, 1504–15

359/56 *Master and fellows of St John's College* v. *Richard Fox et al., feoffees*
Refusal to endow a college with certain lands.
Addressed to: William Warham, Archbishop of Canterbury, 1504–15

368/43 *William Ussher, surety* v. *Dean and Chapter of Windsor*
Claim for alms paid to defendant by principal.
Addressed to: William Warham, Archbishop of Canterbury, 1504–15

401/17 *John Coblay, priest of the chantry* v. *Richard Fynamour et al., stewards*
Profits devised to a chantry of St Mary Magdalen and St Nicholas at Calne.
Addressed to: Thomas Wolsey, Archbishop of York, 1515–18

439/31 *William Raynar* v. *Richard White, son of John*
Land bequeathed to complainant on condition of payment of a yearly obit for twenty years in Foxton Church.
Addressed to: Thomas Wolsey, Archbishop of York, 1515–18

453/65 *Richard Wylkynson et al., executors* v. *Thomas Welby, feoffee*
Refusal to join in a feoffment for a priest to say and sing masses in Harlaxton Church.
Addressed to: Thomas Wolsey, Archbishop of York, 1515–18

463/19 *Thomas Ascheburne in the name of inhabitants of Shenley* v. *William Pygott, heir*

Devise to relieve inhabitants from payment of subsidies.

Addressed to: Thomas Wolsey, Archbishop of York, 1518–29

481/47 *Master and fellows of Trinity Hall* v. *Walter Lombe, heir*

Detention of deeds of lands devised for testator's obit in college chapel; residue for division among fellows and scholars.

Addressed to: Thomas Wolsey, Archbishop of York, 1518–29

492/28 *Laurence Campagius, papal legate* v. *Edward Baynton*

Land devised for maintenance of chantry in Salisbury Cathedral.

Addressed to: Thomas Wolsey, Archbishop of York, 1518–29

499/1 *John Dowman* v. *John Rudstone*

Money for buying land entrusted to defendant for foundation of a grammar school.

Addressed to: Thomas Wolsey, Archbishop of York, 1518–29

517/37 *Robert Hill et al., feoffees* v. *Roger Arundel et al.*

Land devised for eighty years to the church of Uploman.

Addressed to: Thomas Wolsey, Archbishop of York, 1518–29

519/47 *Henry Hunt, executor* v. *Randolph Grymsdyche, feoffee*

Land devised for finding a chantry priest to sing perpetually in parish church.

Addressed to: Thomas Wolsey, Archbishop of York, 1518–29

526/41 *William Hopkyns et al.* v. *William Gorwey et al., feoffees*

Land bought with petitioner's wife's money to maintain an obit.
Addressed to: Thomas Wolsey, Archbishop of York, 1518–29

528/65 *Mayor and burgesses of Hedon* v. *Martin Davison*
Detention of deeds related to the finding of a priest to sing in the parish church of Hedon.
Addressed to: Thomas Wolsey, Archbishop of York, 1518–29

561/100 *Nicholas Rowley* v. *Thomas Taylour, vicar of Christ Church, York, et al.*
Land to guild of Corpus Christi for deceased's soul.
Addressed to: Thomas Wolsey, Archbishop of York, 1518–29

567/15 *Bishop of Chichester* v. *Abbot of Chertsey*
Money paid to a former abbot to repair a house for a chantry.
Addressed to: Thomas Wolsey, Archbishop of York, 1518–29

600/ 35 & 52 *John* ? v. *Robert Northway*
Attempt to destroy petitioner's title by paying rent to feoffees for charitable uses.
Addressed to: Thomas Wolsey, Archbishop of York, 1518–29

601/1 *John Arundell et al., feoffees* v. *John Vyvyan et al., executors*
Failure to pay an annuity, charged on land, for the finding of a priest.
Addressed to: Sir Thomas More, 1529–32

636/19 *John Guyon et al., feoffees* v. *Richard Copsheff*
Dispute concerning land devised for obits.
Addressed to: Sir Thomas More, 1529–32

657/59 *John Mere, chantry priest* v. *William Yonge et al.*
Arrears of annuity payable to priest of the chantry.
Addressed to: Sir Thomas More, 1529–32

677/8 *William Sheperde et al., wardens of parish church of Finchley* v. *William Sheperde et al.*
Land devised for maintenance of the ornaments of the church and performance of an obit. Defendants are surviving witnesses of the testators will.
Addressed to: Sir Thomas More, 1529–32

680/12 *William Trevelian, vicar of Kingsbury* v. *John Chamborn*
Refusal to perform an oral agreement to find yearly a priest to say divine service in Kingsbury church.
Addressed to: Sir Thomas More, 1529–32

697/40 *Richard Bradshawe et al.* v. *John Aschedale et al.*
Land claimed to the use of a chantry.
Addressed to: Sir Thomas Audley, 1532–8

699/40 *Richard Willys et al., churchwardens of Canford* v. *Johanne Gay, executrix*
Money delivered to use of parish church of Canford and for purchase of a chalice.
Addressed to: Sir Thomas Audley, 1532–8

740/19 *John Barker* v. *Thomas Barley et al.*
Lands devised for one year to find a priest in Bromfeld church, and so used for a longer time.
Addressed to: Sir Thomas Audley, 1532–8

753/5 *Thomas Campyon and other parishioners of St Mary Aldermary* v. *Oliver Claymonde, executor*
Action on a bond for a loan towards rebuilding the parish church out of a bequest for a suit of copes.
Addressed to: Sir Thomas Audley, 1532–8

807/49–51 *Richard Rode and Richard Meryham* v. *Thomas Patenden*
Land devised for benefit of church at Goudhurst.
Addressed to: Sir Thomas Audley, 1532–8

813/58 *Thomas Hoore* v. *Edmund Clarke et al.*
Land devised to a chantry in the church of Long Melford.
Addressed to: Sir Thomas Audley, 1532–58

815/30 *Jeffrey Hellott* v. *John Newman, executor*
Money promised for saying masses for the soul of Robert, the testator.
Addressed to: Sir Thomas Audley, 1532–8

841/33 *Thomas Loll et al., churchwardens of Claxby by Willoughby* v. *Thomas Goodwyn*
Money collected to buy a book called 'a Grayle' for the church.
Addressed to: Sir Thomas Audley, 1532–8

858/20–21 *Robert Metham et al., executors* v. *William Vavosour*
Money given to defendant for certain charitable purposes.
Addressed to: Sir Thomas Audley, 1532–8

938/20–21 *William Alyn, heir* v. *William Pooley*
Defendant pleads bequest to pious uses.
Addressed to: Lord Audley, 1538–44

943/42 *Anthony Ayleworthe* v. *Thomas Bossell*
Land bequeathed to a chantry.
Addressed to: Lord Audley, 1538–44

982/32–33 *Anthony Eliott and Robert Chapman, executors* v. *Robert Preston et al.*
Neglect to find a priest to sing for the souls of named persons.
Addressed to: Lord Audley, 1538–44

1014/48–51 *Richard Jamys* v. *Thomas Richemond*
Aid promised for the repair of the church on condition of a gift by the complainant.
Addressed to: Lord Audley, 1538–44

1056/53–54 *Robert Rogeman et al., churchwardens of St Mary's Sutton* v. *Isabel Wright*
Lands devised for foundation of chantry.
Addressed to: Lord Audley, 1538–44

1059/71–73 *John Swynerton, executor* v. *Thomas Chafyn*
Money entrusted to defendant for delivery to churchwardens of Mere to maintain a priest.
Addressed to: Lord Audley, 1538–44

1087/11 *Harry Wayndman* v. *Robert Preston*
Annuity to say masses and pray for soul of Walter in chapel of St Anthony.
Addressed to: Lord Audley, 1538–44

1087/45–48 *John Worssely, heir* v. *Margaret Brudenell*
Defendant pleads bequest to find a priest to sing for the souls of named persons in an action for detention of deeds.
Addressed to: Lord Audley, 1538–44

1094–86 *Archbishop of York* v. *Richard Farclyff*
Devise of profits for maintenance of a chantry and charitable uses.
Addressed to: Lord Audley, 1538–44

1119/1–2 *John Duffeld et al., churchwardens of East Grinstead* v. *Robert Lewknour, et. al.*
Lands devised to the lady chancel of the parish church.
Addressed to: Thomas, Lord Wriothesley, 1544–7

1123/46 *George Atkynson* v. *Edward Sapcottes*
Lands given to a chantry.
Addressed to: Thomas, Lord Wriothesley, 1544–7

1129/59–60 *John Horner, executor* v. *John Standyshe et al.*
Money bequeathed to defendants to maintain poor scholars at a university.
Addressed to: Thomas, Lord Wriothesley, 1544–7

1144/6 *Hughe Mathewe, bailiff, and inhabitants of Tutbury* v. *William & Bartholomew Chaplen*
Legacy for repair of Tutbury bridge.
Addressed to: Thomas, Lord Wriothesley, 1544–7

1146/43–49 *Richard Mondes et al., churchwardens of St Edward, Romford* v. *John Stoker, heir*
Land devised to chapel of St Edward.
Addressed to: Thomas, Lord Wriothesley, 1544–7

1147/21–23 *John Nayler, heir* v. *Thomas Males et al., churchwardens of Balsham*
Land devised to 'church ryvves' of Balsham for purchase of wax and gifts to the poor.
Addressed to: Thomas, Lord Wriothesley, 1544–7

1155/59 *Thomas Rygeley et al., feoffees* v. *Thomas Blyeth*
Land devised to maintain a parish priest at Shenstone.
Addressed to: Thomas, Lord Wriothesley, 1544–7

1169/36–38 *Henry Waynman* v. *Denise Sandes*
Lands devised to find a priest to sing for testator's soul.
Addressed to: Thomas, Lord Wriothesley, 1544–7
(see also 1087/11)

1195/61–64 *Thomas Buller et al.* v. *Thomas Hardynge et al., executors*
Gold bequeathed to petitioners to distribute among poor and other charitable uses.
Addressed to: Richard, Lord Rich, 1547–51

1225/21–22 *John Goodred et al., churchwardens of Launden and other inhabitants* v. *John Byrde*
Land to be used for repair of highways and payments of fifteenths.
Addressed to: Richard, Lord Rich, 1547–51

1312/60–61 *Master of the hospital of St John the Baptist at Meer* v. *Robert Brodbanke, et al.*
Obligation to maintain poor from certain lands.
Addressed to: Thomas Goodrich, Bishop of Ely, 1551–3

1330/45–47 *King's and Queen's tenants of Bolingbroke* v. *Richard Goodriche, executor*
Land to found a school in Bolingbroke diverted by the defendant to a school in Louth.
Addressed to: Stephen Gardiner, Bishop of Winchester, 1553–5

1354/76–77 *Thomas Gregge and other inhabitants of Gonerby* v. *Thomas Knotte*
Land granted for payments to the curate in Lent and for repair of church.
Addressed to: Stephen Gardiner, Bishop of Winchester, 1553–5

1402/97 *William Baker et al., churchwardens of St James's at Bury St Edmunds on behalf of parishioners* v. *Thomas Byrdall et al., executors*
Money bequeathed for rebuilding the church of St James's at Bury St Edmunds.
Addressed to: Nicholas Heath, Archbishop of York, 1556–8

1423/46–48 *Christopher Dyghton et al.*, v. *Thomas Hublethorn, heir*
Land granted for maintenance of a chaplain in church at Horncastle and other religious uses.
Addressed to: Nicholas Heath, Archbishop of York, 1556–8

1427/67 *John Fogge et al., executors* v. *Christopher Eyre*
Legacy (*inter alia*) for marriage of fifty poor maids in Tideswell.
Addressed to: Nicholas Heath, Archbishop of York, 1556–8

1428/52 *John Foster and other churchwardens of Aldenham* v. *Philip Bold et al.*
Money bequeathed to church of Aldenham so that profits may be used for divine service.
Addressed to: Nicholas Heath, Archbishop of York, 1556–8

1458/51–56 *Richard Oye, heir* v. *Robert Clarke*
Land granted for repair of highways in Oadby.
Addressed to: Nicholas Heath, Archbishop of York, 1556–8

1475/4 *Henry Tayllour* v. *Christopher Nelson*
Land granted for the saying of mass in St James in Rychall.
Addressed to: Nicholas Heath, Archbishop of York, 1556–8

1497/46 *Inhabitants of Coppenhall* v. *Thomas Chromeley et al., executors*

Bequest for making a causeway and mending a lane.
Addressed to: Stephen Gardiner, Bishop of Winchester, 1553–5

1506/33 *Maude Kendale* v. *Stephen Kendale et al.*

Procuring from plaintiff a conveyance to religious uses contrary to will of deceased.
Date unknown.

1518/41 *John Yeldham et al.* v. *William Hanford et al., executors*

£40 in gold for an obit in church of St Magnus.
(Date unknown)

Bills and Answers: temp. Elizabeth

P.R.O. citation: C. 2/Eliz./B. 1/16

B. 1/16 *Arthur Henrye, William Wyseman, John Leydon, Anthony Edwards, churchwardens of Burnham* v. *Benjamin Harris*

Bequest to the poor of Burnham.
Bill: 4 February 1595
Answer: 4 February 1595

B. 11/43 *John Bartlett* v. *Robert Wolley et al.*

Money charged on land for charitable uses.
Bill: 1 February 1595
Answer (including a demurrer): 17 January 1596

B. 12/54 *Thomas Parker et al., on behalf of inhabitants of Brentwood* v. *Wistan Browne*

Bill to establish free school and almshouses at Southwelde.
Bill: *temp.* Nicholas Bacon
Demurrer: undated

B. 17/49 *Edward Buggs et al., feoffees for parish of Harlow* v. *William Sompner et al.*

Land to feoffees in trust for poor of Harlow.
Bill: 10 February, 1601
Answer (demurrer): 5 November 1601
(see also H. 17/7)

B. 18/30 *William Buttall et al., churchwardens of Lyndsell* v. *Richard Fitche*
Land for repair of parish church.
Bill: 9 January 1579
Answer and replication: undated

B. 19/47 *Henry Blenkinsopp et al.* v. *Christopher Buckle et al.*
Annuity for certain paupers and a school master in Burgh.
Bill: (?) November 1580
Answer: 5 December 1600

B. 29/44 *John Goodwin et al., churchwardens and overseers of Bocking* v. *John Robinson et al.*
£400 bequeathed for poor of Bocking.
Bill: 10 November 1601
Answer: 20 November 1602

B. 31/49 *Thomas Tychmers et al., churchwardens and feoffees for poor of Barrington* v. *Henry Lancaster*
Land for poor of Barrington.
Bill: 1 October 1597
Answer: 7 November 1597
Replication: undated

C. 6/10 *George Carlton et al., on behalf of inhabitants of Elm* v. *John Blyth et al.*
Legacy to be invested for benefit of poor of Elm.
Bill only: 15 June 1588
(see also E. 5/60)

C. 6/28 *Robert Perott et al., on behalf of inhabitants of Corneworthy* v. *Stephen Cruse*
Land for benefit of parish of Corneworthy.
Bill (for appointment of trustees): 5 February 1589
Answer: undated

C. 22/47 *John Irish et al., and other tenants of manor of Congresbury* v. *Thomas Aishe et al.*
Land to 'divers verye good and godlie uses'.
Bill: (?) October 1586
Answer: (?) 15 November 1586

C. 23/42 *Mayor and citizens of Chester* v. *Robert Brooke et al.*
Land for benefit of apprentices of Chester.
Bill: 1 January 1596
Answer: (?) 7 February 1596

D. 2/57 *Mayor, bailiffs and burgesses of Dartmouth* v. *Nicholas Ball*
Land for poor of, and the repair of the church and harbour at, Clifton Dartmouth.
Bill (for appointment of new trustees): 18 November 1601
Answer: undated

D. 7/35 *John Laymarne et al., churchwardens of Danburye* v. *Thomas Emerye et al.*
Land in trust for poor of Danburye.
Bill: 4 February 1597
Answer: 19 April 1597
(mutilated)

D. 11/47 *Mayor, bailiffs and burgesses of Clifton Dartmouth Hardness* v. *William Furseman et al.*
Land for poor of Dartmouth and other charities.
Bill: 7 February 1596
Answer: 12 February 1596

E. 4/32 *John Blacknall et al., inhabitants of Elksley* v. *Robert Spivy et al.*
Land in trust for said parish.
Bill: 8 June 1597
Answers: 22 September 1597 and undated

E. 5/60 *George Carleton et al., for inhabitants of Elm* v. *John Blyth et al.*
Legacy for inhabitants of Elm.
Bill: *temp.* Christopher Hatton, 1587–91

F. 3/37 *Walter Jenkins et al., inhabitants of Fairford* v. *William Oldisworth*
Legacy to tenants of manor of Fairford.
Bill: (?) 1587
Answer: undated

G. 12/35 — *Richard Estmond et al., inhabitants of Gillingham* v. *Edmond Lawrence*
Land for the support of a charity school at Gillingham.
Bill: 4 January 1597
Answer: 27 January 1597

G. 12/59 — *Christopher Goodson et al.* v. *Henry Monday et al.*
Land to feoffees in trust for repair of highways, about Ailesbury and Hartwell.
Bill: 10 October 1597
Answer: 21 October 1597
Replication: undated

H. 1/34 — *Sir Arthur Havenyngham et al. and other inhabitants of Havenyngham* v. *Thomas Tye*
Land for use of town of Havenyngham.
Answer only: undated

H. 2/26 — *Thomas Sayer et al., overseers to poor of Halingbury Morley* v. *Robert Lambe et al.*
Legacy for poor of Halingbury Morley.
Bill only: 21 October 1602
(see also H. 20/35)

H. 7/57 — *John Huckmore et al., feoffees* v. *John Lang et al.*
Land for poor parishioners of Comb yn Tynhed.
Bill: *temp.* Thomas Bromley.
Answers and replication: undated

H. 10/26 — *William Halle* v. *Master and fellows of St Mary's College of Winchester in Oxford*
Land for scholars and graduates of New College, devised by complainant's grandfather.
Bill: (?) 1594
Answer and replication: undated

H. 17/7 — *Edward Buggs et al., inhabitants of Harlow* v. *Nicholas Sibley*
Land for poor of parish of Harlow.
Bill only: 28 October 1602

H. 20/35 — *Thomas Sayer et al., overseers of poor of Halingbury Morley* v. *Francis Dynne et al.*

Legacy of £20, income to be used for the poor of Halingbury Morley.
Bill only: temp. Thomas Egerton, 1596–1603

H. 21/54 *Edward Heron et al., executors* v. *Richard Sproxton et al.*
Land for free school, almshouses, and the repair of highways in Normanton and Kirkethorpe.
Bill: 8 May 1598
Answer: 22 June 1598

I. 6/24 *William Fisher et al., on behalf of inhabitants of Irchester* v. *Thomas Bletsoo*
Land for poor of, and repair of bridges at Irchester.
Bill: 3 July 1593
Answer: 6 November 1593
Replication: undated

I. 6/31 *John Stocke et al., on behalf of poor of Icklingham* v. *Thomas Page et al.*
Land settled from 'ancient time' for poor of Icklingham.
Bill only: 18 November 1597

I. 6/41 *William Fisher, master of St Mary of Ilford* v. *Anne Seward*
To recover dues, land for relief of poor in Ilford.
Replication only: *temp.* Christopher Hatton

K. 3/50 *Robert Brian et al., inhabitants of Kybworth* v. *Richard Bente et al.*
Land for poor of Kybworth.
Bill: 9 May 1595
Answer: 12 May 1595
Replication: undated

K. 5/55 *Thomas Foxe et al., inhabitants of Kybworth* v. *Richard Bente et al.*
Land for support of a grammar school and schoolmaster at Kybworth.
Bill only: *temp.* Thomas Egerton

L. 3/42 *Z. Babington, master of St John Baptist, Lichfield* v. *Richard Sale et al.*
Land for poor persons in St John Baptist, and for a free grammar school.
Bill: 27 November 1590
Answers: 24 April 1592 and undated

L. 5/18 *Mayor and burgesses of King's Lynn* v. *Thomas Howes*
Land for maintenance of preacher and other charitable uses.
(Badly mutilated).

M. 10/65 *Richard Newton et al., parson and churchwardens of Little Monden* v. *Edward Dane*
Land (*inter alia*) for church at Little Monden.
Bill: (?) November 1597
Answer: 17 November 1597
Replication: undated

N. 4/35 *Mayor and chamberlains of Northampton* v. *John Neale et al.*
Land for charitable uses in Northampton.
Bill: *temp.* John Puckeringe
Answer: undated

P. 3/53 *Edward Grevill et al., feoffees* v. (mutilated)
Land for repair of parish church of Mickleton.
Bill: 4 May 1597
Answers: 13 June 1597 and undated
Replication: undated

P.10/24 *Master and fellows of Pembroke Hall, Cambridge* v. *Robert Russell et al.*
Annuity of 20s. charged on lands in favour of petitioners.
Bill: 7 November 1601
Answer 1: 9 November 1601
Answer 2: 2 February 1602

R. 11/19 *Robert Chambers et al., inhabitants of Reach* v. *Edward Mendham et al.*
Lands for use of poor of Reach.
Bill: 17 October 1590
Answer: 23 January 1591

R. 12/48 *William Rycardes et al., inhabitants of Rodboroughe* v. *Richard Payne et al.*
Land for performance of divine service in a chapel of ease to the said parish. Defendants claim that the land is forfeit to the Crown being given for superstitious uses.
Bill only: *temp.* Christopher Hatton

S. 14/7 *John Stork et al.* v. *Thomas Page et al.*
Land at Icklingham for charitable trusts.
Answer only: undated

S. 20/9 *Sir John Spenser et al., feoffees* v. *Richard Grant et al.*
Rent charged towards payment of 'two fifteenths of the said town'.
Bill: *temp.* Thomas Bromley

S. 26/48 *John Holland et al., collectors for the poor of Stenyng* v. *Robert Grosvenor et al.*
Land for the poor of the parish of Stenyng.
Bill: *temp.* Nicholas Bacon
Answer: 2 May 1578
Replication and rejoinder: undated

T. 4/29 *Edmund and William Salter et al., for poor of Tottington* v. *William Hastings et al., executors*
Land for repair of church and poor of Tottington.
Bill: (?) 1601
Answer: undated

T. 5/46 *Robert Tuttie et al., churchwardens of St Botolph* v. *John Newton*
Land for use of the poor of the parish of St Botolph.
Answer only: 25 June 1595

T. 6/43 *John Arne et al., inhabitants of Towcester* v. *Thomas West, feoffee*
Land for use and endowment of a grammar school.
Bill: 20 November 1589
Answer: undated

T. 11/7 *William Turney et al.* v. *John Buckmaster*
Whether lands were left to charitable or superstitious uses.
Bill: *temp.* Thomas Bromley
Answer: undated

W. 8/57 *Master and bretheren of hospital of Earl of Leicester in Warwick* v. *Robert Lee et al.*
Annuity of £20 to hospital in Warwick.
Bill: 29 November 1599
Answer: 29 April 1600
Replication: undated

W. 9/42 *Henry Hall et al., on behalf of inhabitants of Witham* v. *William Panke*
Land for repair of church and relief of poor.
Bill: 31 January 1596 (for appointment of new trustees).
Answer: 8 April 1596
Replication: undated

W. 13/56 *John Lloyd et al., vicar and churchwardens of Writtle* v. *John Aware et al.*
Land in trust for poor of parish of Writtle.
Bill: 20 January 1595
Answers: one dated 26 April 1597

W. 18/20 *Robert Wyllett et al., churchwardens and inhabitants of Middleton* v. *Agnes Middleton*
Charitable pensions charged on land for benefit of parish.
Bill only: *temp.* Nicholas Bacon

W. 19/51 *John Whitehurst et al., inhabitants of Dulerne* v. *George Warner, feoffee*
Lands for providing a school master and grammar school at Dulerne.
Bill: (?) 9 February 1573
Answer, replication and rejoinder: undated

W. 20/23 *John Fisher et al., inhabitants of Warwick* v. *Robert Philipps et al.*
Land for charitable purposes in Warwick.
Replication only: undated

W. 26/51 *John Rawley, inhabitants of Welborough* v. *Adrian Lewis et al., feoffees*

To appoint new trustees of a charity. Land for repair of parish church.

Bill: *temp.* Nicholas Bacon (for appointment of new trustees)

Answer and replication: undated

P.R.O. citation: C. 3/3/60

3/60 *Thomas Argall* v. *Richard Crane*

Bequest of a silver and gilt cross and 40s. in money to Camborne church.

Bill: 29 May 1562

Answer: undated

13/7 *Nicholas Blomefeld* v. *Thomas Blomefeld*

Lands devised for benefit of Stonham Jernyngham.

Bill: 26 (?) June 1564

Answer: undated

13/59 *Richard Burgin et al.*, v. *William Suzame*

Land for repair of long bridge at Bidyford.

Bill: *temp.* Nicholas Bacon, 1558–1579

14/21 *John Benson, Richard Emscombe, churchwardens of Merstham* v. *Stephen Bateman*

Land for provision of bell ropes, etc.

Bill: 25 (?) April 1572

Answer: undated

29/101 *John Boulde* v. *Sir William Sutton*

Land for Macclesfield Grammar School and for support of its teacher.

Bill: *temp.* Nicholas Bacon

Answer, replication, and rejoinder: undated

77/69 *Master and Fellows of Gonville and Caius College, Cambridge* v. *Roger Manwoode*

Land for foundation of four scholarships at Gonville and Caius under will of Joan Trappes.

Bill: 8 May 1571

Answer: undated

Replications: one undated and one dated 13 June (?) 1575

81/37 *William Hawes* v. *Philip Davis*
Land for foundation of a grammar school at Sevenoaks and almshouses in London.
Bill: *temp.* Nicholas Bacon

109/79 *Thomas Lewyn* v. *Mayor of St Albans*
Land given for foundation of a grammar school in the Lady Chapel at St Albans.
Bill: *temp.* Nicholas Bacon
Answer: undated

110/9 *Dean and chapter of Lincoln* v. *Richard Gyll*
Annuity to the vicar and singers of Leighton Church.
Bill only: *temp.* Nicholas Bacon

110/36 *Dean and chapter of Lincoln* v. *Richard Whalley*
Annuity to vicar and singers, payable out of Car-Colston parsonage.
Bill only: 30 October 1567

111/81 *Vicars and ministers of Lincoln Cathedral* v. *James Bardisey*
Annuity out of Scalford parsonage for benefit of petitioners.
Bill: *temp.* Nicholas Bacon
Answer: undated

111/94 *John Lyndsey, fellow of Jesus College, Cambridge* v. *William Braythwate*
Debt for maintenance of a scholar.
Bill: *temp.* Nicholas Bacon
Answer: undated

115/69 *Mayor of London* v. *Giles Alleyn*
112/78 Bequest for provision of coals for the poor of London forever.
Bill: 8 June 1565
Answer: undated

118/60 *Parson and wardens of St Mary, Milk St. et al.* v. *Thomas Altham*
Land for poor of St Mary, Milk St. and for prisoners in Newgate, Ludgate and The Counters.
Bill only: 6 (?) August 1562

119/23 *Joan Mullyns et al.* v. *John Golde*
Lands bestowed for charitable purposes, for the benefit of the church of Whitchurch.
Bill: *temp.* Nicholas Bacon

119/31 *Robert Manneringe and other inhabitants of Whitegate* v. *Richard Wilbrame*
Land devised for making a road between Darley Hall and Nantwich.
Bill: *temp.* Nicholas Bacon
Answer: undated

122/65 *Robert Mordant and other parishioners of Hempstead* v. *Robert Harte*
Land for the church at Hempstead.
Bill: *temp.* Nicholas Bacon

124/61 *Nicholas Marche et al., churchwardens* v. *Thomas Browne*
Land for maintenance of Modbury church.
Bill: 21 October 1562
Answer, replication, rejoinder: undated

130/73 *Mayor of Maidstone* v. *Richard Colepepir*
Land for repair of church and bridge at Maidstone.
Bill: *temp.* Nicholas Bacon
Answer, replication, rejoinder, surrejoinder, rebutter: undated

133/63 *John Netter et al., churchwardens of Cranbrook* v. *Simon Lynche*
Lands for use of Cranbrook Church.
Bill only: 2 January 1563

145/16 *Sir Thomas Pakyngton and other inhabitants of Droitwich* v. *Richard Blaston*
Lands for foundation of free school at Droitwich.
Bill: 23 January 1564

145/96 *Walter Pykes* v. *George Higgens et al.*
Bequest to St Thomas's Almshouses, Bristol.
Bill: *temp.* Nicholas Bacon
Answers: undated

159/54 *Robert Sturley et al.* v. *Thomas Cooper et al.*
Lands for relief of poor of West Langton.
Bill only: *temp.* Nicholas Bacon

170/27 *Robert Staple and other inhabitants of Halton* v. *Thomas Wynchecombe*
Land for repair of church at Halton.
Bill: 16 May 1571
Answer: undated

173/51 *William Savege and other inhabitants of South Weald* v. *Wystan Browne*
Land for foundation of a grammar school within three miles of Brentwood.
Bill: 10 June 1569
Answer: undated

181/101 *Ralph Turner and other inhabitants of Thaxted* v. *John Bultell et al.*
Distribution of funds among the poor of Thaxted.
Bill: *temp.* Nicholas Bacon
Answers, replication and rejoinder: undated.

183/34 *Edward Unton* v. *William Wyrdnam*
Lands for relief of poor and repair of highway.
Bill: *temp.* Nicholas Bacon
Answer, replication, rejoinder: undated

193/60 *Edward Wyllymot and other inhabitants of Kelshall* v. *Richard Froste*
Lands devised for poor of Kelshall.
Bill: 27 January 1570
Answers: undated
Replication: (?) June 1572

195/41 *John Ward and other churchwardens of Gestingthorpe* v. *John Parke*
Land for poor of Gestingthorpe.
Bill: *temp.* Nicholas Bacon
Answers, replication and rejoinder: undated

195/87 *Edmund Wright* v. *John Latymer*
Bequest for repair of sea walls and ditches.
Bill: *temp.* Nicholas Bacon
Answers, replications and rejoinder: undated

202/65 *Jane Thomas and other inhabitants of Little Hempston* v. *Edward Knolles*
Land for church and poor of Little Hempston.
Bill: 23 January 1567

202/72 *Master of St Mary's Hospital, Nottingham* v. *William Bolles*
Recovery of ornaments bequeathed to St Mary's Hospital, Nottingham.
Bill: 19 April 1564
Answer: undated

214/75 *Henry Mildenhall and other inhabitants of Mildenhall* v. *Robert Suckerman*
Lands bequeathed for foundation of an almshouse.
Bill: 4 November 1586
Answers: undated and 17 November 1586

218/69 *Thomas Yate and other inhabitants of Sutton Courtney* v. *Margaret Androsse*
Bequest for poor of Sutton Courtney.
Bill: 22 May 1582
Answer: undated

219/91 *William Alvye and other inhabitants of Upton* v. *Thomas West*
Land for repair of Upton Church.
Bill only: *temp.* Thomas Bromley 1579–87

227/3 *William Morson* v. *William Waller*
Dispute concerning Oldstoke Charity.
Bill: 8 January 1588
Answer (including a demurrer): 6 February 1588

252/88 *John Heigham and other parishioners of Wickhambrook* v. *Thomas Randall*
New bell for parish church.
Bill only: 8 November 1593

APPENDIX B

SELECTED TRANSCRIPTIONS

C. 1/98/17

To the moste reverend ffader in god John Archbishopp of Caunterbury and Chaunceller of England

[Undated]

Mekely besechyn your good and gracious lordshipp your poore Oratours Richard Joy and Henry Joy of the Towne of Southwold in the Countie of Suffolk Executors of the testament of John Joy Where the seid John by his last wille bequethed to the honor of almyghty god and renewyng of his Churche towards the making of a Crismatorie for the seid Churche *l* xii which late reseid in the keping of your seid Oratours. And for performyng of the seid good dede they had covenanted with oon Sir John Hopton then Vicar which promysed to proveid to the seid churche Crismatorie that noon shuld be like unto yt in Suffolk, And after the same the seid Vicar bargayned with a Goldsmyth at Cambrigge and agreed as he seid to gif to the seid Goldsmyth for the seid Crismatorie *l* xviii and thereuppon wrote with his owne hand to your Beseechers of the seid bargeyn, shewyng ferthermore he had iiii sufficient men bounde for the seid Goldsmyth that he shuld performe his bargeyn and forasmoche as the same vicar wrote ferthermore by his letre that he had bought iii skore unces of broke sylver at iii d the unce. And also that the Goldsmyth wolde have mony in hands he praied your besechers to send hym by his servaunt bringer of the said letre *l* vii xiiis iiiid promysying to answere theym thereof as in the same letre redy to be shewid apperith more of large. Uppon trust of which promeis and writyng and for the good zele which they had to the Churche in this behalf your besechers delyvered to his seid servaunt the seid *l* vii xiiis iiiid which mony came hooly to the hands of the said Vicar as the same servaunt shall testifie afore your good lordshipp. And nowe be yt the day of appoyntment of making and fynysshing of the seid Crismatorie is past over a hole yere or more and your besechers have often tymes requyred the seid Vicar to delyver theym the seid Crismatorie redy made or ells to delyver theym the seid *l* vii xiiis iiiid; yet he that to do hath refused and yet refusith. And forasmuch as your besechers have none Endentures of covenant none of delyvere of the seid money to the seid Vicar nor other especialtie sufficient to demaund the seid money at the comon law they are without remedy unlesse your gracious ayd to theym be shewd in this behalf Pleas yt therefore your gracious lordshipp in augmentyng of honor of godds churche and that hereafter lay people then may be the gladder and better willed to helping of ornaments of the seid Churche, to graunt a Writte Subpena direct to the seid Vicar comaundyng hym by the same to appere before the king in his Court of Chauncerie at a certyn day and under a certyn peyn by your lordshipp to be lymyted there to annswere in the premysses as shal accorde with right and good conscience. And this at the Reverence of god and in the way of charite.

C. 3/118/60

To the Righte honorable Sir Nicholas Bacon Knighte Lord Keeper of the greate Seale of Englande.

[Dated: 7 October 1564]

Mooste humblie complayninge shewithe to youre good Lordshippe youre daylie Oratours the parson and wardens of the paryshes of Sainte Mary Maudelin in milkestreete St. nicholas Acion besydes Lombarde Strete St. benette ffyncke and St. Olave in harte streete in London that whereas John Allen Knyghte Cytzen and Alderman of London deceassed by his laste will and testamente in wryghtinge devysed unto one William Graye his heire and assignes all his sayde lands tenements and heredytaments in plumbestede and wekham in the countie of Kente to the use and intente hereafter followinge That is to saye that he the said William his heires or assignes shoulde from the feaste of penthecoste the laste paste untyll the feaste of penthecoste whiche shall be in the yeare of oure Lorde god a Thousande fyve hundred sixtye and fyve for the full accomplishmente of Twentie yeares weeklie dystribute yeld and deliver unto the poore impotente sicke and nedye paryshyoners of the said foore paryshes and in and amongste the poore prysoners in newgate Ludgate and the Counters in London eight shillings to be bestowed in good newe and sweete bredde in forme followinge That is to weete to the poore paryshioners of every of the saide paryshes wekelye payd for the byenge of everye dossen of bredde accomptinge XIII of bredde to the dossen after the custome of the cyttye and the like dystribution to be made weeklie amongste the prysoners of the said foore prysonns after the rate aforesaid and further wylled by the same his testamente that if the saide william his heirs or assignes omitted and neglected to give or dystrybute the saide eighte shillings as is aforesaide and contrary unto certen convenants betwene the saide Sir John Allen and the said william Graye by Indenture covenanted concerning the premisses that then all suche estate tothe use and Intereste as the saide william had of and in the aforesaide lands and Tenements shoulde utterlie be voyde and of none effecte And then wylled that the parsonns and wardenes of the saide paryshe Churches and every of them so beinge behind unpaide shoolde have use and enjoye the same lands and tenements to them and their successors to doe operate and fulfill that his saide Legacye and bequeste weeklie as is aforesayde duringe the tyme aboute Lymyted as more at large appearithe by the sayde laste will and testament so it is righte honorable Lorde that accordinge to the sayde agreemente and covenante by indenture and the sayde laste will and testament the said william Gray dyd dystribute the saide bredde in forme aforesaide appointed until XIII dayes before Chrystmas daie Anno Domini 1551 and then contrary to the sayde agreemente and will wrongefullie withdrawen and undystributed And thereupon soon after the said william Graye solde the lands and tenements to one Richarde Palladye who hathe solde the same on to one Thomas Altham of London Clothworker and never since the saide XIIIth daye before the saide feaste was distribucion made of the same bredd whereby the poore paryshyoners and prysoners have loste their releyfe and charytable rewarde amountinge in everye yeare to the summe of Twentye pounds syxtene shillings And forasmuch as there yet remaineth foortene years or their abouts resydewe of the saide Twentye years for operation and performance of the saide dystribution And forasmuch allso as the recoverye hereof is not to be had by any ordinarye means of the comen Lawe It maie therefore please youre good Lordeshippe to grante the Queene's majesties mooste gracious wrytte of Subpoena to the sayd Thomas Altham and Richarde palladye to be dyrected commandinge them thereby personallie to appeare before youre good Lordeshippe in the high Courte of Chauncerye at a certen daie and under a certen payne by your Lordeshippe therein to be lymited and appointed then and there to make annsere to the premisses And farther it maie please your good Lordeshippe to take herein such order and dyrection for the continuans of the saide godly and charytable dede to the greate number of poore people in the saide parishes and the like succor for the prysoners of the saide prysonns as to your honorable Lordshippe shall seme herein most mete and conveniente And your saide orators shall daylye praye to god for the prosperous estate of your honorable Lordeshippe with muche encrease of honor long to endure.

C. 2/Eliz./H. 17/7

To the Right honorable Sir Thomas Egerton Knight Lord Keeper of the greate seale of England

[Dated: 28 October 1601]

In all humbleness complayning sheweth unto your honor Your humble Suppliante and daily orator Edward Buggs thelder of Harlowe in the countie of Essex gent John Gladwyn the Elder and John Gladwyn the Younger on the behalf of themselves and of the poore inhabitants of the said parishe of Harlowe That whereas one John Godsalst sometymes of Harlowe aforesaid yeoman was in his life tyme lawfully seised in his demeane as of fee simple according to the custome of the mannor of Harlowbury in the said parishe of and in one coppihold tenement with a garden and two acres of like coppihold land more or lesse thereunto belonging holden by coppie of Court Roll of the said mannor And being thereof so seised did of a good and charitable affection that he bare towardes the relief of the poore and distressed people of the said parish wich then were and yet are very many (by the good liking and allowance of the then Lord of the said mannor and of his then ffarmer thereof) surrender into the handes of the Lorde the said Tenement and Land with the appertenances (as yt then lay and yet lieth metted and bownded and being then and yet knowne thereby) that the

Lord would be pleased to admitt certaine persons to have and to hould to them and their heires in trust to the only use benefitt and profitt of the poore inhabitants of the said parishe wich then and from tyme to tyme in the succeeding ages should be, Whereupon (as well by the appointment of the said John Gadsalst as the good liking of the said Lord of the said mannor) one Anthony Bugges gent Christofer Sompner and William Sompner yeomen were thereunto by the Lord admitted to have and to hould to them and their heires to the use and trust aforesaid, That is to say to the intent and purpose only that the said Tenement and Land should for ever remayne to the said use, and that the profitts thereof should from tyme to tyme be raised and distributed to the use of the poore of the said parishe accordingly as by two severall coppies thereof, the one bearing date the ninth day of June in the tenth yeare of her majesties raigne and the other bearing date the eight and twentieth day of maye in the ffourteenth yeare of her highnes said raigne appeareth. Yet neverthelesse for as much as one roode or thereabouts of the said ground is by the said feoffees (contrary to the said use and trust) alienated by surrender unto one Robert Bateman and his heires, and is by meane conveyance of surrender come to the handes and possession of one Nicholas Sibley of the said parishe yeoman who imployeth the proffitts thereof to his owne use, and not the use of the poore as was intended, Therefore your said orators and others the Overseers for the poore of the said parishe did of late exhibite their complaint unto the comissioners assigned for reformacion of the abuses of trusts in landes and other thinges given to good and charitable uses judicially sitting at Dunmowe in the said countie uppon the same and other like causes. Whereuppon a jury was (according to lawe) impanelled and uppon full evidence given by your Orators and others and the said coppies showed forthe and uppon the confession of the said Nicholas Sibley that the said parcell of ground was part of the said tenement so as aforesaid surrendered and that he the said Nicholas did hould and enjoye the profitts thereof to his owne use, The said Jury did then and there finde and present uppon their corporall othes that the said parcell of grounde so severed from the said Tenement and holden to another use was contrary to the trust whereunto yt was first appointed: ffor reformacion therefore of the said abuse of trust and misimployment and to reduce the said land to the right use whereunto yt was given, The said comissioners did order, adjudge and decree that the said Nicholas Sibley or his heire or heires should at the next court to be holden at or for the said mannor surrender into the handes of the Lord, And (in default of a Court there to be holden) should before the first day of Maye then next ensueing surrender into the handes of the Lord by the handes of the Tenaunts or Bailiff according to the custome of the said mannor the said Tenement or parcell of ground to the use of the said feoffees or the survivor of them to be employed together with the rest for ever hereafter, to the use and benefitt of the poore of the said parishe of Harlowe according to the good and charitable intent and meaning of the Donor, as by the said Decree signed and sealed by Roger Vodl Doctor in Divinitie, Sir Robert Wroth Knight, ffrances Barryington, Henry Maynard, Edward Hubberd, Esquires and others the comissioners appointed as aforesaid and returned into this honorable court and here remayning of Record appeareth: Yet neverthelesse so yt is (Right honorable Lord) that the said Nicholas Sibley neither respecting the reformacion of the said abuse nor regarding the said Decree, did at the next Court holden at the said mannor and yet doth refuse to surrender or yeld the possession thereof to the use aforesaid notwithstanding he hath here sundrye tymes in gentle and easie manner required thereunto: In tender consideracion whereof and for as much as the said proceedings of the said Nicholas Sibley tend not only to the prejudice of the poore by the said misemployment but to the evill example of others by his said refusing to performe the said Decree that your honor will be pleased to award her majesties most gracious processe of subpena to be directed to the said Nicholas Sibley commaunding him thereby at a certaine day and under a certaine paine therin to be lymitted personally to appeare before your good Lordshipp in the said court of Chauncery, Then and there not only to shewe cause whie he should not deliver the possession and the Arrerages of the Rents issues or proffitts of the said parcell of ground to the use aforesaid, according as yt might be resonably lett, But also then and there to answere to the premisses, And to abyde such further order and direction therein as to justice and equitie apperteyneth: And your orators together with their poore inhabitants shall daily pray for the prosperous estate of your honor:

Edward Turner.

C. 2/Eliz./T. 5/46

The Answere of John Newton defendant to the Bill of Complainte of Roberte Cathye and John Aunsell complainants

[Dated: 25 June 1595]

The said defendant sayethe that the said Bill of Complaynt is in many parts thereof (as he is informed) very incerteyne and insufficient in Lawe to be Answered unto, And that yf matters therein were threwe yet the same discloseth not sufficient cause for this honorable courte to hold plea of the same, because the said matters (as the defendant is gyven [to plede] by his councell,) is determynable by the course of the comon lawes of this Realme, And not in this honorable Courte, And therefore he must humbly prayeth that he may [ ][1] from the same and be referred to a tryall at the Comon lawe with his reasonable costs and charge by reason of this his unjust vexacion by him wrongefully susteyned [ ] of he the said defendant shall by the order of this honerable courte be compelled to make Answere to the said byll. Then the excepcions unto the unsufficiencie and incerteinty thereof and unto the jurisdiction of this honorable courte at all tymes hereafter to him saved. The said defendant for soe much as Concerneth his knowledge in the matters mencioned in the same Bill, And for a plaine and manifest declaracion of the trewth thereof saith theat he verely thinketh it to be trewe yf the said William Newton mencioned in the said Bill of Complainte was seised of an estate of inheritance of the messuages and Tenements in the same bill Conteyened, But whether his estate were an estate taile or an estate in ffee simple he the said defendant knoweth not, Neyther yet can he by any waies or meanes as yet understand or learne the same, by reason that the said Margaret by the councell and advise of the said Complainants (as he suposseth) reteyneth the evidences and chests concerninge the said messuages and tenements from the said defendant to whom in lawe the interest and possession of them dothe aperteyne and belonge, And therefore and for the better judginge and descerninge what estate the said William Newton had in the said messuages and tenements, May it please this honorable Courte for to order that

[1] Here and in the following pages, square brackets indicate that words are missing or illegible.

the said Complainants and the said Margaret, who is confederated with them for the disinheritance of this defendant, shall bringe in the said Evidences and writinges concerninge the premisses, And to be delivered by the judgement of this courte to suche person to whom in Right and Lawe they aperteyne, Neyther yet doth this defendant know whether the said William Newton made any will and Testament in writinge bearinge date the XIXth day of November last, or that he did gyve and bequeath the premisses unto Margaret his wiff for and duringe her naturall life. And after her decease unto the poore inhabitinge within the warde of Portsoken within the parishe of St. Buttolphes. And to the use and behoof of the poore of the said warde and parishe at the descrecion from tyme to tyme of the churchwardens and other inhabitantes of the said parishe. And yf the said William Newton should make any such will, eyther it should seeme that he was not in good and perfect memory or els vyolentlye drawen thereunto by his said wiff and some of the inhabitantes of the said parishe in Respect of a covetous minde to benefit themselves, and to disinherit the said defendant, ffor how can it be thought that the said William Newton should so muche forgett his naturall Affection to his Kyndred, beinge both of his blood and name, as to gyve all that he had to his wiff and strangers, and to be mindefull onely of them in his will, and thereby to bestowe nothinge uppon his kindred and blood and name, and not once soe much as to make any mencion of them or any of them in the said supposed will, And especially soe muche to be carelesse and forgetfull of this defendant beinge his brothers sonne, (that is to saie sonne of John Newton brother to the said William Newton deceassed). And uppon whom the said William Newton in all his lifftyme never bestowed any benefitt or good turne other than at one tyme he gave him this defendant XXs to his marriage neyther yet did the said defendant at any tyme offend the said William Newton but alwaies behaved himself towardes the said William in all dutyfull lovinge and obeydient sorte ready to doe and performe any thinge that it should please him to comand, But this streighte course of dealinge must needes be thought to proceede from his said wiff and others who thought as it should seeme all to little for themselves But this defendant hopeth that this honorable court will Adjudge and thinketh it to have beene as charitable an Acte and deede to have bestowed the same uppon the said defendant beinge of his whole blood, and of his name and soe neare of kyn, A Taylor by trade and occupacion, A very poore man havinge a wiff and many children and more is like to have, and possesseth nothinge for the maintenaunce of them all but that which he gayneth and yernethe by his painefull labour and workinge in his said trade and science And therefore yf his said uncle should forgett himself soe muche, and neyther remember this defendant his next kynsman, nor, to have compassion of his poore and distressed estate of soe longe tyme continewed, that neyther in his life, althoughe god havinge blessed him with great plenty of Riches, nor by his will, Accomplishe any parte or duty of nature, that yf lawe by the goodness of god hath cast uppon this defendant some comfortable and smale porcion for the Refreshment of himself, and of his poore wiff and children, that this most honorable court wil be pleased to Afforde him the benefit thereof; And not to deprive him from the possessinge or enjoyinge of the same, cominge thereto by course and discent in lawe without any evill practized or sinister dealinge on his parte that can be alledged or proved against him, without that the said William Newton did the said XIXth day of November gyve the said premisses to his said wiff and after his decease to the poore inhabitinge within the said warde, within the said parishe of St. Buttolphes to the use and behoof of the poore of the said parishe and warde at the discrecion from tyme to tyme of the churchwardens and other inhabitantes of the said parish to the knowledge of this defendant, And yet yf suche gyft were made, yet the same beinge voyde in lawe for that they were not by any suche name persons able to purchase, The said defendant as next heire to the said William Newton by lawe and conscience is to have the said premisses And without that the said William Newton beinge in his death beed beinge moved and required by his said wif that he woulde suffer some parte of the premisses to descend, and come unto the said defendant, the said William utterly denyed, and refused soe to doe and directly Answered as he did divers tymes before that tyme and after Affirme that he had before bene good and beneficiall unto him, And that the poore should have all the said premisses, And that noe parte thereof should by anie meanes come unto the defendant to the knowledge of this defendant, And he verely supposeth that the said William Newton his uncle never used any such speaches because his said uncle never bestowed any other benefitt uppon the said defendant then before in theirs presents is expressed, without that that any other thinge or matter in the said Bill conteyned and herein not sufficiently confessed and Avoyded traversed or denyed is trewe, all which matters, this defendant is ready to Averre and prove, as this honorable Courte shall award, and prayeth as before he hath prayed.

C. 2/Eliz./T. 11/7

The righte honourable Sir Thomas Bromley, Knighte, Lorde Chaunceloure of England

[Undated]

In moste humble wise doe shewe and complaine unto your good Lordshipp youre pore and dayly Orators William Turney and Robart Robartes of Clapton in the countye of Bucks husbandmen that whereas they the saide William and Robart togeather with one Thomas Knighton nowe deceased weare jointlye seased in their demesne as of fee as customarye or copyholde tenaunts accordinge to the custome of the Manor of Laighton Bussarde in the countye of Beddford of and in one halfe yarde by estimation of meadow grounde lyenge theire within the saide Manor and beinge parcell thereof in a place commonly called or knowen by the name of Billingtonlongemeade to the only use entent and purpose to performe and fullfill the last will and testament of one Thomas Knighton also deceassed the which Thomas declared his last will and testament and of a verye good and godlye disposition disposed and bequeathed the same with the rentes issues and profittes thereof arisinge the custome of the saide Manor alwayes to be observed unto the onlye relyfe ease succour and maintenaunce of the pore inhabitantes of Slapton aforesaide and especially of the porest sorte of them declaringe further that his full entent and meaninge was that it shoulde be bestowed by these expresse woords in his saide last will and testament sett downe in manner and forme folowinge that is to saye to the full paiment of the heade silver in Slapton aforesaide soe that the inhabitantes theire and especiallye the pore folke theire dwellinge maye be moste eased and releaved by the same the which his charitable wife dothe fully declare howe well he was affected therein towardes the reliefe of the pore And not for the maintenaunce of any superstitious or of any other unlawfull matters, rites services or seremonies as it hathe byn verye faulslye and untrewlye (as shalbe well and sufficiently proved) surmised and alleadged by one Richarde Buckmaster late of Eaton in the saide county of Beddfordshire yeoman deceased and sense his deathe by one John Buckmaster the elder sonne and nexte heire of the saide Richarde verye unconscionablye maintayned wheereupon so it is righte honourable that the saide Richarde Buckmaster in his lyfe tyme and the saide John his sonne sence his fathers deathe only seekinge their owen private gaine and commodity have of late by what meanes soever possibly they cold invent indevoured and practized not only to gett the possession of the premises fair contrarye to all righte equitye and good conscience but also have obtained and gotten into their handes and now are comme holye into the custodye of the saide John as well by casuall meanes as otherwise other all or the moste parte of the evidences copyes of court roules writinges and munimentes which doe cheifelye conserne and best make for the maintenaunce preservation and defence of the just title and lawfull estate in and to the premisses of your saide pore Oratoures bothe to the greate danger of the utter losse of their rightfull inheritaunce therein accordinge to the custome of the saide Manor and also to the utteroverthrewe of the righte and estate of the Lordes of the saide manor and especially to the cleane extinguishment of that good and godly deede of the saide Thomas Knighton the giver whose meaninge and entent was that it shoolde have had continewaunce to the greate releife and succour of the porest inhabitauntes which shalbe from age to age within the saide parishe of Slapton for evermore unlesse your good Lordshipp accordinge to youre accustomed goodness doe provide somme spedye remedye to prevent and overthrewe these mischevious and unconscionable devises and dealinges of the saide John Buckmaster thelder And for as much as your saide Oratoures knowe not the certaine number of the saide evidences copyes of coorte rooles writinges and munimentes nor the dates thereof and for that they are not conteyned in Boxe or bagge sealed or in Chest locked whereby your saide Oratoures are withowt all remedye by the stricte cause of the common lawes of the Realme for the obteyninge or recoveringe of them or any of them and so consequentlye from declaringe maintayninge or pleadinge as occasion shalbe geven unto them of theire good title to the premisses to the prejudice of the Lordes of the Manor of whome they are holden to your pore Oratoures disinheritinge to the subversion of the wille of the deade proceeadinge of godly and charitable zeale and finally to the greate losse and hinderaunce from time to time for ever of manye pore people unlesse your honourable favour shalbe to them extended in this behalfe. In consideration wheareof Maye it please your honoure of your accustomed goodness to graunte the Queenes majesteyes moste gracious Writt of subpoena to be directed to the saide John Buckmaster thelder commaundinge him thereby personallye to appeare before your good Lordshipp in the queenes majesties honourable Court of Chauncery at a daye certaine and under a certaine paine by your good lordshipp to be limitted and appointed then and thene to abide such ordere and direction concerninge the premisses as to your honour shall seme good and convenient for the remedye of your pore Oratoures in this their lamentable case accordinge to righte, equitye and good conscience and your saide Oratoures shall not sease and accordinge to theire dewties to make theire daylye prayers to allmightie God for the long preservation of your lordshipp in your healthe with increase of honoure.

Potts.

C. 2/Eliz./T. 11/7

The Answere of John Buckmaster defendant to the Bill of complaint of William Turney and Robarte Robarts complaynaunts

[Undated]

The said defendant saith that the said Bill of complainte into this honerable Corte againste him exhibited is uncertain, untrue, and insufficyent in lawe to be annswered unto, and the matters therin conteyned, devised onlie of malice and purpose to putt this defendant to wrongfull charges in the lawe, withoute anye juste grounde or cause so to doe. Nevertheless thadvantage of excepcion to this defendaunte nowe, and at all tymes hereafter saved to the incertaintie and insuffyciencye of the said bill of complainte, The said defendant for further annswerer, and for full and certaine declarcion of a trothe saiethe That true yt is that aboute the xxxth daie of June, in the fyrste yere of the raigne of oure late Soveraigne ladie Quene Marie, the saide Quene beinge seased (as in the righte of her Crowne, by reason of the Statute made in the firste yere of the raigne of the late Kinge, Kinge Edwarde the syxte) of and in one yarde of meadowe, sett, lyinge and beinge in greate Billingdon longe meade; in the parishe of Leighton Bussarde, in the countie of Bedford, beinge gyven for and towardes the maynteynaunce of an Aniversarie perpetuall within the saied Churche or chappell of Billingdon aforesaied, which this Defendant taketh to be the meadowe in the saied Bill specified. And so therof beinge seased, did in consideracion of a certaine some of money, by hir lettres pattents bearinge date the xxxth daie of June in the fyrste yere of her majesties raigne at ffarneham, amongest other thinges, give and graunte to George Rotherham of ffar . . . ey[1] in the countie of Bedford gent, and Roger Barber of Luton in the saied countie yeoman, the saied yarde of meadowe, lyinge in greate Billingdon longe meade aforesaied with thappertenaunces, To have and to houlde amongeste other thinges, all that yarde of meadowe with thappertenaunces to the said George Rotherham and Roger Barber, and to the heyres and assignes of the saied George Rotherham forever, to thonlie use and behoffe of the saied George and Roger and the heyres and assignes of the saied George forever, as by the saied lettres pattentes more at large it dothe and maye appere. By vertue whereof the saied George Rotherham and Roger Barber into the premisses entred and weare therof seased of and in such estate as is aforesayed. And they so thereof seased, as is aforesaied in consideracion of a certaine some of money to them by Rycharde Buckmaster father of the defendant well and trulie paied, did give, graunte, bargaine and sell unto Rycharde Buckmaster all the saied yarde of meadowe in greate Billingdon longe meade aforesaied, To have and to houlde all the saied yarde with thappertanaunces to the saied Rycharde Buckmaster his heyres and assignes forever to the onlye use and behoofe of the saied Rycharde his heyres and assignes forever, as by the saied deede of gyfte more plainlie yt dothe and may appere. By vertue whereof the saied Rycharde into the premisses entred and was therof seased in his demeane as of fee. And he so thereof beinge seased, died thereof, By and after whose deathe, the aforesaied premisses discended and come to the saied defendant, as sonn and heyre to the saied Rycharde Buckmaster deceassed. By reason wherof the saied defendant entred into the saied premisses, and was therof seased in his demeane as of fee, and the fruytes, profyttes and comodites therof comynge hathe ever synce taken and percyved, and yet

[1] Illegible.

dothe perceyve and take, as well and lawfull is for him to doe. Withoute that that the sayed premisses, or and parte or parcell therof, which discended and came to this defendant (to this defendants knowledge) are coppie houlde, but onlye freehoulde. And without that that the saied Thomas Knighton in the bill mencioned, to this defendants knowledge or remembraunce did make and ordeyne anie suche will and testament, as in the saied Bill of complaint is alledged, or if he did, that the whole of the saied will is sett downe. And without that that the saied defendaunte hathe invented, indevoured and practised to gett the possession of the premysses fair contrarie to all righte, equitie and good conscience, otherwyse then righte and lawfull was and is for him to doe, for the gettinge and mayteynyng of his owne righte of Inheritaunce, as in the saied Bill is moste sclaunderouslie suggested. Or that eyther all, or the moste parte of the Evidences, coppies of corte rolles, writinges and mynymentes which doe choiselye concerne, and beste make for the maynteynaunce, preservacion and defence of the juste tytle and lawfull estate in and to the premysses are come to this defendauntes handes, other than the deede from Mr. Rotherham, and Roger Barber, as is lykwyse moste falselye sermysed. And without that that anie other matter or cause in the saied Bill of complaynte conteyned, materiall or effectuall to be annswered unto, and herin by the saied defendant not suffycientlye confessed, or avoyded, traversed, or denyed is true. All which matters the saied defendant is readie to averr and prove (as this honorable corte shall award). And praieth to be dismissed oute of the same with his reasonable costes and charges in that behalfe wrongfullie susteyned.

S. Nagg

C. 2/Eliz./R. 12/48

To the Righte honorable Sir Christofer Hatton knighte Lord Chauncelor of Englande

[Undated]

In most humble manner compleyninge unto your good Lordshippe your dayly Orators William Rycardes John Moore and Edward kynge for themselves and the reste of the Parishioners and inhabitauntes of Rodboroughe in the Countie of Gloucester, That wereas aboute the tyme of Kinge henry the sixte and longe sythens one Margery Breysyn Wyddowe and Edwarde of Rodbury and hughe Nutlinge by their severall deedes in wrythinge of their godly disposicions dyd give graunte enfeoffe and confirme certen Messuages landes and tenements sett and lyinge in Rodborowe aforesaid, to have and to hold to them and their heires unto such uses purposes and behaffe as to the Churchwardens Parshioners and Inhabitaunts of Rodborough aforesaid shod be thought good to celebrate devyne service in a chappell of ease at Rodboroughe aforesaid parcell of the Parrishe of Michynhampton in the said County of Gloucester and to doo and execute with the proffittes thereof charitable Actes and deedes by their discreacions, By force of wich severall deedes the proffittes of the same premisses were by the space of three score years together ymployed by the said Inhabitauntes of Rodboroughe aforesaid to celebrate dyvyne service and to the Relieffe of the poore and other good and charitable Actes. But soe it is Righte honorable Lorde that the Richarde Payne Edward holliday and William holliday, pretendinge to keape the possession of the premisses from your said Orators and the reste of the parrishe, doe take the proffittes to themselves as well by pretence of havinge the said severall Evydences comen to their handes custodie and possession as also by collor thereto An Inquisicion was had taken and found by force of Her Majesties Commission oute of her highness Courte of Exchequere aboute the eighte yeare of her Majesties Reigne that the said premisses were found to be ymployed to superstitious uses wich in ffyve yeres next before the dissolucion of Chaunteryes and chappelles in the first yere of the Reigne of Kinge Edwarde the sixte late kynge of England and that the same Landes were concealed from her Majestie Wherein truthe the said Landes were neyther geven or ymployed to any suche superstitious uses, After wich commyssion so had and founde and her Majestie intitled to the same premisses the same were aboute the same tyme by her Majestie graunted under her grate Letres Patentes unto William Gryte Esquire and Charles Newcommon whose estate in the said premisses were by meane conveyaunce graunted unto the said Richard Payne Edward holliday and William holliday whereupon yf it please your honorable good Lordshippe theis compleynaunts John Moore Edward kinge and William Rychardes dyd for their Relieffe to destroy the sayd practised Comyssion and Inquisicion of fyndinge the said premisses concealed by the statute of primo of Edward the sixte for the dissolucion of the Chauntries Exhibite their Bill of Complaynte againste the said Richard Payne and others for the same premisses and the deteyninge of the same Evidences whereby the same premisses were geven to the Uses aforesaid unto the honorable Courte of her Majesties Exchequere Chamber where aswell the tytle of her Majestie as also theis Complainauntes estate righte and tytle were hard examyned and determyned and the matter dismissed oute of the same Courte, And the said Richard Payne and those that claymed estate by the said supposed tytle of concealemente enjoyned not to pray in Ayde of her Majestie or to be priveledged in the said Courte of Exchequere for the same premisses for that the Queenes Majesties tytle was not found to be of any value or force as by the said Order made in Hillery Terme laste in the said Courte of Exchequer Chamber dothe appear Sythens wich said Order and Dismyssion So it is further Righte honorable Lord that forasmuche as the sayde Rychard payne Edward holliday and William holliday have in theire custodie the said Deedes and evydences tuchinge severall guiftes aforesaid the certentie or certen Dates whereof your said Orator dothe not knowe by reason whereof your said Oratores cannot recover the said premisses at and by the comen lawe to ymploy the proffittes thereof to suche uses and charitable deeds in the said parishe accordinglie as the same premisses were firste geven and ymployed and meant to be geven and ymployed by discreacions of the said Parishioners and Inhabitauntes of Rodboroughe aforesaid but that they had contrived diverse secreate conveyaunces thereof to their owne Uses to diverse persons unknowen, In tendre consideracion whereof and fforasmuche as your said Orators are utterlye voyd of all Remedie for the saide Evidences and Deedes or for the premisses otherwise or else where then in this honorable Courte by your good Lordshippes favoure for that the said Payne holliday and holliday doe pretend some other surmysed tytle to the premisses then under the Queenes Majesties wich is proved to be of no fforce in the sayd Exchequere Maye it therefore please your honor the premisses considered to graunte unto your said Orators the Queenes Majesties most gracious wrytt of Subpena to be directed unto the said Richard Payne Edward holliday and William holliday Comaundinge them thereby at a day certen and under a certen payne therein to be lymited personallie to be and appeare before your good Lordshippe in the Queenes Majesties highe Courte of

Chauncerie then and there tanswere the premisses upon their corporall othes in this honorable Courte and to bringe the sayd Evidences and deedes in their custodie tuchinge the premisses into the said Courte to the Master your Orators Maye in Equity have suche further Order for the premisses therein as to your honors shalbe thought good and your said Orators shall dayly pray to god for your good Lordshippe beinge to Remayne in honor.

C. 2/Eliz./R. 12/48.

The Joynte and severall Replications of William Ricardes John Moore and Edmund kinge Complainauntes to the Jointe and severall Answeares of Richarde Payne Edmond hollidaye and William hollydaye Defendauntes

[Undated]

The said Complainauntes not confessinge anythinge materiall in the said Answeare to be trewe and sauvinge to themselves all advantages of exceptions to the insufficiencye thereof for Replication saye and everie of them saieth, That they do and will averr maynteine and prove their said bill exhibited into this honorable Courte against the said Defendauntes to be sufficiente in law to be Answered unto, and all the matters therein conteyned grounded uppon goode and Juste cause of suett and not uppon any fayned or surmised matter And also that they will do and will averr meynteine and prove all and everie matter clause and sentence in their said bill conteyned to be juste and trewe in such sorte manner and forme as in their said bill the same are sett forthe and alleiged and especially in this that they will averr and prove That the landes Tenements and hereditaments and everie parte and parcell thereof mencioned in the said bill were geven to suche good goodly devine uses searvice and entente for the doinge and executinge with the proffittes thereof charitable actes and deeds in suche manner and forme as in the said bill is alleiged And that the proffittes of the same were ymployed by the space of Three score yeres to suche intent and purpose and in such manner and forme as in the said bill is also truly alleiged And that the said Defendauntes or some of them by coler of havinge of the said dede and evidence of righte belonginge to the complainaunts have and do take the proffittes of the lands, tenements and hereditaments mencioned in the said bill in such manner and forme as in the said bill is also truly alleiged And also that they do and will averr and prove, That as well the title of her Majestie as also these Complainauntes estate right and title of and in the said premisses were heard and determined in her Majesties Courte of Exchequer Chamber and the matter dismissed out of the said Courte And that the said Richard Payne mencioned in the said bill and others that claymed estate by the supposed concealed title Injoyned not to praye in aide of her Majestie to be priviledged in the said Courte of Exchequor for the premisses for that her Majesties title was found not to be of any force or value in such manner and forme as in the said bill is also truly alleiged And that they will averr and prove that the dedes and Evidences mencioned in the said bill provinge the gifte of the premisses to such godly uses ententes and purposes as are in the said bill of Complaint sett fourthe and declared are come to the handes and possession of the said Defendauntes or to the handes of some of them, And that the said Defendauntes or some of them have contrived diverse secreat and unlawfull estates to their owne use to diverse persons unknowen of and in the said premisses in such manner and forme as in the said bill is likewise truly alleiged and declared And that they will averr and prove that the said Defendauntes do pretend a surmised tytle to the said premisses mencioned in the said bill in such manner and forme as in the said bill is also truly alleiged. Without that that the said Robert Bennett Robert Richardes and Johan Ricardes mencioned in the said Joynt and several Answeares or any of them were seised in their demesne as of fee of and in the same Messuages Landes and Tenements mencioned in the said bill or did as their Complainauntes verily thinke geve graunt and confirme unto the said Richard holliday and William holliday and thothers mencioned in the said Answeares all their Landes Tenementes meadowes pastures Rentes Reversions and services in the said County of Gloucester to the use of the said Richard holliday and his heires for ever and in such manner and forme as in the said Joynt and severall Answeares is surmised And without that that by force thereof the said Richard holliday was of the landes and tenements in the said bill mencioned seised untill suche tyme as the said Inquisicion in the said bill mencioned was founde in suche manner and forme as in the said Answeres is most untruly alleiged And without that that by vertue of the Queens Majesties Commission all and singuler the said Messuages landes tenements and hereditaments were found of ancient tyme to be geven ymploied and bestowed unto certayne superstitious uses as in the said and severall Answeres is untruly alleiged or that by reason thereof ought to have bene in our Sovereaigne Laidie the Queenes Majestie or of any of her heighness Ancesters accordinge to that Statute made and provided on that behalfe in the first yere of the reigne of our late Soveraigne Lord Kinge Edward the Sixt in suche manner and forme [ ][1] the said Joynt and severall Answeares is likewise moste untrulie alleiged And without that that the said Defendaunt Edward hollydaye maye lawfull keepe and deteine [ ] Complainauntes any dede or other writinge tuchinge the said premisses mencioned in the said bill in such manner and forme as in the said Joint and severall Answeares is untruly alleiged And without that that the said Defendaunt Richard Payne hath by lawful conveyans and other discentes and meanes derived from and under her heighness [ ] lawfull estate of inheritans in the said messuages landes and tenements in the said bill mencioned, by the name of duryarde and Besseley or hathe and ought to have the Reversion [ ] of one yerely Rentes of twelve shillinges or thereabouts yssuinge out of the said Messuages Landes tenements and heriditaments called hampstede in Besseley after the estate [ ] the said Elizabeth Greve in such manner and forme as in the Jointe and several Annsweares is likewise most untrulie alleiged And without that that by vertue [ ] said Commission her Majestie was intituled unto the said messuages Landes and Tenements mencioned in the said bill, or was thereof seised in her demesne as of fee as in Right of [ ] Crowne of England or that her Majestie had any Righte, by her lettres pattentes to graunt the said messuages Landes and Tenements to the said Grice[2] and Charles [ ][3] and their heires in such manner and forme as in the said Jointe and several Answeares is surmissed And without that that any other matter or thinge materiall or effectual [ ] in the said Jointe and Severall Annsweres nedfull to be replied unto and herein not sufficiently Replied unto confessed and avoyded traversed or denied is true [ ] manner and forme as in the said Answeares[4] is most untrulie alleiged All wich matters those Complainauntes are readie to averr and prove as this honorable Court [ ] awarde and praye as in their said bill they have already prayed.

[1] The MS. is torn on its right-hand side. The last few words of some twelve sentences are therefore lost.

[2] In the bill, his name is given as Gryte; above, p. 216.

[3] From the bill it appears this was Charles Newcommon; above, p. 216.

[4] The answer is badly mutilated.

APPENDIX C

THE CHARITABLE USES ACT, 1597: 39 ELIZABETH I c. 6.

An Acte to reforme Deceiptes and Breaches of Trust, towching Landes given to charitable Uses

Whereas divers Colledges Hospitalles Almes Houses and other Places within this Realme of Englande have bene founded and ordeyned, somme of them by the Quenes most Excellent Majesty and by other her noble Progenytors, and somme by other godly and weldisposed persons, for the Charitable Releife of pore aged and ympotent People maymed Soldyers Scholes of Learninge Orphanes and for such other good charitable and lawful purposes and yntentes: And where divers Landes Tenementes and Hereditamentes Leases Goodes and Chattels have bene given limitted and appointed for the like charitable good and lawfull Uses Intentes and Purposes, as also for Reparacion of Highwaies Amendmentes of Bridges and Sea Banckes, for the Maintenance of Fre Schooles and pore Schollers, as also for the Releife and preferment of Orphanes and fatherles Children, and such like good lawfull and charitable Uses; which Landes Tenementes and Hereditamentes Goods Leases and Chattelles have bene and are still like to be most unlawfully and uncharitably converted to the Lucre and Gayne of somme fewe greedy and covetous persons, contrary to the true intente and meaning of the givers and disposers thereof: To thende such godly and charitable purposes and uses may be from henceforth observed and contynued according to the true intent and meaning of the Givers and Founders thereof, and according to the true entent and meaning of any the foresaid good godly and charitable uses and intentes: Be it enacted by the Queene our Soveraigne Lady the Lordes Spirituall and Temporall and Commons in this present Parliamente assembled, and by the Auctority of the same, That it shall and may be lawfull to and for the Lord Chauncellor or Keper of the Greate Seale of Englande for the tyme being, and for the Chauncellor of the Dutchy of Lancaster for the tyme being for Landes within the County

Palantyne of Lancaster, from tyme to tyme to award Commissions under the Great Seale of Englande or the Seal of the County Palentyne, as the Case shall require, into all or any parte or partes of this Realme respectively according to their severall Jurisdicions as aforesaid, to the Byshop of every severall Dyoces and his Chauncellor, and to other persons of good and sounde behaviour, auctorising them thereby to enquire as well by the Oathes of Twelve lawfull men of the County, as by all other good and lawfull wayes and meanes, of all and singuler such Guiftes Lymittacions and Purposes, and of the Abuses and Misdemeanors Misimploymentes Falsityes defrauding of the Trustes Intentes and Purposes Alyenacions or Mysgovernmentes, which have bene had or at any tyme hereafter shalbe had or made, and of all and every other Matter Thing and Cause whereby or by meanes whereof the good and godly uses aforesaid cannot or may not be maynteyned executed and performed according to the true intent and meaning of the Donours or Founders, and according to the true entent and meaning of any the foresaid good godly and charitable uses and intentes; And after such Inquiry made, uppon hearing and examyning thereof, to set downe such Orders Judgement and Decrees as the said good godly and charitable uses may be truely observed in full ample and most liberall sort, according to the true intent and meaning of the Founders or Donoures thereof; which Orders Judgementes and Decrees, not being contrary or repugnant to the Orders Statutes or Decrees of the Donoures or Founders, shall, by the auctority of this present Parliament, stande fyrme and good according to the teanour and purport thereof.

Provided alwayes, That neyther this Act nor any thing therein conteyned, shall in any waies extende to any Colledges Halles or Howses of Learning within the Universityes of Oxforde or Cambridge, or to the Colleges of Westminster Eaton or Wynchester, or any of them, nor to the Landes Revenues or Possessions thereunto belonging; neyther to any Cathedrall Churche within this Realme of Englande, nor to the Landes or Possessions thereunto appteyning or belonging.

Provided also, That neyther this Acte nor any thing therein shall extende to any Citty or Towne Corporate, or to any the Landes or Tenementes given to the uses aforesaid within any such Citty or Towne Corporate, where there is a speciall Governor or Governors appointed to governe or direct such Landes Tenementes or Thinges disposed to any the uses aforesaid; neyther to any Colledge Hospitall or Free Schole which have specyall Vysitors Governors or Overseers appointed them by their Founders.

Provided also and be it enacted by the auctority aforesaid, That neyther this Acte nor any thing therein conteyned shalbe any way prejudicyall or hurtfull to the Jurisdiction or Power of the Ordynary, but that he may lawfully in every Cause execute and performe the same as thoughe this Acte had never bene had or made.

Provided also, That no person or persons that hath or shall have any of the Landes Tenementes or Hereditamentes Goodes or Chattels, given lymitted or appoynted to or for any the Uses Purposes or Intentes aforesaid, shall intermeddle as a Commissioner in any the Causes aforesaid.

Provided alwayes and it is further enacted by the auctority aforesaid, That all such Orders Judgmentes and Decrees as shalbe so set downe by the said Commyssioners as is aforesaid, shalbe certified under the Seales of the said Commissioners eyther into the Court of the Chauncery of Englande or into the Court of the Chauncery within the County Palatyne of Lancaster, as the Case shall require respectively according to their severall Jurisdiccions, within such convenyent tyme as shalbe lymitted in the said Commyssions; And that the said Lord Chauncellor or Lord Keeper, and the said Chauncellor of the Dutchy shall and may within their said severall Jurisdiccions, take such order for the due Execucion of all or any of the said Judgementes, Decrees and Orders as to eyther of them shall seeme fitt and convenyent: And that yf after any such certyficatt or certyficates made, any person or persons shall finde themselves greived with any of the said Orders Judgementes or Decrees, that then it shall and may be lawfull to and for them or any of them, to complayne in that behalfe unto the said Lorde Chauncellor or Lord Keeper or to the Chauncellor of the said Dutchy of Lancaster, according to their severall Jurisdiccions, for Redresse therin; And that uppon such Complaynte the said Lord Chauncellor or Lord Keeper or the said Chauncellor of the Dutchy, may according to their said severall Jurisdiccions, procede to the examynacion hearing and determyning hereof as to eyther of them in their said severall Jurisdiccions shalbe thought to stande with Equity and good Conscyence; Any Thinge in this Acte conteyned to the contrary hereof in any wyse notwithstanding.

APPENDIX D

THE CHARITABLE USES ACT, 1601: 43 ELIZABETH I c. 4

An Acte to redresse the Misemployment of Landes Goodes and Stockes of Money heretofore given to Charitable Uses

Whereas Landes Tenementes Rentes Annuities Profittes Hereditamentes, Goodes Chattels Money and Stockes of Money, have bene heretofore given limitted appointed and assigned, as well by the Queenes most excellent Majestie and her moste noble Progenitors, as by sondrie other well disposed persons, some for Releife of aged impotent and poore people, some for Maintenance of sicke and maymed Souldiers and Marriners, Schooles of Learninge, Free Schooles and Schollers in Universities, some for Repaire of Bridges Portes Havens Causwaies Churches Seabankes and Highewaies, some for Educacion and prefermente of Orphans, some for or towardes Reliefe Stocke or Maintenance of Howses of Correccion, some for Mariages of poore Maides, some for Supportacion Ayde and Helpe of younge tradesmen Handicraftesmen and persons decayed, and others for releife or redemption of Prisoners or Captives, and for aide or ease of any poore Inhabitantes concerninge paymente of Fifteenes, setting out of Souldiers and other Taxes; Whiche Landes Tenementes Rents Annuities Profitts Hereditaments Goodes Chattells Money and Stockes of Money nevertheles have not byn imployed accordinge to the charitable intente of the givers and founders thereof, by reason of Fraudes breaches of Truste and Negligence in those that shoulde pay delyver and imploy the same: For Redresse and Remedie whereof, Be it enacted by Aucthoritie of this presente Parliament, That it shall and may be lawfull to and for the Lorde Chauncellor or Keeper of the Greate Seale of Englande for the tyme beinge, and for the Chauncellor of the Dutchie of Lancaster for the tyme beinge for Landes within the Countie Palatine of Lancaster, from tyme to tyme to award Commissions under the Greate Seale of Englande, or the Seale of the Countie Palantine as the case shall require, into all or any parte or partes of this Realme respectivelie, according to their severall Jurisdiccions as aforesaide, to the Bishoppe of everie severall Diocesse and his Chanceller, in case there shalbe any Bishoppe of that Diocesse at the tyme of awardinge of the same Commissions, and to other persons of good and sounde behaviour, authorisinge them therebie, or any fower or more of them, to inquire, as well by the Oathes of twelve lawfull Men or more of the Countie as by all other good and lawfull waies and menes, of all and singuler such Giftes Limitacions Assignements and Appoyntments aforesaide, and of the Abuses Breaches of Trustes Negligences Mysimploimentes, not imployinge concealinge defraudinge misconvertinge or misgovernmente, of any Landes Tenementes Rentes Annuities Profits Hereditaments Goods Chattels Money Stockes of Money heretofore given limitted appointed or assigned, or whiche hereafter shalbe given limitted appointed or assigned, to or for any the charitable and godlie uses before rehearsed: And after the saide Commissioners or any fower or more of them, upon callinge the parties interessed in any suche Landes Tenementes Rentes Annuities Profits Hereditaments Goodes Chattels Money and Stockes of Money, shall make inquirie by the Oathes of twelve men or more of the saide Countie, whereunto the saide parties interessed shall and maye have and take their lawfull challenge and challenges; and upon suche inquiry hearinge and examinynge thereof set downe suche Orders Judgments and Decrees, as the saide Landes Tenements Rents Annuities Profits Goods Chattels Money and Stockes of Money may be duelie and faithfullie imployed, to and for suche of the charitable uses and intents before rehearsed respectivelie, for whiche they were given limitted assigned or appointed by the Donors and Founders thereof: whiche Orders Judgements and Decrees, not beinge contrarie or repugnante to the Orders Statutes or Decrees of the Donors or Founders, shall by the Authoritie of this presente Parliamente stand firme and good accordinge to the tenor and purporte thereof, and shalbe executed accordinglie, untill the same shalbe undon or altered by the Lorde Chauncellor of Englande or Lorde Keeper of the Greate Seale of Englande, or the Chauncellor of the Countie Palatine of Lancaster, respectivelie within their severall Jurisdiccions, upon complainte by any partie grieved, to be made to them.

Provided alwaies, That neither this Acte, nor any thinge therein conteined, shall in any wise extende to any Landes Tenements Rents Annuities Profits Goods Chattels Money or Stockes of Money, given limitted appointed or assigned, or whiche shalbe given limitted appointed or assigned, to any Colledge Hall or Howse of Learninge within the Universities of Oxforde or Cambridge, or to the Colledges of Westminster Eaton or Winchester, or any of them, or to any Cathedrall or Collegiate Churche within this Realme.

And provided alsoe, That neither this Acte nor any thinge therein shall extende to any Citie or Towne Corporate, or to any the Landes or Tenements given to the uses aforesaide within any such Citie or Towne Corporate, where there is a speciall Governor or Governors, appointed to governe or directe suche Landes Tenements or Things disposed to any the uses aforesaide; neither to any Colledge Hospitall or Free Schoole whiche have speciall Visitors or Governours or Overseers appointed them by their founders.

Provided also and be it enacted by the Authoritie aforesaide, That neither this Acte nor any thinge therein contained shalbe any way prejudiciall or hurtfull to the Jurisdiccion or Power of the Ordinarie; but that he may lawfullie in everie cause execute and performe the same as thoughe this Acte had never bene had or made.

Provided also and be it enacted, That noe person or persons that hathe or shall have any of the saide Landes Tenements Rents Annuities Profits Hereditaments Goods Chattels Money or Stockes of Money in his Hands or Possession, or dothe or shall pretende Title thereunto, shall bee named Commyssioner or a Juror for any the causes aforesaide, or beinge named shall execute or serve in the same.

And provided alsoe, That no person or persons whiche hathe purchased or obteyned, or shall purchase or obteyne, upon valuable Consideracion of Money or Lande, any Estate or Intereste, of in to or out of any Landes Tenements Rents Annuities Hereditaments Goods or Chattels that have bene or shalbe given limitted or appointed to any the charitable Uses above mencioned, withoute Fraude or Covyn, havynge no Notice of the same charitable Use, shall not be impeached by any Decrees or Orders of Commissioners above mencioned for or concernynge the same his Estate or Interests.

And yet nevertheless Be it enacted, That the saide Commissioners, or any Fower of more of them, shall and may make Decrees and Orders for recompense to be made by any person or persons whoe, beinge put in Truste or havynge notice of the charitable Uses above mentioned, hathe or shall breake the same Truste, or defraude the same Uses, by any Conveiance Gifte Graunte Lease Demise Release or Conversion whatsoever, and againste the Heires Executors and Admynistrators of hym them or any of them, havynge Assettes in Law or Equitie, soe farre as the same Assettes will extende.

Provided alwaies, That this Acte shall not extende to give Power or Authority to any Commissioners before mentioned: to make any Orders Judgments or Decrees for or concernynge any Mannors Lands Tenements or other Hereditaments assured conveied graunted or come unto the Queenes Majestie, to the Late Kinge Henrie the Eighte, Kinge Edwarde the Sixte, or Queene Marie, by Acte of Parliament Surrender Exchange Relinquishemente Escheate Attainder Conveiance or otherwise.

And yet nevertheless Be it enacted, That if any suche Mannors Landes Tenements or Hereditaments, or any of them, or any Estate Rente or Profitte thereof or oute of the same or any parte thereof, have or hathe byn given granted limitted appointed or assigned to or for any the charitable uses before expressed, at anye tyme sithence the begynynge of her Majesties Reigne, that then the saide Commissioners or any fower or more of them shall and maye, as concerninge the same Landes Tenements Hereditaments Estate Rente or Profit soe given limitted appointed or assigned, procede to enquire and to make Orders Judgements and Decrees accordinge to the purporte and meaninge of this Acte as before is mentioned: The saide last Proviso notwithstandinge.

And be it further enacted, That all Orders Judgments and Decrees of the saide Commissioners, or of any fower or more of them, shalbe certified under the Seales of the saide Commissioners or any fower or more of them, either into the Courte of the Chauncerie of Englande, or into the Courte of the Chauncerie within the Countie Palatine of Lancaster, as the case shall require respectivelie accordinge to their severall Jurisdiccions, within suche conveniente tyme as shalbe limitted in the saide Commissions; And that the saide Lorde Chancellor or Lorde Keeper, and the saide Chauncellor of the Duchie, shall and maye, within their saide severall Jurisdiccions, take suche Order for the due Execucion of all or any of the saide Judgments Decrees and Orders as to either of them shall seeme fit and convenient: And that if after any such certificattes made any person or persons shall fynde themselves grieved withe any of the saide Orders Judgments or Decrees, that then it shall and maybe lawful to and for them or anie of them to complaine in that behalfe unto the saide Lorde Chancellor or Lorde Keeper, or to the Chancellor of the saide Duchie of Lancaster, accordinge to their severall Jurisdiccions, for Redresse therein; And that upon suche Complainte the saide Lorde Chancellor or Lorde Keeper, or the saide Chancellor of the Duchie may, accordinge to their saide severall Jurisdiccions, by suche course as to their wisedomes shall seeme meeteste, the circumstances of the case considered, proceede to the examinacion hearinge and determynynge thereof; and upon hearinge thereof shall and may adnull dymynishe alter or enlarge the saide Orders Judgements and Decrees of the saide Commyssioners, or any fower or more of them, as to either of them, in their saide severall Jurisdiccions, shalbe thoughte to stande withe Equitie and good Conscience, accordinge to the true intente and meaninge of the Donors and Fownders thereof; and shall and may taxe and awarde good Costes of Suite by their discrecions againste such persons as they shall fynde to complaine unto them, without juste and sufficient cause, of the Orders Judgments and Decrees before mencioned.

APPENDIX E

A BIBLIOGRAPHICAL NOTE ON THE CAMBRIDGE MS. OF FRANCIS MOORE'S *READING* ON THE STATUTE OF CHARITABLE USES: 43 ELIZABETH I c. 4

The reading was an integral part of the education of the medieval law student, and a necessary exercise for the utter barrister who cast covetous eyes to the Bench of his Inn, the Order of the Coif and a judgeship in the Common Pleas or King's Bench. At one time each reader discoursed on one of the 'old' statutes before Edward III (especially Magna Carta, Merton, Marlborough, Westminster I, Gloucester and Westminster II), but during the sixteenth century readers acquired a wider range of choice; so Coke and Bacon were to read on the Statute of Uses, 1535 and Moore on the Statute of Charitable Uses, 1601.[1] The 'antient readings' are said to have served the apprentices well, particularly as an introduction to the dark intricacies of medieval land law. Coke esteemed them as having five excellent qualities[2]:

> First, they declared what the common law was before the making of the statute, as here it appeareth. Secondly, they opened the true sense and meaning of the statute. Thirdly, their cases were briefe, having at the most one poynt of the common law and another upon the statute. Fourthly, plaine and perspicuous, for then the honour of the reader was to excell others in authorities, arguments, and reasons for proofe of his opinion, and for confutation of the objections against it. Fifthly, they read, to suppresse subtill inventions to creepe out of the statute.

How more favourable than their modern counterparts, mused Coke, which

> having lost the said former qualities, have lost also their former authorities: for now the cases are long, obscure, and intricate, full of new

[1] S. E. Thorne, *Readings and Moots at the Inns of Court in the Fifteenth Century*, Vol. I (1952), Selden Society, LXXI, ix-xvii; and the same author's lecture on 'The Early History of the Inns of Court', printed in *Graya*, no. 50 (Michaelmas, 1959), 79.

[2] Co. Litt. (London, 1832, ed.) 280–280v.

conceits, liker rather to riddles than lectures, which when they are opened they vanish away like smoke, and the readers are like to lapwings, who seeme to bee neerest their nests, when they are farthest from them, and all their studie is to find nice evasions out of the statute.

It ill becomes Coke to castigate others for prolixity, obscurity and intricacy. But his arch condemnation reflected the fact that some readers thought that their chosen task was not to instruct the young but to impress and edify the antients of their Inn with the splendour of their learning. Attendance could not have failed to drop away, and the printed records of the Inns are scattered with entries of fines imposed on students for non-attendance, a phenomenon which becomes more and more marked as Elizabeth's reign progresses.[1] These products of the new grammar schools would have found much of the readers' learning recondite and crabbily pedantic, and have been encouraged in their truancy by the increasing popularity of the printed book whose very existence cast doubt on the utility of an intensely oral and vigorously dialectic method of instruction. It is well known, too, that many an utter barrister viewed the prospect and honour of reading with an enthusiasm that was on the cool side of lukewarm, and bore with equanimity the fine imposed by his Inn (perhaps to be remitted at the instance of a wealthy patron) for failing to do so. The financial penalty imposed by the Middle Temple—between £5 and £10—was mild compared with the frightening expense of the hospitality which the reader was required to lavish on noblemen and members of his Society. So William Dugdale in his *Origines Juridiciales* frankly confessed that[2]

. . . His expenses, during this time of *Reading*, are very great; insomuch as some have spent above six hundred pounds in two days less than a fortnight, which now is the usual time of *Reading*.

Although latter times and examples have added to the Excess; yet heretofore, when they were most frugal, a competent proportion, for entertainment of Strangers (which was held to be a lustre and honour to the House) was ever expected from them, and in some sort hath been prescribed unto them, . . .

Concern was constantly and officially expressed over the failure of incentives either to deliver, or listen to this time-honoured

[1] For example, *Middle Temple Records*, I (London, 1904), 136, 140, 182, 331, 337, 369, 398, 407.

[2] (London, 1666), 207.

exercise. The judges issued to the Inns of Court a succession of orders which sought to ensure that only those 'esteemed for their learning and credit, fit to serve in the common weal, and who have attended the reading in the exercises there two years before their call to that place' should be admitted to read; that no reader should be exposed to the crippling expenses attendant upon reading or should seek to corrupt his position by calling more than three or four to the Bar; and that the reader should be 'plain and perspicuous', always moving 'to make [his] case short, not containing above 2 or 3 points at the most, and those as much upon the Statute read on as may be'.[1] In turn, the Inns attempted to redress the most extravagant abuses,[2] but their reforms were half-hearted and had no lasting impact. As a serious method of instruction in the expertise and science of the common lawyer, the reading did not survive the Civil War. It had outlived its time; it was a ghost of the past and the clanking of its medieval chains was only too audible in the student chambers of the Inns of Chancery and Court.[3]

Francis Moore, delivered his *Reading* in Middle Temple Hall in August 1607,[4] when he was forty-nine years old.[5] Moore enjoyed

[1] *Middle Temple Records*, I, 339 (Hilary Term, 1594). There are other instances in the records of the judges' concern to maintain the integrity and quality of the readings: see, for example, the orders reproduced in the *Middle Temple Records*, I, 200 (1574); and Dugdale, *Origines Juridiciales*, chap. LXX.

[2] See the answer of the Benchers of the Middle Temple, *Middle Temple Records*, I, 340; dated 22 April 1594.

[3] Cf. now W. R. Prest's recently published article, 'The Learning Exercise at the Inns of Court 1590–1640', *Journal of the Society of Public Teachers of Law*, IX (1967), 301. Mr Prest argues that 'the extent of the decline in the system of learning before 1642 has been exaggerated. The main causes of decline . . . were present but dormant. They had little effect on the workings of the system during our period.' There is no doubt that the system did operate in a formal fashion, but Prest has not convinced me that its workings were effective.

[4] In the Middle Temple and the other Inns, readers who read but once were called *single* readers; those who read twice, *double* readers. The single reader always read in the summer: Moore was, therefore, such a reader. See Dugdale, *Origines Juridiciales*, 209.

[5] For much that follows, see Dugdale, *Origines Juridiciales*, 219; J. W. Wallace, *The Reporters*, 3rd ed. (Philadelphia, 1855), 85–7; *Dictionary of National Biography*, XXXVIII (London, 1894), 348–9; W. H. Stevenson and H. E. Salter, *The Early History of St John's College, Oxford* (Oxford, 1939), 319; A. Wood, *Athenae Oxonienses*, ed. Philip Bliss, II (London, 1815), 304. These printed sources are supplemented by the information in C.U.L. MS. Hh. III. 2, fols. 1–5; on which see below, pp. 234–9.

among his fellow-lawyers a high reputation[1] which his *Reading* and his reports confirm for later generations. Many of the 'cases' adduced by him would no doubt have earned Coke's censure for their conceits, but they are nonetheless remarkable examples of the subtle sophistications of the common lawyer's art. Moore was born an orphan and as a child attended Reading Grammar School. He is said to have been a commoner at St John's College, Oxford, in 1574, and although he was later to become Under Steward of that university, he did not graduate from it. Instead he entered New Inn, the satellite Inn of Chancery of the Middle Temple, and became a member of that latter society in 1580. He was a prominent Parliamentarian, entering the House of Commons for the first time in 1588, and being returned again in 1597–8, 1601, 1604–11 and 1614. Moore was a man who earned the friendship and affection of many of the powerful. In his *Reading* he floridly describes how much his advancement was due to a 'grave and wyse' lord, most probably Ellesmere; and in 1603 'at the desire of the Lord Chancellor and Lord Chief Justice', he was admitted 'an associate to the Masters of the Bench until he be called to read either in his own course by antiquity or sooner in default of others, and henceforth to take this place as a Bencher.'[2] Chosen Autumn Reader for the year 1607, seven years later he became Sergeant at Law, and was knighted in 1617. He died in 1621.

There is a long tradition whose origin appears to be the title page and preface of George Duke's *The Law of Charitable Uses*, published in 1676, that Moore was the 'penner' of the Charitable Uses Act, 1601. Duke's work, which has always enjoyed a high reputation,[3] purports to contain collections from

> the Learned Reading of Sr. Francis Moor, Kt. Sergeant at Law, 4 Jacobi, in the Middle Temple Hall, Upon the Statute of 43 Eliz. concerning Charitable Uses, (who was a Member of that PARLIAMENT when that Statute was made, and the Penner thereof.) Abridged by himself, and now Printed by his own Original Manuscript.

[1] For example, it is said that Francis Moore was the first man to practise the conveyancing device of lease and release: see *Barker* v. *Keat* (1677), 2 Mod. 249, 252, *per* Sir Francis North C.J. W. S. Holdsworth accepts this oral tradition; see *A History of English Law*, VII (London, 1937), 360–1.

[2] *Middle Temple Records*, II (London, 1904), 441–2. This Parliament was held at Winchester, during the Treasureship of Bartholomew Man, on 23 November 1603.

[3] See above, p. 14, n. 4.

Who George Duke was is a mystery. There is no reason to think that he was a member of Moore's family. In all probability he was a competent legal hack. His book on the law of charity, with the exception of the extracts from Moore's *Reading*, was largely[1] a faithful reproduction of John Herne's *The Law of Charitable Uses*, first published in 1660 with a second, more comprehensive edition in 1663. Both Herne's and Duke's books were published by the well-known legal publishers of the name of Twyford[2]; and it is not insignificant that whereas Herne supplied the prefaces to both his editions, the obbligato '*to the Reader*' in 1676 was not Duke's but Henry Twyford's. The origins of Moore's abridged manuscript, which wrongly dates the *Reading* as 1606 when it was in fact given in 1607,[3] appear to be as mysterious as the origins of George Duke. The preface does not mention how Twyford acquired the manuscript and it does not now appear to exist.[4] I am suspicious of Twyford's assertion that Moore was the 'penner' of the 1601 Act, although he may well have had a substantial part to play in its drafting. The *Reading* displays a profound knowledge of the statute's provisions and a keen appreciation of its effect on established common law and equity. But the available evidence does not go so far as to confer on Francis Moore the accolade of

[1] There are a few precedents and cases in Duke which are not found in Herne's second edition. So, for example, Duke's pp. 32–34, 41–54, 94 (case 50) and 95–104 are not to be found in Herne. Duke's format is much more pretentious than Herne's, and also contains a fulsome dedication to Charles II.

[2] Herne was published by Timothy Twyford, Duke by Henry Twyford. On the Twyfords, see H. R. Plomer, *A Dictionary of the Booksellers and Printers who were at Work in England, Scotland and Ireland from 1641 to 1667* (London, 1907), 183.

[3] See below, p. 240.

[4] The form of the *Abridgment*, as reproduced in Duke, significantly differs from that of the C.U.L. MS. of the *Reading*. The C.U.L. MS., which is, I believe in Moore's own hand, is in the traditional form of case followed by explanation: below, pp. 237–9. But the *Abridgment* reads more like a simple textbook on the law of charity as found in the statute; the principles of law are boldly and simply set out, divorced from their 'case' context. There is much material in the C.U.L. MS. of the *Reading* which does not find its way into the *Abridgment*. But the *Abridgment* does add some new law which is not found in the C.U.L. MS.

A priori, it is not easy to accept that a lawyer as distinguished and active as Moore would take the trouble to abridge his original text into a form which would appeal and be of help to later generations. However, Twyford's claim that he is printing Moore's own MS. cannot lightly be dismissed; for the *Abridgment* is a sophisticated, coherent and accurate restatement of principles which are diffused throughout the *Reading*. But there is evidence in the printed text of the *Abridgment* of later interpolations.

'penner'. Significantly, he does not claim that honour for himself in his opening speech[1] when it was customary for the new reader to give reasons why he had chosen to expound the statute of his choice.[2] And neither chronicler of the Elizabethan Parliament, Simond D'Ewes,[3] nor Hayward Townshend,[4] deigns to mention him by name as one of the committees, consisting largely of members learned in the law, which considered either the 1597 or 1601 charity statutes[5]; in fact, it was Edward Philips, later to be Speaker and Master of the Rolls, whom Townshend identifies as having drafted the bill, and as presenting to the House of Commons in 1601 the report of the committee which had been charged to 'put into the Bill of Repeal or the Bill of continuance of Statutes', the Statute 39 Elizabeth I c. 6.[6] In all probability, the substance of the Charitable Uses Act 1601 was the work of this committee, a corporate enterprise.

Moore's own manuscript of the *Reading* is preserved in the Cambridge University Library.[7] It is a formidable document. At first sight it appears to contain 280 folios, but many of these folios are blank. Moreover, the numbering of the folios, which is not Moore's, is erratic, and some numbers are for some reason or other omitted. In effect there are 158 folios, 316 pages, with about forty lines to a page. With the exception of the first five folios, which are in English, the whole is written in law French.

Folios 1–3^{v} give a colourful description of the background to the *Reading*. From it we learn that the *Reading*, which began on 3 August 1607, was prematurely determined 'on Friday the 14 of August in respect [of] the plage much increased, the certificatt beinge 77 that weeke of the plage.'[8] We also discover who were

[1] See below, pp. 244–6.

[2] Dugdale, *Origines Juridiciales*, 206.

[3] *Journals of all the Parliaments Held during the Reign of Queen Elizabeth* (London, 1682).

[4] *Proceedings of the last four Parliaments of Queen Elizabeth* (London, 1680).

[5] D'Ewes, *Journals*, 657, 669.

[6] Townshend, *Proceedings*, 285.

[7] C.U.L. MS. Hh. III. 2. It is wrongly described in the C.U.L. *Catalogue of Manuscripts* (Cambridge, 1858), 272, as being upon the statute 43 Eliz. I c. 7, instead of 43 Eliz. I c. 4. The source of this mistake is Moore's MS. itself, fo. 6, which appears to be in Moore's own hand: see below, p. 239.

[8] By tradition the Autumn Reading began on the first Monday in August 'unless this [these] day[s] be festival' (Dugdale, *Origines Juridiciales*, 206–7). It should at this time have lasted for three weeks; but readers often failed to last the course, much to the concern of the judges: see *Middle Temple Records*, I, 339–40 (1594).

Moore's benchers assistants[1]; his cupboard men[2]; the three utter barristers whom it was his privilege as reader to call to the Bar[3]; and the names of those whom he 'specially' admitted 'of the House in my Readinge', which include his three sons Francis, Henry and William.[4] This section of the manuscript[5] concludes with a mouth-watering description of gifts given to Moore at his *Reading*, no

[1] Dugdale, *Origines Juridiciales*, 206, notes that a reader normally only had two benchers assistants, 'being, for the most part, the two next precedent *Readers*'. Moore, however, had five (below, p. 240). Henry Montague, who had read the preceding autumn; Mathewe Dale, a double reader, who had read as long ago as 1576 and 1585: Thomas Pagitt (or Paget), a double reader, who had read in 1584 and 1594; Francis Walron (or Walrond), who had read in 1601; and George Writnighton (or Wrightnighton), who was Lent reader in 1605.

In all cases, and hereafter, the primary spelling is Moore's; the spelling in parenthesis is that adopted in other sources, which is frequently more acceptable. Moore was probably writing from memory or his own rough notes.

[2] Cupboardmen were so named 'because they were stationed at the cupboard, a square or oblong table placed near the Bench table and the centre of ceremonies in the Hall': see *The Middle Temple Bench Book*, 2nd ed. (London, 1937), xix. The four cupboardmen were the four 'antientest Barristers of the House who were to dispute the cases with the reader'; see Dugdale, *Origines Juridiciales*, 203, for further details.

Moore's cupboardmen were Lawrence Hyde (or Hide), Will Swantone (or Swaynton), Francis Harvy (or Harvey), and Edward Cason: see below, p. 240, and *Middle Temple Records*, II, 487. All these were to become readers. This confirms that it was the practice of the Middle Temple at this time only to choose as cupboardmen those who resolved to read. The cupboardmen could appoint deputies to perform their duties, but only with due excuse. Robert Smith and Anthony Benn deputised for Moore's cupboardmen. Below, p. 240, Moore was a cupboardman in 1606 and 1607.

[3] This privilege had been considerably abused. At this date the Middle Temple was making an earnest effort to control the reader's discretion. So it was the practice of that House to confirm in its Parliament the calls of its readers; to fine them for calling 'unfit persons'; to disallow the calls; and to regulate the number of members its readers could call (*Middle Temple Records*, I, 189, 303 and 391).

Moore called to the Bar: John Mercer, Edward Latton and Francis Keate (or Keat): below, p. 240. Normally a single reader was allowed only two calls so that Moore was given a special privilege, which is not noted in the formal records of the Society. His calls were confirmed in the Parliament held on 30 October 1607: see *Middle Temple Records*, II, 484.

[4] The others mentioned by Moore are: Robert Knollys, George Wattnighton (?) (below, p. 240); a Mr Smith; and a Mr Angell (or Aungell). The *Middle Temple Records*, II, 483, also give the name of Richard Lewknor. In none of these cases, save Angell's, was a fine demanded from the member. Those members of the Inn who were specially admitted would generally wish to be admitted for purely social reasons. The Inns at this time were one of the fashionable meeting-grounds of London, most desirable clubs to which young gentlemen would aspire to belong.

[5] See below, pp. 242–3.

doubt for the reader's feast, which Moore, contrary to custom,[1] paid for out of his own pocket.

Then follows (fols. 4–5) 'his speech at the beginninge', which casts some valuable biographical light on Moore and explains why he chose to read on the statute. He pays an elaborate and punning tribute to his 'two superiors', the Middle Temple and the 'Grave and wyse Senator of the State, who next under the Septer serves the Magistrey of the Kingdom', no doubt an allusion to Ellesmere. The speech concludes with an encomium on the value of the ancient custom of reading and with a self-effacing account of his own personal inadequacies.

In the course of his *Reading* Moore presents to his audience seventy cases arranged in seven divisions, which comprise the remainder of the manuscript. Moore's seven divisions (which are closely followed in Duke's book) are as follows[2]:

1. What is a charitable use within the statute?
2. When is the commission, issued under the statute, well awarded and executed?
3. What is a sufficient inquisition?
4. What is a good decree?
5. What cities, towns, etc., are exempted from the statute?
6. What can be said to be a purchase for valuable consideration of money or land?
7. What can be said to be a defrauding of the charitable use?

There may have been an eighth division dealing with the power of the Ordinary and with the question of Crown exemption; but it has not survived either in the C.U.L. manuscript or in Duke's book. Certainly Moore's 'heads of divisions' (fo. 6) suggest that he intended to discuss these topics. It is possible that he never did

[1] Dugdale, *Origines Juridiciales*, 207, narrates: 'although it be called the *Readers Feast*, yet he bears no part of the charge, the same being imposed on four gentlemen of the House; whom they call Stewards of the Feast; whereof two are Utter-Barristers, and the other two under the Bar, whose charge is now at the least x[l] a piece; but heretofore less: for by an Order made 34 Eliz. they were to be at no farther charge than five pounds a man.'

By an order of the Middle Temple Parliament, dated 4 November 1586, the Stewards were required to bear the costs equally between them: see *Middle Temple Records*, I, 287. In fact Moore's Stewards contributed £8 a piece, and 'I performed the feaste at myne own costes.' See below, p. 241.

[2] What follows is a summary and not a transcription of Moore's seven divisions, which are set out in full in fo. 6. The divisions are thereafter only noted in *marginalia* in the body of the MS.

so. It is also possible that he did, but that the cases are lost; for it is clear from internal evidence that the C.U.L. manuscript was at one time in its history carelessly bound or rebound.[1]

A presentation by division and case, followed by an exposition, was traditional. The prime purpose of the case was to illustrate the contents of the particular division, but there is also in each case an extremely full and learned discussion of relevant principles of common law and equity and whether these principles must or must not give way to the letter or equity of the statute. Indeed, this collateral analysis of common law rules should have been more important to the student than Moore's exposition of the nuances of the law of charity. It must be confessed, however, that many of Moore's cases would have driven even the most dedicated and conscientious apprentice to despair. Take his first case, which involves complicated questions of disseisin and coparcenary, which is learnedly illustrated by medieval citation and which extends over nine closely written pages[2]:

a disseisor of two parceners of land in London grants rent by indenture to one of them in fee to find bows and arrowes for infants between the ages of seven and seventeen; and makes a lease for life of the land to another, the remainder in fee to the grantee and avows for the rent. The disseisor devises the land to be sold on the death of the tenant for life and the money distributed to twenty of the poorest of his kin: and he makes the tenant for life his executor and dies. The tenant for life surrenders by fine to the heir and dies without issue. Here are two charitable uses, one for the rent, the other for the land, within the statute.

The case, put at New Inn to the fledgling law students, is perhaps even more intimidating[3]:

A lord grants his seignory, that a horse be found, and rent in fee on condition of finding a perpetual rider to train all wards in the county to manage a war horse. The tenant makes a feoffment to the grantor and grantee to the intent that the grantee and his heirs will find the horse, the grantee releases to the grantor on condition that he and his heirs

[1] So, division six (fols. 244–80^{v}) follows division seven (fols. 205–41) in the C.U.L. MS. Again, fols. 17–18^{v} should follow fols. 11–14, being a part of the discussion of Moore's second case and not his third case, fols. 15–15^{v}. Fo. 16 is blank.

[2] Fols. 7–10^{v}.

[3] Fols. 47–48. The case is transcribed in appendix G.

will find both. He [the grantor] fails during the year [to find both] because there are no wards in the county. A commission [under 43 Eliz. I c. 4] is awarded to the Bishop, his chancellor, an Italian rider and the grantor and grantee, who [all of whom] execute the commission. It is well awarded and well executed.

The quality of these hypothetical facts may explain why it was not uncommon for a reader to find that he had no audience on his arrival at the Inn of Chancery.[1]

Moore is very careful to note in the margin which case was argued, and this was the only case which appears to have been put at an Inn of Chancery. All the remaining cases were argued at the Middle Temple. The selection of the case or cases from each division for argument was not the reader's, but the prerogative of the most junior cupboardman.[2] Having chosen the case, the cupboardman argued 'to oppose the *Reader's* conclusion'; the next cupboardman against him, and so on.[3] The benchers then joined in the fun; as did those judges and sergeants of the Society who happened to be present, and who, by tradition, supported the reader's arguments. The reader brought the proceedings to an end by maintaining 'his own conclusion', and the assembly, intellectually satiated, feasted.[4]

The C.U.L. manuscript contains no hint of any interjection by the cupboard, but there are a few cases which suggest either that Moore changed his mind or that he modified his original conclusion in the light of the disputation following the case. A particularly striking example is case six of Division III, fols. 252–4. Moore had originally concluded on the particular facts that the feoffee would be

[1] *Black Books of Lincoln's Inn*, II (London, 1898), 293. (This event is recorded as having happened in 1630, when the reader from Lincoln's Inn arrived at Furnival's Inn.) On the Inns of Chancery, see Sir Cecil Carr's introduction to the *Pension Book of Clement's Inn* (1960), Selden Society, LXXVIII, *passim*.

[2] Twelve cases appear to have been argued by the cupboardmen: they are I–2 (Division I, case 2) (fo. 11); II–1 (fo. 47); II–3 (fo. 55); III–2 (fo. 91); IV–2 (fo. 131); V–1 (fo. 167); V–2 (fo. 170); V–3 (fo. 173); VI–3 (fo. 252); VI–6 (fo. 264); VII–2 (fo. 209); VII–6 (fo. 225).

On the whole, these cases are more complex than those which were not argued. It is significant, too, that division five, where Moore considers which colleges and cities, etc, were *exempt* from the statute, was the subject of the greatest debate.

[3] Dugdale, *Origines Juridiciales*, 206.

[4] But after dinner there might be further disputation and discussion. The scene at the reading is well set by Dugdale, *ibid.* 203 ff. and by Edward Waterhouse in his *Fortescutus Illustratus* (London, 1663), 544–6.

charged with two charitable uses. He then struck out that sentence and wrote above it that he was bound by the second but not the first charitable use. The body of the text is also altered and a substantial section of it which supports his original conclusion is deleted. These corrigenda are in the same hand as the original text. Such evidence—and there are many other examples[1] of spontaneous addenda and corrigenda—leads me to conclude that the MS. is in Moore's own hand. It is highly unlikely that it is the work of a copyist, who misread his primary source; and any suggestion that a copyist, having transcribed from Moore's own text, corrected the master's findings of law seems to me to be wholly unrealistic.

Moore's *Reading* adds much to the account of the contemporary law of charity in Duke's book. But it is important in a wider context. It supplements in a significant way our knowledge of early seventeenth-century equity, and graphically explains why Moore was so esteemed amongst his contemporaries for his technical mastery of the minutiae of the common law: his arguments and conclusions of law are lucidly stated; he makes effective use of verbal antithesis; his citation of medieval authority is (unlike that of some of his contemporaries) relevant; and his references to recent cases decided by the chancellor, whose source must have been his own notebook, are telling. Less ostentatious and contrived than Coke's *Reading*,[2] less metaphysical and finely spun than Bacon's *Reading*,[3] Francis Moore's *Reading* on the statute of 43 Elizabeth I c. 4 is an impressive and comprehensive illustration of the technique and learning of a generation of common lawyers who were highly influential in adapting ancient learning to the needs of an independent and aggressively expansionist society.

[1] See, for example, fols. 43–43^{v}, 51–53, 95–96^{v}, 173–4^{v}, 193–193^{v}, 197–198^{v}.

[2] *Reading on the Statute of Uses, 1535* (27 Hen. VIII c. 10): B.M. MS., Stowe, 424.

[3] *Reading on the Statute of Uses, 1535*, ed. W. H. Rowe (London, 1804).

APPENDIX F

FRANCIS MOORE'S NOTES AND HIS *SPEECH AT THE BEGINNINGE*

[Fo. 1] I begann my readinge on Mondaye 3 Auguste 1607 Anno 5 Jacobi regnis—in the middle temple.

I had benchers assistants[1] at my beginninge Sir Henry Montague knight, Recorder of London and of the Kinges counsaile by patent, with a clause to be against the Kinge for the City of London if question growe betweene them.

Mathewe Dale a Dubble Reador, and one of the two judges of the Sheriffs Cort of London.

Thomas Pagitt a Dobble Reador and of the Countey of Northampton dwellinge at Walgrove.

Frances Walron, a single Reador, dwellinge in Thistleworth in Middlesex.

George Writnighton, a single Reador.

I had for my Cubbardmen[2] assigned

Lawrence Hyde of the Countey of Middlesex.

Wil Swantone of the Countey of Dorset.

Fraunceys Harvy of the Countey of Northampton.

Edward Cason of the Countey of Hertford.

All which were attendant the first weeke, and as they departed there came in their places

Robart Smith of Suffolk.

Anthony Benn of Surrey, then Reador of Newe Inn.

I ended my readinge on friday the 14 of August in respect the plage much increased, the certificatt beinge 77 that weeke of the plage.

I called 3 utterbarresters.[3]

Jhon Mercer, sonne of Rafe Mercer of Whitley in the Countey of Berkshire, gent.

[1] See above, p. 235, n. 1.

[2] See above, p. 235, n. 2.

[3] See above, p. 235.

Edward Latton, sonne of Jhon Latton of Kingston Bagespius in the Countey of Berkshire, Esquire.

Francis Keate, sonne of Edward Keate of Estlockinge, gent.

[Fo. 1] The Stewards of my ffeaste[1] were these.

Edward Harris utterbarrister sonne of Thomas Harris thelder knight and sergiant at Lawe.

Mr. Culpeper utterbarrister of the Countey of Kent.

Mr. Denton of prioers Cort in the Countey of Berkshire.

Mr. Lake sonne of Doctor Lake of the Civill Lawe.

Every of these paid £8 contribution and I performed the feast at myne owne costes.

I admitted of the house in my Readinge.[2]

1. Robert Knollys sonne and heire apparant of Sir Francis Knollys of Readinge in the County of Berkshire knight.

2. George Wattnighton[3] gente, clerk of the poore of the Countey of Berkshire.

3. Fraunceys Moore, myne eldest sonne.

4. Henry Moore, my second son.

5. William Moore, my third sonne.

6. The corrector of the Lawe printe, Smith.

7. The sonne of Mr. Angell the fishmonger.

Readers of the other Howses were at this tyme.

Thomas Chamberlayn Esquior of the County of Oxfordshire at Grayes Inn.

Rychard Delabere esquior of the Countey of Glocestshire at Lincolnes Inn.

Jhon Walter esquior of the countey of Oxfordshire at the Inner Temple.

This yere, the 5 of August, being the daye of the Kinges delivery from the treason of Earle Gowrey in Scotland; fell to be the first wensday in August, which day all the Readors forbeare their Readinge and heard two sermons, one in the forenone an other in thafternone. And ffor us of the Temple, Mr. Carewe Chapleine to

[1] See above, p. 236, n. 1.

[2] See above, p. 235, n. 4.

[3] In all probability this was George Wrightnighton, son of the single reader and Master of the Bench; above, p. 235.

the Lord Ellesmere Lord Chauncelor in the forenone, and Mr. Deneson also his Lord's Chapleine preached in thafternone at my request.

[Fo. 2] Giftes at my readinge[1]

Wyne	Francis Englefeild, esquior	— 2 Hoggesheds	— £xii x^s
	Francis Fytton, esquior	— a Hoggeshed	— £vi v^s
	The Company of Vintners	— a Hoggeshed	— £vi v^s
	The Middle Temple	— a Hoggeshed	— £vi x^s
	Sir Jhon Whitbroke	— a Hoggeshed	— £vi v^s
Money	Sir Edward Hungerford, Knight		— £x
	Jhon Chamberlayne, gent		— £x
	Thomas Pagitt, esquior		— £v
	William Minterne, esquior		— xl^s
	Jhon Carlile, esquior		— xl^s
	Edmund Duniche (?) esquior		— xx^s
	Sir Francis Palmer, knight		— xx^s
	Sir Jhon Bois, knight		— xx^s
	Edward Clerk, esquior		— xx^s
	The towne of Readinge		— £x
Sugar	Francis Englefeild, esquior	— loaves	— 3
	Oates Gare, gent	— loaves	— 2
	Sir John Egerton thelder	— loves	— 3
	Peter Vantore	— loves	— 2
	Lawrence Hale, esquior	— loves	— 1
	Samuell Backhowse, esquior	— loves	— 1
	Mr. Alden	— loves	— 2
	Mr. Gye	— loaves	— 1
	Mr. Elias Wood	— loves	— 2
	Mr. Moile	— loves	— 1
	Mr. Edward Clerk	— loves	— 2
	Mr. Crompton, my chamber fellow	— loves	— 3
	Mr. Phillips, warden of the fflete	— loves	— 1
	Mr. Edward Keate of Leckinge	— loves	— 2

[1] The donors included relatives and friends of Moore, members of his Inn, and others, like the corrector of the law print, Smith, whose son he had admitted, who were in one way or another indebted to him.

[Fo. 2^v]

Peppar	Mr. Wood the grocer	— xii^s
	Mr. Alderman Bowler	— xii^s
Sturgeon	Mr. Wilson of Wyndsore	— a ferkin
	Mr. Blake of Readinge	— a ferkin
	Mr. Manwaringe of Cullendgham	— a ferkin
	Mr. Jhon Brewster	— a kegg
	Doctor Hamond	— a kegg
Swannes	The Company of Vintners	— 2
	Mr. Mann of the benche	— 2
	Mr. Jhon Loveden	— 3
Salmon	Mr. Angell	— 1
	Mr. Jhon Brewster Mr. Jermy	— 2 baked
Trowts	Mr. Hungerford of Weston	— xiii
Marchpanes	Baron Sotherton	1
	Edward Cason, esquior	1
	Mr. Hodzor	1
	The corrector of the Lawprint Doctor Hamond	1
Poultry, Fowls, Chese	Mr. Wollascott	— 10 chicken, 8 tirkeis, 12 pullitts, 10 partriges
	Mr. Blandy	— 4 capons, 2 tirkeis, 6 cheses
	Mistris Brabroke	— a fesant, a pehenn, 14 quails 2 capons, 2 pulletts, 6 cheses
	Mr. Keate of Estlockinge	— 12 partriges, 12 quails, 3 dozen pigeons
	Mr. Robert Wirdynain ffrom ffalley	— 5 geese, 5 tirkeis, 50 capons
	Mistress Grunter	— a turkye
	Myne uncle Church	— 12 capons, 2 dozen of pigeons, 12 chickens
	Mistris Purcell	[No entry]
	My sister Apleton	— a fatt shepe and a fatt lambe
	Mr. Overbury	— a banbury cake and 6 cheses

[Fo. 4][1] *My speech at the beginninge*

When I first forsawe the burthen of this busines falinge towards

[1] Fols. 3 and 3^v are blank.

me, I caste myne eye uppon the kalender of Statutes, and fromthence I selected into my meditacion 3 Statutes to have reade uppon one after thother as I was variably conceited. The first was the Statute of Accomptaunts,[1] the second the Statute of Bankrupts,[2] the third was this of charity whereuppon I am settled. I affected that of Accomptaunts in respect of extraordinary resceits I hold from two Superiors, that raises a desire in me to knowe how to accompt, and what was subject to myne arreriages. But examininge myself a while uppon my charity and dischardge I might see as in a transparent glasse thorough mine owne conscience, that the totall of myne dett was more than my meanes to satisfie, which made me feare, yf I spent my muses in that Lawe, I shold saye, *Dolor meus in Conspectu meo semper.*[3]

Whereuppon I diverted my Cogitacions to the Statute of Bankrupts from whence disperate debtors use to take ease by payenge but ratable parts to their creditors. But after a Little readinge in that Corse I sawe yt cold not fit me, for that I was not able to paye a mighte in the pounde.

Then loathe to waste my wittes in Laboures of renewinge greife, I lefte that, and betoke me to this of charitye, whereby I might be enable at the leaste, to extoll, and advaunce deeds of charity in Givers and Forogivers. Resolvinge never to plede either plee to my Creditors, then, *Habilis Confitentem Reum* (?)[4]; and to conclude with praises and thanckesgivinge to god for them, and to them for my selfe. [Fo. 4^{v}] The two Superiors to whom I was accomptable and yet am, are these: The first, this reverent learned and lovinge Societie of the middle temple who when I was younge, rude, and ignorant receaved me, instructed me, and prepared me for all that Little which I am come to since. Thother is that great, grave and wyse Senator of the State, who next under the Septer sirves the magisterry of the kingdom, and who of his honorable bountey,

[1] 13 Eliz. I c. 4, and 27 Eliz. I c. 3.

[2] 34 & 35 Hen. VIII c. 4; 13 Eliz. I c. 7; 1 Jac. I c. 15. Although Moore was not to read on these statutes, he did incidentally discuss some of their provisions: see, for example, fols. 35–35^{v}, 128, 209–212^{v}, 217–218^{v}, 252–254^{v}. He was no doubt determined that his skirmishing researches should not be wasted.

[3] Psalms, xxxvii, 18:

Quoniam ego in flagella paratus sum,
et dolor meus in conspectu meo semper.

[4] Query if Moore intended to quote Petronius' *Satyricon*, 130: 'numquam tamen ante hunc diem usque ad mortem deliqui: habes confitentem reum.' (I am indebted to Mrs W. A. F. P. Steiner for this suggestion.)

toke me into his favoure callinge me to his feete in publick and to his elbowe in private. What shold I saye? Concerninge this poore frehall or cotage whereof I do consist. For the first materialls of foundacion and walles to the middle temple, for the coveringe and fyrnishinge I stand most bound to that greate Lorde, my patron and protector. Therefor to either of these two I do accompt that I owe more then my selfe, and that for a deed of charity which is my Statute, thone for educacion, thother for preferment of me an orphane.

To the middle temple I am nowe called to give an accompt of above 27 yeres spent if not mispent, wherein I must confess I receive discourogement by 3 thinges.

1. The necessity of this service.
2. Thexspectation raised of yt.
3. The excellent performaunce of my predecessors.

The necessity consisteth in this, that as wee are a voluntary society professinge the Study and practize of the Lawes for the use of the people, So by that function wee undertake to be Learned in the Lawes as the propfitt David saith, *Erudimini qui iudicatis terram.*[1] And becawse this exercise of of Readinge is the Cheifest wee have for attayning Learninge therefore it especially behoveth the Reador to be Learned, And in this custome of Readinge wee do assimulate our selves to a naturall body, that as in a naturall body every vayne conduceth one to an other, and from the [f. 5] greate Sinowes in the hed is conveyed mocion and sense to all other parts; So by our mutuall conferences wee are instructed one by an other, and by the judiciall experience of the greate Auncients distilled into the younger by their arguments and Readinges. All stand enabled to exercise their vocacions redily and skilfully. From these principalles it must nedes be concluded that a Reador of necessitye shall be complete in Learninge and practize to illuminate others. And that Reador that failes in either of these deceaves ordinary expectacion; which my predecessors have not done beinge men of the rarest gifts in learning, practize, eloquence and affability, besides their greate bountey. Thinges that shold much dismaye me, when I remember, *Nosce te ipsum.*

[1] Psalms, ii, 10:
Et nunc, reges, intelligite;
erudimini, qui judicatis terram.

Nevertheless my desire to doe the howse service doth conquere all manner of passion in my self and makes me bold that shold be bashful for *ingratum si dixeris omnia dixeris*; for avoidinge whereofe I have chosen to putt my wants and weaknes uppon your judgments who I knowe will be contented rather to err a little in a point of favoure to me, then to expose my reputacion to stricter Justice then yt may beare.

APPENDIX G

A CASE FROM FRANCIS MOORE'S *READING*

Put at New Inn: division II, case I[1]

[Fo. 47] Segnior grant son segniorie de chivalline et rent in fee, sur condicion de trouver Ryder perpetuall de ensign touts gards deins le Countey de mannage chivall de guerr. Tenant infeff grauntor et grauntee al entent que grauntee et ses heires trovera le chivall, grauntee releas al grauntor sur condicion que il et ses heires trovera ambodeux. Il faile per Annum quia nul gard in le Countey. Commission est agard al Evesque, son chauncelor, Italian rider, grauntor et grauntee quex execute le commission. Est bien agard et bien execute.

Quant segniorie est graunt, et le tenant infeff grauntor et grauntee, ceo nest attornment. Mes ove le circumstaunce de nostre case, il est attornment. Car le segniorie esteant graunt pur trover le Rider, quel est le consideracion del graunt et impose sur le grauntee, quant le tenant infeff grauntor et grauntee al entent que grauntee trovera le chivall,[2] il est implicite un approvement del former graunt de garder le Rider quia le Rider et chivall sont Correlatives, et le tenant demonstrate per le paroll (le) chivall que il voit aver mesme le chivall trove sur que le Rider chivachera et enseignera les infants, pur le paroll *Illud*[3] vies *Bossoms* Case.[4]

Le second chose est si per feffment del tenant al grauntor et grauntee le Condicion le grauntor et le segniory del grauntee et ex consequence le charitable use soit tout ale. Et tout ceo materiall al forme del case: car si le condicion remayne, le grauntor est pretendor de title et ne poit estre Commissioner si nul charitable use nul commission agardable. Et quant a ceo est avoire coment le case estoit enter eux cesty, le grauntee ad le segniorie a son use demesne, chardge ove trust et condicion. Il ove le segnior sont infeffes del tenancy, mes ceo est al sole use le grauntee, le quel est

[1] I have omitted the marginalia.

[2] But *trover* would make better sense.

[3] *Illud* seems the most likely reading, but the word is virtually illegible.

[4] Or *Bosomes* case (1582), Moo. K.B. 496; the report is a matter of lines and does not help to supply the illegible word in the MS.

prove per le sole chardge impose sur luy de trover le chivall, per que il est de necessity que il avera sole property in le ter, et issint le feffment est a son use sole chardg ove trust auxi del charitable use, dont ensuist que le grauntee ayant le segniorie a son use demesne, et esteant infeff del tenancy a son use demesne, le segniorie nest save per le proviso de lestatute de 27 h.8. Uses. Si le segniorie ne soit save al grauntee, le question est si le condicion anexx al segniorie poit estre save al grauntor, Et semble que cy. Et uncore il ayant Condicion est infeff al auter use. Mes nota que il nad condicion in le chose dont il est infeff al auter opus, cest le tenancy mes son condicion est in le segniory, le quel segniory est per son acceptaunce demesne extinct il esteant pone al ambodeux uses. [Fo. 47v] Le objecion que le charitable use serra ale ad deux braynches. Le premier que le Segniory sur que il est chardge est extinct, et *Debile fundamentum ruit opus*, lauter, que le condicion que limitt et preserve le charitable use est extinct per act le donor mesme, et pur ceo auxi le use faile. Et si sic, le Commission nest bien agard. A le premier est destre respoigne, Que le profitt et fruit del segniory remayne per cession de payment in luy que doit ceo paye, et que est auxi chardg ove le trust del charitable use, per que le remayne equity que cesty partie faira le charitable use, autrement si le segniory ewst estre evict hors de ses maynes, Auxi il serroit encountre conscience, que per son act demesne cest per purchase del tenauncy il defeatera le charitable use. Et quia les commissioners sur cest statute ont mixt powre de faire orders accoret al ley ou equity, cest use est orderable per eux, pur le second, est respoign, que parolls condicionall sont le instrument de limitacion et appointment de charitable use, et le feare del condicion gard et preserve le charitable use in exercise et in vie, mes auxi cy pres que le use est limitt, la est tiere person interessted in equity et ceo est le Commonwealth et le majesty divine pur quel honor charitie est fait et commaund. Et pur ceo, coment que le Condicion soit extinct que est le bulward de defence al use uncore le use nest destroy, mes poit estre repaire et support per rules de equity. Et a ore lestatute viengot in lewe de tiels assurances et fortificacons queux estre plant per les foundors sont ruinate per frawds, negligences, ou auter acts del people; mes sur ceo difference est conceave, lou le condicion est destroy per foundor et lou per auter car si foundor mesme ayant powre de revoke releas le condicion ou sil ayant nul powre enter pur le condicion infrant, il semble reasonable que le use serra determine, *quia cuius est dare eius est disponere*. Mes si le heire le donor release le Condicion, le use nest extinct, Et si enter pur le condicion infrant, il serra subject de meynteyne le charitable use. Et quant al entencion ou act le donor in nostre case, il nad fait releas del condicion ne enter pur condicion infrant mes per son acceptaunce de joint feffment ove party charged ove le condicion del segniory, le condicion semble extinct in extremity del ley, et encountre lentent del donor expresse car lexpresse entent de feffment quel in [ ] est, que le use estoyera. Et ceo est prove per le limiting del graunte et feffment que il trovera (le) chivall, le quel est chivall pur le Rider de chivase quel rider est destre maynteyne per le entent de Condicion, per que semble in equity le use don remayne et decree sur le equity poit estre fait, et issint commission agarder.

Le releas fait per grauntee al grauntor sur condicion que il maynteynera le Rider et le chivall est void in ley, quia le releas ne curre a cesty que nad riens quia le grauntee per le use del feffment (cesty a trover le chivall) est sole tenant, et grauntor execute, uncore ceo monstre le entent de tout eux que le charitable use estoyera nient obstant le feffment. [Fo. 48]. *Encounter le* agard del Commission poit estre object que la nest misimployment, ne negligence demployment quia le cession fuit quant nul gard fuit in le Countey come le case de tenure repaire castell, meason, Sale, porte etc. et castle gard quel que tenure cessera cy longment que nest castell tanque soit repaire et que est destre dit cest manner de charitable use nest destre compare al auters cases: car in lauter case le castle doit preced le garding ou repairing mes in nostre case le Rider et le chivall doit preced le teaching in preparacions. Et le partie poit garder Rider et chivall coment que ne soit garde al entent dattender cy pres que gard escue mes in lauter case nest possible de garder castle ou repaire castle tanque soit castle, per que le commission bien agard pur le non trover de Rider et chivall, et ceo est negligence del charitable use coment que ne soit pas gard.

Encounter lexecucion del commission est destre dit que covient estre 4 commissioners al meynes free excepcion, le quel nest in nostre case car le grauntor pretend title per condicion et auxi il est chardgable per acceptaunce del releas sur condicion de trover ambodeux. Et le grauntee ad le chose et ad fait le default, Et le Italian est alien nee et issint nest de good or sound behaviour, per que excepcion esteant al trois des Commissioners que execute le

Commission, le Commission nest bien execute. Et que est destre respoigne, que le grauntor ned ascun title ne pretend per le condicion ne per le releas come est avaundit. Mes le graunte est clerlement disable le Alien nee nest disable destre Commissioner coment que il ne poit estre retorne (come 13 h.4) de Jury? car le Roy nad ascun alien enemy, per que alien enemy coment que il ne soit denizen poit execute authority come il poit executorship, ou powre de vouch ter etc. Et issint levesque, son Chauncelor, le grauntor et le Italian sont 4 Commissioners sans excepcion que execute le commission et pur ceo bien execute.

APPENDIX H

Inquisitions before the Charity Commissioners: 1597–1787 [1]

English Counties

County	1597–1649 (39 Eliz. I–24 Car. I)	1649–1688 (1 Car. II–4 Jas. II)	1689–1714 (1 Wm. & M.–13 Anne)	1714–1787 (1 Geo. I–28 Geo. III
Beds.	13 (5)[2]	12	2	0
Berks.	14 (9)	21	5	3
Bucks.	22 (9)	28	23	5
Cambs.	14 (5)	20	18	17
Ches.	10 (5)	19	3	0
Cornwall	1 (1)	0	0	0
Cumb.	3 (2)	11	0	0
Derby.	11 (7)	10	0	17
Devon	23 (12)	28	2	0
Dorset	5 (2)	6	3	0
Dur.	1 (1)	8	1	0
Essex	30 (8)	27	11	5
Glos.	17 (9)	18	7	1
Hants.	9 (5)	12	0	0
Hereford	5 (1)	7	0	2
Herts.	18 (6)	13	4	2
Hunts.	3 (2)	4	0	1
Kent	20 (7)	35	7	1
Lancs.	4 (4)	38	8	1
Leics.	8 (5)	15	10	3
Lincs.	22 (11)	22	6	8
Middx.	34 (11)	109	24	5
Mon.	1 (0)	10	0	0
Norfolk	23 (7)	13	7	11
Northants.	17 (8)	43	3	1

[1] The jury, in each inquisition, might find breaches of more than one charitable trust: above, p. 44. The commissioners would then make separate decrees in respect of each charitable trust: see appendix I.

[2] The figures in brackets indicate the number of inquisitions temp. Jas 1.

English Counties (contd.)

Northumb.	4 (3)	1	2	0
Notts.	7 (4)	6	10	0
Oxon.	29 (14)	50	17	1
Rutland	0	7	0	0
Salop.	9 (3)	6	0	0
Somerset	7 (3)	19	0	21
Staffs.	13 (8)	5	2	23
Suffolk	20 (10)	18	8	19
Surrey	16 (11)	28	0	11
Sussex	7 (1)	12	1	0
War.	18 (9)	10	1	0
Westmorland	6 (4)	21	8	0
Wilts.	5 (2)	5	20	2
Worcs.	19 (7)	11	1	1
Yorks.	33 (15)	127	57	38
TOTALS	521 (236)	855	271	199

Inquisitions before the Charity Commissioners: the Commonwealth to the Revolution

English Counties

County	1649–1660 (1 Car. II–12 Car. II)	1661–1671 (13 Car. II–22 Car. II)	1671–1688 (23 Car. II–4 Jas. II)
Beds.	6	5	1
Berks.	11	4	6
Bucks.	3	9	16
Cambs.	10	4	6
Ches.	1	16	2
Cumb.	0	1	9
Derby.	1	2	7
Devon	4	5	19
Dorset	0	4	2
Dur.	1	3	4
Essex	4	7	16
Glos.	8	3	10
Hants.	5	3	4
Hereford	1	2	2
Herts.	5	3	5
Hunts.	0	0	4
Kent	0	3	32
Lancs.	2	4	32
Leics.	5	0	10
Lincs.	6	4	12
Middx.	23	23	63
Mon.	1	5	8
Norfolk	2	5	6
Northants.	5	12	26
Northumb.	0	0	1
Notts.	2	0	6
Oxon.	10	17	23
Rutland	0	0	7
Salop.	3	1	2
Somerset	4	1	15

English Counties (contd.)

Staffs.	1	2	2
Suffolk	7	6	5
Surrey	7	8	13
Sussex	5	1	6
War.	4	3	3
Westmorland	1	8	12
Wilts.	3	2	0
Worcs.	4	4	3
York.	10	58	59
TOTALS	165	238	459

Inquisitions before the Charity Commissioners: 1597–1787

Welsh Counties

County	1597–1649 (39 Eliz. I–24 Car. I)	1649–1688 (1 Car. II–4 Jas. II)	1688–1714 (1 Wm. & M.–13 Anne)	1714–1787 (1 Geo. I–28 Geo. III)
Brecon.	0	2	1	0
Carmarthen	0	2	5	0
Caernarvon	2	2	0	0
Denbigh	3	2	0	0
Flints.	2	8	0	0
Glam.	0	6	0	0
Merioneth	0	1	0	0
Montgomery	1	1	0	0
Pemb.	0	2	0	0
Radnor	1	1	0	0
TOTALS	9	25	6	0

APPENDIX I

DECREES MADE BY THE CHARITY COMMISSIONERS: 1597–1787

English Counties

County	1597–1625 (39 Eliz. I–23 Jac. I)	1625–1649 (1 Car. I–24 Car. I)	1649–1660 (1 Car. II–12 Car. II)	1661–1688 (13 Car. II–4 Jac. II)	1689–1701 (1 Wm. & M.–14 Wm. III)	1702–1787 (1 Anne –28 Geo. III)
Beds.	11	8	19	8	1	1
Berks.	77	15	28	27	5	4
Bucks.	38	27	11	81	18	30
Cambs.	13	17	27	24	15	40
Ches.	31	4	14	38	3	0
Cornwall	1	0	0	0	0	0
Cumb.	2	8	0	19	0	0
Derby.	30	15	2	13	0	30
Devon	40	49	9	35	0	2
Dorset	17	0	0	7	0	4
Dur.	1	0	28	42	8	0
Essex	48	48	9	72	13	44
Glos.	16	15	76	19	9	4
Hants.	19	5	16	18	0	0
Hereford	2	39	16	64	0	4
Herts.	17	40	11	17	8	4
Hunts.	5	0	0	5	0	1
Kent	31	50	0	42	7	4
Lancs.	5	0	22	61	12	1
Leics.	6	10	13	13	0	15
Lincs.	37	20	35	18	0	25
Middx.	43	49	56	140	24	23
Mon.	0	1	14	72	0	0
Norfolk	15	29	2	15	5	21
Northants	24	29	8	71	1	3

English Counties (contd.)

Northumb.	4	0	0	1	4	0
Notts.	60	11	4	16	14	0
Oxon.	89	42	15	60	7	20
Rutland	0	0	0	12	0	0
Salop.	8	9	3	3	0	0
Somerset	3	15	10	22	0	33
Staffs.	23	6	16	16	6	47
Suffolk	83	22	18	15	14	31
Surrey	34	26	21	42	0	11
Sussex	1	13	22	13	5	0
War.	21	17	12	34	4	0
Westmorland	28	34	0	37	7	2
Wilts.	4	2	10	6	0	24
Worcs.	36	16	20	21	2	1
Yorks.	134	39	102	185	56	82
TOTALS	1057	730	669	1404	248	511

Welsh Counties

Brecon.	0	0	18	1	0	1
Carmarthen	0	0	0	2	18	1
Caernarvon	20	0	0	0	0	0
Denbigh	2	4	6	0	0	0
Flints.	0	3	0	17	0	0
Glam.	0	0	1	1	0	0
Merioneth	0	0	1	0	0	0
Montgomery	0	3	0	3	0	0
Pemb.	0	0	22	1	0	0
Radnor	0	1	1	0	0	0
TOTALS	22	11	49	25	18	2

APPENDIX J

THE MORTMAIN ACT, 1736: 9 GEORGE II c. 36

An act to restrain the disposition of lands, whereby the same become unalienable.[1]

Whereas gifts or alienations of lands, tenements or hereditaments, in Mortmain, *are prohibited or restrained by* Magna Charta, *and divers other wholsome laws, as prejudicial to and against the common utility; nevertheless this publick mischief has of late greatly increased by many large and improvident alienations or dispositions made by languishing or dying persons, or by other persons, to uses called* Charitable uses, *to take place after their deaths, to the dishersion of their lawful heirs;* for remedy whereof be it enacted by the King's most excellent majesty, by and with the advice and consent of the lords spiritual and temporal, and commons, in this present parliament assembled, and by the authority of the same, That from and after the twenty fourth day of *June*, which shall be in the year of our Lord one thousand seven hundred and thirty six, no manors, lands, tenements, rents, advowsons, or other hereditaments, corporeal or incorporeal, whatsoever, nor any sum or sums of money, goods, chattels, stocks in the publick funds, securities for money, or any other personal estate whatsoever, to be laid out or disposed of in the purchase of any lands, tenements, or hereditaments, shall be given, granted, aliened, limited, released, transferred, assigned, or appointed, or any ways conveyed or settled to or upon any person or persons, bodies politick or corporate, or otherwise, for any estate or interest whatsoever, or any ways charged or incumbered by any person or persons whatsoever, in trust, or for the benefit of any charitable uses whatsoever; unless such gift, conveyance, appointment, or settlement of any such lands, tenements, or hereditaments, sum or sums of money, or personal estate (other than stocks in the publick funds) be and be made by deed indented, sealed and delivered in the presence of two or more credible witnesses twelve calendar months at least before the death of such donor or grantor (including the days of the execution and death) and be inrolled in his Majesty's high court of *Chancery*, within six

[1] I have omitted the marginalia.

calendar months next after the execution thereof; and unless such stocks be transferred in the publick books usually kept for the transfer of stocks six calendar months at least before the death of such donor or grantor, (including the days of the transfer and death) and unless the same be made to take effect in possession for the charitable use intended, immediately from the making thereof, and be without any power of revocation, reservation, trust, condition, limitation, clause, or agreement whatsoever, for the benefit of the donor or grantor, or of any person or persons claiming under him.

II. Provided always, That nothing herein before mentioned relating to the sealing and delivering of any deed or deeds twelve calendar months at least before the death of the grantor, or to the transfer of any stock six calendar months before the death of the grantor or person making such transfer, shall extend, or be construed to extend, to any purchase of any estate or interest in lands, tenements, or hereditaments, or any transfer of any stock, to be made really and *bona fide* for a full and valuable consideration actually paid at or before the making such conveyance or transfer without fraud or collusion.

III. And be it further enacted by the authority aforesaid, That all gifts, grants, conveyances, appointments, assurances, transfers, and settlements whatsoever, of any lands, tenements, or other hereditaments, or of any estate or interest therein, or of any charge or incumbrance affecting or to affect any lands, tenements, or hereditaments, or of any stock, money, goods, chattels, or other personal estate, or securities for money to be laid out or disposed of in the purchase of any lands, tenements, or hereditaments, or of any estate or interest therein, or of any charge or incumbrance affecting or to affect the same, to or in trust for any charitable uses whatsoever, which shall at any time, from and after the said twenty fourth day of *June*, one thousand seven hundred and thirty six, be made in any other manner or form than by this act is directed and appointed, shall be absolutely, and to all intents and purposes, null and void.

IV. Provided always, That this act shall not extend, or be construed to extend, to make void the dispositions of any lands, tenements, or hereditaments, or of any personal estate to be laid out in the purchase of any lands, tenements, or hereditaments, which shall be made in any other manner or form than by this act is directed, to or in trust for either of the two universities within that part of *Great Britain* called *England*, or any of the colleges or houses of learning within either of the said universities, or to or in trust for the colleges of *Eton*, *Winchester*, or *Westminster*, or any or either of them, for the better support and maintenance of the scholars only upon the foundations of the said colleges of *Eton*, *Winchester*, and *Westminster*.

V. Provided nevertheless, and be it enacted by the authority aforesaid, That no such college or house of learning, which doth or shall hold or enjoy so many advowsons of ecclesiastical benefices as are or shall be equal in number to one moiety of the fellows or persons usually stiled or reputed as fellows, or, where there are or shall be no fellows or persons usually stiled or reputed as fellows, to one moiety of the students upon the foundation, whereof any such college or house of learning doth or may by the present constitution of such college or house of learning consist, shall from and after the twenty fourth day of *June*, one thousand seven hundred and thirty six, be capable of purchasing, acquiring, receiving, taking, holding or enjoying any other advowsons of ecclesiastical benefices by any means whatsoever; the advowsons of such ecclesiastical benefices as are annexed to, or given for the benefit or better support of, the headships of any of the said colleges or houses of learning, not being computed in the number of advowsons hereby limited.

VI. Provided always, That nothing in this act contained shall extend or be construed to extend to the disposition, grant, or settlement of any estate, real or personal, lying or being within that part of *Great Britain* called *Scotland*.

APPENDIX K

THE POOR RELATION CASES

The courts were frequently asked to consider the fate of legacies to 'poor relations.' But not until *Mahon* v. *Savage* (1803), 1 Sch. and Lef. 111 and *Att.-Gen.* v. *Price* (1810), 17 Ves. 371, did any question turn on whether the legacies were or were not charitable.

In the majority of cases the testator had bequeathed personalty to his poor relations, to be distributed among them at the discretion of his executors. The primary question which confronted the courts was to determine *which* of the testator's poor relations could take.

The eighteenth-century law on this topic is an intractable bog of conflicting decisions, made more intractable by confused and incompetent reporting: see, for example, *Isaac* v. *De Friez* (1754), Ambl. 595 and *Att.-Gen.* v. *Bucknall* (1741), 2 Atk. 328. The balance of authority suggests that the Statute of Distribution, 1670 (22 and 23 Car. II c. 10), was deemed to be 'the best measure for setting bounds to such general words; otherwise it would be endless to find out everybody that were relations'. See, generally, *Carr* v. *Bedford* (1678), 2 Chan. Rep. 146; *Griffith* v. *Jones* (1686), 2 Chan. Rep. 394; *Att.-Gen.* v. *Bucknall* (1741), 2 Atk. 328; *Edge* v. *Salisbury*, *Goodinge* v. *Goodinge* (1749), Ambl. 70; (1749), 1 Ves. Sen. 231, Ves. Sen. Sup 222; *Isaac* v. *De Friez* (1754), Ambl. 595; *Brunsden* v. *Woolredge* (1765), Ambl. 507 (and Dick. 380, where the defendant is called *Woolridge*); *Widmore* v. *Woodroffe* (1766), Ambl. 636, Dick. 392. But cf. *Jones* v. *Beale* (1700), 2 Vern. 381; *Anon.* (1709), 2 Eq. Cas. Abr. 190, pl. 3.

No eighteenth-century case holds that a simple legacy to 'poor relations' was incapable of being charitable, and it is doubtful if the courts would have cured the uncertainty inherent in such a legacy if it had been thought to be non-charitable: see Parker L.C.'s observations in *Att.-Gen.* v. *Hudson* (1720), 1 P. Wms. 675. It is true that in a few cases (e.g. *Anon.* (1714), 1 P. Wms. 327, and *Widmore* v. *Woodroffe* (1766), Ambl. 636, 640, *per* Lord Camden), the court construed the will as if the word 'poor' was not in it, for there are 'no distinguishing between the degrees of poverty'. But these were exceptional decisions. Generally the word 'poor' was interpreted to mean 'most necessitous': see, for example, *Att.-Gen.* v. *Buckland* (1742), Ambl. (Blunt ed.), 71n.; *Gower* v. *Mainwaring* (1740), 2 Ves. Sen. 87, 110, Ves. Sen. Supp. 283; *Brunsden* v. *Woolredge* (1765), Ambl. 507, and cases there cited. It would be rash, therefore, to conclude that because the courts restricted the class of 'poor relations' to those within the Statute of Distributions, they thereby concluded that the legacy was not capable of being charitable. The question did not directly arise.

There were, moreover, sound reasons why it would have been advantageous, in some cases, for poor relations to claim that the particular gift was not charitable. A devise of land to poor relations *eo nomine* would be outside the mischief of the Mortmain Act, 1736: see *Brunsden* v. *Woolredge* (1765), Ambl. 507, *semble*, and *Grieves* v. *Case* (1792), 4 Bro. C.C. 67, 1 Ves. Jun. 548, 2 Cox, 301, discussed in the text, above.

In the early nineteenth century, judges imposed a gloss on these earlier authorities and sought to distinguish the charitable from the non-charitable legacy to 'poor relations'. So, Lord Redesdale, Lord Chancellor of Ireland, in *Mahon* v. *Savage* (1803), 1 Sch. and Lef. 111, contrasted a legacy to 'poor relations' with one to 'such poor relations or such other objects of charity as should be mentioned in his private instructions to his executors'—no instructions being left. In the former case, the court had to distribute the money among relations within the Statute of Distribution. In the latter, the executors could exercise their discretion in favour of any relation, whatever his or her degree of relationship to the testator, for the 'testator's design was to give to them as objects of charity, and not merely as relations'. 'It was nothing more than ascertaining a number of objects of charity who could not claim except they were such.'

A different explanation of the early cases was given by Sir William Grant M.R. in *Att.-Gen.* v. *Price* (1810), 17 Ves. 371. In that case land had been devised in 1581 to devisees to distribute the income at their discretion 'amongst my poor kinsmen and kinswomen and amongst their offspring and issue which shall dwell within the county of Brecon . . .'. The defendants pleaded in answer to an information brought at the relation of three poor relations that the devise was void for uncertainty. The Master of the Rolls rejected that plea. 'This seems to be just as much in the nature of a charitable bequest as [*Isaac* v. *De Friez*, above]. It is to have perpetual continuance in favour of a particular description of poor; and is not like an immediate bequest of a sum to be distributed among poor relations.' See also *White* v. *White* (1802), 7 Ves. 423.

For the modern authorities, see *Re Compton* [1945], Ch. 123; *Re Scarisbrick* [1951], Ch. 622; *Tudor on Charities*, 6th ed. (London, 1967), 21–2.

INDEX

actions, representative, 20. *See also* information

adequacy of consideration, 99

administration of estates by the church, 3

African society, 125, 132

aggrieved parties, 45

Altham, Thomas, 16

anatomical exhibitions, 125

answers, chancery, 9, 17. *See also* appendix A

appointments *inter vivos:* bargain and sale as, 62; covenant to stand seised as, 62; defective conveyances as, 68–70; defective gifts as, 55; defective transfers as, 60–5; defective wills as, 64–5; land in knight service, of, 72

Arden, Sir Richard Pepper (Master of the Rolls), 106, 119, 138, 144, 145, 146, 155, 158

assets: in equity, 96–7; in law, 96; insufficiency of, 5; marshalling of, 96–7, 156–9

assistants, benchers', Moore's, 235, 240

Attorney-General, informations brought by, *see* information

Awberry, Master, 92

Babington, Chief Justice, 66

Bacon, Sir Francis (Lord Keeper), 65, 74–5, 97

Bacon, Sir Nicholas (Lord Keeper), 16, 17

bankruptcy, priority of charity on, 95–6

bargain and sale: as an appointment, 62; void, perfecting, 60–1

bastards, support of, 28

Bateman, Robert, 76

Bathurst, Lord (Lord Chancellor), 152

Baxter, Richard, 81

begging by highways, 30

bells, provision of, 31, 128

benefit, public, 27; in definition of charity, 121–2; private charity and, 126–7

benevolence and legal charity, 122–7

bequests, charitable, in Chancery (*temp.* Eliz.), 17–18

Berkeley, Mr Justice, 35

Bills, Chancery, charitable gifts and, 7–8; number of 9, 16–19. *See also* appendix A

Bishop, the, as a commissioner, 40; as Ordinary, 4, 20–1, 226

bona fide purchaser: mortmain and the, 112; notice of charitable uses, 97–101, 135

Bold, Grace, 84

bows and arrows as charitable objects, 27, 29–30

botanical garden, 128

bridges, repair of, 4, 29, 124

British Museum, 129

Bromley, Sir Thomas (Lord Chancellor), 92, 94, 97. *See also* appendix A

Brougham, Henry, 163–4, 167–8

Buckland, Edward, 76

Buller, Mr Justice, 145

Burges, Henry, 8

Burnham, Poor of, 17

Cambridge, University of, 27, 111

Camden, Lord (Lord Chancellor), 122, 128, 138

Camps, Symon, 7

candles, gifts for, 3

canon law, 3–5, 74

capacity, legal: at common law, 65–6; of charity commissioners, 40; of feoffees to charitable uses, 36, 65–70, 91; of feoffors to charitable uses, 71

Carew, Master, 92

Carlele, William, 7

case, A, from Francis Moore's *Reading*, 247–50

catechising, schools of, 33–4

Catholics, *see* Roman Catholics

causes, pious: Chancery Bills and, 7–8; definition of, 3, 57–8; legal charity and, 15, 57–8; obligation to support, 3–4; privileges given to, 9; Reformation and, 10. *See also* superstitious uses

causeways, repair of, 27
Cecil, Robert, 77
challenge to jury, 24, 43
Chancellor, the Lord: appeals to, 46; contempt, committing for, 51–2; enforcement of legacies by, 6; issues commissions, 39–40; jurisdiction over charitable uses, 33–7; power to give costs, 46; powers of, 51–2; the trust and, 6–7
Chancery, Court of: delays in, 160–1; pleading in, 7–9, 16–18
Chancery Bills and Answers, 7–8, 9, 18–19. *See also* appendix A
Chancery *Decree Rolls*, 9
Chancery decrees, 9, 18
Chancery *Entry Book of Decrees and Orders*, 9, 18
Chancery pleading, 7–9, 16–18
Chancery procedure, 7–9, 16–18; inadequacy of, 19–20, 22–3, 160–8
Chantries, 3; attack on, 10–13; defective devise to, 65–6; gifts to, 13–15. *See also* superstitious uses
Chaplains: maintenance of, 81; to celebrate communion, 31; to celebrate divine service, 32–3. *See also* preaching ministers
charitable donations, registration of, 165
charitable legacies, *see* legacies, charitable
charitable objects: definition of, 26–37, 57–8, 120–127, 132–3; eighteenth century, 120–1; excluded from 1601 Act, 37–9, 51; excluded from 1736 Act, 111; mortmain and, 107–8, 128–133; preamble and, 25, 26–37, 57–8, 120–7, 132–3; public benefit in, 121–2, 133; Reformation, effects of, 10–15. *See also cy-près*
charitable uses and trusts: bills to enforce, 7–8, 18–19. *See also* appendix A; charity commissions (43 Eliz.) and, 22ff.; enforcement of, 160–8; information and, 34–7, 54–6, 69–70, 88, 120, 160–8; Parliamentary commission and, 167–8; petition (under 1812 Act) and, 165–7; outside the preamble, 31ff., 57–8
Charitable Uses Act, 1597, debates on, 23–6. *See also* Table of Statutes
Charitable Uses Act, 1601, debates on, 23–6. *See also* Table of Statutes
charity commission (under 43 Eliz.), *see* commission, charity (under 43 Eliz.)
charity commissioners (under 43 Eliz.), *see* commissioners, charity (under 43 Eliz.)
charity, private, 126–7
charity, privileges of, *see* privileges of charity
Charles I, 78, 79, 88, 89–90
Charles II, 90
Charnock, Robert, 84
childbirth, poor women in, 28
Christ's Hospital, 89, 90
church: administration of estates by the, 3; legacy to the, 5; repair of, 4, 31, 121
churchwardens, personalty vested in, 67
Clarke, Sir Thomas (Master of the Rolls), 132, 158
Coke, Sir Edward (Chief Justice), 13, 47, 92
commission, charity (under 43 Eliz.): defects of, 53; demise of, 54–6; exemption of Crown from, 236–7; general charity, jurisdiction over, 89; hearing, the, 44; inquisitions, 44; interested parties, 44; issue of, 39–40; jury and, 24, 42–3, 44; notice of, 41–2; parties aggrieved, 45; perfecting gifts, 50
commissioners, charity (under 43 Eliz.): achievement of, 52–6; awarding costs, 46; capacity of, 40; *cy-près* application by, 49–50; decrees, exceptions to, 45–6; inquisitions before, 251–4; number of, 40, 255–7; jurisdiction of, 33–6; powers of, 47–51; pretending title, 40–1
committal for contempt, 51–2
common law: capacity at, 65–6; wills at, 6
communion, celebration of, 31
communion table, 31
conditions, bare, 70
consideration: adequacy of, 99; executed and executory, 99; good, 98; jewels as, 98; *laesio enormis*, 98–9; marriage, 98; mixed, 98; of land, 98; plate as, 98; supplied by another, 101

constructive notice, 100
contempt, committal for, 51–2
copyholds: charity commissioners and, 49; mortmain and, 119; surrender of, to charity, 72; wills of, 137, 138
corn, grinding of, 27, 30
corporation sole, 66
corporations, and the 1601 Act, 37–9; as trustees, 38–9; wrongfully created, 66, 79–80
costs: information, of, 161–4; jurisdiction to award, 46
Cottington, Lord, 78
counsellor, notice to, 100
courts, ecclesiastical: expense and delay in, 5; favoured pious causes, 4–5; remedies in, 6; unpopularity of, 5
covenant to stand seised as an appointment *inter vivos*, 62
Coventry, City of, Chantry statute (I Edw. VI.) and, 13
Coventry, Thomas, Lord (Lord Keeper), 35, 43, 62, 88
creditors of bankrupts, 95
Croke, Mr Justice, 35
Crown, the: applying illegal charitable endowments, 147, 151–3; as guardian of charity, 21, 77; charity commissions and, 236–7; charity statute and, 51; concern for charity, 22–3; forfeiture of property to, 13–15, 82–3. *See also cy-près*
cupboardmen, Moore's, 235, 240
cy-près, 5, 51; alteration of charitable objects, 73–5; canon law, in, 74; commissioners' powers, 49–50; criticised, 107; general and specific charitable intention, 144–53; illegality, 76–87, 140–3, 143–8; indefinite charitable objects, 73–5, 88–91, 140, 148–153; initial impossibility, 73–5, 138, 140–4; judicial, 73–5; judicial bewilderment, 138–9; mortmain and, 119; origins, 72–3; prerogative, 75–91, 147, 151–3; Roman law, in, 73–4; supervening impossibility, 138; surplus funds and, 155–6

Davenport, Sir Humphrey (Chief Baron), 78
de excommunicato capiendo, 6
debts, charitable legacies and paying, 5, 96–7, 156
decayed persons, 28
Dekon, John, 8
declarations *inter vivos*. *See* appointments *inter vivos*
decrees: charity, 19, 255–7; charity, exceptions to, 45–6; enrolling, 9, 18
decretal of Gregory IX, 3
definition of charity, 26–37, 57–8, 87–8, 120–7; mortmain and, 107–8, 128–33; public benefit in, 121–2, 126–7, 133
delays in Chancery, 160–1
devises, pre-1736, and mortmain, 114
dinners, wedding, 30
dissenters, Erastian judges and, 141–2; trusts for, 76–82, 141–2
divine service, celebration of, 32–3
Divinity, teaching of, 32
donations, charitable, registration of, 165
dower, charity limited on an estate in, 70
Duke, George, *The Law of Charitable Uses*, 54, 232–3
Dykes, 4
Dynne, Francis, 17

East Grinstead church, 7
ecclesiastical courts, *see* courts, ecclesiastical
Edward VI, attack on chantries, 10–15
Egerton, Lady, 82
Egerton, Sir Thomas (Lord Keeper), 14, 68, 82, 97
Eldon, Lord (Lord Chancellor), 106, 122, 123–5, 132, 133, 134, 138, 140, 141–2, 146, 148, 149–50, 152–3, 154, 155, 156, 161, 166
Elizabeth I, 13
entails: as valid appointments, 62; barring, defeating charity, 137
estates, administration of, 3
Eton College, 37, 111
exceptions by aggrieved parties, 45
executed consideration, 99
execution, 1601 Act and process of, 52
executory consideration, 99
executors: actions against, 17–18; control of, 5–6
exempt charities: and 1601 Act, 37–9; and 1736 Act, 111

Exeter, Lord, 77
exhibitions, anatomical, 125

fees, payment of, 25
felons not commissioners, 40
feoffees to charitable uses, incapacity of, 65–70, 91
feoffees to impropriations, 77–81
feoffors to charitable uses, capacity of, 71
Finch, Henry, 22
Flemming, Sir Thomas (Chief Justice), 61, 62
forfeiture, to the Crown, 13–15, 82–7. *See also cy-près*
form, defect of, perfecting, 60–5, 135–8. *See also* appointments *inter vivos*
frank marriage, charity and gifts in, 70
fraternities, 13
frauds, statute of: breaking in on, 115–16; charity and, 136. *See also* Table of Statutes
freeholds, marshalling against, 157–8
Fryer, Henry, 88
funds, mixed, mortmain and, 119

general charitable intention, 144–53
good consideration, 98
Goudhurst, the church at, 8
Grant, Sir William (Master of the Rolls), 122, 123–5, 126, 132, 143, 147
Gray, William, 16
Gregory IX, decretal of, 3
guilds and fraternities, 13

Halingbury Morley, inhabitants of, 17
Hardwicke, Earl of (Lord Chancellor), 47, 112–19, 121–37, 143, 148, 151, 154, 157–8, 159
Harris, Benjamin, 17
Harris, Sergeant, 24
Harcourt, Lord (Lord Chancellor), 106, 136, 141
Hartwell, Vicar of, 255
Hastings, Sir Francis, 24
havens, repair of, 29
heir: mortmain, protecting the, 107, 109–11, 115; natural right to land of, 117–18
Henry III, 4
Henry VIII attacks chantries, 10–15
herdsmen, finding of, 29
Herne, John, *The Law of Charitable Uses*, 54, 233
Hervey, Lord, 111
Highmore, Anthony, appreciation of Hardwicke, 113
highways: begging by, 30; gravelling, 29
Hobart, Chief Justice, 65
Hobbie, Sir Edward, 24
Holt, Sir John (Chief Justice), 65
hospitals, 4; imperfect gifts to, 21

illegality of charitable objects, 76–87, 140–3, 143–8
impossibility: initial, 73–5, 138, 140–4; supervening, 138
impropriations, feoffees to, 77–81
imputed notice, 100
incapacity, 36; of feoffees, 65–70
incense, gifts for, 3
incorporation, wrongful, 66, 79–80
indefinite charitable objects, 88–91, 140, 148–53
infancy, notice of charitable use during, 99
infants, legacies to, 18
information: cost of, 161–4; enforcing charitable trusts, 8, 21, 26, 34–6, 36–7, 54–6, 69–70, 120; inadequacy of, 160–8; indefinite charitable objects, 88; intrusion, of, 21; relator's role, 161–2
initial impossibility, 73–5, 138, 140–4
Inns of Court, reading exercises in the, 229ff.
inquisitions before charity commissioners, 251–4; importance of, 44
instruction in surgery, 28
insufficiency of assets, payment of debts on, 5, 96–7, 156
intention, general charitable, 144–53
intention, specific charitable, 144–53
interest, payment of, 48
interested parties under 1601 Act, 42–3
intestate, fate of, 3
intrusion, information of, 21
Italian rider, 247–50

James I, 52, 76
James II, 83, 84
Jekyll, Sir Joseph (Master of the Rolls), 110, 113, 121

Jesuba, trust for a, 143
Jesuits, trusts for, 82. *See also* superstitious uses
jewels as consideration, 98
Jews, trusts for, 142–3
jointure to bar dower as an appointment *inter vivos*, 63
Jones, Gaynor, 83-6
judges: attitude to charity of, 23–5, 105–8; orders to Inns of Court, 231
judicial *cy-près*, *see cy-près*
jurors, challenges to, 24, 43
jury, task of, and 1601 Act, 42–3, 44

Kenyon, Sir Lloyd (Master of the Rolls), 145
King, Lord (Lord Chancellor), 141, 150
knight service, land held in, 71–2

laches, 93
laesio enormis, 98–9
Lambe, Robert, 17
Lancaster, County of, 84
land: bequests from sale of, 118; consideration of, 98; heir's right to, 117–28; held in knight service, 71–2. *See also* mortmain
lands and tenements, meaning of, within 1601 Act, 37–8
Laud, Archbishop, 78, 88, 90
Leach, Sir John (Vice Chancellor and Master of the Rolls), 127, 129–30
leaseholds: marshalling against, 157–8; mortmain and, 118–19
legacies, charitable: in Chancery, 95; indefinite, 5, 7–8, 88–91, 148–53; marshalling, 96–7; payment of debts and, 96–7; suits to enforce, 7–8, 17–18
legal personality, 65–7
lessor, notice of charitable use, 98
liberality and legal charity, 122–7
limitation, statutes of, charitable uses and, 93–4, 134. *See also* Table of Statutes
Loughborough, Lord (Lord Chancellor), 119, 129, 147
Lynn, town of: bequest to, 8; chantries in, 13

Macnaghten, Lord, 124
maimed and suffering, bequests for, 4
manor, lord of, notice by, 100
marriage consideration, 98
marriage money, 38
married women, legacies to, 18
marshalling of assets, 96–7, 156–9
Mary I, 13
masses, gifts for, 3. *See also* superstitious uses; Roman Catholics
Merchant Taylors' Company, 8
Meryham, Richard, 8
midwife, public, 28, 68
mills as charitable objects, 27, 30
ministers: non-conformist, 76–82, 141; poor, 129; preaching, 34–5
Mitford, John (Lord Redesdale), 123, 166
mixed consideration, 98
Modestinus, 73
Montague, Sir Henry, 65, 76, 240
Moore, Sir Francis, 24, 27, 31–2, 33ff., 83, 231ff.
Moore, Sir George, 24
More, Sir Thomas (Lord Keeper), 19
mortgages of turnpike tolls, 119
mortmain, 7, 11, 68, 96; amendments to 1736 Act, 111; background to 1736 Act, 109–13; bequests of pure personalty, 113, 114, 130–2; *bona fide* purchase, 112; buildings, improving, 115; copyholds, 119; *cy-près*, 119; definition of charity, 107–8, 128–33; devises, pre-1736, 114; dislike of charity, 108–9; drafting of 1736 Act, 112–13; exempt charities, 130–2; express charge against realty, 159; extrinsic evidence, 115; funds, mixed, 119; heirs, 107, 109–11, 115, 117–18; imperfect gifts, 36–7, 55; infringement of, 48; interpretation of 1736 Act, 113–19; leaseholds, 118–19; marshalling after 1736, 157–9; next-of-kin, 107, 109–11, 119; object of 1736 Act, 116; secret trusts, 115–16; terms of 1736 Act, 110, 257–9; turnpike tolls, 119

Natural History, 125
next-of-kin, Mortmain Act and, 107, 109–11, 119
non-conformist ministers, 76–82, 141
North, Sir Francis (Lord Keeper), 81, 87, 90, 91, 151
Notes, Francis Moore's, 240–6

Northington, Lord, 114–17, 131, 135, 158
notice, of charitable uses, 96, 98–101; of charity commission, 41–2; constructive, 100; imputed, 100; during infancy, 99; lessor and, 98; of manorial rights, 100; purchasers with, 99, 101. *See also bona fide* purchaser; of rent charge, 100; of tenant in tail, 98
Nottingham, Lord (Lord Chancellor), 36, 55, 69–70, 71, 72, 73, 88, 90
Noy, William (Attorney-General), 78–9
nuncupative wills, 64–5

obits, gifts for, 3
objects: benovelent and liberal, 122–7; charitable, *see* charitable objects
orders, judges', *see* judges
Ordinary, the, 4, 20–1, 226
orphans, poor, 143
outlaws not commissioners, 40
Oxford, University of, 37, 111

Palgrave, Francis, appreciation of Hardwicke, 113
parents, disabled, 28
Parker, Sir Thomas (Lord Chancellor), 156
Parliamentary commissions (Brougham), charities and, 167–8
parson, legal personality of, 67
parties, aggrieved, 45
Patenden, Thomas, 8
Pember, Sir Francis, 34–5
Perceval, Spencer, 124
perpetuity, mischief of, 71
personalty: bequests of pure, mortmain and, 113, 114, 130–2; chantry statutes and bequests of, 13–15; churchwardens and gifts of, 67; from sale of land, 118
petition (under 1812 Act) to enforce charity, 165–7
petitioners, class of, in Chancery, 8, 16. *See also* Bills, Chancery; information
Petitions, Chancery, *see* Bills, Chancery
pews, repair of, 31
philanthropy, *see* charitable objects; causes, pious
Philips, Edward, 24, 234
picture galleries, 125
pious causes, *see* causes, pious
plate as consideration, 98
pleading in Chancery, 7–9, 16–18
Plumer, Sir Thomas (Master of the Rolls), 126
poor: bequests for, 4; legacy to, 5; relief of, 4, 22ff., 45
poor ministers, 129
poor orphans, 143
poor relations, 128–9, 260–2
poor recusants, 82
poor women, 28
Portington, Lady, 86
ports, 124
possibilities, remote, 70
prayer books, 31
preaching ministers, 34–5
preamble (to 43 Eliz.), definition of charity and, 25, 26–37, 57–8, 120–7, 132–3
prerogative *cy-près*, *see cy-près*
pretending title, 40–1
prisoners, relief of, 28
private charity, 126–7
privileges of charity, 5, 9, 18, 59–101, 134–59; *bona fide* purchase and, 97–101, 112, 135; criticised and scrutinised, 106–8; *cy-près*, 72–91, 138–53; defect of form, 60–5, 135–8; forty, shilling suits, 94–5, 134; incapacity at law, 65–70; legacy suits not remitted, 95; limitation period, 93–4; limits, 70–2; marshalling of assets, 96–7, 156–9; origins, 59; surplus funds, 91–3, 153–6
procedure in Chancery, 7–9, 16–18; inadequacy of, 19–20, 22–3, 160–8
property, repairing of, 48
public benefit, 27; in definition of charity, 121–2, 133; private charity and, 126–7
public passages, 27
public works, 21
pulpit, repair of, 31
purchase, in name of another, 101
purchaser, *bona fide*: defence of, 97–101, 135; mortmain and, 112. *See also* notice
purposes, charitable or public, 127, 129

Queen Anne's Bounty, 109, 111

reading exercises, in the Inns of Court, 229ff.
Reading (MS.) on 43 Eliz. I c. 4, 234–6
realty, marshalling against, 156–9
recusants, poor, 82
Reformation, the, law of charity and, 10–15
registration of charitable donations, 165
relations, poor, 128–9, 260–2
relator's role in the information, 161–2
religious uses, 76–87. *See also* Roman Catholics; preaching ministers; superstitious uses
remainder, estate in, to charity, 71
remote possibilities, 70
rent charge, notice of, 100
rents: proviso to 1601 Act, and, 38; to charity, 92–3
repair: of bridges, 4, 29, 124; of churches, 4, 31, 121; of havens and ports, 4, 29, 124; of pews, 31; of property, 48; of pulpit, 31; of seabanks, 29
replies, Chancery, 9. *See also* appendix A
representative actions, 20. *See also* information
resulting trusts, surplus funds and, 154–5
revenue, Royal, 71–2. *See also cy-près*
reversion, grant of, as an appointment *inter vivos*, 63
rich, the, as objects of charity, 29–30
Richards, Richard, 122, 123
rider of a warhorse, 247–50
roads, repair of, 4
Rode, Richard, 8
Roman Catholics, trusts for, 82–7, 143. *See also* masses, superstitious uses
Roman law, *cy-près* in, 73–4
Royal Academy, prizes for, 132

Sackville, Thomas, 77
St John's College, Cambridge, 69
St Leonard's Shoreditch, 151, 152
St Mary Abchurch, 8
St Mary Maudlin, Milke St, 16
St Paul's Cathedral, 89–90
satisfaction of debts, 5, 96–7. *See also* marshalling of assets
scholars, presentation of, 29
schools of catechising, 33–4
Schools, Welsh Circulating, 142
scrivener, knowledge of charity by, 100
seabanks, repair of, 29
secret trust, 82, 115–16
sermon, trust for, 128
Sewell, Sir Thomas (Master of the Rolls), 138
Shaftesbury, Lord, 94
Shenley, inhabitants of, 8
ships as charitable objects, 29
sign manual, 81, 88, 147, 151–3. *See also cy-près*
Slaney, John, 76
soldiers, sick, 28
Speech at the Beginninge, Francis Moore's, 240–6
spring water, bequest for, 128
statutory interpretation in the sixteenth century, 14
stock for young tradesmen, 28
Suckerman, Robert, 17
summons of interested parties, 43
superstitious uses, 11–15, 31–3, 57, 82–7, 143, 147
supervening impossibility, 138
surgery, instruction in, 28
surplus funds: 91–4, application of, 153–6; *cy-près* doctrine and, 155–6; heir's claim to, 154–5; resulting trusts and, 154–5

tail, tenant in, notice of charitable uses, 98
taxes: charity statutes and, 29; relief of, 28
tenures, abolition of, 72
testament, the, *see* will, the
Thurlow, Lord (Lord Chancellor), 132, 147, 155
tolls, turnpike, mortmain and, 119
tracing property, 95–6
tradesmen: as commissioners, 41; stock for young, 28
Trevor, Baron, 80
trust, the: advantages of, 7; disposal of land via, 6; secret, 84, 115–16. *See also* charitable trusts; commissions, charity; commissioners, charity
trusts, variation of, *see cy-près*

trustees lacking capacity, 65–70, 91
Twyford, Henry, 233

Unitarians, trusts for, 142
universities, the, scholars at, 29. *See also* Cambridge; Oxford

Venables, Sara, 76–9
vestments, gifts for, 3

Walmesley, Mr Justice, 92
war, civil, effect of, on charity commissions, 25–6
warhorses, 247–50
wards, 247–50
water, spring, bequest for, 128
wedding dinners, 30
wedding rings, 30
Welsh Circulating Schools, 142
Westminster School, 37, 111
Weston, Lord, 78, 79, 80
Wetherell, Sir Charles (Solicitor-General), 129
Wheatley church, 144
Whitchurch, churchwardens of, 16
wills: copyholds, of, 137, 138; nuncupative, 64–5; of personalty, 4; void, as appointments, 64–5. *See also* mortmain; charitable legacies
Williams, Bishop (Lord Keeper), 64
Williams, Peere, 137
Wilmot, Chief Justice, 61, 138, 139
Winchester College, 37, 111
Wolsey, Cardinal, 19
women, poor, 28
Wotton, Anthony, 76
Wroth, Sir Robert, 24